The Single Chip
Microcomputer

S. J. CAHILL

*Department of Electrical and Electronic Engineering,
University of Ulster, N. Ireland, UK*

Prentice-Hall PHI International

Englewood Cliffs, NJ   London   Mexico   New Delhi
Rio de Janeiro   Singapore   Sydney   Tokyo   Toronto

To Aaron, whose arrival between Chapters 7 and 8
nearly canceled the rest of the project, and to Noreen
who has since had to put up with both of us.

Library of Congress Cataloging-in-Publication Data

Cahill, S. J., 1948–
  The single chip microcomputer.

  Bibliography: p.
  Includes index.
  1. Microprocessors. I. Title.
TK7895.M5C33   1987   621.391′6   86–30438
ISBN 0-13-810581-2 (pbk.)

British Library Cataloguing in Publication Data

Cahill, S. J.
  The single chip microcomputer.
  1. Microcomputers   2. Microprocessors
  I. Title
  621.391′6   TK888.3

  ISBN 0-13-810581-2

Prentice-Hall Inc., *Englewood Cliffs, New Jersey*
Prentice-Hall International (UK) Ltd, *London*
Prentice-Hall of Australia Pty Ltd, *Sydney*
Prentice-Hall Canada Inc., *Toronto*
Prentice-Hall Hispanoamericana S.A., *Mexico*
Prentice-Hall of India Private Ltd, *New Delhi*
Prentice-Hall of Japan Inc., *Tokyo*
Prentice-Hall of Southeast Asia Pte Ltd, *Singapore*
Editora Prentice-Hall do Brasil Ltda, *Rio de Janeiro*

Printed and bound in Great Britain for
Prentice-Hall International (UK) Ltd,
66 Wood Land End, Hemel Hempstead, Hertfordshire, HP2 4RG
at the University Press, Cambridge.

1 2 3 4 5 91 90 89 88 87

ISBN 0-13-810581-2

Contents

Preface

The year 1969 was momentous in the fields of electronics and computer science. For in that year Busicom, a Japanese calculator manufacturer, approached a year-old US company making semiconductor memories, with a proposal to produce a set of custom-designed integrated circuits for a new line of calculators. Intel designer Marcian Hoff's background in minicomputers led to the suggestion that an alternative approach to the problem was to integrate a simple computer central processor unit into silicon. This would move the emphasis away from the conventional hardware random structure towards a software-oriented regime. Thus was conceived the first microprocessor – the 4004, described at the time as a 'microprogrammable computer on a chip'.

The 4004 microprocessor (MPU) integrated 2,300 transistors on a single silicon chip, and represented the state of the art in 1971. The virtual doubling of fabrication density each year over the succeeding decade was reflected in the growth of complexity of these microprocessors within which two main thrusts can be identified. The most visible of these is the expansion of the processor width. The 4004 handled data in 4-bit nybbles. The 8008, introduced as soon as 1972, was the first 8-bit (byte) device. As progenitors of the species, the 4004 and 8008 were naturally somewhat primitive. The second generation of 8-bit microprocessors, introduced from 1974 on, gave a tenfold increase in throughput, and were much easier to use. The 8080 MPU circuit requires 5,000 transistors in its fabrication.

Although the 8-bit MPU continued to be refined throughout the decade, e.g., the Motorola 6809 is a 15,000-transistor device, the main movement along this path led to 16-bit processors. As early as 1974, National Semiconductor introduced its 16-bit PACE unit, but the first popular MPU of this size, the Intel 8086, appeared at the end of the decade. This 29,000-transistor design represented a further order of magnitude increase in throughput. The Motorola 68000 circuit, which was introduced shortly after, requires over 60,000 transistors, but is internally designed with a 32-bit product in mind. This is identified as the 68020, and became commercially available in the mid 1980s.

The 8008 was sold in an 18-bit package, and required at least 20 other integrated circuits for memory and interface. Although later devices reduced the minimum support chip count to single figures, e.g.; the 40-pin 8080 MPU requires six, it is clear that an alternative use of the extra resources provided by the improved fabrication density is to include more of the support and interface requirements of a microcomputer on a single chip. The first concrete expression of this approach led to the Texas Instruments TMS-1000 family of 4-bit microcomputer chips (MCUs). This was followed in 1976 by Intel's 8048 MCU, which put an 8-bit CPU, RAM and ROM memory and interface on the one die. Shortly after, Motorola introduced the first of two large families of 8-bit MCUs, coded the 6801 and 6805 series. By the mid 1980s 16-bit MCUs began to appear, exemplified by the Philips 68070 device (a derivative of the 68000 family).

MCUs are not designed to replace fully fledged microcomputers. Rather they appear, often in multiples working in tandem, as the intelligence of dedicated systems ranging from vending machines, through automobile circuits to smart laboratory instruments. Indeed, reflecting this application field, MCUs are often known as *microcontrollers*.

It is difficult to generalize the facilities available in a MCU. Taking the Motorola MC68705R3 as a typical example, this comprises an 8-bit CPU, with around 4 k bytes of EPROM program memory, 112 bytes of RAM, four parallel interface ports, a timer and a 4-channel analog to digital converter. The implementation requires around 70,000 transistors, over 15% more than the 68000 MPU!

The overall objective of the book is of course the transfer of information to the reader concerning single-chip microcomputers. In order to make this efficient and enjoyable, the following criteria were used in structuring the text.

1. Only an introductory knowledge of microprocessor hardware and software to be assumed as background.
2. A rounded and accurate skeleton of design technique should be presented with a broad enough coverage to give the reader an overall picture.
3. A pragmatic philosophy be adopted, whereby the reader acquires the detailed knowledge (and confidence!) to design a real MCU-based system.

Part 1 of the tripartite structure has a broad function, dealing with the background and theory necessary for single-chip microcomputers. Covering CPU, serial and parallel digital ports, decoding, interrupt handling, analog/digital conversion and timing, I have expanded the material to allow this section to stand alone as a treatise on microprocessor interface. Real chips and examples are used throughout. A microprocessor is used as the example CPU at this point to avoid premature specialization.

Part 2 looks in detail at real MCU devices. Architecture, hardware and software are covered, together with programming your own internal MCU memory from both an external EPROM or personal computer. As a natural progression from the 6802 microprocessor of Part 1, members from the 6805 family are used as illustrative material. Use of a single family not only avoids submerging the reader in a morass of data but permits the level of detail to be high enough to lay the foundation for the project of Part 3.

The final part takes a project through from specification to a finished prototype product. There is enough meat in the chosen project, a temperature/time annuciator, to be illustrative of real applications, but not so difficult as to bog the reader down in overcomplex hardware and software circuits. Only simple equipment is used in this section, allowing the project to be completed in any normally equipped workshop or laboratory. In an industrial environment, where time is money, the use of sophisticated equipment, such as in-circuit emulators and logic analyzers are of course essential. However, for the student who will eventually graduate to such dizzy heights, the baptism of fire engendered by the simple approach espoused here is more than justified by the educative experience.

I should like to acknowledge the cooperation of Motorola, Analog Devices, Ferranti, Intersil, RS Components and Texas Instruments in granting permission to reproduce data. In particular Graham Livey of Motorola's Semiconductor Product Division, Glasgow, for his invaluable help.

S. J. C.

List of Acronyms and Abbreviations

A	Accumulator/Accumulator A
ACR	Analog Control Register
A/D	Analog to Digital convertor/conversion
ALU	Arithmetic Logic Unit
ARR	Analog Result Register
ASCII	American Standard Code for Information Interchange
B	Accumulator B
BA	Bus Available
C	Carry flag
CAD	Computer Aided Design
CCR	Code Condition Register
CL	Clear (flip flop)
CMOS	Complementary Metal-Oxide Semiconductor
CPU	Central Processor Unit
CR	Capacitor-Resistor (time constant)
D/A	Digital to Analog convertor/conversion
DAC	Data ACcepted (handshake line)
DAV	DAta Valid (handshake line)
DDR	Data Direction Register
DIL	Dual In-Line (package)
DMA	Direct Memory Access
E	Enable (clock signal ϕ_2)
EEPROM	Electrically Erasable PROM
EOC	End Of Conversion (A/D)
EOR	Exclusive-OR
EQU	EQUivalent (pseudo operation)

FCB	Form Constant Byte (pseudo operation)
FCC	Form Constant Character (pseudo operation)
FDB	Form Double Byte (pseudo operation)
FSK	Frequency Shift Keying
H	Half-Carry flag
HMOS	High density MOS
I	Interrupt mask
IC	Integrated Circuit
INT/INT2	INTerrupt request
ICE	In-Circuit Emulation
IRQ	Interrupt ReQuest
I/O	Input/Output
IX	IndeX register
LED	Light Emitting Diode
LSB	Least Significant Bit or Byte
LSTTL	Low-power Schottky TTL
MCU	MicroComputer Unit
MDS	Microprocessor Development System
MOR	Mask Option Register
MOS	Metal-Oxide Semiconductor (transistor)
MPU	MicroProcessor Unit
MR	Memory Ready/Miscellaneous Register
MSB	Most Significant Bit or Byte
N	Negative flag
NMI	Non-Maskable Interrupt
NMOS	N-channel Metal-Oxide Semiconductor (transistor)
ns	Nanosecond (10^{-9}s)
ORG	ORiGin (pseudo operation)
PC	Program Counter
PCR	Programming Control Register
PIA	Peripheral Interface Adapter
PIT	Programmable Interval Timer
PR	Preset (flip flop)
PSK	Phase Shift Keying
PWM	Pulse Width Modulation

RAM	Read/write Random Access Memory
RE	RAM Enable
ROM	Read-Only Memory (also covers PROM & EPROM)
RST	ReSeT
R/$\overline{\text{W}}$	Read/$\overline{\text{Write}}$ (control line)
SC	Start Convert (A/D converter)
SCI	Serial Communication Interface
S/H	Sample and Hold
SP	Stack Pointer
TCR	Timer Control Register
T_{cyc}	Cycle time (ϕ_2 period)
TINT	Timer Interrupt
TTL	Transistor Transistor Logic
TTY	Tele TYpewriter
UART	Universal Asynchronous Receiver Transmitter
V	OVerflow flag
VMA	Valid Memory Access (control line)
Z	Zero flag
μs	10^{-6}s (microseconds)
%	Binary prefix
$	Hexadecimal prefix
( )	Contents of
$\rightarrow$	Transfers into; becomes

PART ONE

Microprocessor Systems

The single-chip microcomputer unit is fundamentally a microprocessor integrated with memory and software configurable peripheral interface circuitry. Thus as a foundation to the main topic of this text, we require an understanding of both the microprocessor and its interaction with the outside world.

1

In the Beginning

The origin of most specific microcomputer units (MCU) lies with a progenitor microprocessor (MPU), rather than representing an entirely new development. This is certainly the situation for the MCU we have chosen to illustrate this book. Thus we will begin by looking at an ancestor MPU.

1.1 THE 6802 MICROPROCESSOR

Advances in integrated circuit technology by the early 1970s permitted the fabrication of complete digital systems on one silicon chip. To take advantage of the economics of mass production, such a system had to be flexible and powerful enough to be used in a large number of applications. The earliest of these standard systems mimicked the central processor unit (CPU) of a computer. This integrated CPU, known as a *microprocessor,* is the most important of the many general purpose integrated systems currently available.

The first commercial 8-bit MPU was the Intel 8008, quickly followed by the 8080 device. As a response, Motorola produced the 6800 MPU in 1974. The 6800 is a memory-oriented MPU as opposed to the register-based 8080. This distinction has been retained in the 8-bit developments of both families and their offspring, up to the present time.

As the density of device fabrication increases, the complexity of microprocessors similarly follows the trend. An early (1977) example of this is the 6802 MPU, which is basically the 6800 processor with an integral 128-byte read/write random-access memory (RAM) and clock oscillator. The 6808 MPU is similar, but lacks the integral RAM. As the 6802 is the ancestor of the 6805 MCU chosen to illustrate this text, it will be useful to build the foundations of our explorations on this microprocessor.

The internal structure of a typical microprocessor can be partitioned into three broad areas:

(a) The mill.
(b) Register array.
(c) Control circuitry.

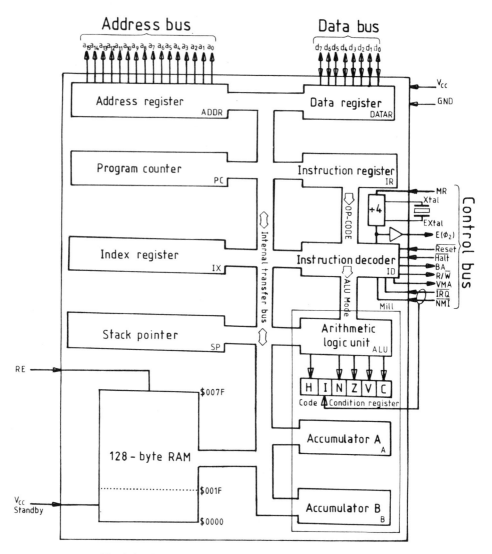

Fig. 1.1   The internal structure of the 6802 microprocessor

Fig. 1.1 shows a simplified schematic of the 6802 MPU, giving the interconnection of these elements.

THE MILL

An 8-bit arithmetic logic unit (ALU) gives the system its processing power. Data, normally obtained via the data bus, is operated upon, and is deposited in one of two general purpose registers, known as *accumulators*. For example, it is possible to add the constant six to the contents of Accumulator A, with the sum ending up in that accumulator; symbolized as ADDA #6. The final register associated with the mill, is the code condition register. This consists of four flip flops (or flags) yielding status information on the last relevant ALU operation; viz., Z set for a zero result, C giving a carry/borrow-out, N set for a negative result (bit 7 = 1) and V for a 2s complement overflow. The I mask can be set by the programmer to lock out interrupt requests, as described in Section 2.3. The two unused bit positions are permanently logic 1, as shown in Fig. 1.7.

REGISTER ARRAY

For those readers familiar with the 8080/Z80 family of MPUs, a glance at Fig. 1.1 shows a paucity of registers. The 6800 family rely chiefly on obtaining data from memory, processing the data in the MPU, and the return of the new data back to memory. The procedure is then repeated. Normally this data is channelled through an accumulator, e.g., Load Accumulator A with data from location $40 (LDAA $40) for incoming data, and Store Accumulator A at location $41 (STAA $41) for outgoing data.

Besides the code condition register, all other registers accessible to the programmer are associated with addressing data out either in memory or in a peripheral device, and therefore deal with manipulating the address bus. All these registers have a 16-bit capacity, to match this bus.

Program instructions are stored sequentially in memory, as is shown in Fig. 1.2. The program counter register holds the location of the current program byte to be fetched. Normally as the program progresses this register keeps track by automatically incrementing (or counting). However, some instructions such as branch or jump override this autoincrement, forcing a skip to another program segment (see Section 1.2).

The *index register* is used when a computed address facility is desired. For example, the index register may be set up to address the first element of a table of constants. The programmer can access the nth element of this array by augmenting the contents of the index register by n, and then loading the accumulator with data at this new address. This is symbolized as LDAA n,X, as described in Section 1.2. The index register can also be incremented or decremented, and thus can systematically step through tabular data, in a program loop, or even act as a convenient 16-bit counter.

The *stack pointer register* is used to identify an area of RAM used as a temporary storage area for subroutines and interrupt purposes. The interaction of these procedures with the stack is discussed in Sections 1.3 and 2.3.

The 6802 has a 16-bit *address bus,* which is used in conjunction with external hardware to select between devices on the data bus. Up to 2^{16} (65,536) different address codes can thus be produced. The address register stores these outgoing codes, and buffers the signals to drive up to four LSTTL loads. Such addresses may originate from the program counter, in which case program bytes are being accessed, or from the instruction itself where data bytes are being communicated.

The address register/buffer is invisible to the programmer, as is the corresponding data register/buffer. However, the latter interface is rather more complex, in order to deal with the bidirectional nature of the *data bus*. As this bus is only eight bits wide, all data is brought in or sent out in byte-sized packets. If necessary, larger data word sizes can be built up by bringing down or sending out several bytes in sequence. Both buses are discussed in more detail in Chapter 2.

The 6802 MPU has an internal 128-byte RAM automatically responding to addresses $0000–$007F (the Hitachi 6802W has a 256-byte RAM). When an operation is performed on a location in this range, e.g. LDAB $40, the external data bus is not used, and the information is internally transferred. The internal RAM may be disabled and the external data bus used for its address range by bringing RAM enable (RE) low.

RAM enable is an example of the miscellaneous collection of control and timing signals collectively known as the *control bus*. Whilst the address and data buses are relatively standard features of all microprocessors, the control bus varies considerably between families, and indeed between individual members. Here we will briefly list the 6802's control signals.

Read/$\overline{Write}$ (R/$\overline{W}$)

This status signal is associated with the data bus. It tells the outside world whether data is being sent out (R/$\overline{W}$ = 0) or brought in (R/$\overline{W}$ = 1), see Figs. 2.2 and 2.3. The 8080 family uses two signals for this purpose, viz., $\overline{Memory Write}$ and $\overline{Memory Read}$, both active low.

Valid Memory Address (VMA)

VMA is a status signal associated with the address bus. The 6802 MPU will occasionally activate the address bus during an internal processing cycle. VMA is used as a strobe to prevent such false addresses accidentally enabling external circuitry, see Figs. 2.2 and 2.3.

$\overline{Reset}$ ($\overline{RST}$)

The starting location of the string of codes making up the program may lie anywhere in available address space $0000–$FFFF, as chosen by the designer. Upon reset, the program counter must be made to point to that address, so that the program can commence operation. In the 6800 family, resetting the MPU forces the addresses $FFFE and then $FFFF onto the address bus. The resulting two data bytes are loaded into the program counter, constituting a type of indirect jump to the start of the program. In cases where no memory physically exists at these locations, the address decoders will normally be designed to enable the upper two bytes of any existing memory to respond to $FFFE/F (see Section 2.1). For example, the 68705R3 MCU has ROM between $0100 and $0FFF, with no memory above. The *reset vector* here is at $0FFE/F. The designer must ensure that the start address is programmed into the reset vector before the program runs (see also Fig. 1.5).

$\overline{Halt}$

When $\overline{Halt}$ is brought low, the MPU finishes its current instruction and goes into an idle state. $\overline{Halt}$ signals are usually sent by circuits wishing to take over the microprocessor's buses, to directly access memory (DMA).

Bus Available (BA)

This forms a pair with $\overline{Halt}$. When the MPU has halted, BA goes high to tell the outside world that it can take over the buses. The data bus goes open circuit, but due to a design oversight the address bus does not (as erroneously stated in early Motorola data sheets). In the 6800 MPU all buses and R/$\overline{W}$ go low on $\overline{Halt}$.

$\overline{Interrupt\ Request}\ (\overline{IRQ})$

A low level on this input signals an interrupt request from an external device. Provided that the I mask flag is not set, this is accepted as described in Section 1.3.

$\overline{Nonmaskable\ Interrupt}\ (\overline{NMI})$

This is similar to $\overline{IRQ}$, but is activated by a low-going edge rather than level. Also it cannot be ignored by the MPU (see Section 1.3).

RAM Enable (RE)

This enables the on-chip RAM which can then respond to MPU accesses between $0000–$007F. This pin may also be used to disable writing to the RAM during a power-down situation.

V_{cc} Standby (4.75–5.25V)

This pin supplies the d.c. voltage of the lowest 32 bytes of internal RAM, and the RE control logic. This permits a guaranteed retention of data during power-up or -down conditions, provided that RE is low, at least three clock cycles before power-down.

Extal and Xtal

The 6802 has an integral oscillator timed by a quartz crystal connected between these pins. This gives an internal clock signal (see Figs. 2.2 and 2.3) of one fourth of the crystal resonance frequency. Crystals between 400 kHz and 4 MHz can be used. The lower 100 kHz clock frequency bound is necessitated by the dynamic nature of some of the internal registers.

Enable (E)

This supplies a clock signal used to synchronize external circuits to the MPU clock cycle, as shown in Figs. 2.2 and 2.3. This is a buffered version of the internal clock, and is thus one fourth of the crystal frequency. It is sometimes called ϕ_2.

Memory Ready (MR)

This is a control input to the clock oscillator. By bringing MR low, an external memory or peripheral device can freeze the oscillator, subject to a limiting total cycle time of 10 μs. This gives slow devices time to accept or generate data by the end of the clock cycle (see Figs. 2.2 and 2.3).

1.2   INSTRUCTING THE MPU

Given that the MPU is a hardware circuit whose 'intelligence' is controlled by a stored string of instructions; a knowledge of the structure of these program bytes is a necessary precursor to the understanding of the hardware-software interaction. We can acquire this with the aid of Fig. 1.2, which shows a highly simplified 6802 MPU together with part of its address space. The memory map shows three zones. The lower of these is devoted to RAM. This area is mainly used for the temporary storage of variables and status indicators, and is often referred to as *scratchpad memory*.

In a microprocessor system dedicated to one task, such as illustrated in Part three, the program is fixed. This implies the use of ROM, as shown in the middle zone of Fig. 1.2. In the same situation the reset address is also fixed, and in the 6800 series is stored in the reset vector $FFFE/F (see Fig. 1.5); although in practice this will usually lie at the top of available program ROM.

To illustrate the rhythm of the MPU, Fig. 1.2 shows a short program segment which takes the data out of location $0000 (call it X), adds the constant decimal 32 ($20) to it, and puts the resulting sum (Y = X + 32) in location $0001. Three instructions are used for this:

I   Load Accumulator A (LDAA)
     This brings down (reads) the data X, and puts it in Accumulator A.
II   Add to Accumulator A, immediately (ADDA #)
     This adds the specified constant ($20) to the contents of Accumulator A, which is overwritten by the sum.
III Store contents of Accumulator A (STAA)
     This takes the data in Accumulator A(Y) and puts (writes) it away at the specified address.

Examination of the format of each of these instructions shows a 2-part structure. The first byte is always a code for the instruction itself. These 1-byte op-codes are unique to the operation, and in this case are $96 for LDAA; $8B for ADDA # and $97 for STAA (remember of course that these are actually stored in binary).

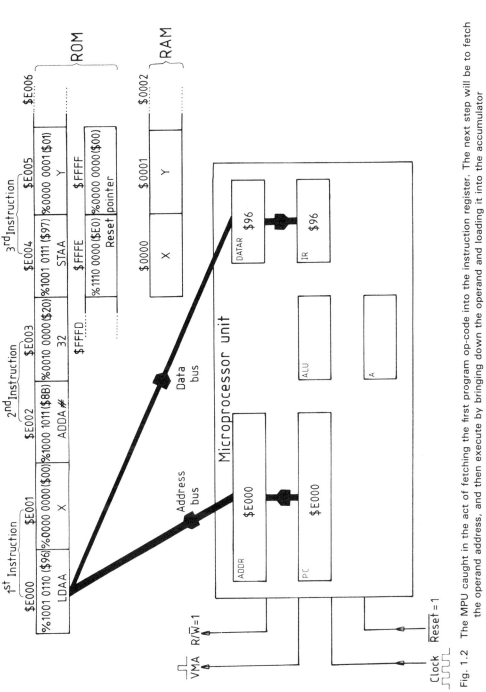

Fig. 1.2 The MPU caught in the act of fetching the first program op-code into the instruction register. The next step will be to fetch the operand address, and then execute by bringing down the operand and loading it into the accumulator

The second part of each instruction carries the address of the data to be operated upon (e.g., STAA at $0001) or else the data itself (e.g., ADDA #$20). These are only two of the many ways of telling the MPU where this data can be got, and we will look at some more later in this section.

Once the program counter has been pointed to the beginning of the string of instructions (e.g., at reset), the MPU begins its *fetch and execute* rhythm by bringing down the op-code to the instruction decoder. This decides on the remaining steps to be taken to implement the instruction, which usually requires the fetching down of one or more bytes relating to the data address, before executing the operation on the targeted data. The program counter is automatically incremented during each fetch, so that prior to execution it will always point to the following op-code. This fetch and execute sequence continues indefinitely unless the MPU is in a reset or halt state, or has just executed a wait (WAI) instruction (i.e., stop).

Up to this moment we have only examined three instructions: load, add and store. The 6802 MPU has a repertoire of 72 operations. As these form the basis of the MCU's instruction set used later, we will briefly summarize these in this and the next section.

ARITHMETIC INSTRUCTIONS

The 6802 MPU, in common with most 8-bit microprocessors, can basically only add and subtract. These operations set the carry/borrow flag appropriately. The add/subtract with carry instructions allows the programmer to perform arithmetic functions on operands larger than eight bits. Thus the addition of say two 24-bit operands could be implemented by adding the two least signficant bytes; then the two middle bytes with the resultant carry, and finally the two upper bytes plus carry. The carry from this addition is the twenty-fifth bit of the sum. See Section 1.4 for an example of multiple-precision addition.

The contents of any location in read/write memory (M) can be incremented by one, e.g., INC $0040. Similarly the contents of any accumulator can be incremented, INCA; INCB. Increment does not produce a carry. Thus, if the contents of Accumulator A are %11111111, an INCA operation gives (A) = %00000000, without the carry flag being set to indicate an overflow. In this respect increment is not identical to ADDA #01. Decrement is the subtractive counterpart to increment.

Decimal adjust (DAA) implements the correction algorithm on Accumulator A, necessary when binary addition is used to sum two BCD bytes (each BCD byte holds two BCD digits). As this algorithm relies on information regarding the carry between the lower and upper four bits, DAA can only be used after instructions which activate the H flag. In the 6802 MPU, this means that BCD subtraction cannot be directly accomplished. Although our 6805 MCU does not provide a DAA operation, the H flag is retained to give the designer the capability of constructing an equivalent process.

Table 1.1 reviews these instructions, giving a brief description of the operation carried out, and its effect on the status flags. The V flag has been omitted, as it is not implemented by the 6805 MCU. The symbol ⌐ has been used to show a flag operating normally, while · indicates not affected. M indicates anywhere in memory, A and B are the two accumulators. The symbol → may be read as 'transfers to'. A full legend is given at the end of Table 1.7.

Table 1.1   A summary of 6800/2 arithmetic operations

Operation		Mnemonic	Flags HNZC	Description
Add				Binary addition
	to A	ADDA	√√√√	A + M → A
	to B	ADDB	√√√√	B + M → B
	B to A	ABA	√√√√	B + A → A
with Carry				Includes carry
	to A	ADCA	√√√√	A + M + C → A
	to B	ADCB	√√√√	B + M + C → B
Decimal Adjust				Corrects binary addition
	A	DAA	·√√√	to BCD format
Decrement				Subtract one, no carry
	memory	DEC	·√√·	M − 1 → M
	A	DECA	·√√·	A − 1 → A
	B	DECB	·√√·	B − 1 → B
Increment				Add one, no carry
	memory	INC	·√√·	M + 1 → M
	A	INCA	·√√·	A + 1 → A
	B	INCB	·√√·	B + 1 → B
Subtract				Binary subtraction
	from A	SUBA	·√√√	A − M → A
	from B	SUBB	·√√√	B − M → B
	B from A	SBA	·√√√	A − B → A
with Carry				Includes carry (borrow)
	from A	SBCA	·√√√	A − M − C → A
	from B	SBCB	·√√√	B − M − C → B

Table 1.2   Data manipulation instructions

Operation		Mnemonic	Flags H N Z C	Description
Clear				Replaces data by 00
	memory	CLR	· R S R	00 → M
	A		· R S R	00 → A
	B		· R S R	00 → B
Load				Puts data into
	A	LDAA	· ✓ ✓ ·	M → A
	B	LDAB	· ✓ ✓ ·	M → B
Rotate left				Circular shift through Carry
	memory	ROL	· ✓ ✓ b_7	M
	A	ROLA	· ✓ ✓ b_7	A
	B	ROLB	· ✓ ✓ b_7	B
Rotate right				Circular shift through Carry
	memory	ROR	· ✓ ✓ b_0	M
	A	RORA	· ✓ ✓ b_0	A
	B	RORB	· ✓ ✓ b_0	B
Shift left, arithmetic				Linear shift left into Carry
	memory	ASL	· ✓ ✓ b_7	M
	A	ASLA	· ✓ ✓ b_7	A
	B	ASLB	· ✓ ✓ b_7	B
Shift right, logic				Linear shift right into Carry
	memory	LSR	· ✓ ✓ b_0	M
	A	LSRA	· ✓ ✓ b_0	A
	B	LSRB	· ✓ ✓ b_0	B
Store				Put data away
	A	STAA	· ✓ ✓ ·	A → M
	B	STAB	· ✓ ✓ ·	B → M
Transfer				Move between Accumulators
	A to B	TAB	· ✓ ✓ R	A → B
	B to A	TBA	· ✓ ✓ R	B → A

DATA-MANIPULATION INSTRUCTIONS

The 6800 series MPUs provide several instructions which essentially move data about. We have already met load and store, which respectively move data into or out of an accumulator. The clear operation can be thought of as moving an all-zero byte to anywhere in read/write memory or an accumulator. It is also possible to transfer data directly between the two accumulators using the transfer instruction.

Somewhat more complex are the shifting operations. These essentially move data one bit to the right or left. In Table 1.2, these instructions have been divided into two groups, depending on what happens to the bit shifted out. The linear shift operations place this bit in the carry flag. Thus if we wish to examine bit 2, we could shift the byte right (LSR) three times, after which the state of the carry flag is that of the bit under investigation.

The other category of shifting operations are known as the *rotate* instructions. These circulate data through the carry flag, which is used as the ninth bit. Rotate instructions are mainly used to perform multiple-precision shifts. This is shown in Fig. 1.3, where a 24-bit data word is shifted once left. The least significant byte is linearly shifted left, with bit 7 moving into the carry flag. The middle byte is then rotated, with the carry bit moving into bit 0 of this byte and the overflow from bit 7 replacing it. A final rotate (or alternatively a linear shift) is used for the most significant byte.

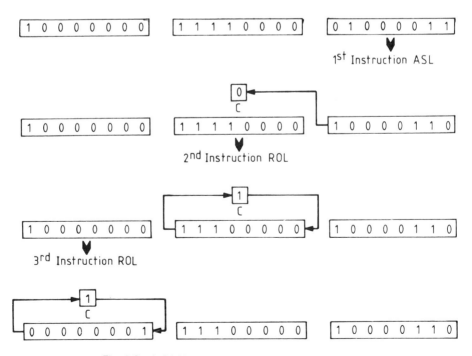

Fig. 1.3 A 24-bit shift left using the rotate instruction

In Table 1.2 we are using R to show a flag which is always reset to zero by that operation, and S for always set to one.

LOGIC OPERATIONS

The three basic logic operations of AND, OR and NOT (complement) are provided, together with Exclusive-OR (see Table 1.3). The NOT operation inverts each bit in any memory location or accumulator. For the AND operation, the 8-bit contents of an accumulator are bitwise ANDed with the data byte. Thus (A7 A6 A5 A4 A3 A2 A1 A0) $\cdot$ (D7 D6 D5 D4 D3 D2 D1 D0) = A7 $\cdot$ D7 A6 $\cdot$ D6 A5 $\cdot$ D5 A4 $\cdot$ D4 A3 $\cdot$ D3 A2 $\cdot$ D2 A1 $\cdot$ D1 A0 $\cdot$ D0. ANDing with logic 0 always gives zero, while logic 1 does not alter the original data. Thus if the contents of A were %00110111, then the operation ANDA #%11110000 would yield (A) = %00110000.

The AND function may be used to clear any bit or bits, conversely the OR function can set bits. For example, the operation ORA #%10000000 will force bit 7 of Accumulator A high, and leave all other bits unaltered.

The Exclusive-OR (EOR) operation can be used to invert any bits, or check for a change in data. Consider the EOR truth table:

D	A	F
0	0	0
0	1	1
1	0	1
1	1	0

Two observations can be made. First, if the data bit is logic 0, then the output equals A, while for D = 1, F = $\overline{A}$. Thus EORA #%10000000 will invert bit 7, but leave the other bits unchanged.

The second observation notes that the output is always logic 1 if the inputs differ. Thus if we were monitoring a bank of switches, waiting for a change, we could continuously EOR the current reading with the first reading. If they agree, the no change will be signaled by an all-zero result. For example:

```
     10110000       1st Sample
⊕    10110000       Nth Sample
     ────────
     00000000       EOR (Difference word)
```

```
     10110000       1st Sample
⊕    10010000       (N + 1)th Sample
     ────────
     00100000       EOR (Difference word)
```

Thus by examining the Z flag after EOR we can tell if a change has occurred; furthermore, by shifting and examining the carry flag we can also determine which

Table 1.3 Logic operations

Operation		Mnemonic	Flags H N Z C	Description
AND				Logic bitwise AND
	A	ANDA	• ✓ ✓ •	A•M → A
	B	ANDB	• ✓ ✓ •	B•M → B
Complement				Logic bitwise NOT
	memory	COM	• ✓ ✓ S	M̄ → M
	A	COMA	• ✓ ✓ S	Ā → A
	B	COMB	• ✓ ✓ S	B̄ → B
Exclusive-OR				Logic bitwise EX-OR
	A	EORA	• ✓ ✓ •	A⊕M → A
	B	EORB	• ✓ ✓ •	B⊕M → B
OR				Logic bitwise OR
	A	ORAA	• ✓ ✓ •	A + M → A
	B	ORAB	• ✓ ✓ •	B + M → B

bit or bits have changed. By ANDing the difference word with the sample word, the polarity of change can be determined.

DATA-TESTING OPERATIONS

For all but the most primitive of systems, a degree of response to changing external conditions is required. It is implicit in this requirement that the central processor must be able to compare data to either a fixed or variable reference (see Table 1.4). To do this we must be able to test and compare data bytes.

We can use the AND function to test any bit of an accumulator. For example, to check the state of bit 2 of Accumulator A we perform the operation ANDA # %00000100. If bit 2 was logic 0 then the final result will be all zero and the Z flag will be set. Otherwise Z will be cleared. A series of bits may be checked by systematically ANDing with different 'masks'. Unfortunately ANDing is a destructive test, in that the accumulator content is changed, although only the state of the Z flag is of consequence, not the resulting byte. To get around the necessity of restoring the original data after each test, the 6800 series uses the bit test (BIT) operation. This works in the same way as AND, e.g., BITA # %00000100 tests bit 2, but does not alter the accumulator contents in any way.

Comparison of the magnitude of data in memory with the contents of an accumulator requires a different approach. For example, we may be interested if (A) is higher than, equal to or lower than (M), where we are using parentheses to

Table 1.4   Data-testing operations

Operation		Mnemonic	Flags H N Z C	Description
Bit Test				Non-destructive AND
	A	BITA	• ✓ ✓ •	A • M ((A) unchanged)
	B	BITB	• ✓ ✓ •	B • M ((B) unchanged)
Compare				Non-destructive subtract
	with A	CMPA	• ✓ ✓ ✓	A-M ((A) unchanged)
	with B	CMPB	• ✓ ✓ ✓	B-M ((B) unchanged)
Test for Zero or Minus				Non-destructive subtract zero
	memory	TST	• ✓ ✓ R	M-00
	A	TSTA	• ✓ ✓ R	A-00
	B	TSTB	• ✓ ✓ R	B-00

signify contents of. Mathematically this can be done by subtracting (M) from (A). Depending on the state of the carry and zero flags, their relative magnitudes may be deduced thus:

(A) *Higher than* (M) : A − M will give C = 0, Z = 0
(A) *Equal to* (M)   : A − M will give C = 0; Z = 1
(A) *Lower than* (M) : A − M will give C = 1; Z = 0

remembering that the subtraction of a larger from a smaller number will always generate a borrow (C flag).

The subtract operation can be used for comparison purposes, but like ANDing this is a destructive test. The compare operations perform the same subtraction, setting the Z and C flags appropriately, but do not overwrite the contents of the accumulator with the difference. The test for zero or minus instructions offers a convenient comparison of any memory location or accumulator contents with zero. As test activates the N flag, as well as the Z flag, this can also be used to check the state of bit 7. Like compare, test does not alter any data.

In our discussion of magnitude comparison, unsigned numbers have been assumed. When a 2s complement signed representation is used, the same compare instruction can be used. However, the state of the N and V flags are then pertinent. As our MCU does not have a V flag, we will not discuss this feature further.

To enable the MPU to respond to the state of the code condition register, a group of conditional operations must be provided. These usually move the program counter to a different segment of the program on the basis of the state of one or more flags.

SKIPPING OPERATIONS

All conditional operations in the 6800 series take the form of a branch instruction. These cause the program to skip *n* places in response to the instruction BRA n. The branch always (BRA) operation is made irrespective of the state of the flags. True conditional branching is provided on the state of one or more of the CCR bits. In the context of this book, the most important of these are the Z flag, N flag, C flag and if either or neither the C and Z flags are set. These are detailed in Table 1.5.

Two other instructions affecting the program counter are shown. The unconditional jump is not relative, in that the program counter is set to the specified value, e.g., JMP $0300 forces PC to $0300. The no operation (NOP) instruction does literally nothing. It takes two clock cycles (typically 2 μs) to do it, and by virtue of the auto increment during the fetch, advances PC by one notch. The 6805 and 6809 MPUs have a branch never (BRN) instruction. This is an elaborate NOP, but takes four cycles to do nothing!

Some of the flags in the code condition register can be directly cleared or set, as shown in Table 1.6. Of most interest to us is the carry flag and interrupt mask (see Section 1.3).

The full instruction set for the 6800/6802 MPUs is shown in Table 1.7. A close inspection shows several instructions ignored in our summary. Some of these are not implemented by the 6805 MCU and are, therefore, not of immediate interest, while those covering interrupt handling, the index register and stack pointer will be discussed in the next section.

In observing the layout of the instruction set, notice that instructions have

Table 1.5   Skipping operations

Operation	Mnemonic	Description
Branch Always	BRA	Always branches, irrespective of flags
Branch if Equal to Zero	BEQ	Branches if Z flag set (= 1)
Branch if Not Equal to Zero	BNE	Branches if Z flag not set (= 0)
Branch if Minus	BMI	Branches if N flag set (bit 7 = 1)
Branch if Plus	BPL	Branches if N flag not set (bit 7 = 0)
Branch if Carry Set	BCS	Branches if (Acc.) lower than*
Branch if Carry Clear	BCC	Branches if (Acc.) higher or equal*
Branch if Lower or Same	BLS	Branches if C or Z flag set*
Branch if Higher	BHI	Branches if neither C or Z flag set*
Jump	JMP	Jumps always, irrespective of flags
No Operation	NOP	Only increments Program counter

*After a Subtract or Compare operation

Table 1.6 Flag operations

Operation	Mnemonic	Flags I H N Z C	Description
Clear Carry flag	CLC	· · · · R	$0 \rightarrow C$
Set Carry flag	SEC	· · · · S	$1 \rightarrow C$
Clear Interrupt mask	CLI	R · · · ·	$0 \rightarrow I$
Set Interrupt flag	SEI	S · · · ·	$1 \rightarrow I$

between one and four distinct op-codes for the same operation. These differences indicate to the instruction decoder how the operand is to be obtained. We have already met two of these address modes in Fig. 1.2. The first instruction LDAA $00 used op-code $96 not only to indicate Load Accumulator A but to state that the following byte is the address at which the data is to be found. The final store instruction uses the same address mode. However, the addition instruction uses a different address mode. Here the second byte is the data itself. It is possible to use this mode with the load instruction, e.g., LDAA #$00 is another way of clearing Accumulator A. This time we see from our instruction set, the op-code is $86.

There are six address modes used in the 6802 MPU.

Inherent | Op-code |

These are single-byte instructions which inherently address an internal register. For example, INCA = $4C adds one on to the contents of Accumulator A. No address as such is needed.

Immediate | Op-code | Single-byte data |

The second byte of this instruction is the actual data. This address mode is used to manipulate constants, as its value is part of the program in ROM. For example, ADDA #$32 = 8B-32 results in the constant $32 being added to the accumulator, symbolized as #. Only constants between 0 and 255 can be handled in this way, but note that the index and stack-pointer registers having a 16-bit capacity can operate on double-byte data (see Section 1.3).

Direct | Op-code | Lower-address byte |

The following byte in this case is the lower byte of a 16-bit address, the upper byte being assumed $00. Thus the instruction ADDA $32 = $9B-32 in effect takes data from $(00)32 and adds it to the accumulator's contents. The direct-address mode can be used only for data stored between addresses $0000 and $00FF. Most microprocessors with few internal registers (this also includes the 6502 series) have

Table 1.7 The 6800/2 instruction set (reproduced by courtesy of Motorola Limited)

ACCUMULATOR AND MEMORY INSTRUCTIONS

OPERATIONS	MNEMONIC	IMMED OP	~	=	DIRECT OP	~	=	INDEX OP	~	=	EXTND OP	~	=	IMPLIED OP	~	=	BOOLEAN/ARITHMETIC OPERATION (All register labels refer to contents)	H	I	N	Z	V	C
Add	ADDA	3B	2	2	9B	3	2	AB	5	2	BB	4	3				A + M → A	↕	●	↕	↕	↕	↕
	ADDB	CB	2	2	DB	3	2	EB	5	2	FB	4	3				B + M → B	↕	●	↕	↕	↕	↕
Add Acmltrs	ABA													1B	2	1	A + B → A	↕	●	↕	↕	↕	↕
Add with Carry	ADCA	89	2	2	99	3	2	A9	5	2	B9	4	3				A + M + C → A	↕	●	↕	↕	↕	↕
	ADCB	C9	2	2	D9	3	2	E9	5	2	F9	4	3				B + M + C → B	↕	●	↕	↕	↕	↕
And	ANDA	84	2	2	94	3	2	A4	5	2	B4	4	3				A · M → A	●	●	↕	↕	R	●
	ANDB	C4	2	2	D4	3	2	E4	5	2	F4	4	3				B · M → B	●	●	↕	↕	R	●
Bit Test	BITA	85	2	2	95	3	2	A5	5	2	B5	4	3				A · M	●	●	↕	↕	R	●
	BITB	C5	2	2	D5	3	2	E5	5	2	F5	4	3				B · M	●	●	↕	↕	R	●
Clear	CLR							6F	7	2	7F	6	3				00 → M	●	●	R	S	R	R
	CLRA													4F	2	1	00 → A	●	●	R	S	R	R
	CLRB													5F	2	1	00 → B	●	●	R	S	R	R
Compare	CMPA	81	2	2	91	3	2	A1	5	2	B1	4	3				A − M	●	●	↕	↕	↕	↕
	CMPB	C1	2	2	D1	3	2	E1	5	2	F1	4	3				B − M	●	●	↕	↕	↕	↕
Compare Acmltrs	CBA													11	2	1	A − B	●	●	↕	↕	↕	↕
Complement, 1's	COM							63	7	2	73	6	3				M̄ → M	●	●	↕	↕	R	S
	COMA													43	2	1	Ā → A	●	●	↕	↕	R	S
	COMB													53	2	1	B̄ → B	●	●	↕	↕	R	S
Complement, 2's	NEG							60	7	2	70	6	3				00 − M → M	●	●	↕	↕	①	②
(Negate)	NEGA													40	2	1	00 − A → A	●	●	↕	↕	①	②
	NEGB													50	2	1	00 − B → B	●	●	↕	↕	①	②
Decimal Adjust, A	DAA													19	2	1	Converts Binary Add. of BCD Characters into BCD Format	●	●	↕	↕	↕	③
Decrement	DEC							6A	7	2	7A	6	3				M − 1 → M	●	●	↕	↕	④	●
	DECA													4A	2	1	A − 1 → A	●	●	↕	↕	④	●
	DECB													5A	2	1	B − 1 → B	●	●	↕	↕	④	●
Exclusive OR	EORA	88	2	2	98	3	2	A8	5	2	B8	4	3				A⊕M → A	●	●	↕	↕	R	●
	EORB	C8	2	2	D8	3	2	E8	5	2	F8	4	3				B⊕M → B	●	●	↕	↕	R	●
Increment	INC							6C	7	2	7C	6	3				M + 1 → M	●	●	↕	↕	⑤	●
	INCA													4C	2	1	A + 1 → A	●	●	↕	↕	⑤	●
	INCB													5C	2	1	B + 1 → B	●	●	↕	↕	⑤	●
Load Acmltr	LDAA	86	2	2	96	3	2	A6	5	2	B6	4	3				M → A	●	●	↕	↕	R	●
	LDAB	C6	2	2	D6	3	2	E6	5	2	F6	4	3				M → B	●	●	↕	↕	R	●
Or, Inclusive	ORAA	8A	2	2	9A	3	2	AA	5	2	BA	4	3				A + M → A	●	●	↕	↕	R	●
	ORAB	CA	2	2	DA	3	2	EA	5	2	FA	4	3				B + M → B	●	●	↕	↕	R	●
Push Data	PSHA													36	4	1	A → MSP, SP − 1 → SP	●	●	●	●	●	●
	PSHB													37	4	1	B → MSP, SP − 1 → SP	●	●	●	●	●	●
Pull Data	PULA													32	4	1	SP + 1 → SP, MSP → A	●	●	●	●	●	●
	PULB													33	4	1	SP + 1 → SP, MSP → B	●	●	●	●	●	●
Rotate Left	ROL							69	7	2	79	6	3				M	●	●	↕	↕	⑥	↕
	ROLA													49	2	1	A	●	●	↕	↕	⑥	↕
	ROLB													59	2	1	B	●	●	↕	↕	⑥	↕
Rotate Right	ROR							66	7	2	76	6	3				M	●	●	↕	↕	⑥	↕
	RORA													46	2	1	A	●	●	↕	↕	⑥	↕
	RORB													56	2	1	B	●	●	↕	↕	⑥	↕
Shift Left, Arithmetic	ASL							68	7	2	78	6	3				M	●	●	↕	↕	⑥	↕
	ASLA													48	2	1	A	●	●	↕	↕	⑥	↕
	ASLB													58	2	1	B	●	●	↕	↕	⑥	↕
Shift Right, Arithmetic	ASR							67	7	2	77	6	3				M	●	●	↕	↕	⑥	↕
	ASRA													47	2	1	A	●	●	↕	↕	⑥	↕
	ASRB													57	2	1	B	●	●	↕	↕	⑥	↕
Shift Right, Logic	LSR							64	7	2	74	6	3				M	●	●	R	↕	⑥	↕
	LSRA													44	2	1	A	●	●	R	↕	⑥	↕
	LSRB													54	2	1	B	●	●	R	↕	⑥	↕
Store Acmltr.	STAA				97	4	2	A7	6	2	B7	5	3				A → M	●	●	↕	↕	R	●
	STAB				D7	4	2	E7	6	2	F7	5	3				B → M	●	●	↕	↕	R	●
Subtract	SUBA	80	2	2	90	3	2	A0	5	2	B0	4	3				A − M → A	●	●	↕	↕	↕	↕
	SUBB	C0	2	2	D0	3	2	E0	5	2	F0	4	3				B − M → B	●	●	↕	↕	↕	↕
Subtract Acmltrs.	SBA													10	2	1	A − B → A	●	●	↕	↕	↕	↕
Subtr. with Carry	SBCA	82	2	2	92	3	2	A2	5	2	B2	4	3				A − M − C → A	●	●	↕	↕	↕	↕
	SBCB	C2	2	2	D2	3	2	E2	5	2	F2	4	3				B − M − C → B	●	●	↕	↕	↕	↕
Transfer Acmltrs	TAB													16	2	1	A → B	●	●	↕	↕	R	●
	TBA													17	2	1	B → A	●	●	↕	↕	R	●
Test, Zero or Minus	TST							6D	7	2	7D	6	3				M − 00	●	●	↕	↕	R	R
	TSTA													4D	2	1	A − 00	●	●	↕	↕	R	R
	TSTB													5D	2	1	B − 00	●	●	↕	↕	R	R
																		H	I	N	Z	V	C

LEGEND:

OP	Operation Code (Hexadecimal);		+	Boolean Inclusive OR;
~	Number of MPU Cycles;		⊙	Boolean Exclusive OR;
=	Number of Program Bytes;		M̄	Complement of M;
+	Arithmetic Plus;		→	Transfer Into;
−	Arithmetic Minus;		0	Bit = Zero;
·	Boolean AND;		00	Byte = Zero;
MSP	Contents of memory location pointed to be Stack Pointer;			

Note − Accumulator addressing mode instructions are included in the column for IMPLIED addressing

CONDITION CODE SYMBOLS:

H	Half-carry from bit 3;
I	Interrupt mask
N	Negative (sign bit)
Z	Zero (byte)
V	Overflow, 2's complement
C	Carry from bit 7
R	Reset Always
S	Set Always
↕	Test and set if true, cleared otherwise
●	Not Affected

Table 1.7   The 6800/2 instruction set (reproduced by courtesy of Motorola Limited)
(*continued*)

CONDITION CODE REGISTER MANIPULATION INSTRUCTIONS

OPERATIONS	MNEMONIC	IMPLIED OP	~	#	BOOLEAN OPERATION	COND. CODE REG. 5 H	4 I	3 N	2 Z	1 V	0 C
Clear Carry	CLC	0C	2	1	$0 \rightarrow C$	●	●	●	●	●	R
Clear Interrupt Mask	CLI	0E	2	1	$0 \rightarrow I$	●	R	●	●	●	●
Clear Overflow	CLV	0A	2	1	$0 \rightarrow V$	●	●	●	●	R	●
Set Carry	SEC	0D	2	1	$1 \rightarrow C$	●	●	●	●	●	S
Set Interrupt Mask	SEI	0F	2	1	$1 \rightarrow I$	●	S	●	●	●	●
Set Overflow	SEV	0B	2	1	$1 \rightarrow V$	●	●	●	●	S	●
Acmltr A → CCR	TAP	06	2	1	$A \rightarrow CCR$	⑫					
CCR → Acmltr A	TPA	07	2	1	$CCR \rightarrow A$	●	●	●	●	●	●

CONDITION CODE REGISTER NOTES: (Bit set if test is true and cleared otherwise)

1   (Bit V)   Test: Result = 10000000?
2   (Bit C)   Test: Result = 00000000?
3   (Bit C)   Test: Decimal value of most significant BCD Character greater than nine?
          (Not cleared if previously set.)
4   (Bit V)   Test: Operand = 10000000 prior to execution?
5   (Bit V)   Test: Operand = 01111111 prior to execution?
6   (Bit V)   Test: Set equal to result of N⊕C after shift has occurred.

7   (Bit N)   Test: Sign bit of most significant (MS) byte = 1?
8   (Bit V)   Test: 2's complement overflow from subtraction of MS bytes?
9   (Bit N)   Test: Result less than zero? (Bit 15 = 1)
10   (All)   Load Condition Code Register from Stack. (See Special Operations)
11   (Bit I)   Set when interrupt occurs. If previously set, a Non-Maskable
                Interrupt is required to exit the wait state.
12   (All)   Set according to the contents of Accumulator A.

INDEX REGISTER AND STACK MANIPULATION INSTRUCTIONS

POINTER OPERATIONS	MNEMONIC	IMMED OP	~	#	DIRECT OP	~	#	INDEX OP	~	#	EXTND OP	~	#	IMPLIED OP	~	#	BOOLEAN/ARITHMETIC OPERATION	COND. CODE REG. 5 H	4 I	3 N	2 Z	1 V	0 C
Compare Index Reg	CPX	8C	3	3	9C	4	2	AC	6	2	BC	5	3				$X_H - M, X_L - (M+1)$	●	●	⑦	↕	⑧	●
Decrement Index Reg	DEX													09	4	1	$X - 1 \rightarrow X$	●	●	●	↕	●	●
Decrement Stack Pntr	DES													34	4	1	$SP - 1 \rightarrow SP$	●	●	●	●	●	●
Increment Index Reg	INX													08	4	1	$X + 1 \rightarrow X$	●	●	●	↕	●	●
Increment Stack Pntr	INS													31	4	1	$SP + 1 \rightarrow SP$	●	●	●	●	●	●
Load Index Reg	LDX	CE	3	3	DE	4	2	EE	6	2	FE	5	3				$M \rightarrow X_H, (M+1) \rightarrow X_L$	●	●	⑨	↕	R	●
Load Stack Pntr	LDS	8E	3	3	9E	4	2	AE	6	2	BE	5	3				$M \rightarrow SP_H, (M+1) \rightarrow SP_L$	●	●	⑨	↕	R	●
Store Index Reg	STX				DF	5	2	EF	7	2	FF	6	3				$X_H \rightarrow M, X_L \rightarrow (M+1)$	●	●	⑨	↕	R	●
Store Stack Pntr	STS				9F	5	2	AF	7	2	BF	6	3				$SP_H \rightarrow M, SP_L \rightarrow (M+1)$	●	●	⑨	↕	R	●
Indx Reg → Stack Pntr	TXS													35	4	1	$X - 1 \rightarrow SP$	●	●	●	●	●	●
Stack Pntr → Indx Reg	TSX													30	4	1	$SP + 1 \rightarrow X$	●	●	●	●	●	●

JUMP AND BRANCH INSTRUCTIONS

OPERATIONS	MNEMONIC	RELATIVE OP	~	#	INDEX OP	~	#	EXTND OP	~	#	IMPLIED OP	~	#	BRANCH TEST	COND. CODE REG. 5 H	4 I	3 N	2 Z	1 V	0 C
Branch Always	BRA	20	4	2										None	●	●	●	●	●	●
Branch If Carry Clear	BCC	24	4	2										$C = 0$	●	●	●	●	●	●
Branch If Carry Set	BCS	25	4	2										$C = 1$	●	●	●	●	●	●
Branch If = Zero	BEQ	27	4	2										$Z = 1$	●	●	●	●	●	●
Branch If ≥ Zero	BGE	2C	4	2										$N \oplus V = 0$	●	●	●	●	●	●
Branch If > Zero	BGT	2E	4	2										$Z + (N \oplus V) = 0$	●	●	●	●	●	●
Branch If Higher	BHI	22	4	2										$C + Z = 0$	●	●	●	●	●	●
Branch If ≤ Zero	BLE	2F	4	2										$Z + (N \oplus V) = 1$	●	●	●	●	●	●
Branch If Lower Or Same	BLS	23	4	2										$C + Z = 1$	●	●	●	●	●	●
Branch If < Zero	BLT	2D	4	2										$N \oplus V = 1$	●	●	●	●	●	●
Branch If Minus	BMI	2B	4	2										$N = 1$	●	●	●	●	●	●
Branch If Not Equal Zero	BNE	26	4	2										$Z = 0$	●	●	●	●	●	●
Branch If Overflow Clear	BVC	28	4	2										$V = 0$	●	●	●	●	●	●
Branch If Overflow Set	BVS	29	4	2										$V = 1$	●	●	●	●	●	●
Branch If Plus	BPL	2A	4	2										$N = 0$	●	●	●	●	●	●
Branch To Subroutine	BSR	8D	8	2											●	●	●	●	●	●
Jump	JMP				6E	4	2	7E	3	3				See Special Operations	●	●	●	●	●	●
Jump To Subroutine	JSR				AD	8	2	BD	9	3					●	●	●	●	●	●
No Operation	NOP										01	2	1	Advances Prog. Cntr. Only	●	●	●	●	●	●
Return From Interrupt	RTI										3B	10	1		⑩					
Return From Subroutine	RTS										39	5	1		●	●	●	●	●	●
Software Interrupt	SWI										3F	12	1	See Special Operations	●	●	●	●	●	●
Wait for Interrupt *	WAI										3E	9	1		●	⑪	●	●	●	●

*WAI puts Address Bus, R/W, and Data Bus in the three-state mode while VMA is held low.

a page-0 mode like this. Specifying only the lower byte of the address not only saves one byte of memory space but executes in one less clock cycle. Essentially microprocessors of this kind are using these external 256 bytes of RAM as an additional register array. The 6809 MPU even has a page register, which is used to hold the upper byte for direct addressing. With this set at $00, page 0 is accessed as described. However, the page register can be changed to any value as the program progresses.

Extended | Op-code | Upper-address byte | Lower-address byte |

This is the general version of direct addressing applicable to any address. For example, ADDA $038F = $8B-03-8F operates on data in location $038F. Some manufacturers refer to this address mode as absolute. In the 6800/2 MPUs, several instructions do not have a direct mode; e.g. to clear RAM location $32 we have to use the instruction CLR $0032 = 7F-00-32. In the 6805 MCU, the converse is the case.

Relative | Op-code | Signed   PC   offset |

This address mode is only used for branching instructions. Where the branch condition (if any) is fulfilled, the program counter is augmented by the single-byte offset. This offset is in the form of an 8-bit signed 2s complement number. Thus to branch forward four places, the offset is %0,0000100. For example, BRA $04 (20-04) with PC at $0316 has the following effect:

$$
\begin{array}{ll}
0000\ 0011\quad 0001\ 0110 & \text{PC, } \$0316 \\
+\ \underline{(0000\ 0000)\ 0000\ 0100} & \text{Offset, } +4 \\
0000\ 0011\quad 0001\ 1010 & \text{PC, } \$031A
\end{array}
$$

the PC effectively skipping forward four places.

Branching can be backwards, provided that a negative offset is used. Thus to go back four places we use the offset %1,111 1100($FC), which is the 2s complement of four. In the same situation BRA $FC will have the following effect:

$$
\begin{array}{ll}
0000\ 0011\quad 0001\ 0110 & \text{PC, } \$0316 \\
+\ \underline{(1111\ 1111)\ 1111\ 1100} & \text{Offset, } -4 \\
(1)\ 0000\ 0011\quad 0001\ 0010 & \text{PC, } \$0312
\end{array}
$$

a move back by four. Notice the way the sign bit has been extended to match the 8-bit offset to the 16-bit program counter capacity.

When a program is being translated by hand (see Section 1.4), the programmer must remember that the program counter has already gone forward two places during the fetch phase to point to the next instruction. Thus counting forwards or backwards should begin at the instruction following the branch.

Indexed	Op-code	Positive	IX	offset

The second byte of an instruction using this mode will be added onto the current contents of the 16-bit index register to form the true or effective address. Thus if the index-register contents are $0E00 at the time when the instruction ADDA $32,X is executed, data at $0E32 will be fetched and added. We will elaborate on the role of the index register in Section 1.3, meanwhile note the use of the appellation ,X to indicate indexed addressing.

In the instruction set of Table 1.7, each instruction is listed with its op-codes for the applicable address modes. The number of clock cycles for each instruction version is indicated under the column headed ~ , while the number of bytes comprising the instruction is under the heading # . Thus ANDA extended is a 3-byte instruction taking four cycles to implement. At a clock frequency of 1 MHz, cycles may be read as microseconds.

1.3   ADDRESS POINTERS

Looking at Fig. 1.1, we see that the 6802 MPU has three 16-bit registers associated with the address bus. We have already seen that it is the duty of the program counter to keep track of the location of the next program byte to be processed. But there is more up in memory space than just the program. Arrays of data, either variables in RAM or constants in ROM, are frequently used. During the execute phase, the address of one of these array elements must be sent out to access the data. If we use the *index register* to point to this element, then the use of the index address mode will facilitate this access.

As an example, let us take the problem of checking all RAM locations between $0000 and $1FFF. We can do this by sending out a test signature (typically %10101010) to each cell in turn and verify that it has been correctly stored. The crude method of doing this is to place the signature in an accumulator, then store it at $0000 and compare its contents with that in the accumulator. If they equate then repeat the store and compare routine for each RAM location; a total of 8,192 program segments. Rather a long program! Here is a better version:

10		LDX	#0	Clear index register
20		LDAA	#%10101010	Put signature in accumulator
30	LOOP	STAA	0,X	Send out signature
40		CMPA	0,X	Has it got there OK?
50		BNE	ERROR	IF not THEN go to error routine
60		INX		ELSE move pointer up one
70		CPX	#$2000	Check that we haven't overshot yet
80		BNE	LOOP	IF not THEN next byte
90		– – –	– – –	ELSE next portion of program

In this program the actual send and check routine comprises the same three instructions repeated in a loop 8,192 times. Steps 60–80 update the index register, which is being used as a data pointer.

When manipulating the contents of the index register, the programmer must remember that a 16-bit register is being handled in an 8-bit environment. Thus, if it is desired to store the contents of the index register in memory (perhaps to retrieve later), the STX M instruction has the problem of moving two bytes of data to one address M. This is overcome by moving the higher byte IXH to M and the lower to M + 1. For example, STX $0020 results in $\boxed{\text{IXH}\,|\,\text{IXL}}$ in $0020/1. The index register is similarly loaded from memory. The immediate load and compare instructions both use double-byte operands.

The *stack-pointer register* plays a completely different role. Like the index register it has a 16-bit capacity and points to a memory location. Normally an area of memory, known as the *stack,* is set aside for use in conjuction with the stack pointer. The stack is primarily used to facilitate the efficient use of subroutines and interrupts.

A *subroutine* is a program segment implementing a particular procedure. This segment is generally separate from the main program, which can call up the subroutine whenever it is desired to implement that algorithm. A simple example is given in Section 1.4, where a byte in memory is to be multiplied by a constant in the accumulator. Anytime the main program wishes to multiply, the constant is placed in Accumulator A and the subroutine is called up.

Using a straightforward jump to get to the subroutine is not satisfactory. As can be seen from (a) in Fig. 1.4, the problem lies in the return. If the subroutine is to be capable of being called up from more than one place in the main program, or even from another subroutine, then how is the program counter to be returned to its jumping-off value at the end of the procedure? Obviously the initial (jumping-off) PC value must be stored in RAM prior to the call, and reinserted at the return. Both the 8080 and 6800 families use the stack to do this automatically. The 6800's jump to subroutine (JSR) pushes the higher byte of PC into the location pointed to by the stack pointer, decrements the pointer, pushes the lower byte into the stack, again decrements the pointer to point to the next empty stack location; and only then implements the jump. This is shown in (b) in fig. 1.4.

At the end of the subroutine the inherent instruction 'return from subroutine' (RTS = $39) causes the stack pointer to move up two places, in the process returning the contents (i.e., the old value) to the program counter. This effectively returns the MPU to its jumping-off point irrespective of where the subroutine was called. For those readers with an 8080/Z80 family background, the subroutine instructions are *call* and *return*. The stack pointer in this case always points to the last-used stack location.

Automatic use of a stack in this manner, rather than using two fixed RAM locations, permits the use of nested subroutines, where one subroutine calls up another. Each additional call simply pushes the stack down two further places, while on return the sequence is opposite. In order to use this push-down stack, the programmer must set aside an area of RAM, big enough to deal with all contingencies, and set the stack pointer to point to the top of this RAM. In the 6802 MPU

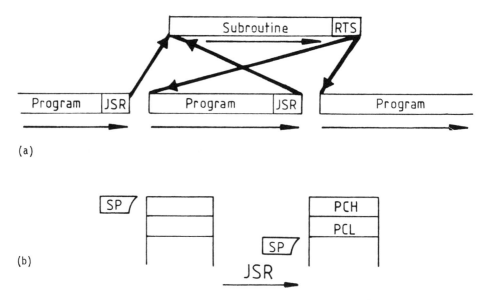

Fig. 1.4 How the 6800 family handles subroutines
(*a*) Subroutine programming
(*b*) Automatically saving the return address
(PCH-PCL) on the stack before the jump

the internal RAM is often used as a stack, and in this situation one of the initialization instructions must be LDS # $007F (8E-00-7F). If subroutines are nested up to ten deep, then the top 20 bytes ($006C-$007F) must not be used for any other purpose.

One of the distinguishing features of a microprocessor-based system involves its quality of interaction with external events. We have already observed that one form of interaction involves the MPU branching to a different program segment depending on the magnitude or pattern of a word in memory space. As we shall see in Chapter 2, this is usually the state of an external peripheral device. This form of interaction is entirely controlled by the MPU, which tests the state whenever it likes. However, some external events are too urgent to wait on a possibly tardy response from the system controller.

A simple example of a time-sensitive requirement is shown in Fig. 1.5. Here we wish to measure the elapsed time between external events to a precision of 0.1 ms. An external counter totalizes the 0.1 ms 'ticks' provided by a precision 10 kHz oscillator. If the MPU reads the state of the counter on the occurrence of each event, it can subtract the present from previous reading to form a difference. But it must react to the occurrence of an event within 100 μs to stay within the stated precision.

All current microprocessors have one or more inputs labeled *interrupt*. An external circuit can activate this input and thereby cause the MPU to jump to a special subroutine, known as an *interrupt service routine*. Thus in Fig. 1.5 we have

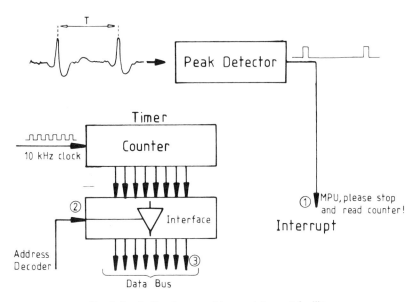

Fig. 1.5   A situation requiring an interrupt facility

the following sequence of events:

1   Event detector signals the MPU to interrupt whatever it is doing.
2   The MPU then jumps to the service routine which addresses the counter interface.
3   And the MPU then reads the data into an internal register.

The hardware implications of this are covered in Chapter 2; here we will look at how the 6800 family handles interrupt requests and the role of the stack pointer in this procedure.

In Section 1.2 we saw that the 6802 has two interrupt pins labeled $\overline{\text{IRQ}}$ and $\overline{\text{NMI}}$. We will concentrate on the former (sometimes known as a *hardware interrupt*), as this is the most commonly used.

When an external device pulls $\overline{\text{IRQ}}$ low, the following sequence of events occur:

1   The MPU completes execution of its current instruction.
2   If the I mask is set the interrupt is ignored and the next instruction fetched. Go to Step 1.
3   The contents of the program counter are saved on the stack, in the manner of (b) in Fig. 1.4. However, additionally the following registers are also pushed into the stack; IXH, IXL, A, B and CCR (see Fig. 1.6).
4   The I mask is set, thus blanking out any further interrupt request.
5   The start address of the IRQ service routine is fetched from $FFF8/9 and placed in the program counter. This effectively causes a jump to the service routine.

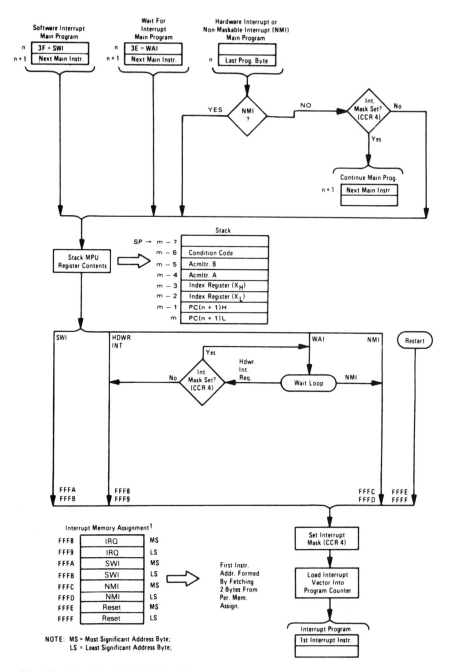

Fig. 1.6   How the 6800/2/8 handles interrupts (reproduced by courtesy of Motorola Limited)

6   The last instruction of the interrupt service routine must be 'return from interrupt' (RTI = $3B). This is similar to RTS but causes the stack to offload all its register contents, not just those of the program counter. Thus the MPU returns to its original preinterrupt state, and continues as if it had never had cause to pause. The return of the CCR flags effectively means that the I mask is reset (see Step 4), and the MPU can now immediately service another interrupt request. Of course, the signal on the $\overline{\text{IRQ}}$ pin from the just-serviced peripheral must have been lifted at this time. Go to Step 1.

The sequence of events is shown diagrammatically in Fig. 1.6. Notice especially the view of the stack presented in the middle of the diagram. The instruction 'wait for interrupt' (WAI = $3E) will dump the register contents onto the stack automatically and then idle the MPU until an interrupt comes along. As an external interrupt is by definition random, this automatic stack dump ensures that no corruption of internal data will occur irrespective of where in the program the interrupt strikes.

As the programmer can set and clear the I mask at will (SEI and CLI, see Table 1.6), $\overline{\text{IRQ}}$ can be locked out in sensitive areas. It is for this reason that a reset will always set the I flag, as it is desirable to have the various peripheral interface devices set up prior to permitting an interrupt service (see Chapters 2 through 5).

The non-maskable interrupt ($\overline{\text{NMI}}$) is similar to the maskable variety, but as it cannot be locked out by the I flag has a higher priority. Thus a $\overline{\text{NMI}}$ can interrupt an IRQ service routine. The starting address for the NMI service routine must be stored in $FFFC/D. As $\overline{\text{NMI}}$ is edge sensitive, it is not necessary to ensure that the signal is lifted by the end of the service routine. Due to its nonmaskability, $\overline{\text{NMI}}$ is normally used only for an overriding system emergency, such as an impending power failure.

A third interrupt is shown in Fig. 1.6, viz., the software interrupt (SWI). This is strictly not an interrupt as we have described it, as it is triggered by the instruction SWI (= $3F). The forces the system stack dump as described, and the MPU vectors to the start of the SWI service routine via $FFFA/B. SWI is used mainly as a software debug tool, effectively moving the state of the internal registers out into RAM, where they can be examined by the microprocessor development system; perhaps by using the SWI service routine to print them out.

Reset is also listed in Fig. 1.6 as an interrupt. This is true in the sense that it is an external signal which causes the MPU to drop whatever it is doing and go to a service routine. This time the service routine is in effect the main program, which is vectored via $FFFE/F. However, as the stack dump is not used, no evidence remains of the MPU's previous life.

Some microprocessors, such as the 6502 series, do not save anything but the program counter contents on the stack on an interrupt. The 6809 MPU has a $\overline{\text{FIRQ}}$ interrupt (fast $\overline{\text{IRQ}}$) which saves the PC and CCR only. In such cases the state of any register which will be used during the service routine must be saved somewhere. Both MPUs have push and pull (sometimes known as *pop*) instructions for pushing register contents onto the stack and pulling them back. Thus in the 6502 MPU,

PSHA moves the accumulator contents out into the stack and decrements the pointer; whilst PULA increments SP and moves the byte back to the accumulator. The 6809 MPU allows a selection of all internal registers to be pushed or pulled in one instruction. The 6802 MPU has PSHA; PSHB and PULA; PULB operations, which can be used for the convenient saving and retrieval of accumulator data and for building up arrays. However, because of the use of the stack for subroutine and interrupt purposes, great care must be exercised in these circumstances. The 6809 MPU has two stack pointers, and thus can keep its two stacks entirely separate.

1.4   SOME PROGRAM EXAMPLES

To give the reader who is unfamiliar with the 6800/2 MPU some feeling for the software aspects of this microprocessor, we will look at three realistic programming examples. We choose these routines to exemplify programming technique and with an eye to our project's future software requirements. To facilitate the student, Fig. 1.7 shows a programmer's view of the 6802's accessible registers.

As our first example let us look at the problem of noise in analog signals. For our project we will be reading an analog voltage proportional to temperature. This

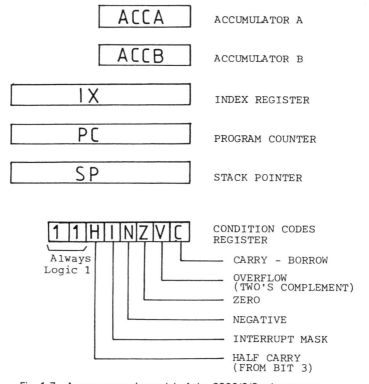

Fig. 1.7   A programmer's model of the 6800/2/8 microprocessors

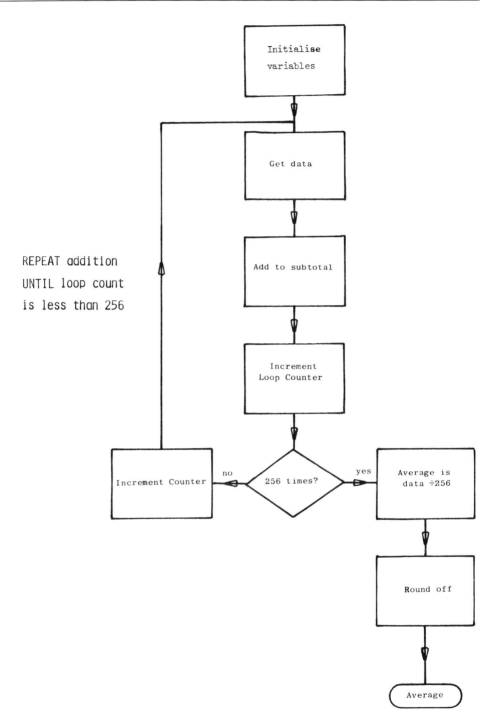

Fig. 1.8   A software noise reduction algorithm

will be changed to a directly readable digital equivalent using an analog to digital converter. Now these analog signals will inherently be noisy. Noise may be internally generated by the digital circuitry or may be induced from outside; e.g., mains frequency pickup. This can be reduced, but not eliminated, by following layout and shielding stratagems. Further improvements can be achieved by including frequency sensitive filtering in the analog circuitry. Alternatively the filtering may be done by the MPU on the digital equivalent. One of the simplest digital filtering algorithms is that of averaging. The parameter is sampled and summed n times. The final value is this sum divided by n. Provided that the sampled quantity, e.g., temperature, has not significantly altered during this process and that the noise is random, then the signal-to-noise ratio is improved by the factor $\sqrt{n}$.

For this example we use $n = 256$, to simplify the division process. After adding 256 8-bit numbers, the resulting 16-bit sum will occupy two bytes, thus:

$$\boxed{\text{Upper byte}} \quad \boxed{\text{Lower byte}} \quad \bullet \quad \text{(sum of 256 8-bit numbers)}$$

The sum is a whole number, as shown by the notional binary point to the right of the 16-bit sum. In binary numeration the movement of the binary point left by k places gives a division factor of 2^k. Thus a shift of eight places divides by 256:

$$\boxed{\text{Upper byte}} \quad \bullet \quad \boxed{\text{Lower byte}}$$

and we can then take the upper byte of the sum as the average of 256 summations. The accuracy of the result is enhanced if the upper byte is incremented when the lower byte has its most significant bit $= 1$ (i.e., lower byte $\geqslant \frac{1}{2}$).

The algorithm flow chart for this program is shown in Fig. 1.8. The central portion of this is in the form of a *loop*, where the data is continuously fetched and added to the double-byte subtotal. In order to exit this loop after 256 goes, Accumulator B is used as a counter. This is initially cleared and is then incremented after each loop pass. It will return to zero after 256 passes.

The listing for this example follows. We have divided the listing into three zones. The leftmost of these is known as the *source program*. This is written in a programmer-readable form, using operation mnemonics and names for the various memory locations. The center zone is the object program. This is machine-readable code (but in hexadecimal), listing the program byte in each location. The rightmost field is for documentation purposes only. Good and clear documentation is essential to aid in the production of accurate software, and in the debugging of such programs. When complete lines of commentary are included, this is indicated with a * label following the line number.

We have used pseudo operations EQU and ORG to pass information concerning the name of locations and the start position of the machine code. Pseudo instructions do not produce machine code in themselves, they are used to provide information to the translator of source to object code.

Source Code	Object Code				Commentary
10*	This subroutine averages over 256 samples				
20*	Locations used: $0040/41; A; B; CCR				
30*	ENTRY: No conditions				
40*	EXIT: Rounded-off average in Acc.A				
50*	EXIT: Acc.B cleared. $0040/1 holds sum of 256 additions				
60 LBYTE	EQU	$0040			This is the lower byte of the sum
70 UBYTE	EQU	$0041			and the upper byte
80 A/D	EQU	$000F			This is the A/D Data register
90	ORG	$0A00			Subroutine starts at $0A00
100*	Clear workspace				
110 INDATA	CLR	LBYTE	$0A00/1/2	7F-00-40	Clear data workspace
120	CLR	UBYTE	$0A03/4/5	7F-00-41	Note, clear has no extended mode
130	CLRB		$0A06	5F	Acc.B used as loop counter
140*	Add Nth sample to sum total				
150 LOOP	LDAA	A/D	$0A07/8	96-0F	Get latest sample
160	ADDA	LBYTE	$0A09/A	9B-40	Add it to the lower byte
170	STAA	LBYTE	$0A0B/C	97-40	and restore it
180	LDAA	UBYTE	$0A0D/E	96-41	Now get upper byte of sum
190	ADCA	#00	$0A0F/10	89-00	Add carry only
200	STAA	UBYTE	$0A11/2	97-41	and restore it
210*	256 times yet?				
220	INCB		$0A13	5C	One more time
230	BNE	LOOP	$0A14/5	26-F1	IF not finished THEN again
240*	Divide by 256 and round off				
250	LDAA	UBYTE	$0A16/7	96-41	ELSE get sum/256
260	TST	LBYTE	$0A18/9/A	7D-00-40	Examine remainder for bit 7 = 0
270	BPL	END	$0A1B/C	2A-01	IF not THEN don't add one
280	INCA		$0A1D	4C	ELSE roundup
290 END	RTS		$0A1E	39	Exit with answer in Acc.A

Let us briefly summarize the listing. Steps 110–120 clear the two sum bytes. Extended addressing is used here (and in Step 260) as no direct mode exists for these instructions. Accumulator B is used as the loop counter, Step 130.

Inside the loop itself the single-byte data is added to the double-byte sum. The two lower bytes are added normally, Steps 150–170, while the resultant carry plus zero (the conceptual data upper byte) is then added to the sum upper byte, Steps 180–200.

The loop test is accomplished in Steps 220–230 by incrementing the loop counter, which will set the Z flag when this overflows back to zero. If the count is not zero, the conditional branch of Step 230 will return the program counter back to Step 150. As the PC is already pointing to the next instruction following the fetch, an offset of $-$\$0F is required. The 2s complement of \$0F is \$F1.

Finally the upper byte is brought down to Accumulator A, and the remainder in $0041 tested for negative (N flag set if bit 7 = 1). The branch-if-plus operation of Step 270 will cause the PC to skip the increment of Step 280 if bit 7 = 0.

As the listing is written in the form of a subroutine, it is terminated by RTS. Any time the main program requires a reading, it will simply call up this module. No data are required to be transferred to the subroutine.

The machine code in this listing has been *hand-assembled*. That is, each instruction in the source program has been translated by hand using Table 1.7 together with manual branch offset calculation. Also names and labels have been manually converted to their actual equivalent. For programs of any practical length, this process is time-consuming and error-prone. Furthermore, making even a single alteration can mean nearly a complete rewrite of the entire program.

Translation from source to object code is essentially a rote process, and so is an ideal candidate for computerization. An *assembler* is a program which takes source code as typed in by the operator, and produces machine code with no further manual intervention. The assembler is usually paired with a *text-editor* program. This allows the operator to enter the source code on a terminal, and permits the correction of current or previous typing errors. The editor-assembler package may either run on the microcomputer which will eventually run the machine code, or operate in an entirely separate computer. The former is known as a *resident editor-assembler*. The listings shown in the rest of the text are produced using a *cross-assembler-editor* running on an Apple IIe personal microcomputer. We will use our second example to illustrate the syntax of this editor-assembler.

It is desired to implement a subroutine to multiply two 8-bit numbers. The multiplicand is in location $0040, while the multiplier is passed to the subroutine in Accumulator A. The 16-bit product is to be returned in $0042/3.

Firstly we need an algorithm for binary multiplication. Following the familiar decimal technique, consider the following case:

$$
\begin{array}{rl}
1011 & \text{Multiplicand} \\
\times\ 0110 & \text{Multiplier} \\
\hline
0000 & \\
1011 & \\
1011 & \Big\}\ \text{Partial products} \\
+\ 0000 & \\
\hline
1000010 & \text{Product}
\end{array}
$$

An inspection of the resulting partial products show that the *n*th subproduct is the multiplicand shifted *n* places left multiplied by the *n*th multiplier bit, either 0 or 1. As a shift left one place is a multiplication by 2, we can express the product *P* as:

$$P = \sum_{n=0}^{k} D \times 2^n \times R(n)$$

where D is the multiplicand, 2^n is a shift n places-left operator and $R(n)$ is the *n*th multiplier bit.

Implementing the shift-and-add multiplication algorithm will then involve a loop in which the multiplicand is shifted left once and conditionally double-precision added to the subproduct. The condition being the state of the *n*th multiplier bit. By shifting the multiplier once right during each loop pass, and examining the C flag, each multiplier bit can be examined sequentially moving to the left. The flowchart (b) of Fig. 1.9 exits whenever the residue multiplier is zero. This is faster and more efficient than counting eight loop passes to completion.

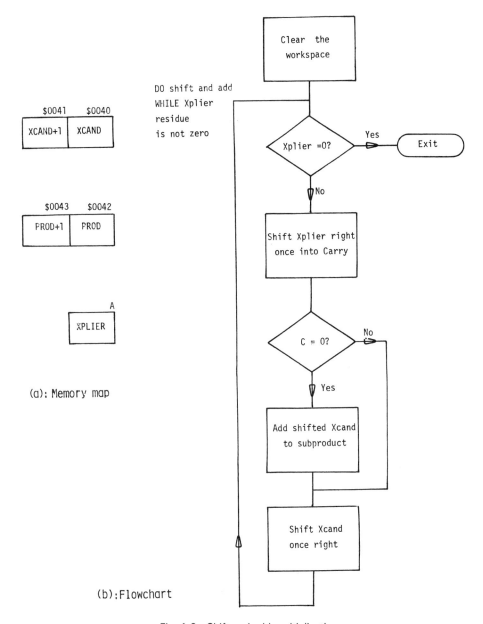

(a): Memory map

(b):Flowchart

Fig. 1.9   Shift-and-add multiplication

The memory map (a) of Fig. 1.9 gives the location of the multiplicand, multiplier and product. Since the multiplicand byte is to be shifted progressively left as n increases to k, then an overflow byte at \$0041 is provided to accommodate this maneuver.

The source program for this subroutine is given in Listing 1.1, exactly as entered using the editor. Zone divisions are indicated by a space, with an * identifying a comment. An additional blank after the line number signifies no label for that line. The listing has been segmented by comment lines to correspond with the

```
10 * This subroutine multiplies two unsigned bytes
20 * Locations used : $0040-43; A; CCR
30 * ENTRY : Multiplier in A; Multiplicand in $0040
40 * EXIT  : Product in $0042/3 (LSB/MSB)
50 * EXIT  : Multiplicand and Multiplier destroyed; A=00
60 * ******************************************************
70 XCAND EQU $0040 *This is where the Multiplicand is
80 PROD EQU $0042 *This is where the product will be
90  ORG $0A30 *Machine code commences at $0A30
100 * Clear the workspace
110 MULT CLR XCAND+1 *Clear the Multiplicand overflow
120  CLR PROD *and both the product bytes
130  CLR PROD+1
140 * A zero multiplier?
150 LOOP TSTA
160  BNE XSHIFT *IF not THEN next loop pass
170  RTS  *ELSE finished
180 * Now shift multiplier once into Carry
190 XSHIFT LSRA
200 * Examine the nth bit in the C flag
210  BCC MSHIFT *IF zero THEN do not add
220 * If bit n is 1 THEN add the shifted multiplicand to the product
230  PSHA  *First save multiplier residue on the Stack
240  LDAA PROD *Now add lower byte to subproduct
250  ADDA XCAND
260  STAA PROD
270  LDAA PROD+1 *Then the upper byte plus Carry
280  ADCA XCAND+1
290  STAA PROD+1
300  PULA  *Get back the multiplier residue
310 * Shift the multiplicand once left
320 MSHIFT ASL XCAND *First the lower byte
330  ROL XCAND+1 *Then the upper byte
340  BRA LOOP *Go do it again
```

Listing 1.1   Source program for the multiplication subroutine

flowchart (b) symbols of Fig. 1.9. Each function is relatively simple, usually taking no more than three instructions. However, note the double-precision addition of Lines 230–300. As the multiplier residue is in Accumulator A, we should use Accumulator B for addition during this operation. This has not been done here in order to emulate the 6805 MCU which has only one accumulator. Instead the residue multiplier has been moved out of the way in Line 230 by using a push operation. It is returned after the additions by pulling it back off the stack in Line 300. Lines 320 and 330 perform a double-precision shift left in the manner illustrated in Fig. 1.3.

Once the source program has been entered, it can be passed from the editor to the assembler program. This performs the same operation as our hand translation of the previous example, and also checks for certain syntax errors. The pseudo operations ORG and EQU are used in this situation to pass information from the programmer to the assembler. For example, 'I want you to take the label PROD to mean \$0042 anytime you see it used in the program'. i.e., PROD EQU \$0042. Most assemblers can do simple arithmetic with labels; thus PROD + 1 becomes \$0043 in Line 130 of Listing 1.2.

Most assemblers produce listings in three zones. In Listing 1.2, the leftmost zone gives the machine or object code. This gives the location and value for each byte in program memory in hexadecimal. The middle zone is a formatted version of the original source code of Listing 1.1, followed by any comment. As an assembled listing shows both source and object code, only this type of listing will be shown in future programs.

Our final example of this section involves division. Division is an algorithm whereby the number of times a divisor can be subtracted from a dividend is recorded. A software implementation of division by repetitive subtraction is relatively simple to program, but usually results in a long execution time. A fast division can be accomplished by using the binary equivalent to decimal long division. For example, to divide %1011 by %10, we perform the following operations:

$$
\begin{array}{ll}
\begin{array}{r} 1101 \\ \div\ \underline{10} \end{array} & \\[2ex]
\begin{array}{r} 1101 \\ \div 10\ \underline{} \end{array} & \text{Align } (N = 2) \\[2ex]
\begin{array}{r} 1101 \\ -\ 10 \\ \hline 0101 \end{array} & \begin{array}{l} \text{and} \\ \text{subtract} \qquad Q = 1 \end{array} \\[2ex]
\begin{array}{r} -\ \ 10 \\ \hline 0001 \end{array} & \begin{array}{l} \text{shift divisor} \\ \text{subtract} \qquad Q = 11 \end{array} \\[2ex]
\begin{array}{r} -\ \ 10 \\ \hline 0001 \end{array} & \begin{array}{l} \text{shift divisor} \\ \text{cannot subtract} \quad Q = 110 \end{array}
\end{array}
$$

MULT-OBJECT

        Line Machine code   Source code   Comment

```
 10   *This subroutine multiplies two unsigned bytes
 20   *Locations used : $0040-43; A; CCR
 30   *ENTRY : Multiplier in A; Multiplicand in $0040
 40   *EXIT  : Product in $0042/3 (LSB/MSB)
 50   *EXIT  : Multiplicand and Multiplier destroyed; A=00
 60   *******************************************************
 70        (0040) XCAND  EQU   $0040        *This is where the Multiplicand is
 80        (0042) PROD   EQU   $0042        *This is where the product will be
 90        (0A30)        ORG   $0A30        *Machine code commences at $0A30
100   *Clear the workspace
110   0A30 7F-0041 MULT  CLR   XCAND+1      *Clear the Multiplicand overflow
120   0A33 7F-0042       CLR   PROD         *and both the product bytes
130   0A36 7F-0043       CLR   PROD+1
140   *A zero multiplier?
150   0A39 4D      LOOP  TSTA
160   0A3A 26-01         BNE   XSHIFT       *IF not THEN next loop pass
170   0A3C 39            RTS                *ELSE finished
180   *Now shift multiplier once into Carry
190   0A3D 44      XSHIFT LSRA
200   *Examine the nth bit in the C flag
210   0A3E 24-0E         BCC   MSHIFT       *IF zero THEN do not add
220   *If bit n is 1 THEN add the shifted multiplicand to the product
230   0A40 36            PSHA               *First save multiplier residue on the Stack
240   0A41 96-42         LDAA  PROD         *Now add lower byte to subproduct
250   0A43 9B-40         ADDA  XCAND
260   0A45 97-42         STAA  PROD
270   0A47 96-43         LDAA  PROD+1       *Then the upper byte plus Carry
280   0A49 99-41         ADCA  XCAND+1
290   0A4B 97-43         STAA  PROD+1
300   0A4D 32            PULA               *Get back the multiplier residue
310   *Shift the multiplicand once left
320   0A4E 78-0040 MSHIFT ASL  XCAND        *First the lower byte
330   0A51 79-0041       ROL   XCAND+1      *Then the upper byte
340   0A54 20-E3         BRA   LOOP         *Go do it again
```

Listing 1.2   Assembled program for the multiplication subroutine

In essence this procedure can be summed up as:

I   Move divisor over N places to align with dividend.
II   Repeat Steps III to V for $k = N$ to 0, step -1.
III   Try to subtract divisor. If successful $Q = 1$, else $Q = 0$.
IV   Shift divisor right one place.
V   Next k. Go to Step III.
VI   If the remainder is more than divisor/2, then round up quotient.

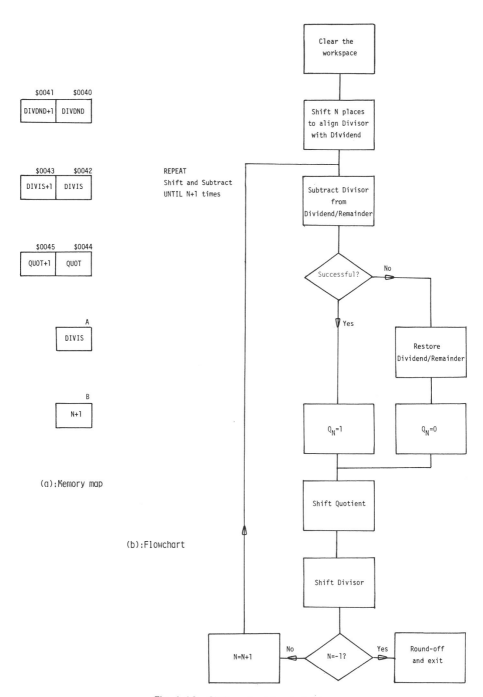

(a):Memory map

(b):Flowchart

Fig. 1.10 Shift-and-subtract division

```
 10   *This subroutine divides a 16-bit dividend by an 8-bit divisor
 20   *ELSE round off Quotient
 30   *ENTRY : Divisor in A
 40   *ENTRY : Dividend in $0041/0 (MSB/LSB)
 50   *EXIT  : Quotient in $0045/4 (MSB/LSB), rounded off
 60
 70        <0040>  DIVDND  EQU   $40          *Dividend/Remainder lives in $40/1
 80        <0042>  DIVIS   EQU   $42          *Divisor moves to $0042/3
 90        <0044>  QUOT    EQU   $44          *Quotient ends up in $0045/4
100        <0A60>          ORG   $0A60        *Subroutine starts here
110   ********************************************************************************
120   *Clear workspace
130   0A60 7F-0043 DIVIDE  CLR   DIVIS+1      *Divisor overflow cleared
140   0A63 7F-0044         CLR   QUOT         *and Quotient space
150   0A66 7F-0045         CLR   QUOT+1
160   0A69 5F              CLRB               *Align count = 00 (N)
170   0A6A 97-42           STAA  DIVIS        *Move Divisor up to $0042
180   *Now align Divisor with Dividend
190   0A6C 5C      ALIGN   INCB               *One more for the align count N
200   0A6D 92-43           SBCA  DIVIS+1
210   0A6F 79-0043         ROL   DIVIS+1
220   0A72 2A-F8           BPL   ALIGN        *IF bit7 not 1 THEN one more shift
230   0A74 5C              INCB               *ELSE make N one more
240   *N+1 in Acc.B = number of digits to left of Quotient's binary point
250   *
260   *Now do the 16-bit subtraction
270   0A75 96-40   SUB     LDAA  DIVDND       *First sub the LSBs
280   0A77 90-42           SUBA  DIVIS
290   0A79 97-40           STAA  DIVDND
300   0A7B 96-41           LDAA  DIVDND+1     *Now the MSBs
310   0A7D 92-43           SBCA  DIVIS+1
320   *IF a borrow has been produced THEN an unsuccessful subtraction
330   0A7F 24-09           BCC   SUCCESS      *IF successful THEN omit restore
340   0A81 96-42           LDAA  DIVIS        *ELSE restore LSB
350   0A83 9B-40           ADDA  DIVDND       *By adding the LSB Divisor back again
360   0A85 97-40           STAA  DIVDND       *Note the MSB has not been altered
370   0A87 0C              CLC                *Make Qn = 0
380   0A88 20-03           BRA   NEWQUOT      *by shifting in Carry flag
390   *Yes a successful subtraction
400   0A8A 97-41   SUCCESS STAA  DIVDND+1     *New MSB of Remainder
410   0A8C 0D              SEC                *Set C to 1, the new Quotient bit
420   *Shift Quotient left
430   0A8D 78-0044 NEWQUOT ASL   QUOT         *Shifts in Carry as new bit0
440   0A90 79-0045         ROL   QUOT+1
450   *Now shift divisor right
460   0A93 74-0043         LSR   DIVIS+1      *Upper byte
470   0A96 76-0042         ROR   DIVIS        *Into Lower byte
```

Listing 1.3   The 16-bit by 8-bit division program

(continued)

```
480  *Shift count N = 0 yet?
490  0A99 5A              DECB
500  0A9A 26-D9           BNE   SUB         *IF not THEN DO subtract again
510
520  *ELSE round off Quotient
530  0A9C 78-0040         LSL   DIVDND      *Multiply Remainder by 2
540  0A9F 25-04           BCS   RDUP        *IF 9-bit Remainder THEN must be > Divisor
550  0AA1 96-42           LDAA  DIVIS       *Compare with Divisor
560  0AA3 91-40           CMPA  DIVDND      *Carry = 0 if Divisor <=, C=1 for > Divisor x2
570  0AA5 96-44    RDUP   LDAA  QUOT        *Get Quotient LSB
580  0AA7 89-00           ADCA  #00         *Add Carry only
590  0AA9 97-44           STAA  QUOT
600  0AAB 96-45           LDAA  QUOT+1
610  0AAD 89-00           ADCA  #00
620  0AAF 97-45           STAA  QUOT+1
630  0AB1 39              RTS               *Quotient now rounded off
```

Listing 1.3   The 16-bit by 8-bit division program

For the purposes of this example we are dividing a 16-bit dividend by an 8-bit divisor. This yields a quotient which can be up to 16 bits in size. The location of these variables is given in the memory map (a) of Fig. 1.10. Notice that a 1-byte overflow has been provided (DIVIS + 1) to permit the alignment of the divisor (DIVIS) with the 16-bit dividend (DIVDND + 1/DIVDND).

The program of Listing 1.3 is directly based on flowchart (b) of fig. 1.10. In this program, alignment has been performed by double-precision shifting the divisor left (Steps 210–220) until bit 15 is high (Step 230). Accumulator B totalizes the number of shifts, with one added (Step 240) to give the number of quotient places, $N + 1$, for the main loop. This loop commences with a double-precision subtract, Steps 270–310. If this produces a final borrow/carry, the subtraction has not been successful, $Q_k = 0$ (Line 370) and the old value of remainder or dividend has to be restored, Lines 340–360. If no borrow is produced, the subtraction is consumated in Line 400, and $Q_k = 1$ in Line 410. The new quotient is formed by double-precision shifting the existing quotient left, with the new bit 0 being 0 or 1 as appropriate, Lines 430–440. Finally the divisor is shifted right once and the procedure repeated, Lines 460–500.

After the shift-and-subtract procedure has been completed, the resulting quotient is rounded off. This is done by multiplying the remainder by two. If this either gives a 9-bit result (Line 530) or an 8-bit result larger than the divisor, Lines 540–550, then one is added to the quotient (carry flag = 1 in Line 570).

One software bug exists in this implementation. With a zero divisor the program will loop forever through Lines 200–230 trying to align. If desired, this can be avoided by testing the contents of Accumulator A at the beginning of the subroutine. If (A) = 00 then an approximate quotient of $FFFF could be returned.

Listing 1.3 implements a 16-bit/8-bit division. Only the round-off routine need be altered where a 16-bit divisor is used, although of course this cannot be passed to the subroutine in an 8-bit accumulator. The same algorithm can be used for fractional numbers. For example, allowing three bytes for each variable and shift/subtracting $(N + 1) + 8$ times, will produce a 16-bit plus 8-bit fractional quotient from a 16-bit $\div$ 8-bit whole number division.

2

Is There Anyone Out There?

In Chapter 1 we examined the innards of a typical microprocessor. Now we must take a wider view and see how the MPU controls and interfaces to its surrounding circuitry. The methods employed give each system a distinctive architecture, even though its heart is a standard microprocessor.

In this chapter we use standard low power Schottky transistor transistor logic (LSTTL) integrated circuits (ICs) for our example implementations. Later chapters will use N-channel metal-oxide semiconductor (NMOS) devices. Although most microprocessors themselves are NMOS circuits, their buses are buffered to generate and accept TTL-level signals. For example, the 6800 family generally have drive capabilities of four LSTTL loads. When greater numbers of circuits must be driven, appropriate buffering must be used.

2.1 THE ADDRESS BUS

A large proportion of an MPU's operating time is spent simply in moving data to and from external devices and memory. All current MPUs use a common data bus organization, illustrated in a highly simplified form in Fig. 2.1. For clarity a 4-bit MPU is shown with a 12-bit address bus, but the structure is the same irrespective of bus width.

The microprocessor obtains practically all its information via the one data bus, which is also used to send out data. This single bus is common to all external devices such as memories and peripheral interface circuits. Communication is always between the MPU and an external device, only one of which must be active at any one time to avoid interference on the common bus. Most input devices are three-state, and therefore float when disabled. The MPU performs the necessary managerial role by using its address bus to identify the target device to be activated. Taking a 16-bit address bus as an example, there are 2^{16} (65536) unique combination of bits, i.e., addresses, which can be used for this identification. Thus, if the hardware designer decides that peripheral interface n is to respond to the address %1100 0000 0000 0000 ($C000), then circuitry must be provided to detect this pattern, and hence strobe the interface. Thus the instruction LDAA $C000 will result

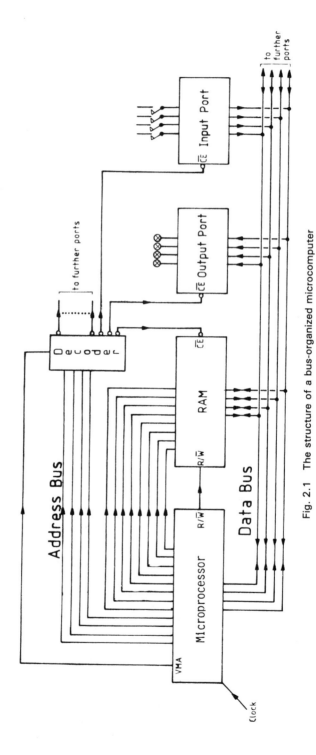

Fig. 2.1 The structure of a bus-organized microcomputer

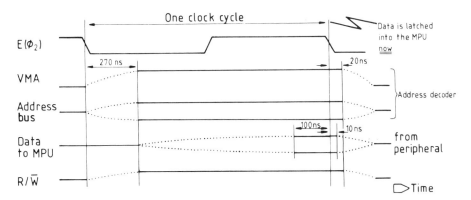

Fig. 2.2 How the MPU reads data from a peripheral device. Worst-case times are
shown

in the address $C000 appearing on the address bus, which is detected by the *address decoder*. This in turn enables peripheral device *n*, and the resulting data is taken off the data bus into the accumulator.

Before looking at the design of address decoders, let us examine the timing relationship between the major buses on the 6802 MPU for the execution of an instruction such as LDAA $C000 (see Fig. 2.2). All signals are synchronized at the start of the clock cycle by the falling edge of ϕ_2. The address (e.g., $C000) appears within 270 ns of this time, together with the associated VMA status signal. These are detected by the external address decoder, which then enables the device (or memory cell) at the specified address. Provided that this responds within 100 ns before the end of the clock cycle (typically 1 μs in duration), the resulting valid data sitting on the data bus at this instant are grabbed by the MPU. Data should be held for at least a further 10 ns to ensure a successful grab. Within 20 ns after this traumatic event, the address- and control-bus signals collapse to their value of the following cycle, and the external device is taken off the bus. The R/$\overline{\text{W}}$ signal is high during this cycle to indicate that the MPU is doing a read operation.

The process of sending out data is broadly similar, as is shown in Fig. 2.3. A typical software instruction would be STAA $C000; here we are assuming that the device responding to $C000 can accept data. Address and VMA are sent out by the MPU following the falling edge of the clock, in the same manner as our previous case. However, this time R/$\overline{\text{W}}$ is low to signify a writing action. Data (in our example from the accumulator) are impressed on the data bus by the MPU, within 225 ns following the middle of the cycle.

Within 20 ns of the end of the clock cycle the address and control signals collapse, leaving the device which is enabled by the address decoder no more than 10 ns to grab the data before they too are gone. Relying on the end of the address decoder's output to trigger the peripheral device is dangerous, as there is a competition between the propagation delay through the decoder and the 10 ns to data collapse. To avoid this hazardous *race*, it is usual to further qualify the address decoder's strobe for output devices (and this includes RAM) by the clock pulse

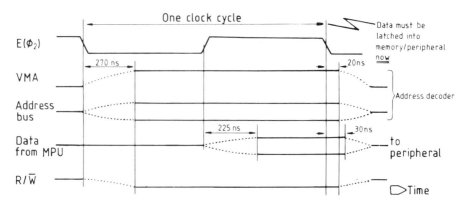

Fig. 2.3   How the MPU writes data to memory or a peripheral device. Worst-case times
are shown

itself, ϕ_2. Thus the device is triggered 30 ns less the decoder's propagation delay before data collapse.

From the foregoing discussion we see that address decoding is a straightforward code detection task; thus we can use standard combinational logic such as gates, natural decoders and equality comparators. Normally the system designer takes the entire range of addresses available and allocates within this, location areas for the various memories and peripheral interfaces. This technique, known as *memory mapping*, is applicable to all types of MPUs, although particular devices will place restraints on this allocation. For example, the 6800 and 6502 families expect ROM to be in the highest locations, as this will hold the reset and interrupt vectors. Similarly the lowest locations are usually RAM, to permit data manipulation using the more efficient direct address mode. Peripheral devices usually lie somewhere in the middle.

A gate-implemented address decoder servicing four peripheral devices is shown in Fig. 2.4. An 8-input AND gate/inverter array detects whenever a_{15} a_{14} a_{13} a_{12} a_{11} a_{10} a_9 = %1100000 and VMA are high. Thus any legitimate addresses from $C000 and $C1FF will activate this gate. This base signal in turn enables four front-line NAND gates, which add a further address line to the decoder function. Thus $\overline{\text{Chip Enable 1}}$ will detect the pattern %1100 000X XXXX XXX1, with X indicating omitted variables. Taking these as 0 gives $\overline{\text{CE1}}$ activated for address $C001. Using further front-line gates operating on other address lines, or combination of these, the number of enable lines can be increased as necessary. When output devices are being enabled, the clock signal ϕ_2 may also be used to enable the front-line gates, to avoid the critical race previously discussed.

The simple circuit of Fig. 2.4 exhibits several interesting properties. Since eight address variables are not used for any given output (e.g., $a_1 - a_8$ for $\overline{\text{CE1}}$), then their state is irrelevant. Thus $\overline{\text{CE1}}$ will also detect %1100 0001 1111 1111 or $C1FF. In deed $\overline{\text{CE1}}$ will respond to $2^8 - 1 = 255$ *image addresses* between $C003 and $C1FF inclusive. Although image addresses mean that memory space is not being used

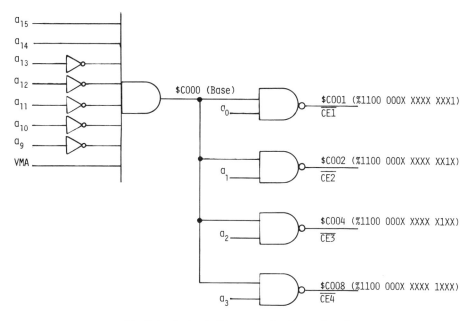

Fig. 2.4   A simple linear-select address decoder

efficiently, in many dedicated small- and medium-sized systems only a small fraction of available space is required, and cost-effective hardware is more important.

The linear-selection principle shown in Fig. 2.4 has a less desirable property, that of *multiple selection*. For example, the address $C00F = %1100\ 0000\ 0000\ 1111$ will activate all four outputs simultaneously. Although this will not happen when the program has been correctly written, it can inadvertently occur during the software-development phases.

The address circuit of Fig. 2.4 represents a small local decoder, serving several peripheral interfaces. Taking an overall system, a primary decoder is frequently used to divide the available address space into zones or pages. For instance in Fig. 2.5, a single 3- to 8-line natural decoder splits the 64K memory space into eight 8K pages. In a typical situation the lowest two pages might be used for RAM; page 4 for peripheral interface and the top zone for program ROM. Each page will have its own secondary decoder, to enable the n devices inhabiting this page. In the situation shown in Fig. 2.5 we have subdivided page 7 into four 2K slots, each comprising a 2516/2716 EPROM, using a secondary 2- to 4-line natural decoder.

Alternatively a gate array, similar to that of Fig. 2.4, could be used as a secondary decoder. To a microprocessor, an m-byte memory chip appears as m separate devices or cells. For example, the 2716 EPROM has an on-board 11 to 2,048 decoder acting on address lines $a_{10} - a_0$, selecting one of the 2,048 read-only cells, provided the overall chip is enabled by the secondary decoder. This on-board decoder may be considered as a tertiary decoder.

If only one EPROM is required for page 7, then the secondary decoder may

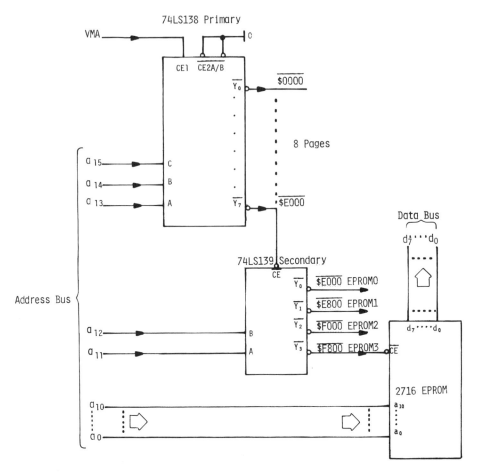

Fig. 2.5   A partial-decoding scheme, showing how an EPROM is selected

be dispensed with, and the $E000 base used directly. In the case of a 2716 EPROM, address lines a_{10} a_{11} will not be part of the decoder equation, and each EPROM cell will have three images. The top two EPROM addresses $E7FE/F will then image to $FFFE/F, the reset vector.

2.2   INPUT/OUTPUT PORTS

In Fig. 2.5 we saw how an EPROM chip could be interfaced to the system bus. RAM chips are dealt with in the same way, except that the address strobe must be qualified with ϕ_2 to prevent the writing race. As a RAM cell is both read and write, the MPU's R/W̄ must be used to drive the R/W̄ RAM control, as shown in Fig. 2.1.

Memory chips are specifically designed for easy interface to microprocessor

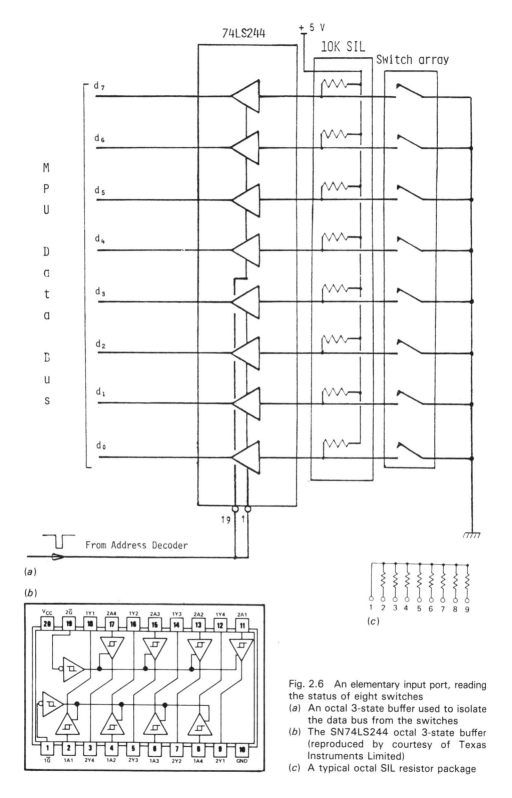

74LS244

+ 5 V

10K SIL

Switch array

M
P
U

D
a
t
a

B
u
s

d_7
d_6
d_5
d_4
d_3
d_2
d_1
d_0

19 1

From Address Decoder

(a)

(b)

V_{CC}	$2\overline{G}$	1Y1	2A4	1Y2	2A3	1Y3	2A2	1Y4	2A1
20	19	18	17	16	15	14	13	12	11

1	2	3	4	5	6	7	8	9	10
$1\overline{G}$	1A1	2Y4	1A2	2Y3	1A3	2Y2	1A4	2Y1	GND

1 2 3 4 5 6 7 8 9

(c)

Fig. 2.6 An elementary input port, reading
the status of eight switches
(a) An octal 3-state buffer used to isolate
the data bus from the switches
(b) The SN74LS244 octal 3-state buffer
(reproduced by courtesy of Texas
Instruments Limited)
(c) A typical octal SIL resistor package

buses. However, matching up the panoply of external circuits and signals to the rhythm of the MPU is a different situation entirely. For example, how could we use a microprocessor to read the state of eight switches or digital signals? We cannot connect these switches directly to the data bus, since this bus must be shared with other devices. Any interface interposed between switches and bus must have the property of passing through the switch states unaltered when enabled, and floating when disabled.

A simple solution is shown in Fig. 2.6. Here an octal 3-state buffer acts to isolate the data bus from the outside world, except when enabled by the address decoder. The propagation delay of these buffers is short, and there are no time-related problems with this type of interface port. Where mechanical single-pole or electromechanical switches are being read, as in Fig. 2.6, pull-up resistors are used to give a good logic 1 when the contact is open. For convenience octal arrays of resistors with one commoned end are available in single-in-line packages.

The converse problem arises when we wish to arrange for the microprocessor to control external devices, e.g., eight small relays. The interface in this case must be capable of sampling the state of the data bus and holding this constant until again

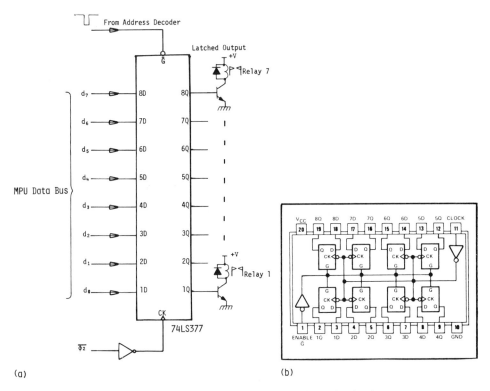

(a)   (b)

Fig. 2.7   A simple 8-bit output port, driving relay loads
(a) Connecting the flip flop array
(b) The SN74LS377 octal D flip flop (reproduced by
    courtesy of Texas Instruments Limited)

strobed. A straightforward solution uses an octal D latch or D flip flop as the sample and hold element, as shown in (a) in Fig. 2.7. Here the address decoder output is used to enable the flip flop array. The 74LS377 octal D flip flop in (b) of Fig. 2.7 loads data when enabled AND clocked by a rising edge. Inverting ϕ_2 both provides a rising edge at the end of the clock cycle (see Fig. 2.3) and avoids the output race hazard.

When the output port is to drive non-TTL loads, appropriate buffer circuitry must be provided. If such loads take on appreciable current, surges may be reflected back into the MPU's power supply. In this situation opto-couplers or pulse transformers are often used to isolate the two systems, which run off separate power supplies.

Both ports have been shown for octal signals. However, any number of signals can be accommodated by increasing the number of ports, each enabled by a separate address decoder output.

2.3   INTERRUPT HANDLING

The raison d'être for interrupt processing was discussed in Section 1.3, together with the internal response of the 6800/2 MPU to such events. Here, we will look at some practical considerations when external circuitry seeks to use this feature.

As an illustrative example, let us consider the problem of creating a real-time clock facility, where the current time in hours, minutes and seconds is continuously available in three memory locations. One approach to this would be to create a delay loop of slightly less than one second, and then add one second to the time array before repeating. A delay loop is usually a software routine idling the time away by counting. The major problem with this type of implementation is that the MPU is hung up in what is essentially an endless loop. This precludes the microprocessor doing anything other than this one task.

A more efficient way of tackling this requirement would be to arrange for an external 1 Hz oscillator to interrupt the MPU each second. The interrupt service routine would then update the time array and return to the task in hand. If we assume that the service routine takes approximately 100 μs to execute, then we find that 99.99% of execution time is available for other background tasks. The price to pay for this efficiency is the cost of the additional hardware, primarily the precision oscillator. This may be a self-standing crystal-controlled astable circuit, or more simply the MPU clock ϕ_2 divided by the appropriate ratio.

Directly feeding the $\overline{\text{IRQ}}$ pin from the oscillator will lead to some spectacular timekeeping. This is because after the MPU returns from its interrupt service routine it finds $\overline{\text{IRQ}}$ still low, and immediately jumps back to the update service routine. It will continue to do this as long as the oscillator remains low. Most microprocessor interrupt inputs are level sensitive, like the 6800/2's $\overline{\text{IRQ}}$ input. Using an edge-sensitive interrupt like $\overline{\text{NMI}}$ will eliminate this problem; but the use of a non-maskable interrupt is only recommended to service system emergencies.

Insertion of a narrow-pulse generator (typically a capacitor-resistor network) after the oscillator will effectively convert $\overline{\text{IRQ}}$ to an edge-triggered mode. The

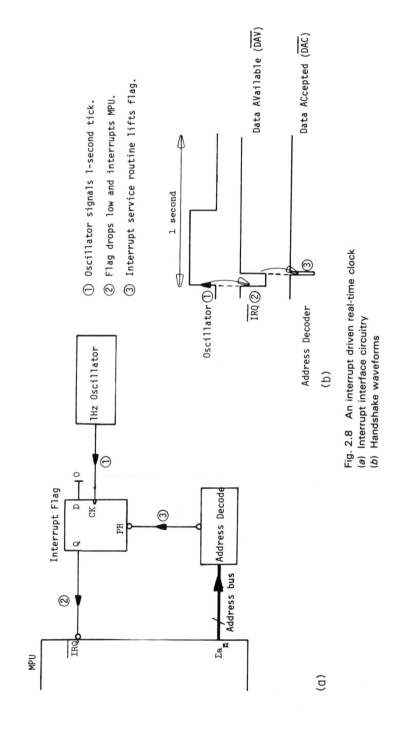

MPU

Interrupt Flag

1Hz Oscillator

Address Decoder

Address bus

① Oscillator signals 1-second tick.

② Flag drops low and interrupts MPU.

③ Interrupt service routine lifts flag.

Oscillator ①

IRQ ②

Address Decoder ③

1 second

Data AVailable ($\overline{DAV}$)

Data ACcepted ($\overline{DAC}$)

(a)

(b)

Fig. 2.8 An interrupt driven real-time clock
(a) Interrupt interface circuitry
(b) Handshake waveforms

pulse length should be less than the shortest possible service routine but longer than
the MPU clock cycle. For greater reliability over a range of conditions a synchronous handshake technique is normally used, such as shown in Fig. 2.8. Here the
oscillator clocks a flip flop, which then flags the $\overline{IRQ}$ input. As part of the resulting
service routine, the flag must be raised. Thus on return $\overline{IRQ}$ will have been deacti-
vated. In the diagram, one of the address decoder's outputs is connected to the
flip flop's preset ($\overline{PR}$) input. With this hardware configuration, the flag may be lifted
by any instruction which refers to the allocated address, see Step 130 in Listing 2.1.

The data bus is not shown in Fig. 2.8, as no information is being acquired
during the service routine, other than the implied fact that one second has elapsed
since the last interrupt. A different situation exists in Fig. 1.4 where the state of the
external counter is to be fetched on interrupt. In this case the output of the peak
detector will drive the interrupt flag of (a) in Fig. 2.8. The counter-timer itself will
be interfaced to the data bus using a 3-state buffer, identical to that of Fig. 2.6.

The waveforms of (b) in Fig. 2.8 will still apply to this situation, but signal 1
refers to the peak detector's output. The interrupt request to the MPU can be
regarded as signaling that there is new data available, $\overline{DAV}$. In response to this alert,
the input port is read. The address decoder strobe could then be labeled. Data have
now been accepted, $\overline{DAC}$. This status protocol, i.e. 'here is some data for you' –
'thanks, data now accepted' is a simple example of a 2-line handshake. If we connect
the $\overline{DAC}$ signal to the interrupt flag's $\overline{PR}$ input, then the MPU's response to $\overline{DAV}$,
viz., reading the counter, will automatically cancel the interrupt request.

Let us return now to the real-time clock situation and develop the software
component of the system (see Fig. 2.9). Assuming for this example that the clock
routine originates at $0E00, then on receiving an interrupt the MPU will vector via
$FFF8/9 to $0E00, provided that we have cleared the I mask in the code condition
register. We assume a stack has been set up to allow a succesful return.

The first task of the interrupt-service routine is to produce a $\overline{DAC}$ signal to lift
the interrupt. In Line 130 we assume that this is represented by the output of an
address decoder sensitive to $C000 and connected to the flip flop's $\overline{PR}$ input.

The remainder of the routine is involved in adding one second to the total
time. Normally one is added to the second's count, unless this already totals 59, in
which case it is returned to zero and the process is repeated for minutes. Assuming
a 24-hour clock format, the overflow condition for the hours byte is 23, otherwise
the procedure is the same. In all cases RTI is physically the last instruction. Listing
2.1 shows a possible software implementation.

If the accuracy of the clock is to be maintained, then care must be taken with
systems supporting multiple interrupt sources, that one of the other interrupt
routines does not last for more than one second, otherwise a tick will be lost. This
is more likely for higher precision clocks; e.g., when mains frequency is used as the
interrupt source, then each tick lasts only one fiftieth or one sixtieth of a second.
But given only one $\overline{IRQ}$ pin, how does the 6800 family handle interrupts from more
than one source?

There are several techniques used to handle multiple interrupt sources, usually
trading speed against hardware costs. One of the simplest of these, applicable to any

CLOCK-OBJECT

Line	Machine code	Source code			Comment

```
10   *This interrupt routine implements a 1s real-time clock
20   *Locations used : $0051-53
30   *ENTRY : SEC in $0051; MIN in $0052; HRS in $0053
40   *EXIT  : (SEC in $0051; MIN in $0052; HRS in $0053)+1second
50   *************************************************************************
60      <0051>  SEC     EQU    $0051          *Seconds stored here
70      <0052>  MIN     EQU    $0052          *Minutes stored here
80      <0053>  HRS     EQU    $0053          *Hours stored here
90      <C000>  DAC     EQU    $C000          *Address to lift the Interrupt flag
100     <0E00>          ORG    $E00           *Routine starts at $0E00
110
120  *Reset Interrupt flag
130  0E00 B7-C000 TIME  STAA   DAC            *Pulse flipflop's PR to lift flag
140  *Check seconds
150  0E03 96-51         LDAA   SEC            *Get seconds
160  0E05 81-3B         CMPA   #59            *Is it 59?
170  0E07 27-04         BEQ    MINS           *IF it is THEN clear and update minutes
180  0E09 7C-0051       INC    SEC            *ELSE one more second
190  0E0C 3B            RTI                   *and return
200  *Check minutes
210  0E0D 7F-0051 MINS  CLR    SEC            *Seconds zeroed
220  0E10 96-52         LDAA   MIN
230  0E12 81-3B         CMPA   #59
240  0E14 27-04         BEQ    HOURS
250  0E16 7C-0052       INC    MIN
260  0E19 3B            RTI
270  *Check hours
280  0E1A 7F-0052 HOURS CLR    MIN
290  0E1D 96-53         LDAA   HRS
300  0E1F 81-17         CMPA   #23
310  0E21 27-04         BEQ    MIDNITE        *IF 23 hours THEN +1 = midnight
320  0E23 7C-0053       INC    HRS            *ELSE one more hour
330  0E26 3B            RTI
340  0E27 7F-0053 MIDNITE CLR  HRS            *00:00:00 = midnight
350  0E2A 3B            RTI
```

Listing 2.1   A real-time clock interrupt-service routine

type of MPU, uses the method of *polling*. Essentially this entails a search of the various interrupt sources, until a set flag is found. As there is only one interrupt pin, the N sources must be ORed together to give a single $\overline{\text{IRQ}}$ signal. Similarly with only one IRQ vector, this will result in a jump to the one common interrupt-service program. The initial portion of such a routine will then poll the N peripheral interrupt flags, causing a jump to the appropriate routine when the actual source has been identified.

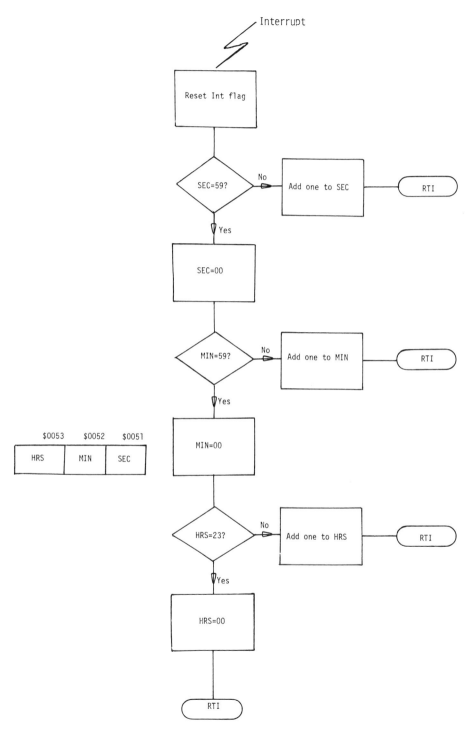

Fig. 2.9 A flowchart for a real-time clock

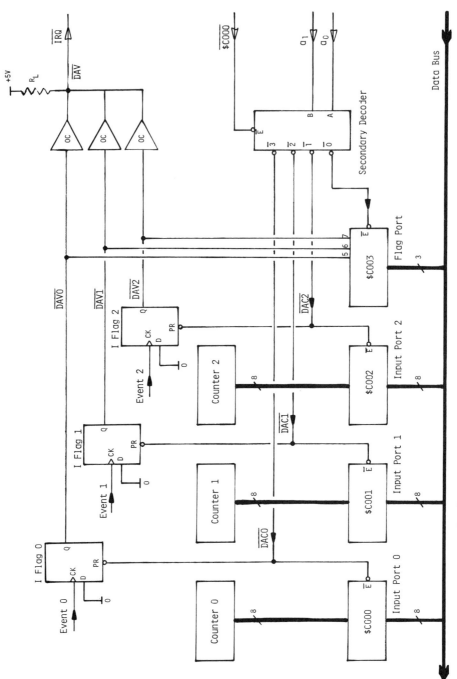

Fig. 2.10 Servicing three peripheral devices requesting an interrupt

As an example, consider the extension of Fig. 1.4 to the situation where the duration of three different events are to be timed. As is shown in Fig. 2.10, three counter/input ports are used. Each counter is clocked at the appropriate rate, not shown in the diagram. Associated with the counters are interrupt flags, activated by the appropriate event occurrence. These three 'cries for help' are commoned using open-collector buffers to give a single interrupt request to the MPU. When the interrupt is serviced, the state of the three flags can be read at a status port, whence the actual originating event can be deduced. A simple program doing this is:

```
10*          This program segment polls for the interrupt source
20 POLL   LDAA                    *Get status of flags
30           BITA #%10000000       *Event 2?
40           BEQ PROG2             *IF so THEN go off to Program 2
50           BITA #%01000000       *Event 1?
60           BEQ PROG1             *IF so THEN go off to Program 1
70 PROG0  ---- ----               *By elimination, must be Event 0
```

Once the event has been identified, then the appropriate counter is read. In Fig. 2.10, the act of reading counter k automatically resets interrupt-flag k. If more than one flag is set simultaneously, then the priority will be dependent on the order of reading by software, the interrupt of next priority will be dealt with on return from the interrupt routine. If we assume a common clocking rate of 10 kHz, the duration of the longest interrupt routine should not be more than 33 μs, to keep full accuracy independent of conditions. When this is not acceptable, the counters may be buffered from the port using a latch triggered by the $\overline{DAV}$ signal. In this case the duration of the interrupt software can be up to one third of the shortest event duration.

When very large numbers of interrupt sources are involved, polling can be very slow. In situations like this, hardware priority encoders can be used to create the binary number of the interrupt flag. This can even be forced onto the data bus whenever the interrupt vector is being fetched, to force a direct jump to the appropriate routine. To facilitate this, MPUs such as the Z80 and 6809 have an interrupt acknowledge signal $\overline{INTA}$, which tells this outside circuitry that the interrupt vector is in the process of being fetched.

3

One Byte at a Time

In Chapter 2 we looked at elementary techniques for getting data into the system, or conversely getting it out. We also developed the technique of interrupt handling together with its associated idea of handshake protocol. The facility of parallel input/output (I/O) with interrupt and handshake facilities is virtually a universal requirement for microprocessor systems. In view of the economics of integrated circuits (ICs), it makes sense to produce a general-purpose interface port which is flexible enough to fit the majority of parallel applications.

Such a general-purpose parallel port is by its nature complex. Provision must be made to enable the designer to choose various options, such as configuring the port as input or output, choosing the interrupt flag to trigger on a rising or falling edge. Early devices required a change in hardware wiring to effect these options. However, the pin count is dramatically reduced if these are chosen by setting up a configuration pattern in an internal control register. This makes possible the production of general-purpose microcomputer circuitry, with fixed hardware but configurable by software. A further advantage of software configurable I/O is that their function can be altered dynamically as the program advances.

All major microprocessor manufacturers produce general-purpose parallel I/O ports. These are given various names, such as the Intel PIO (programmable input/output); Rockwell's VIA (versatile interface adapter) and Motorola's PIA (peripheral interface adapter). Some advanced versions have additional features such as timer-counters and integral memory. In this chapter we examine the PIA as a typical example of the genre.

3.1   THE PERIPHERAL INTERFACE ADAPTER

A simplified functional diagram of the 6821 PIA is shown in Fig. 3.1. This also applies to the 6520, 6820 and 6822 devices, which however differ slightly in timing and drive specifications. The PIA comprises two separate 8-bit parallel input/output ports. Except for minor differences both ports behave in an identical fashion.

The central feature of any I/O port is the data register, which interfaces the MPU's data bus to the peripheral device. In the PIA this register comprises a flip flop

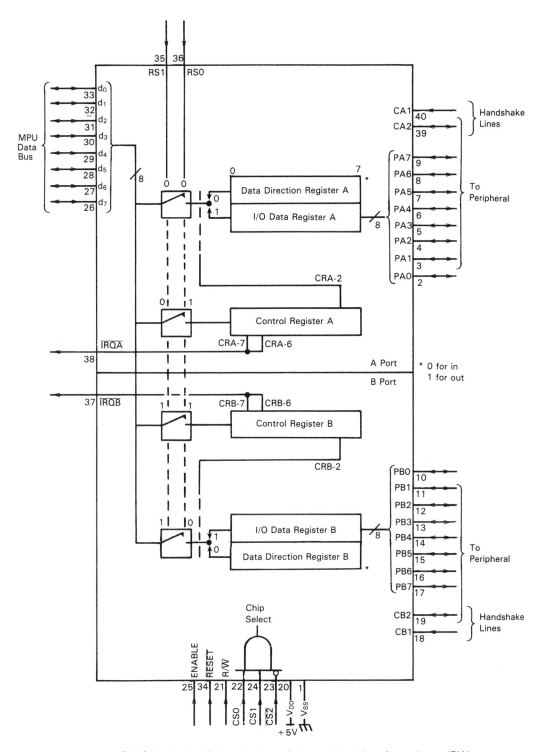

Fig. 3.1 A simplified equivalent of the peripheral interface adapter (PIA)

array for storing outgoing data as in Fig. 2.7, with an octal 3-state buffer for incoming data (Fig. 2.6). The actual status of this circuit as either input or outut depends on the state of an associated *data direction register* (DDR). Thus to use Port A as an output, DDRA must be set to %11111111, whereas if DDRA is cleared, Port A is an input. As each data register bit has a corresponding DDR bit, a port can be a mixture of input and output lines. Thus if DDRA is set up to %11110000, then PA0–PA3 are input lines, whilst PA4–PA7 act as latched output lines. Should the MPU read lines designated as outputs, then the response can depend on the port. In Port A the state of the actual PIA pin will be read. Provided that the loading on (current into or out of) that pin is such that logic 1 is not pulled down below 2.0V and logic 0 is not above 0.8V, then the correct state will be recorded. Port B output lines have additional buffering, and the recorded state is independent of what goes on at the pin. Data sent to a data register configured as an input will be written into the flip flop array, but will not appear at the output pins until the port is reconfigured as an output. This can be useful to set up an initial output after reset, which automatically configures the data register as input.

The PIA has six user-accessible internal registers. The actual register called into conversation by the MPU is a function of the select pins RS0 and RS1. RS1 selects between ports A and B for RS1 = 0 and 1 respectively. RS0 selects between registers within a port, with RS0 = 0 giving the data register and RS0 = 1 the control register.

As the data direction register is normally set up at the beginning of the program only, it shares the same internal address as the frequently used data register. They are shown paired in Fig. 3.1 to emphasize this. The actual register accessed at this address depends on bit 2 of the *control register*. For example, if CRA2 is 0, then DDRA is accessed on RS1 RS0 = 00; whereas CRA2 = 1 enables DRA under the same conditions. As the data direction register is so infrequently used, the software overhead resulting from this 2-port access procedure is very small, and saves the hardware overhead of an additional register select pin.

In Section 2.3 we saw that an interrupt-handling facility is important to interfacing peripheral devices. Each of the 6821's ports has two handshake lines, to enable a peripheral to request access to the MPU, and for the MPU to acknowledge this request. Taking Port A as an example, CA1 permits a peripheral to set a flag on either a rising or falling edge. This flag, which is equivalent to the D flip flop of Fig. 2.8, is actually read as bit 7 of the control register. If bit 1 is logic 0, a falling edge sets CRA-7 high; whereas CRA-1 = 1 makes the rising edge active. Furthermore if CRA-0 = 1, the active edge will send an interrupt to the MPU through $\overline{\text{IRQA}}$. Subsequently reading data register A will automatically signal $\overline{\text{Data Accepted}}$ ($\overline{\text{DAC}}$) and the flag will be cancelled, in the manner shown in Fig. 2.10.

Handshake line 1 is always an input, accepting cries for help from the peripheral device. However, handshake line 2 can be either input or output depending on the state of control bit 5. Thus, if CRA-5 is 0, then CA2 will act in the same manner as CA1, with CRA-4 setting the active edge, CRA-3 enabling $\overline{\text{IRQA}}$ and CRA-6 being the interrupt flag. As before this is cleared by reading the data register.

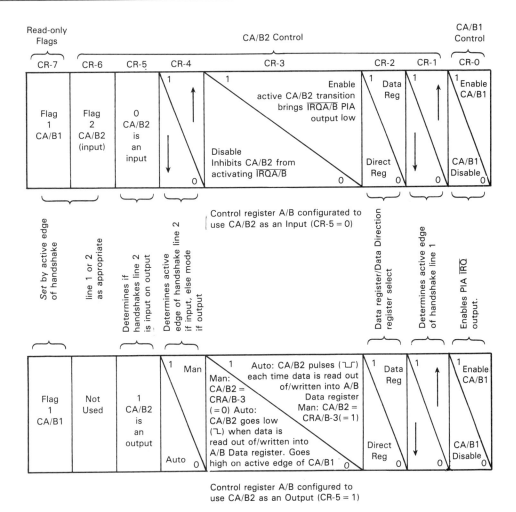

Fig. 3.2   Configuring the PIA using the control register

The MPU can determine whence the interrupt request originated by examining (polling) both flags in turn.

Setting control bit 5 high makes handshake line 2 an output. In this situation control bits 3 and 4 act in a different fashion, as shown in the lower half of Fig. 3.2. When CRA-4 is logic 1, handshake line 2 will simply follow the state of CRA-3. Thus, to make CA2 go high CRA-3 is set. Line 2 will stay high until CRA-3 is cleared.

As an alternative to this manual mode, by making control bit 4 = logic 0, it is possible to have line 2 pulse automatically in response to a certain sequence of events. Now if CRA-3 is logic 1, CA2 will pulse low each time data is read from data register A. This tells the peripheral device that data has been accepted ($\overline{\text{DAC}}$).

The duration of this pulse is that of the MPU's clock cycle, usually around 1 μs. If CRA-3 is 0, then CA2 will go low when the Data register is read. However, it will stay low indefinitely until the peripheral responds by activating the CA1 input. These two sets of waveforms are shown in Fig. 3.3

The automatic line 2 handshake is a little different for the B side. Here CB2 pulses when data is *written* into data register B. Thus with CRB-5, 4, 3 = 100, CB2 goes low when the MPU writes to data register B. This tells the peripheral device that

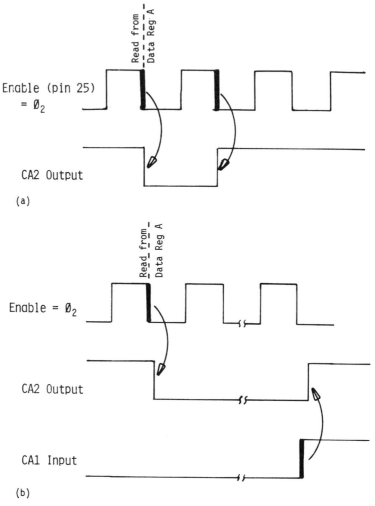

Fig. 3.3 Automatic handshake waveforms
(a) Auto mode (CRA5/4/3 = 101). CA2 pulses low on read (Port B similar, but pulse on write and synchronized by the rising edge of E)
(b) Auto mode (CRA5/4/3 = 100) CA2 goes low on read. Canceled on active edge of CA1, shown rising here. Port B similar, but CA2 goes low on the rising edge of E following a write

data is now available. After a time the data is ready by the external device, which then pulses CB1. This releases CB2, and also (if CRB-0 is logic 1) interrupts the MPU, in effect telling the MPU that at last its data has been accepted. To clear the interrupt, the MPU must read data register B. The actual data is unimportant, but the act of reading automatically lifts the interrupt flag CRB-7.

Some further PIA handshake examples are given in Section 3.2.

Interfacing the PIA to the MPU buses is straightforward. Looking at the outside connections we have:

PERIPHERAL DATA LINES A: PA0 through PA7 (Pins 2–9). These TTL compatible lines go to the peripheral device either directly or through suitable buffers. When programmed as outputs they can drive up to eight LSTTL loads. As inputs they represent typically 20 LSTTL loads.

PERIPHERAL DATA LINES B: PB0 through PB7 (Pins 10–17). These are similar to Port A's peripheral lines, but with different output buffers. As outputs the fan-out is 8 LSTTL loads, but with a minimum of 1 mA guaranteed into the base of a Darlington-connected transistor. As inputs, no more than 10 μA are taken at TTL logic levels.

HANDSHAKE LINES: CA1, CA2, CB1, CB2 (Pins 40, 39, 18, 19). Handshake lines with CA1 and CB1 only input, and CA2 and CB2 being either input or output. Their specific action is a function of the control-register setting. Electrical characteristics are the same as those of their respective port's peripheral data lines.

DATA LINES: d0 through d7 (Pins 33–26). The 8-bit data bus is directly connected to that of the microprocessor.

READ/WRITE: R/W (Pin 21). Directly driven by the MPU, this controls the direction of data transfer within the PIA.

ENABLE: E (Pin 25). Normally driven by microprocessor clock ϕ_2, this input is used for internal timing purposes. Its use eliminates the write-to hazard discussed in Section 2.1.

CHIP SELECT LINES: CS0, CS1, $\overline{\text{CS2}}$ (Pins 22, 24, 23). These are used by the MPU to enable the PIA at a specific address. Both CS0 and CS1 must be high, and CS2 low for a successful data transfer. This must occur well in advance of the rising edge of the E clock (see Figs. 2.2 and 2.3), typically 160 ns for a 1 MHz 6821. For this reason the address decoder should not be qualified with ϕ_2 (see Section 2.1). This also applies to the ACIA and PIT devices of Sections 4 and 5. If VMA is not included in the address decoder equation, then it may be applied directly to CS0 or CS1.

RESET: $\overline{\text{RST}}$ (Pin 34). This clears all internal registers to zero, and by implication all ports are inputs and interrupts are disabled.

INTERRUPT REQUEST LINES: $\overline{IRQA}$, $\overline{IRQB}$ (Pins 38, 37). These are open-collector lines which may be tied together to the single MPU $\overline{IRQ}$ lines, in the manner shown in Fig. 2.10. A 3.3 kΩ pull-up resistor is recommended for this purpose. A large number of interrupt lines from additional PIA's and other devices can be tied to this one point. The number N is limited by the voltage drop in the pull-up resistor caused by the N off-leakage currents, but is typically over 50. For the 6821 PIA, leakage is no more than 10 μA for each interrupt line, with a sink logic 0 current of 3.2 mA.

REGISTER SELECT: RS1, RS0 (Pins 35, 36). These are used by the PIA to select which internal register is to communicate with the MPU. They are normally connected to the MPU's two lower address lines, as shown below.

A simple configuration showing the interconnection of the PIA and MPU is given in Fig. 3.4. Using the address decoder of Fig. 2.5 as shown, the PIA-base address is %100X XXXX XXXX 1100 ($800C). When more than one PIA is used, different combinations of address lines a_3a_2 with CS0 CS1 can be used to select between devices. Sometimes the address lines a_1a_0 are transposed from the shown connection. This has the effect of placing both data registers in adjacent addresses, and likewise the control registers. It allows the programmer to change the contents of say both control registers with a single store index register (STX) instruction.

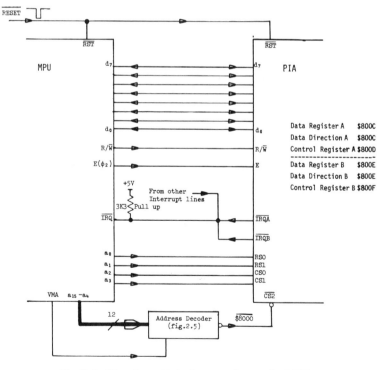

Fig. 3.4   Showing a typical connection to the MPU

3.2   INTERFACING WITH THE PIA

Although the interconnection between MPU and PIA is relatively standard, the interface to the peripheral depends very much on the characteristics of that device. In this section we will give two examples to illustrate some typical configurations.

Our first example involves the use of the MPU as a data logger. An analog signal, perhaps representing temperature, will be sampled periodically. The sampling frequency is to be determined by an external oscillator, which can be used as the timing element for a real-time clock (see Fig. 2.8). Each time a sample is requested the MPU is to be interrupted, and an analog-to-digital (A/D) converter coaxed into giving a digital equivalent of the analog signal. We will discuss analog-to-digital converters in Chapter 6; here it suffices to say that this is done by pulsing start convert (SC) low. The converter responds by bringing $\overline{\text{End of Convert}}$ $(\overline{\text{EOC}})$ high to say that it is now busy doing the conversion. When the conversion is complete $\overline{\text{EOC}}$ goes low. The converted data is now available for reading.

A suggested interface between PIA, sampling clock and A/D converter, together with handshake protocol, is shown in Fig. 3.5.

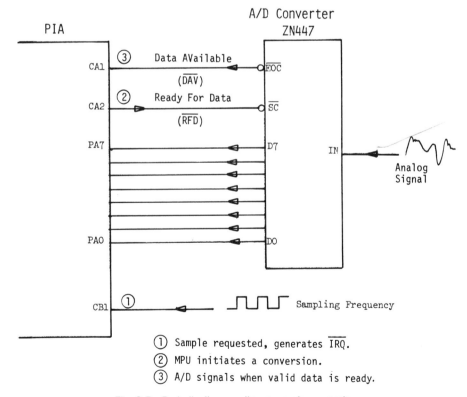

① Sample requested, generates $\overline{\text{IRQ}}$.
② MPU initiates a conversion.
③ A/D signals when valid data is ready.

Fig. 3.5   Periodically sampling an analog quantity

In configuring the PIA the following options are chosen:

Port A   : Input;   DDRA = $00
CA1   : Active on negative-going edge;   CRA1 = 0
         : Interrupt disabled;   CRA0 = 0
CA2   : Output;   CRA5 = 1
         : Automatic response mode;   CRA4 = 0
         : Pulses on data-read;   CRA3 = 1
CB1   : Active on negative-going edge;   CRB1 = 0
         : Interrupt enabled;   CRB0 = 1

Listing 3.1 gives appropriate initialization software.

Two points can be made about this listing. Firstly on reset all registers are cleared. Thus the first two instructions may be omitted in such a situation. The setting of DDRB is irrelevant to this example. In some circumstances interrupt requests occurring during the initialization phases should be canceled to allow the main program to start with a clean sheet. This can be done by reading both data registers before the MPU's interrupt mask is cleared for action.

The actual interrupt-service program, entered on each active edge of the sample oscillator, is straightforward, as shown in Listing 3.2. Assume that the A/D data is to be placed in location $0040 before return.

In Step 20 of Listing 3.2, the CA2 line is automatically pulsed on reading data register A. When an A/D converter is used which requires a longer $\overline{\text{Start Convert}}$ pulse than is produced by this means (2 μs with a 1 MHz ϕ_2 clock), then the manual mode with a software delay may be used. Step 30 cancels the Interrupt flag represented by control bit 7, by simply reading data register B. The MPU then continually monitors bit 7 of control register A, which is set via CA1 when the A/D's $\overline{\text{EOC}}$ goes low. Branch if plus (BPL) is not satisfied when bit 7 is low, and allows

```
10   *The PIA initialization module
20   *Port A
30            CLR   $800D        *Clears control register A's bit 2, selects DDR
40            CLR   $800C        *All DDR bits zero; Port A is an input port
50            LDAA  #%00101100   *Control register A configured as discussed above
60            STAA  $800D        CRA2=1 switches from DDRA to data register A
70   *Port B
80            LDAA  #%00000001   *Control register B configured to enable CB1 to
90            STAA  $800F        *interrupt MPU on negative edge
100  *Initialization module for next device
110           ------
120  *Last instruction clears interrupt mask, which will have been
130           CLI                *set on the MPU's reset
140  *Main program starts here
```

Listing 3.1   Initializing the PIA interface to the analog/digital converter

```
*This is the interrupt service routine for PIA $800C
SAMPLE  LDAA  $800C       *Pulse CA2 by reading Data register A
        LDAA  $800F       *Cancel interrupt flag (CRB7) by reading Data register B
EOC?    TST   $800D       *Check state of Control register B; is bit7 set?
        BPL   EOC?        *IF not THEN check for End Of Conversion again
        LDAA  $800C       *ELSE get valid data
        STAA  $40         *put it in $0040
        RTI               *and exit
```

Listing 3.2   Operating the A/D converter on a sample command

the program to move on to the next stage, when the valid data is brought in and stored in $0040 before returning.

Our second example involves the opposite process of digital-to-analog (D/A) conversion. Without regard to the actual process (see Section 6.1), a typical D/A converter appears to the PIA as a latch register, the $\overline{\text{Enable}}$ of which must be brought low to accept the digital data. After the new data has been entered, the analog equivalent appears at the output after a short delay. For the purposes of this example let us assume that the D/A converter is part of a 16-channel data acquisition system. A 16-channel version of Fig. 3.5 (see Fig. 6.5) is used to regularly sample each of the input channels. The last 256 samples of each channel are stored in one of 16 arrays.

The system output display peripheral is an X–Y plotter, which is to show all 16 traces on the one sheet of paper. In order to meet the single-sheet criterion, the output Y-axis D/A converter must provide the analog equivalent of the channel data, plus a d.c. offset proportional to the channel number. This effectively super-imposes the trace on a separate Y level for each channel.

The proposed interface for the Y-axis is shown in Fig. 3.6. The channel number N is sent out by the MPU to the upper four bits of the 12-bit D/A converter, giving the offset. The channel data is then sequentially stored at data register B, which drives the lower 8-bits, giving the necessary fine resolution. After each channel datum is sent out, the whole 12 bits are loaded into the converter by pulsing $\overline{\text{WRITE}}$ low. Also shown is a pen-lift signal.

It is necessary to lift the pen at the end of the cycle, so that the retrace to the start of the following channel trace is not recorded.

The PIA configuration for this scheme is as follows:

Port A	: Lower four bits are outputs;	DDRA = $0F
CA2	: Output;	CRA5 = 1
	: Manual mode;	CRA4 = 1
	: Output initially zero (pen up);	CRA3 = 0
Port B	: All outputs;	DDRB = $FF
CB2	: Output;	CRB5 = 1
	: Automatic mode;	CRB4 = 0
	: Pulses on writing to data register B;	CRB3 = 1

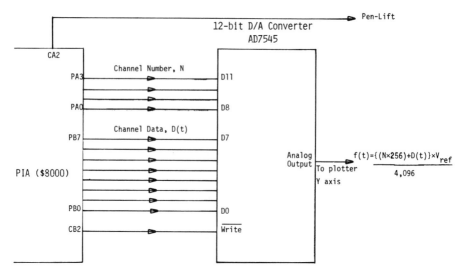

Fig. 3.6   Interface to a 12-bit digital-to-analog converter

A typical initialization module is given in Listing 3.3. We assume that the PIA is based at $80C0, to avoid overlap with the data acquisition PIA at $8000 (try designing a suitable address decoder).

In a practical system a further D/A converter would be necessary to move the pen in the X direction. Each time a new channel sample is output, the X count is incremented. This effectively creates a ramp, which is applied to the X-plotter input. For a channel array of dimension 256 an 8-bit D/A is sufficient, while a 12-bit converter would be adequate for array sizes up to 2,048.

```
*The $80C0 PIA initialisation module
*Port A
        CLR     $80C1           *Clears Control register A's bit2, selects DDRA
        LDAA    #%00001111      *Set up lower four bits as output
        STAA    $80C0
        LDAA    #%00110100      *Configure CA2 as manual output = 0;
        STAA    $80C1           *switch from DDRA to Data register A
*Port B
        CLR     $80C3           *Clears Control register B's bit2, selects DDRB
        LDAA    #%11111111      *Set up Port B as all output
        STAA    $80C2
        LDAA    #%00101100      *Configure CB2 as auto pulse mode
        STAA    $80C3           *Switch from DDRA to Data register B
*Next initialisation module
```

Listing 3.3   Initializing the D/A PIA

The driving software for this example is beyond the scope of this text. Such software would have to perform the following tasks.

I	For C = 0 to 15 do:
II	Send out channel number C to Port A
III	X count = 0: short delay for the plotter's inertia
IV	Pen down
V	For N = 0 to 255 do:
VI	Send out Nth channel sample to Port B: X count to PIA X
VII	N = N + 1: X = X + 1: Short delay
VIII	Go to V (next sample)
IX	Pen-lift
X	Go to II (next channel)
XI	Stop

The plot may be speeded up by drawing every other channel backwards.

As the data acquisition of Fig. 3.5 is interrupt driven, the arrays may be updated during the display procedure. This is especially useful when a continuous oscilloscope display is being used, rather than a plotter.

4

One Bit at a Time

The concept of a common data bus snaking between the various memory and peripheral interface devices cannot easily be extended to long distances. When normal digital circuits are used, the physical extent of the bus should not exceed 30 cm (1 ft). To some extent, this limitation is due to attenuation and noise problems. Also, when the propagation time of pulse signals is longer than their rise and fall times, bus conductors act as transmission lines, with their attendant problems of reflections.

Bus length can be extended by using suitable buffering, which enhances noise immunity and matches signals to the transmission line. However, elaborate buffering is required when distances of more than a few meters are employed. The cost of providing this circuitry and the necessary multicore cabling for not only the data bus but at least a subset of the address and control buses make this technique prohibitively expensive.

The normal solution to the problem of long-distance data communication between the MPU and its peripherals is to modify the bus structure in some way to reduce the number of conductors. The IEEE 488 system uses an 8-bit data bus which is switchable to an address bus. Together with handshake and control lines, a total of 16 conductors are used. Generally this is a very expensive technique, and its maximum range of 20 meters limits its use to interlaboratory instrumentation networks.

A more economically effective solution is illustrated in Fig. 4.1. Here the eight data lines are latched by the output interface, and sent to the remote peripheral device one bit at a time. As far as the microprocessor is concerned, the interface looks similar to a normal output port, but the sending rate is independently controlled by a transmission clock. Only one buffer is required in this situation. A receiver port based on this scheme is also possible, and here the input port acts as a serial-to-parallel converter.

In a practical situation, some elaboration will be necessary. For example, the MPU needs to know if the byte previously stored at the transmitter has completely gone, before sending the next word. Also a receiver must have some means of telling the MPU that a new word has been shifted in and is ready for collection. The requirement for this serialization function is sufficiently common to warrant the production of dedicated serial ports, generically known as the *universal asynchronous*

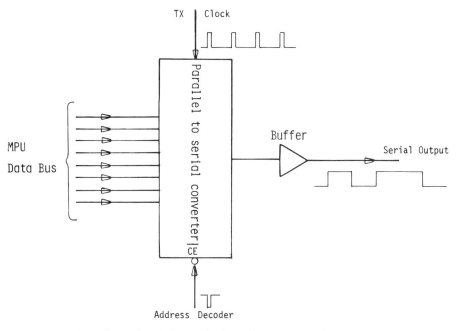

Fig. 4.1   A simple solution to the long-distance transmission problem

receiver transmitter (UART). In Section 4.1 we will examine a typical software configurable UART, while Section 4.2 looks at long-distance transmission.

4.1   THE UNIVERSAL ASYNCHRONOUS RECEIVER TRANSMITTER

One of the features of early computer development (during the 1940s and 1950s) was the extensive use of existing technology. An essential adjunct of any computer-oriented installation is a data terminal. This allows the operator to enter data, and the computer to printout information. At this time, as is still the case, the communications industry made considerable use of teletypewriters (literally a 'typewriter from afar'; Greek, *tele* = far). These TTYs are used for the Telex service, whereby alphanumeric characters are sent over telephone and radio links. As these links are inherently single-channel media, such data is sent in a serial fashion. Data is converted between serial and parallel formats in the terminal itself.

Until comparatively recently, TTYs were electromechanical machines, driven by a synchronous electric motor. Thus synchronization between remote terminals could be guaranteed only for short periods. To get around this problem, each word transmitted was preceded by a start bit and followed by one or more stop bits. A typical example is shown in Fig. 4.2. While the line is idling, a logic 1 (break level) is transmitted. A logic 0 signals the start of a word. After the word has been sent, a logic 1 level terminates the sequence. Depending on the system, this stop level must

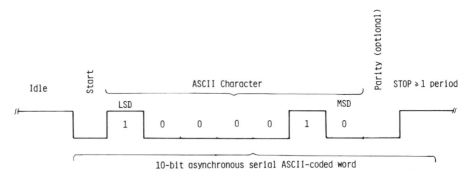

Fig. 4.2 Transmitting the character '!' in ASCII (%010001) using the asynchronous serial mode, with even 1s parity and one stop bit

be held for a minimum of 1, $1\frac{1}{2}$ or 2 periods before the next word is sent. Electro-mechanical terminals typically print 10 characters per second, and require 2 stop bits. This gives a transmission rate of 110 bits per second, or 110 *baud*. Faster rates, applicable to electronic terminals, only use one stop bit; thus a baud rate of 2,400 will output up to 240 characters per second to a visual display unit (VDU).

As terminals deal with alphanumeric data, each character must be represented in code. The *American Standard Code for Information Interchange* (ASCII code) is the commonest of these. The 7-bit version given in Table 4.1, provides for 96 characters including DELete, plus 32 control commands. These latter provide con-

Table 4.1   The 7-bit ASCII code

Least significant character (hex)

	0	1	2	3	4	5	6	7	8	9	A	B	C	D	E	F
0	NUL	SOH	STX	ETX	EOT	ENQ	ACK	BEL	BS	HT	LF	VT	FF	CR	SO	SI
1	DLE	DC1	DC2	DC3	DC4	NAK	SYN	ETB	CAN	EM	SUB	ESC	FS	GS	RS	US
2	SP	!	"	#	$	%	&	'	(	)	*	+	,	-	.	/
3	0	1	2	3	4	5	6	7	8	9	:	;	<	=	>	?
4	@	A	B	C	D	E	F	G	H	I	J	K	L	M	N	O
5	P	Q	R	S	T	U	V	W	X	Y	Z	[	\	]	^(↑)	_(←)
6	`	a	b	c	d	e	f	g	h	i	j	k	l	m	n	o
7	p	q	r	s	t	u	v	w	x	y	z	{	|	}	~	DEL

Most significant character (hex)

NUL	All zero		LF	Line feed		ETB	End of transmission block
SOH	Start of heading		VT	Vertical tabulation		CAN	Cancel
STX	Start of text		FF	Form feed		EM	End of medium
ETX	End of text		CR	Carriage return		SUB	Substitute
EOT	End of transmission		SO	Shift out		ESC	Escape
ENQ	Enquiry		SI	Shift in		FS	File separator
ACK	Acknowledge		DLE	Data link escape		GS	Group separator
BEL	Audible signal		DC1,DC2,DC3,DC4 Device controls		RS	Record separator
BS	Backspace		NAK	Negative acknowledge		US	Unit separator
HT	Horizontal tabulation		SYN	Synchronous idle		SP	Space
						DEL	Delete

trol facilities such as BEL (rings bell) and CR (carriage return). A rather more limited 6-bit ASCII code is given in Appendix 2.

The standard serial format, shown in Fig. 4.2, employs an 8-bit word length. The eighth bit is frequently a parity bit, which makes the number of logic 1s always even (or odd), and thus provides for a limited error-checking capability at the receiver. As the use of the TTY as a computer terminal was almost universal for some twenty years, this asynchronous format has become the common serial standard, even though development in terminal technology is such that more efficient synchronous serial schemes are feasible. Synchronous serial transmission essentially brackets each burst of words with a start and stop character.

Although we have been talking in terms of computer terminals, the 8-bit word format is ideal for general purpose data communication with microprocessors. For example, a remote transducer may convert to digital (see Section 6.2) and send its data in series to the MPU at a considerable distance away. Furthermore, several such transducers may be connected to the one serial link. Each station in this case must be intelligent enough to recognize its own code, and if called, to take over the link. In this situation, an MPU may be used in each station together with its own UART.

The 6850 software configurable UART is shown in Fig. 4.3. This specific

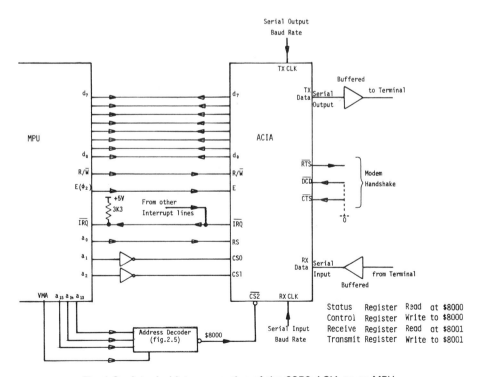

Fig. 4.3   A typical interconnection of the 6850 ACIA to an MPU

device is known as an *asynchronous communication interface adapter* (ACIA). To the MPU the ACIA looks like two memory locations, targeted by register select (RS), which is normally driven by address line a_0. The other connections are the standard data bus, $R/\overline{W}$, $E(\phi_2)$ and interrupt. Like the PIA, three chip selects are used in conjuction with the address bus to enable the device.

Signals at the terminal side of the ACIA can be split into three categories. The transmitter comprises the serial link together with its baud-rate clock. A similar pair are used for the receiver. The remaining three signals are used for modem hand-shake, and are discussed in Section 4.2.

The internal structure of the ACIA is shown in Fig. 4.4. The output section comprises a double-buffered transmit register. Double buffering enables data to be stored in the transmitter at the same time as the previous byte is being shifted out. Data destined to be transmitted is put into the transmit data register (e.g., STAA $8001, with the address decoding of Fig. 4.3) and is internally transferred to the transmit shift register for serialization, provided that this is empty.

The receive section is similarly double-buffered, allowing the previously received byte to be held in the receive data register while the new word is being shifted into the receive shift register. When a complete word has been received it is transferred to the receive data register, provided that this is empty (the previous word having been read). The receive data register is at the same address as the transmit data register, but is enabled when the MPU does a read (e.g., LDAA $8001).

The status of the receive and transmit data registers can be determined by reading the status register as follows:

Bit 0: Receive Data Register Full

This is set whenever a new word has been received and passed to the receive data register. It is inhibited when $\overline{DCD}$ is high (bit SR2), and cleared when this word is read by the MPU.

Bit 1: Transmit Data Register Empty

This is set whenever a word has been passed from the transmit data register to the transmit shift register, and signifies that the way is clear to send the next word. It is inhibited when $\overline{CTS}$ is high (bit SR3) and cleared when a second word is sent before the first word has been shifted out.

Bit 2: $\overline{Data\ Carrier\ Detect}$

This is set whenever the modem fails to find a receive carrier (see Fig. 4.6). It is cleared whenever the modem signals that a carrier is present ($\overline{DCD}$ on Pin 23) and the status followed by receive data register is read.

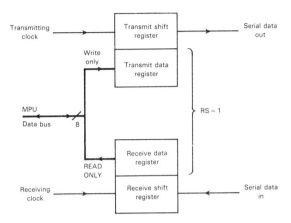

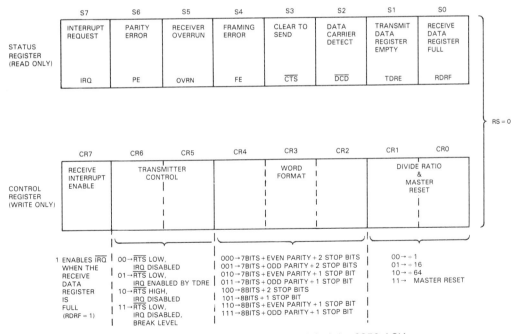

Fig. 4.4   A programmer's model of the 6850 ACIA

Bit 3: *Clear to Send*

This follows the state of the modem's $\overline{\text{Clear to Send}}$ output. If high, it indicates that the modem is unable to accept data for transmision.

Bit 4: *Framing Error*

A high FE indicates that a stop bit was not received, implying loss of synchronization.

Bit 5: *Receiver Overrun*

When high, OVRN indicates that one or more words have been received, and thus lost, since the MPU last read the receive data register.

Bit 6: *Parity Error*

When set, this bit indicates a lack of parity in the word currently held in the receive data register.

Bit 7: *Interrupt Request*

This is the interrupt flag for the ACIA. It can be set when the receive data register is full; the transmit data register is empty; or there is a loss of the modem's receive carrier (if used). These options are set up by the control register. IRQ is cleared by reading or writing as appropriate to the pertinent data register.

The control register is addressed at the same location as the status register, but is enabled when the MPU writes. The setting of this register provides software control over the word format, clock rate and interrupt options.

Bits 0 and 1: *Divide Ratio and Master Reset*

The 6850 ACIA has no hardware reset pin, although it will detect a power-on situation and reset the status register bits (except $\overline{\text{DCD}}$ and $\overline{\text{CTS}}$). To release this power-on reset logic, control bits 0 and 1 must subsequently be set to 11. After this first store, the $\overline{\text{RTS}}$ line can be used (if desired) to wake up the modem by manipulating control bits 5 and 6.

It is unusual to use the receive clock to shift in received data ($00 = \div 1$) directly, as this would require synchronization to the data-pulse train. Ideally the ACIA should sample around the midpoint of each data bit. Taking Mode 01 ($\div 16$) as an example, the receive clock is set to 16 times the bit frequency; e.g., 19.2 kHz for a 1,200 baud rate. The ACIA synchronizes the incoming bit pattern by sampling on the positive transitions of the receiver clock. If the input remains low for nine consecutive samples, the bit is assumed to be a valid start bit. Furthermore, the approximate midpoint has been found, and each subsequent 16-receive clock pulses will find the centerpoint of the following bits. Mode 10($\div 64$) is similar, but 33 samples are used to confirm the start bit and hence the midpoint. Switching between Modes 01 and 10 can be used as crude software control of baud rate. In the example quoted above, Mode 10 gives a baud rate of 300. The mode division ratio also applies to the transmit clock.

Bits 2;3;4: Word Format

Eight word formats are listed in Fig. 4.4, and apply to both transmitter and receiver. When a 7-bit plus parity format is used, the parity bit is replaced in the receive data register by bit 7 = 0.

Bits 5 and 6: Transmit Control

This permits the ACIA to interrupt the MPU when the transmit data register is empty (01). It is also used to manipulate the $\overline{RTS}$ modem control. Initially $\overline{RTS}$ should be brought low and IRQ disabled. When the modem wakes up, it activates $\overline{CTS}$ and the ACIA can then continue. A break level (11) is the continuous transmission of a logic 0.

Bit 7: Receive Interrupt Enable

This permits the ACIA to interrupt the MPU when there is a new word waiting in the receive data register. It also permits the loss of a modem carrier ($\overline{DCD}$) to send the interrupt.

In common with all software-configurable I/O (see Chapter 3), the ACIA is normally set up at the beginning of the main program, and before the interrupt mask is cleared. If we take a typical example using a $\div 16$ mode (01), with an 8-bit + 1 stop bit word format (101), no interrupt from transmitter (00) and an interrupt on receive word (1); the initialization routine would be:

```
*    The $8000 ACIA initialization mode
*    Reset
     LDAA #%00000011        Master reset to control register
     STAA $8000
*    Format
     LDAA #%10010101        1;00;101;01 to control register
     STAA $8000
```

A typical receive-interrupt routine getting valid data based on the above format, and placing it in $0040, would be:

```
*           The $8000 ACIA receive routine
            TST $8000               Check ACIA receive interrupt flag
            BPL OTHER               IF not set THEN another routine
            LDAA $8000              ELSE get status
            NEGA                    Inverting makes it easy to check
            BITA #%00110001         OVRN, FE & RDRF all = 0
            BNE ERROR               IF any not = 0, THEN go to error routine
            LDAA $8001              ELSE get data
            STAA $40                and put it in $0040
            RTI                     before returning
*           Error routine
ERROR   LDAA #$FF                   IF corrupt data return
            STAA $40                with ASCII for DELete
            RTI
*
*           Some other non-ACIA interrupt service routine
OTHER   ──────                      ──────
```

The action taken on occurrence of an error depends on the system. For example, a blank or ? may be printed where a terminal is the eventual destination. In the example above I have indicated an error with the ASCII for DELete.

4.2   DISTANCE COMMUNICATIONS

Given the requirement for long-distance transmission, it is obvious that the limited drive capability of standard logic circuits must be buffered in some way. One of the first of these buffering techniques uses current-loop signaling. This provides for two current levels to represent the binary signals. In early electromechanical terminals, these currents directly actuated the input relays. Although this requirement is no longer a feature of any consequence, current-loop signaling remains an ad hoc standard. Normally 20 mA is used for logic 1, with no current for logic 0.

Current signaling is useful for distances up to several kilometers as, barring leakage, current injected at the transmitter will be maintained irrespective of line length. However, a current source is equivalent to a voltage source in series with a large resistance. This leads to long-time constants and severe line-impedance mismatch, both of which restrict the signaling speed. Thus current loops rarely operate above 300 baud.

Both the Electronic Industries Association (EIA) in the USA and the Comité Consultatif International de Téléphonie et de Télégraphie (CCITT) in Europe have developed a series of standard signaling techniques based on voltage levels. The first of these, and still the most common, is the RS-232/V24 standard, published in 1962. This typically transmits + 12 V to represent logic 0 and − 12 V for logic 1. The receiver sensitivity is ±3 V. Data rates of around 2,400 baud over a range of 15 meters are easily accomplished, and with care longer installations are possible.

A newer, but broadly compatible, specification permits transmission at 1,200 baud for up to 1 km. RS-423 features an improved receiver sensitivity of ±200 mV, and a lower transmitter-output impedance.

Both RS-232 and RS-423 standards are single-ended schemes, where the receiver measures the potential between signal line and ground reference. Even though the transmitter and receiver grounds are connected through the transmission-line return, as shown in Fig. 4.5, the impedance over a long-distance connection may support a significant difference in the two ground potentials. Any ground shift is superimposed on the received voltage levels, and will degrade the noise performance.

The RS-422 standard, shown in Fig. 4.5, employs differential transmission, considerably enhancing the speed-distance product. In this case a push-pull pair of balanced signal lines are used. Thus logic 0 may be represented by a signal +5 V/0 V, and logic 1 by 0 V/+5 V. The receiver detects differences down to ±200 mV across its differential input. Signal lines can have a common voltage difference from receiver ground of up to ±7 V without degradation of performance. Furthermore, the output impedance of RS-422 drivers matches the characteristic impedance of 100 Ω twisted-pair line.

Line lengths can be extended by including receiver/transmitter pairs as repeaters to regenerate the signal at appropriate intervals. However, this technique is likely to prove expensive for very long lengths, not only to install but to maintain. A viable alternative in such cases is to use existing communication links, such as the public telephone network or radio channels. When high speed signaling is envisaged, it may be economic to rent a special link installed by the telephone utility company.

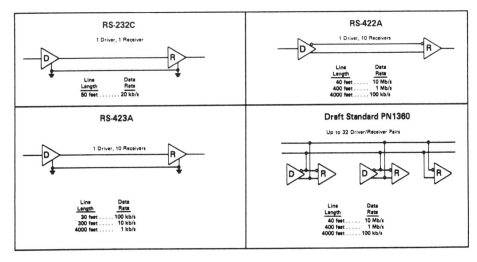

Fig. 4.5   Some voltage signaling configurations (reproduced by courtesy of Texas Instruments Limited)

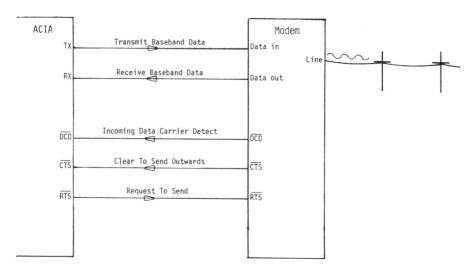

Fig. 4.6 Driving a modem from an ACIA UART

Now, a telephone channel has a bandwidth of 300-3,400 Hz. Thus it is not possible to impress the digital signals directly on to the line. Instead, these baseband signals are used to modulate a tone. Typically a normal telephone line can support one simultaneous bidirectional (duplex) communications channel at up to 300 baud using frequency-shift keying (FSK) modulation. Here the low band uses 1,070 Hz for logic 0 (space) and 1,270 Hz for logic 1 (mark). The high band uses 2,025 and 2,225 Hz for space and mark respectively. Alternatively a single simplex (unidirection) 1,200 baud channel can be supported. The term *half-duplex* is used to indicate a channel carrying nonsimultaneous bidirectional movement of data.

Rather than using FSK modulation, a more efficient technique shifts the phase of the carrier. Phase-shift keying (PSK) typically shifts $0°$, $90°$, $180°$, $270°$ from the last tone to represent dibits 00, 01, 10, 11 respectively. Tribit data with $45°$ differential shifts are also used. PSK systems allow simplex or half-duplex transmission over normal telephone lines of up to 3,600 baud, with rates of up to 9,600 baud on specially compensated lines leased from the telephone company. PSK, and to a lesser extent FSK, are also used to modulate data which are to be stored on magnetic tape and disk.

Of course relatively complex circuitry is required both to *mod*ulate and *dem*odulate the carrier. This modem will also generate status signals indicating the readiness of the channel to participate in the communication. Suitable coupling to the line, either electrical or acoustic will have to be provided. A simplified architecture of a long-distance link is illustrated in Fig. 4.6. Although an ACIA is shown, most MPU-compatible UARTs will have suitable modem handshaking facilities.

5

What Time Is It?

One of the more common functions required in a processing system is the measurement of intervals between external events and the generation of signals of a precisely controllable duration or frequency. All these functions can be implemented in software; e.g., the period between events can be timed by using registers or memory locations as a counter, incremented each pass around a software delay loop. However, by their nature, such implementations require the full attention of the microprocessor, essentially just marking time.

When the MPU is to undertake any but the most trivial additional task, the use of external hardware specifically designed to generate or to measure periods of time should be considered. We have already given an example in Fig. 1.4 where an external counter happily counts ticks from an oscillator, while the MPU goes about its tasks. The only intervention required is the reading of the counter whenever an event occurs. Counters may also be used, together with comparator circuits, to generate either single pulses or pulse trains of a controllable mark:space ratio.

Rather than designing specific hardware to implement a particular time-related task, software programmable timer ICs are available, where the internal configuration is chosen according to the bit pattern loaded into a control register. This is the same technique adopted by the parallel and serial interface chips discussed in Chapters 3 and 4. Here, we will examine the 6840 *programmable interval timer* (PIT) as a typical example of a software-configurable counter-based device.

5.1   THE PROGRAMMABLE INTERVAL TIMER

The 6840 PIT (sometimes designated *programmable timer module*, PTM) essentially comprises three 16-bit down-counters together with associated control registers and a status register. As seen from outside, each counter can be externally clocked via its input CK1, CK2, CK3 in Fig. 5.1. The maximum clock rate is approximately 400 kHz for a 1 MHz system clock ϕ_2. Each counter can used to generate output waveforms to a predetermined time relationship at an output terminal O1, O2, O3. Periods of external events at the gate inputs G1, G2, G3 can be measured. A typical

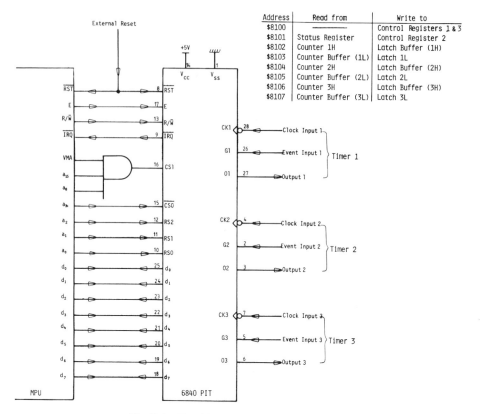

Address	Read from	Write to
$8100	─────	Control Registers 1 & 3
$8101	Status Register	Control Register 2
$8102	Counter 1H	Latch Buffer (1H)
$8103	Counter Buffer (1L)	Latch 1L
$8104	Counter 2H	Latch Buffer (2H)
$8105	Counter Buffer (2L)	Latch 2L
$8106	Counter 3H	Latch Buffer (3H)
$8107	Counter Buffer (3L)	Latch 3L

Fig. 5.1   The 6840 PIT as seen from outside

connection of the PIT to the MPU-bus system is given in Fig. 5.1. There are 16 internal registers accessible to the programmer, and, with one exception, are chosen
using the three register select inputs RS2, RS1, RS0. These registers are split into
a read-only and write-only group, as tabulated in the diagram. The $R/\overline{W}$ control is
used to select between these groups. Thus, using the address decoder shown in Fig.
5.1 as an example, storing to $8101 will write data into control register 1, while
loading an accumulator from $8101 will read data from the status register. Care
must be taken not to use read-modify-write instructions (e.g., increment) in these
circumstances, as they work by getting in the data ($R/\overline{W} = 1$); modifying it (e.g., add
one) and restoring it ($R/\overline{W} = 0$). Thus INC $8101 will end up copying the contents
of control register 1 plus 1 into the status register!

The counting section illustrated in Fig. 5.2 shows that each of the three 16-bit
counters has an associated 16-bit latch register. Whenever a counter is initialized,
e.g., on a negative-going gate input, it is loaded from its associated register. When
the PIT is externally reset, all latch registers are set to $FFFF, and this is transferred
into the counter registers. Thus, whenever counting commences, the counter will

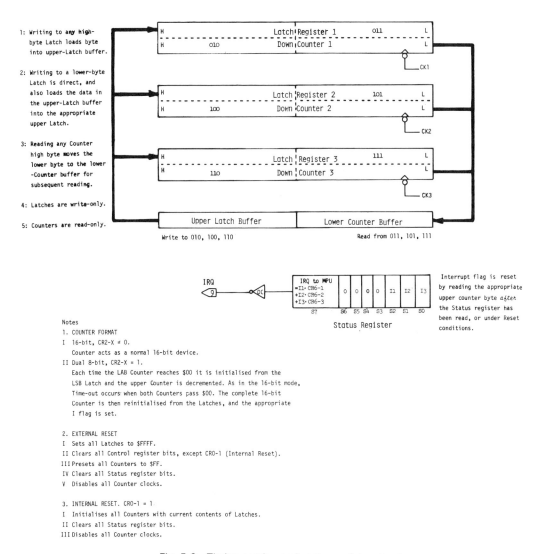

1: Writing to any high-byte Latch loads byte into upper-Latch buffer.

2: Writing to a lower-byte Latch is direct, and also loads the data in the upper-Latch buffer into the appropriate upper Latch.

3: Reading any Counter high byte moves the lower byte to the lower-Counter buffer for subsequent reading.

4: Latches are write-only.

5: Counters are read-only.

Write to 010, 100, 110

Read from 011, 101, 111

IRQ

IRQ to MPU
= I1· CR6-1
+ I2· CR6-2
+ I3· CR6-3

	S7	S6	S5	S4	S3	S2	S1	S0
	0	0	0	0	I1	I2	I3	

Status Register

Interrupt flag is reset by reading the appropriate upper counter byte *after* the Status register has been read, or under Reset conditions.

Notes
1. COUNTER FORMAT
I 16-bit, CR2-X = 0.
   Counter acts as a normal 16-bit device.
II Dual 8-bit, CR2-X = 1.
   Each time the LAB Counter reaches $00 it is initialised from the
   LSB Latch and the upper Counter is decremented. As in the 16-bit mode,
   Time-out occurs when both Counters pass $00. The complete 16-bit
   Counter is then reinitialised from the Latches, and the appropriate
   I flag is set.

2. EXTERNAL RESET
I   Sets all Latches to $FFFF.
II Clears all Control register bits, except CR0-1 (Internal Reset).
III Presets all Counters to $FF.
IV Clears all Status register bits.
V   Disables all Counter clocks.

3. INTERNAL RESET. CR0-1 = 1.
I   Initialises all Counters with current contents of Latches.
II Clears all Status register bits.
III Disables all Counter clocks.

Fig. 5.2   Timing section and status register structure

decrement from $FFFF down through $0000, when it *times out*. This requires 65,536 clock pulses.

A latch register can be set to any 16-bit value, as appropriate to the application. For example, it may be necessary to interrupt the MPU whenever 20 events (clock pulses) have occurred. In this case, the latch register would be set to initialize the associated counter register to $0013(19). After 19 events the counter will be $0000, and the twentieth event will cause time-out and, if selected, an interrupt will be generated. After this event the counter has been reinitialized to $0013. In general, a latch setting of N results in a time-out after N + 1 clock pulses.

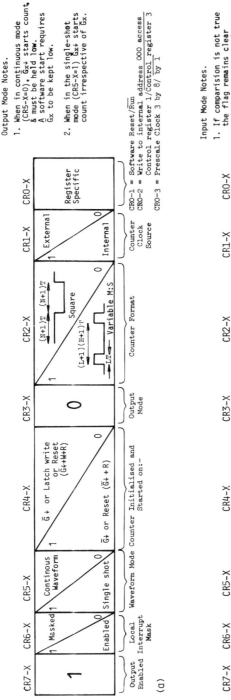
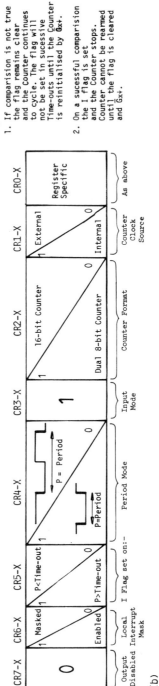

Output Mode Notes.

1. When in continuous mode (CR5-x=0), G̅x↓ starts count & must be held low. A software start requires G̅x to be kept low.

2. When in the single-shot mode (CR5-x=1) G̅x↓ starts count irrespective of G̅x.

Input Mode Notes.

1. If comparision is not true the flag remains clear and the Counter continues to cycle. The flag will not be set in sucessive Time-outs until the Counter is reinitialised by G̅x↓.

2. On a successful comparison the I flag is set and the Counter stops. Counter cannot be rearmed until the flag is cleared and G̅x↓.

(a)

CR7-X	CR6-X	CR5-X	CR4-X	CR3-X	CR2-X	CR1-X	CR0-X
1	1 Masked	1 Continous Waveform	1 G̅↓ or Latch write or Reset (G̅↓+W+R)	0	1	1 External	Register Specific
	0 Enabled	0 Single shot	0 G̅↓ or Reset (G̅↓ + R)		0	0 Internal	
Output Enabled	Local Interrupt Mask	Waveform Mode Counter Initialised and Started on:-		Output Mode	Counter Format	Counter Clock Source	

(N+1)T̅ (N+1)T
Square
(L+1)(H+1)T̅ LT̅ Variable M:S

CRO-1 = Software Reset/Run̅
CRO-2 = Write to internal address 000 access Control register 1/Control register 3
CRO-3 = Prescale Clock 3 by 8/ by 1

(b)

CR7-X	CR6-X	CR5-X	CR4-X.	CR3-X	CR2-X	CR1-X	CR0-X
0	1 Masked	1 P<Time-out	1	1	1	1 External	Register Specific
	0 Enabled	0 P>Time-out	0		0	0 Internal	
Output Disabled	Local Interrupt Mask	I Flag set on:-	Period Mode	Input Mode	Counter Format	Counter Clock Source	As above

P = Period
P=Period

16-bit Counter
Dual 8-bit Counter

Fig. 5.3 One of the three control registers

(a) Configuration of the three control registers when the PIT generates output signals (bit 3 = 0)
(b) Configuration of the three control registers when the PIT measures input events (bit 3 = 1)

Besides the simple 16-bit counting mode just described, an alternative dual 8-bit mode can be selected. In this situation the counter register acts as two separate 8-bit counters. After intialization the lower counter decrements to zero. The next clock pulse then decrements the upper counter and reloads the lower counter from the lower latch (in the 16-bit mode the lower counter always goes to $FF). Time-out occurs on the first event after both counters reach zero. For example, if we initialize the counters to $0109, then the sequence will be $0109; 0108; 0107; 0106; 0105; 0104; 0103; 0102; 0101; 0100; 0009 (lower counter reinitialized to $09); 0008 $- - -$ 0000; (time-out); 0109. A full 16-bit count would sequence $0109 $- - -$ 0101; 0100; 00FF; 00FE $- - -$. In general, the dual 8-bit mode will time-out after $(H + 1)(L + 1)$ clock pulses, $2 \times 10 = 20$ in this example.

A problem arises in matching the various 16-bit timer registers to the 8-bit data bus. For instance, altering the latch register one byte at a time may cause a glitch if a time-out occurs in the middle of this procedure. To avoid this problem the 6840 PIT has an upper latch buffer register. To change the contents of a latch register in one go, the upper byte is first stored in the buffer. When the lower byte is sent out to the lower byte of the latch register, this action simultaneously moves the contents of the latch buffer register to the upper byte of the latch register. If we use the circuit of Fig. 5.1 as an example, latch register 1 can be set to $0109 as follows: LDAA #1; STAA #8102; LDAA #9; STAA $8103. Note that there is only one latch buffer register, although it responds to any of the three tabulated addresses.

Digesting the 16-bit counter at one gulp presents similar problems. Reading the upper byte of a counter register automatically moves the lower byte to the lower counter buffer register, where it can be read at any subsequent time.

Any of the three timer sections can raise a flag on an appropriate event. The status register uses its three lower bits as flags for these sections. A flag-raising event can be used to interrupt the MPU, depending on the state of bit 6 of the appropriate timer control register (see Fig. 5.3). Bit 7 of the status register is the interrupt flag for the entire chip, and is a composite of each individual timer's flag together with its local interrupt mask.

Each of the three timer sections can be set up to its operating mode by means of an associated control register. With the exception of bit 0, all control bits have an identical function. Timer modes can be categorized as input, when signal periods at a gate are measured in terms of clock pulses (control bit 3 = 1), or output, where waveforms are generated at the appropriate output terminal (control bit 3 = 0).

In the case of the former, summarized in (a) in Fig. 5.3, generated waveforms are initiated on reset (either hardware at pin 8 or software, by setting bit 0 of control register 1), or by a negative-going edge at the associated gate (Gx↓). A software initiated start is possible if control bit 4 is clear when the attendant latch register is written to. The four waveform synthesis (*output*) modes are as listed.

OUTPUT MODE 0: Continuous square-wave synthesis

With control bits 5 and 2 = 00, a square wave will be generated with both mark and space durations of $(N + 1)$ counter clock intervals. A space is generated first after initiation. The associated gate must be kept low for as long as it is desired to generate the signal. For example, if a 1 MHz system clock is used as the counter clock (control bit 1 = 0), then a latch register setting of N = 49($31) gives a division ratio of 100; resulting in a 10 kHz square wave.

A timer set to this mode can be persuaded to generate an interrupt on each time-out, by setting control bit 6 high. Thus, e.g., if it is desired to inform the MPU that 20 events have occurred at the clock input, then the latch register should be set to 19($13). After generating the interrupt on time-out, the counter will continue cycling, and the interrupt flag should be cleared by reading the status register followed by the counter in question. As the output signal is not of interest in this application, it may be disabled by clearing control bit 7. The associated gate should be kept low.

OUTPUT MODE 1: *Continuous asymmetrical-wave synthesis*

This is similar to Mode 0, but using the dual 8-bit counter configuration, control bits 5 and 2 = 01. Here, the total cycle length is (H + 1)(L + 1) clock periods, with the mark lasting L periods. Thus with H = 49($31) and L = 1, a division ratio of 100 will result, with a mark:space ratio of 1:99. As with Mode 0, the space comes first after initiation, and the timer may be used as an event counter.

OUTPUT MODE 2: *Single-slot pulse*

With control bits 5 and 2 = 10, a single pulse will be generated on initiation. The pulse appears after one clock cycle delay, and will remain high for N clock cycles. The counter will continue to cycle, but no further pulse will be produced until a new initiation. Initiation requirements are similar to Mode 0, but the gate need not remain low for the duration of the output waveform. It should however remain low long enough to be recognized by the system clock plus hold and set-up times, typically 1.25 μs for a 1 MHz clock. When a software initiation is used (control bit 4 = 0), the state of the gate is immaterial.

OUTPUT MODE 3: *Variable delay single-shot pulse*

When dual 8-bit counting is used (control bits 5 and 2 = 11) a single high-pulse of duration L clock cycles results after a delay of (L + 1)(H + 1) − L cycles. As in Mode 2, the counter continues cycling and timing-out behind the scenes, and thus can be used as an event totalizer.

In all of the preceding modes its should be remembered that gate (and clock) inputs are synchronized by the system clock ϕ_2. This causes a certain amount of time jitter, as they will not be recognized by the PIT unless they are present for a minimum of 200 ns before the falling edge of ϕ_2 (for the high-speed 68B40 2 MHz PIT, the set-up time is 75 ns) and held for at least 50 ns afterwards.

When control bit 3 is set high the associated timer is set to measure periods of signals applied to the appropriate gate input. Once again there are four basic operating modes.

INPUT MODE 0: Frequency measurement

With control bits 4 and 5 = 00 the timer will measure the period between successive negative-going edges of the gate signal, provided that this is less than the counter time-out period. The counter will be initialized to the associated latch register on the first falling edge, and will proceed to count down at the clock rate. If the second edge occurs before time-out, the counter will stop and set the appropriate status register flag. If control bit 6 is high, this event will also send an interrupt to the MPU. When the MPU reads the status register followed by the counter in question, the flag and interrupt are lifted. Only then is the counter rearmed to repeat the process. The period, and by inference frequency, is the difference in clock periods between the latch register setting and the state of the counter. If the latter is set to $FFFF and a 16-bit counting mode is used (control bit 2 = 0), this can simply be obtained as the complement of the counter state.

If the measured period is longer than time-out, then the counter continues cycling and does not set the interrupt flag. It is reinitialized on the next falling gate edge.

INPUT MODE 1: Frequency comparison

In this situation, the interrupt flag is set when the counter times-out before the second falling edge. The counter then stops, and be rearmed only when the interrupt flag has been cleared (read status followed by read counter) and a falling edge is impressed at the gate. If the falling edge occurs before time-out, then the counter will be reinitialized automatically as the interrupt flag is not yet set. This mode is set up with control bits 4 and 5 = 01.

INPUT MODE 2: Period measurement

With control bits 4 and 5 = 10, the timer acts in a similar manner to Mode 0, but time is measured between a falling edge on the gate (which rearms the counter) and the next rising edge. Provided that this rising edge occurs before time-out, the counter will stop and the interrupt flag will be set. This must be cleared before the counter can once again be reinitialized, except by reset. As only the down-time of the input signal is measured, no assumption can be made for frequency, unless the signal is square.

INPUT MODE 3: *Period comparison*

This is the down-time counterpart of Mode 1. It is set up with control bits 4 and 5 = 11.

Looking at Fig. 5.3, it can be seen that control bit 0 plays a register-dependent role. In control register 1, bit 0 acts as a software reset. If this bit is set, all counters are preset with the contents of the corresponding latch registers, and are frozen; all outputs are disabled and interrupt flags cleared. The other control bits and the latch registers may be altered during a software reset, and when finally CR0-1 is cleared the PIT will commence its programmed operations. An external hardware reset will always set this bit, and clear all other control bits. Unlike a software reset, bringing pin 8 low sets all latch bits to 1.

In control register 3, bit 0 enables a divide-by-8 prescaler in series with counter 3's clock input. This prescaler is effective both for an external clocking source (control bit 1 = 0) or when the system clock ϕ_2 is used as the source (control bit 1 = 1).

Both control registers 1 and 3 live at the same address. Bit 0 of control register 2 is used to select between them, rather in the manner of the PIA's data and DDR register couplet. This is illustrated in Section 5.2.

5.2   BEAT-TO-BEAT VARIATION

As an example illustrating the setting-up procedure of the PIT, let us consider the following problem. The jitter of the human heart rate is an important physiological measure of nervous degeneration in long-term diabetic patients. In order to measure the beat-to-beat variation, the period between successive heart contractions must be measured to a resolution of better than 1 ms. If we assume the analog-processing circuitry detecting the peak of the electrocardiogram (ECG) waveform, then the system input will be represented by the upper pulse waveform of Fig. 5.4. Here we must measure the elapsed time between each pair of negative-going edges.

A first approach could be to use this signal to gate one of the counters configured to input mode 0. This will return the period between falling edges, with the counter stopping at the second edge. However, a moment's thought should convince you that as the counter has now stopped, it will not restart until the next again falling edge (provided that it is rearmed by this time). Thus every second beat will be missed! Obviously two timers working in tandem must be used to circumvent this problem.

To ensure the alteration of the two counters, the input waveform is phase-split; one possibility being shown in the two lower waveforms of Fig. 5.4. In this situation the down period is to be measured, and input mode 2 will be applicable. Whenever one timer section stops, the other timer will start. By the time this other timer in turn stops, the first timer will have been read and hence rearmed.

The maximum count in any timer section is 65,536 clock periods. Thus using

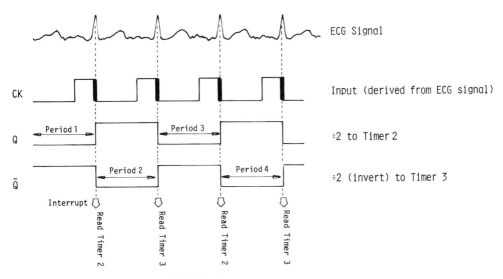

Fig. 5.4   System timing waveforms

the system clock ϕ_2 of 1 MHz restricts the duration of the count to 0.06536 s. In the situation being depicted here, durations of around 2 seconds are possible. A time-base of 10 kHz would extend the count to over 6 s, and falls within the specified resolution. Rather than employing an external oscillator to generate the 10 kHz master clock, the remaining unused timer can be used to divide the 1 MHz clock by 100. Output mode 0 will provide the necessary signal, which is then used to drive the clock inputs of the two-period counters; as shown in Fig. 5.5. Here a toggling JK flip flop is used to phase-split the incoming ECG-derived pulse, giving the waveforms depicted in Fig. 5.4.

As in all software programmable interfaces, the PIT must be configured during the initialization program just following the MPU reset. The setting of control register 1 will be %10000010 for output enabled with no interrupt, continuous waveform started when latch register 1 is set up, output mode, 16-bit counter clocked by ϕ_2 and with bit 0 zeroed to release the software reset. Setting the associated latch register to $0031 (49) gives the ÷ 100 ratio ((N + 1) + (N + 1)).

Control register 3 will be set up to %01011000 to disable the output, enable the interrupt generated if the down period is less than time-out, input mode, 16-bit counter clocked by an external signal and with no prescale. Control register 2 is similarly set up, bit 0 is used to select between registers 1 and 3 in this case.

Based on the address decoder of Fig. 5.1, the program of Listing 5.1 configures the PIT according to our specification. We assume that the PIT has been hardware reset.

Some comment is called for concerning the initialization of locations $0060/1 to $4000. To illustrate the use of the PIT in action, we will update a 256 double-byte circular array of heartbeat periods. This array is to be stored in RAM between $4000

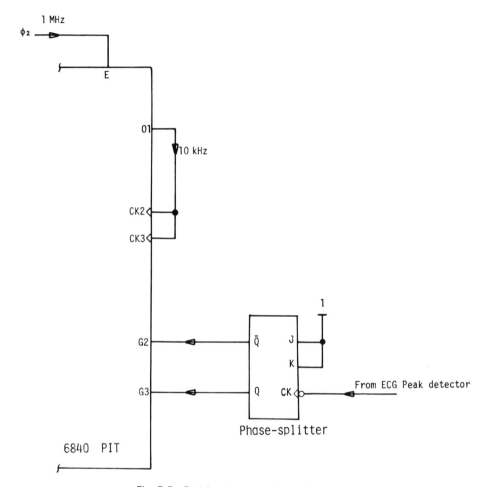

Fig. 5.5 Peripheral connection to the PIT

and $41FF. The pointer to the last updated element will be kept in $0060/1, which has been initialized to point to element 0 in Lines 220–240 of Listing 5.1. When the array is filled, the pointer will be wrapped around to the beginning of the array, hence the term *circular array*. At any time the last 256 beat-timings are available relative to this pointer. The program is given in Listing 5.2.

At the beginning of the service routine, the array pointer is moved into the index register, where it is used in conjunction with the indexed address mode to add two new bytes to the array (Lines 450 and 490). The origin of the interrupt (counter 2 or 3) is determined by testing bit 2 of the status register in Steps 390–400, after which the appropriate counter's upper byte is read in either Line 410 or 430. This moves the associated lower byte to the counter buffer register, to be read later in Line 470. The routine terminates by checking that the twice incremented index

```
10      (0060)  POINTER EQU   $0060
20      (8100)  PITBASE EQU   $8100
30   *
40   *This routine configures the PIT
50      (0100)          ORG   $0100
60   0100 86-58          LDAA  #%01011000   *Set up Control register3
70   0102 B7-8100        STAA  PITBASE      *at PITBASE
80   0105 86-59          LDAA  #%01011001   *Do the same for Control register2
90   0107 B7-8101        STAA  PITBASE+1    *& switch over PITBASE to Control register1
100  010A 86-80          LDAA  #%10000000   *Now can setup Control register1
110  010C B7-8100        STAA  PITBASE
120  010F 7F-8102        CLR   PITBASE+2    *By clearing High-byte Latch buffer
130  0112 86-31          LDAA  #$31         *and sending $31 to Low-byte Latch register2
140  0114 B7-8103        STAA  PITBASE+3    *Latch register1 is set up to $0031
150  *
160  0117 7F-0061        CLR   POINTER+1    *Set up POINTER/POINTER+1 to $4000
170  011A 86-40          LDAA  #$40
180  011C 97-60          STAA  POINTER
190  *
200  *Next initialisation routine starts here
210  *After all peripherals initialised, clear interrupt mask
```

Listing 5.1   Setting up the PIT

```
230  ************************************************************************
240  *This interrupt service routine updates the heart-period array
250  *Locations used : $0060/1; $4000-$41FF
260  *ENTRY          : $0060/1 points to last updated value
270  *EXIT           : $0060/1 points to new value
280  ************************************************************************
290     (0E00)          ORG   $0E00
300  0E00 DE-60  BEAT    LDX   POINTER      *Move contents of POINTER/POINTER+1 into IX
310  0E02 08             INX                *Point to next array upper byte
320  0E03 B6-8101        LDAA  PITBASE+1    *Examine PIT Status register
330  0E06 85-04          BITA  #%00000100   *Look at Timer3's flag
340  0E09 27-05          BEQ   TIMER2       *IF clear THEN must be Timer2
350  0E0A B6-8106        LDAA  PITBASE+6    *Read Counter3's high byte
360  0E0D 20-03          BRA   HAWAY        *Skip Timer 2's read
370  0E0F B6-8104 TIMER2 LDAA PITBASE+4     *Get Counter2's high byte
380  0E12 40     HAWAY   NEGA               *Change down-count to up-count
390  0E13 A7-00          STAA  0,X          *And put it away in the array
400  *
410  0E15 08             INX                *Point to next array point's lower byte
420  0E16 B6-8105        LDAA  PITBASE+5    *Get byte from Lower Counter buffer
430  0E19 40             NEGA               *and convert to up-count
440  0E1A A7-00          STAA  0,X          *and put it away
450  *
460  0E1C 8C-41FF        CPX   #$41FF       *Check for endpoint of array
470  0E1F 26-05          BNE   UPDATE       *IF not THEN do not reset POINTER
480  0E21 CE-4000        LDX   #$4000       *ELSE reset to beginning of array
490  0E24 DF-60  UPDATE  STX   POINTER      *Update array pointer
500  0E26 3B             RTI
```

Listing 5.2   Adding a new double-byte element to the period array

register has not passed the end of the array, and moves its value back to the array pointer ($0060/61).

The array as described here comprises absolute period magnitudes. Variability elements are obtained by doing a double-precision subtraction from the previously stored absolute values, giving $\Delta t(n) = t(n) - t(n-1)$.

6

Take the Rough with the Smooth

Microprocessors speak in bits and bytes. The real world speaks in continuously variable volts and amps: or at least after the physical parameter has been converted to an analogous electrical quantity by the transducer. Betwixt and between the rough digital world of the MPU-based system and the smooth analog signals provided by the real world lies an analog-digital conversion interface.

Analog-to-digital (A/D) conversion is required when the MPU wishes to read an analog signal, while digital-to-analog (D/A) conversion provides the means of controlling an analog quantity. In our project of Part 3, our concern is to measure the analog-quantity temperature. As a prelude to that discussion, Chapter 6 looks at D/A and its extension to A/D conversion.

6.1   DIGITAL-TO-ANALOG CONVERSION

D/A conversion can be defined as the production of an analog signal, typically voltage or current, whose amplitude is proportional to the quantitative magnitude of the input-digital word.

One rather crude way of providing this relationship is known as *pulse-width modulation* (PWM). Here, a pulse train of constant repetition rate has its mark duration altered in a proportional manner to the digital magnitude. Thus a small number gives a skinny pulse, which when smoothed out by a low-pass filter translates to a low voltage. Conversely, a large digital number leads to a correspondingly large mark : space ratio, which in turn after smoothing yields a high voltage. PWM can easily be produced using a hardware counter in tandem with a comparator. The latter compares the continuously incrementing counter with the digital number N. When the count reaches N a latch is set, and remains thus until the end of the cycle when the counter overflows to zero and the latch is then reset. The counter-comparison action can be simulated in software, but in this case most of the MPU's computing time is tied up in the one task.

PWM conversion can be very accurate, essentially depending on the precision of the mark and space voltages, and is simple to implement. However, very extensive filtering is required to remove harmonics of the pulse rate. This filtering by definition makes the conversion slow to respond to changes in the digital input. Normally PWM is used to control heavy loads, such as motors or heaters, where the inertia of these devices provides the smoothing action. Furthermore, the pulse nature of the signal is ideally suited to control power transistors and thyristor-firing circuits.

Natural binary code is weighted in ascending order of powers of two. Thus an 8-bit binary number can be written as:

$$N = (b_7 \times 2^7) + (b_6 \times 2^6) + (b_5 \times 2^5) + (b_4 \times 2^4) + (b_3 \times 2^3)$$
$$+ (b_2 \times 2^2) + (b_1 \times 2^1) + (b_0 \times 2^0)$$

where b_n is the nth binary digit, either 0 or 1. In general:

$$N = \sum_{k=0}^{M-1} b_k \times 2^k$$

for an M-digit word.

With this definition in mind, the use of a suitably weighted resistor network is suggested. Using eight resistors, each driven by one digital line and feeding into the virtual earth of an operational amplifier summing junction will give a composite output which is a function of the digital pattern and the resistor weights. Thus using a 128 kΩ resistor in series with b_0, 64 kΩ for b_1 down to 1 kΩ for b_7 will feed currents in ascending orders of two into the summing junction.

Obviously for any useful accuracy, the raw digital voltage levels cannot be used directly to feed the resistor network. Instead the logic signals are used to control precision switches which, in turn, feed an accurate noise-free reference voltage to the network.

In a practical situation the use of weighted resistors leads to severe accuracy problems. These are the result of the wide range of resistance values (1 : 2,048 for a 12-bit network) leading to a correspondingly large range of currents carried by the precision switches; not to mention the difficulties in selecting resistors of a suitable accuracy. Because of these difficulties, a resistor network based on a ladder topology is used.

An example of such a network is shown in (a) in Fig. 6.1. To analyze this circuit we make use of Thevenin's theorem which states that any linear circuit may be replaced, insofar as its external behavior is concerned, by its open-circuit voltage and internal resistance. In (b) in Fig. 6.1, we iteratively Thevenize the network one section at a time moving from left (least significant bit) to right. This shows that each stage attenuates all previous voltages by the desired factor of two. Furthermore, the resistance looking left at any node is always 2R (R + 2R//2R). If the load resistor of Fig. 6.1 is made 2R, then the network is symmetrical, and the resistance at any node looking right must also be 2R. Thus as seen from *any* switch, the total resistance is always 2R + 2R//2R = 3R; hence the switch current is always the same irrespective of position.

For clarity our analysis has been for three bits, this can be extended by simply moving the leftmost 2R-terminating resistor over and inserting the requisite number of sections. This does not affect the resistance seen left of the node, and therefore does not change the conditions of any of the rightmost sections.

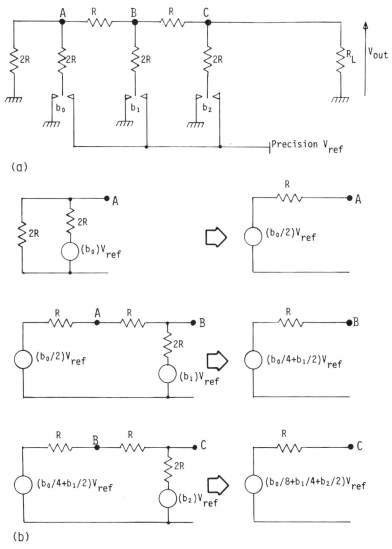

Fig. 6.1   R-2R digital-to-analog conversion
(*a*) A 3-bit R-2R ladder network
(*b*) Thevenizing the network

An inspection of our analysis shows that nowhere does the absolute value of resistance appear. In fact the accuracy of the analysis depends only on the R:2R ratio. While it is relatively easy to fabricate accurate ratioed resistors on a silicon die, this is certainly not the case for absolute values. Thus R:2R networks are mandatory for monolithic (one silicon chip) D/A converter devices.

A typical MPU-compatible 8-bit D/A converter is shown in Fig. 6.2, which illustrates its internal structure. Conversion time is around 1 μs, depending on the

D to A CONVERTER

ZN428E-8
ZN428J-8

8 Bit Latched Input Monolithic D to A Converter

FEATURES

- Contains DAC with data latch and on-chip reference.
- Guaranteed monotonic over the full operating temperature range
- Single +5V supply
- TTL and 5V CMOS compatible
- 800 ns settling time
- ZN428E-8   Commercial temperature range   0°C to +70°C
- ZN428J-8   Military temperature range   −55°C to +125°C

GENERAL DESCRIPTION

The ZN428 is a Monolithic 8 bit D to A converter with input latches to facilitate up-dating from a data bus. The latch is transparent when $\overline{\text{Enable}}$ is LOW and the data is held when $\overline{\text{Enable}}$ is taken HIGH. The ZN428 also contains a 2.5 volt reference the use of which is pin optional to retain flexibility. An external fixed or varying reference may therefore be substituted.

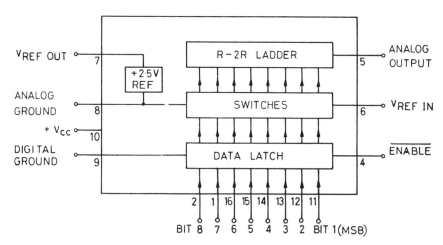

Fig. 6.2   The ZN428 8-bit monolithic D/A converter (reproduced by courtesy of Ferranti Electronics Limited)

capacitance of the analog load. The schematic shows that an internal 2.55 V generator is provided. This may be used to furnish the precision R-2R reference voltage ($V_{REF\ IN}$ connected to $V_{REF\ OUT}$), which may alternatively be sourced from outside (connected to $V_{REF\ IN}$). One internal voltage generator can provide the reference for several ZN428 D/A converters, providing excellent matching and temperature tracking characteristics.

As seen by the MPU, the ZN428 looks like a normal 8-bit output port, similar to that of Fig. 2.7. It is the integral data register that qualifies such D/A converters with their appellation *microprocessor compatible*. Figure 6.3 shows a direct connection of such a circuit to the MPU's data bus. Note the qualification of the address decoder's output with ϕ_2 to avoid the writing critical race of Section 2.1.

An alternative indirect interface technique is shown in Fig. 3.4. Here the converter's data register is permanently enabled, and a PIA is used in its place. This

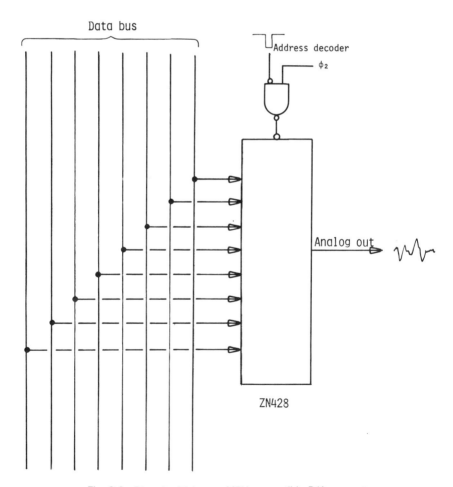

Fig. 6.3   Directly driving an MPU-compatible D/A converter

technique can reduce noise induced in the analog signal by the constantly jiggling data bus, inherent to the direct connection.

6.2   ANALOG-TO-DIGITAL CONVERSION

The alternative transformation direction of analog to an equivalent digital quantity is by far the more complex of the two. One possible scenario involves an array of analog comparators. A known reference voltage is applied to a string of N equal resistors, giving a series of ascending voltage steps of V_{REF}/N. The unknown incoming analog voltage V_{IN} is compared to the voltage at each resistor node. Thus whenever the fixed quantum voltage exceeds V_{IN}, that comparator output will be logic 0, and logic 1 signals nodes whose voltage is less than V_{IN}. This generates an N-line digital pattern, which is a simple function of the fraction V_{IN}/V_{REF}. One stage of digital processing then yields the K-bit binary code.

Parallel, or 'flash', converters are expensive, as an array of 2^k analog comparators are needed (e.g., 256 comparators for an 8-bit word). Nevertheless, they are very fast, and are the only feasible technique when dealing with situations such as real-time video digitization.

For most microprocessor applications, the short conversion times of flash converters is an embarrassment, demanding direct memory-access procedures to make full use of their conversion rate. Instead, most MPU-compatible A/D converters make use of the more prosaic technique of *successive approximation*. This is the electronic equivalent to the beam balance. Consider an unknown weight placed in one pan of such a balance, and a range of known weights in powers of two available to the operator. A systematic approach to the determination of the unknown weight is to start with the largest known weight. If this is too light, then it is left in situ, otherwise it is removed. The same procedure is carried out in descending order until the smallest known weight has been used. The solution is then the assemblage of weights in the pan, to a resolution of the smallest weight.

A typical A/D converter using this approach is shown in Fig. 6.4. When the ZN427 is reset, by pulsing $\overline{\text{Start Convert}}$ $(\overline{\text{SC}})$ low, the successive approximation register (SAR) is set to %10000000 (half scale). The R-2R network then transforms this to $V_{REF}/2$, which is compared to V_{IN} using an analog comparator. If $V_{REF}/2 \leqslant V_{IN}$ then bit 7 is left at logic 1, otherwise it is cleared. The same process is repeated after each bit in descending order, until bit 0 ($V_{REF}/256$) has been tried. The bit pattern in the SAR is then the nearest digital equivalent. This is signaled to the outside world by end of conversion (EOC) going high.

An indirect interface strategy for an A/D converter is shown in Fig. 3.4. Here, a PIA is used to create the appropriate handshake, and act as an input port. Alternatively the ZN427 may be connected directly to the MPU's data bus, by virtue of the integral 3-state buffer. To read the SAR, the MPU simply pulses $\overline{\text{Output Enable}}$ $(\overline{\text{OE}})$ low.

Unfortunately fast A/Ds are just as good at converting noise spikes as they are at processing the desired signals. We have already discussed some noise reduction

A/D CONVERTER

ZN427E-8
ZN427J-8

8 Bit Successive Approximation A/D Converter

FEATURES
- Fast; 15 μs conversion time guaranteed
- 3-state outputs, TTL compatible
- Internal or external reference
- No missing codes over operating temperature range
- Unipolar and bipolar input ranges
- Ratiometric conversion
- +5V and –3V to –30V supplies
- ZN427E-8   Commercial temp. range   0°C to +70°C
- ZN427J-8   Military temp. range   –55°C to +125°C

DESCRIPTION
The ZN427 is an 8-bit A to D converter with 3-state outputs to permit bussing on common data lines. It contains a voltage switching D to A converter, a 2.5 volts precision reference, a fast comparator and successive approximation logic.

The use of the on-chip reference voltage is pin optional to retain flexibility. An external fixed or varying reference may therefore be substituted.

Only passive external components are required. For basic operation these are an input resistor, a reference resistor and capacitor and a resistor from R_{EXT} (pin 5) to the negative rail (V_-).

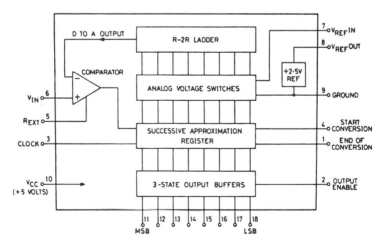

Fig. 6.4   The ZN427 8-bit monolithic A/D converter (reproduced by courtesy of Ferranti Electronics Limited)

techniques in Section 1.4. In severe cases opto-isolation may be used to separate the converter entirely from the rest of the digital circuitry. Converters of 12-bit or more resolution are especially sensitive to noise. In such circumstances alternative slow conversion strategies may be used. Typically the analog signal is integrated as an internal counter goes from zero to full scale (i.e., a fixed time). On overflow the integrator is ramped down by a reference voltage. When the integrator reaches zero the count stops. The time, and therefore count, is proportional to the magnitude of the original analog signal. Such dual-slope A/D converters have conversion times of up to 50 ms but the integrating action tends to smooth out high-frequency noise perturbations. This is particularly true if the integrating time is made equal to one mains cycle.

One question arises, especially when the converter takes an appreciable processing time. What happens if the analog signal is changing during this period? Normally the result will lie somewhere between the digitized equivalent at the start and end of conversion. Obviously when the analog change during this time exceeds the resolution (1-bit equivalent) of the converter, then that parameter is effectively degraded. An example will clarify.

The ZN447 A/D converter has a guaranteed conversion time of not more than 9 μs. If the uncertainty factor is not to exceed its 1-bit resolution, what is the maximum frequency of a full-scale sinusoid which can be successfully converted?

Now, the scale range of the ZN447 is 0–2.55V, giving a 1-bit resolution of 10 mV (FS/255). A full-scale sinusoid can be expressed as $f(t) = FS(\frac{1}{2} + \frac{1}{2} \sin \omega t)$, i.e., a sine wave superimposed on a $\frac{1}{2}$-scale bias.

Differentiating gives the rate of change thus:

$$\frac{df(t)}{dt} = (FS/2)\omega \cos \omega t$$

which is maximum when ωt equals 0^0 (cos $\omega t = 1$). Therefore, the maximum rate of change equals $\omega(FS/2)$, and the total change in 9 μs will then be approximately

$$\omega(FS/2) \times 9 \times 10^{-6} \text{ volts}$$

which must not exceed FS/255. Thus,

$$\omega(FS/2) \times 9 \times 10^{-6} = FS/255$$

$$\omega = \frac{2 \times 10^6}{9 \times 255} = 871 \text{ radians s}^{-1}$$

$$f \approx 140 \text{ Hz}$$

In practice the picture is not so bleak as this result apparently indicates. In a wide spectrum signal, such as speech, the higher frequency content is small in amplitude, and therefore adds less to the rate of change. However, the problem is compounded with converters having more than 8-bit resolution. For example, a similarly specified 12-bit conversion has a full-scale sinusoid limitation of less than 9 Hz!

In situations where quickly varying signals are being handled, an analog *sample-and-hold* circuit is usually inserted between analog source and A/D converter input. This is the analog equivalent to the digital D latch. In its simplest form it consists of a switch and capacitor. When the switch is closed (sample) the capacitor voltage follows the input signal. When the switch opens, the capacitor holds its charge for a relatively long period of time. The A/D converter is then free to begin processing. A typical sample-and-hold circuit has an uncertainty time (known as *aperture time*) of 50 ns or less. However, the time between data capture and the output setting down (the acquisition time) can be as long as 10 μs, depending on the capacitor size. Conversion must not begin before this time. A 50 ns aperture time will permit error-free 8-bit conversion of a full-scale 7 kHz signal.

This discussion leads on to an additional question. How often should a signal be sampled? The *sampling theorem* states that a sampling rate of twice the highest frequency component of the signal will be sufficient to ensure that no information is missed. Thus, e.g., a band-limited signal of 200 Hz, must be sampled at least 400 times per second. Any component of the sampled signal above half the sampling rate will give rise to distortion which cannot subsequently be removed by filtering. This distortion can be avoided by low-pass filtering the analog signal, which even if band-limited will contain some high-frequency noise. This filter stage should be placed prior to the sample-and-hold circuit, where this is used. Using a sampling rate somewhat above the theoretical limit also helps.

In many situations analog information from more than one source has to be acquired by the MPU, e.g., see Section 3.2. Essentially there are two approaches to this problem. One uses a separate A/D converter for each channel. This provides the fastest means of multichannel conversion, but is expensive.

If speed is not a prime consideration, then a single A/D converter fed by an analog mutiplexer is an economical solution. Here the N analog channels feed into an N to 1-line multiplexer. The MPU must first latch in the channel address M. This switches through channel M to the A/D converter, which can then start processing.

Some A/D converter chips are available with 8- and 16-channel multiplexers built in. The National Semiconductor ADC0816/7 device featured in Fig. 6.5 is typical of these. The ADC0816 has an integral 4-bit address latch enabled by address latch enable (ALE). In the configuration of Fig. 6.5, when ALE is pulsed high, data from the lower four bits of the data bus are loaded into this latch. Thus to select analog channel 7, a typical software sequence would be: LDAA #$7:STAA $9000. The $9000 decoder output is qualified with ϕ_2 to avoid the write-to race hazard. After no more than 2.5 μs the selected analog signal, which appears at the common-out pin, settles to its stable value. This is normally connected through to the A/D input, as shown in the diagram.

The ACD0816 is now ready to start its conversion. This is done by pulsing SC high, which resets the successive approximation register. With a recommended maximum clock frequency of 640 kHz, conversion takes around 100 μs, after which end of conversion (EOC) goes high. In Fig. 6.5, a polling approach is used to sense this event, with EOC being 3-state gated through to data line 7. A typical polling software procedure would then be TEST TST $9003:BPL TEST. Remember that TST sets the N flag if bit 7 is high.

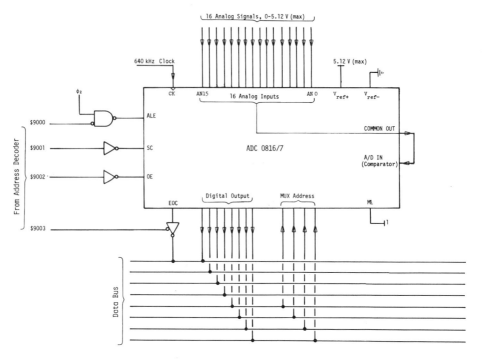

Fig. 6.5   A multichannel A/D converter

An alternative interrupt-driven handshake protocol can be implemented by using EOC to set an interrupt flag in the manner of Fig. 2.8.

In situations when the 100 μs conversion time is too long, a sample and hold circuit may be inserted between the multiplexer output and A/D converter input. This will be activated after the address latch has been clocked (if the channel is being changed). Conversion must not now be started until after the sample-and-hold's acquisition time.

The multiplexer enable (ME) input is provided to facilitate the expansion of the channel capacity by using external analog multiplexers. For example, an extra latched address bit could switch between the internal multiplexer (ME = 1) and an external 16 to 1-line analog multiplexer (ME = 0). The outputs of the two multiplexers are connected into the common-out pin. The total capacity will now be 32 channels.

PART TWO

The Microcomputer Chip

With the growth in fabrication density since the first microprocessor devices became available, a logical progression path involves moving more of memory and peripheral interface onto the one device, creating in essence a mirocomputer on a chip.
Having spent some time studying microcomputer architecture, we now need to investigate such a practical single-chip microcomputer unit (MCU).

7

At the Heart of the 68705R3 MCU

At the time of writing there are over 30 variant MCUs loosely classified as the 6805 family, if we include the closely allied 6305 series. Fortunately these are all based on a common core CPU, which only shows a slight intrafamily variation, generally reflecting the size of the supported ROM/EPROM. By implication, the same holds for 6805 software.

Part 3 of this text develops a project based on the 68705R3 MCU, and because of this we will in the main concentrate our discussion on this device. However, due to the commonality exhibited across the 6805/6305 range, much of this material is universally applicable. Some of these differences are pointed out as the text progresses, but to avoid confusion Chapter 11 has been set aside to discuss the features of other family members. The appellation 6805 is used when general family traits as opposed to specific devices are being discussed.

7.1   ITS CPU

For the purposes of our discussion, the core of the 6805 series MCU may be partitioned into three interacting entities, viz., memory, program registers and CPU.

Practically all family members provide on-board memory of various kinds, the size and type of which differs according to device. The 68705R3 provides a total of 4K bytes of memory (see Fig. 7.1). At the bottom of the memory spectrum lies 16 bytes of register storage, from $000 to $00F; mainly used as control and data registers for the various peripheral interfaces. We will discuss these in detail in Chapter 8. Next, lying between $010 and $07F, is 112 bytes of read/write RAM. This functions both as a stack ($060–$0FF) and as scratchpad (for small amounts of temporary storage). The remaining memory space up to $FFF is occupied by ROM. Of this, all but 191 bytes ($F39–$FF7) is EPROM, destined for user programs, permanent data and reset/interrupt vectors. The 191 bytes of mask-programmed ROM is permanently stored software to enable the designer to program the internal EPROM in the appropriate hardware environment; this is the subject of Chapter 10.

A 4K memory space requires a 12-bit internal address bus, and a correspondingly sized program counter. Other 6805 variants have program counter capacities

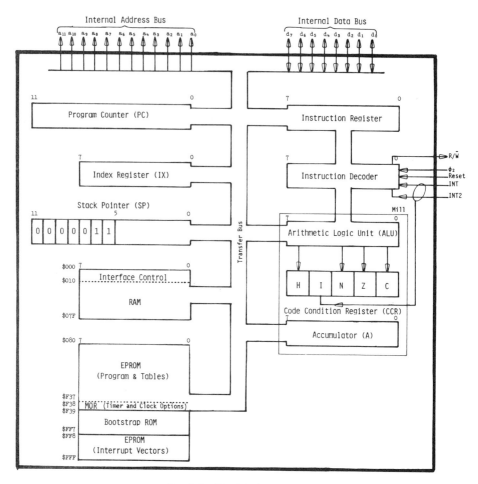

Fig. 7.1   The 68705R3 CPU

of 11 bits (e.g., the 6805P3) or 13 bits (e.g., the 68HC05C4) to match memory spaces of 2K and 8K bytes respectively. In a similar manner the stack pointer is also sized to match the internal address bus.

The index register is peculiarly sized at eight bits. Unlike the 6802's 16-bit index register, which can point anywhere in memory, the 6805's counterpart can be thought of as accessing a page of memory. Taken together with an expanded set of indexed address modes, as discussed in Section 9.1, arrays of up to 256 elements can be accessed anywhere in memory. Users of 6502 MPUs will have learned to live with a truncated index register, albeit two in this case. An 8-bit index register does have one advantage, in that it can be used as a single-byte internal storage register partially to compensate for the absence of a second accumulator. Thus, e.g., the transfer operations TBA and TAB of the 6802 MPU become TXA and TAX respectively.

The 6805 mill is a somewhat shrunken version of the 6802 counterpart. The ALU has roughly the same power, but all signed branch operations have been removed, together with the associated V flag. However, the other 6802 flags have been retained. Only one accumulator is provided as the target for ALU exertions. As these MCUs find their primary application in input/output (I/O)-intensive control functions, when only modest demands are placed on the processor, the shift in resources away from CPU to I/O on the same area of silicon satisfies both the architectural and cost requirements of this area of the market.

All versions of the 6805 have an internal clock generator. The frequency of this generator can be regulated in four ways using the XTAL and EXTAL inputs (Pins 5 and 6):

Mode I

An AT-cut parallel resonance crystal across XTAL-EXTAL gives an accurately defined frequency ϕ_2 of Fc/4, where Fc lies between 400 kHz and 4 MHz. Recommended capacitor loads for the crystal are given in Fig. 12 of Appendix 1. The expense of a crystal is justified where software loops are being used for timing purposes or ϕ_2 is being utilized to clock the internal timer.

Mode II

An external TTL-compatible signal of between 400 kHz and 4 MHz may be used directly to drive EXTAL. As in Mode I, ϕ_2 is the external frequency divided by four. This mode is useful when several 6805s are to be used together, when one accurate oscillator can replace many crystals.

Mode III

Connecting a single resistor between XTAL and V_{cc} gives a low-cost low-accuracy master clock. A resistor value around 3.3 kΩ gives $\phi_2 \simeq 500$ kHz $\pm$ 25% (see Appendix 1, Fig. 14).

Mode IV

The lowest cost of all utilizes a direct link between EXTAL and XTAL. This gives a typical ϕ_2 of 200 kHz $\pm$ 50%.

The internal oscillator must be configured to operate in the appropriate mode. In the case of mask-programmed 6805 devices (e.g., the 6805R3 is the masked ROM counterpart of the 68705R3 EPROM-based device), the desired option is specified to the manufacturer at the time of ordering, in a similar format to that outlined in Fig. 11.4. During manufacture, the mask is designed to configure the oscillator appropriately.

With EPROM-6805 devices, a byte of EPROM is set aside to simulate the mask options listed in Fig. 11.4. Most of these relate to the internal timer, and will

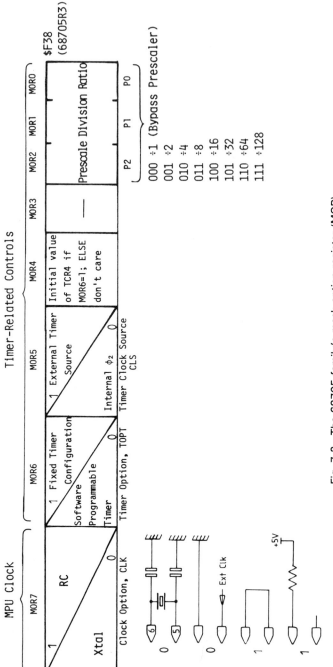

Fig. 7.2 The 68705 family's mask option register (MOR)

be discussed in Section 8.3. However, bit 7 of the *mask option register* (MOR) is used to select the clock configuration, as shown in Fig. 7.2. During EPROM programming the MOR must be set to the appropriate bit pattern. Even though the MOR is described as a register, it cannot be subsequently modified under program control. See also Sections 8.3 and 14.4. The MOR is normally placed just under the bootstrap ROM, which places it at $F38 in the 68705R3, as shown in Fig. 8.1.

7.2   HANDLING INTERRUPTS

The highest priority interrupt in any CPU will always be reset. When a 6805 series CPU recognizes a reset request (pulse $\overline{RST}$ low), it will vector to the start of the user program at the address stored in the highest two memory locations. In the 68705R3 this is at $FFE/F (in EPROM), as shown in the memory map of Fig. 8.1.

The internal circuitry connected to the $\overline{RST}$ pin includes a pull-up resistor and Schmitt trigger buffer (see Appendix 1, Fig. 10). Connecting an external capacitor of 1 μF, or greater, to this point will provide a 'cold-start' facility when V_{cc} power is first applied. The CR charging delay will be sufficient to permit the internal clock generator time to start up and stabilize before the $\overline{RST}$ voltage rises above the logic 1 threshold (about 3 V).

During the time $\overline{RST}$ is low, the peripheral contol and direction registers are initialized, as is the stack pointer. Also, the interrupt circuitry is disabled. These intialized states will be examined in more detail in Chapter 8. After $\overline{RST}$ is released, the contents of the mask option register (see Fig. 7.2) are moved to their targets in the oscillator circuitry and timer control register. The start address is then loaded into the program counter from top of memory, and the user's program commences. This is summarized in the interrupt flow diagram of Fig. 7.3.

All the 6805 MCUs have at least one interrupt pin, and the 68705R3 has two. Both of these interrupt inputs, $\overline{INT}$ (Pin 3) and $\overline{INT2}$ (Pin 18), are triggered by a negative-going edge (as is the $\overline{NMI}$ of the 6802 MPU). Looking first at the input circuitry of $\overline{INT}$ as shown in Fig. 7.4, we see that in effect an internal interrupt flag has been provided, acting in a similar manner to the D flip flop of Fig. 2.9. This D flip flop is clocked to logic 1 on a negative-going edge at $\overline{INT}$. Provided that the I mask in the code condition register is cleared, an interrupt request will be passed to the CPU. If the I mask is set, the INT flag will remain set, and the interrupt will be recognized at any future time when the I mask is cleared.

The CPU will respond to an internal interrupt request only when the current instruction execution has been completed. Its first action will be to clear the INT flag, and this clear will be held until the interrupt service routine has been terminated by the RTI operation. This means that any further interrupt request (negative-going edge at $\overline{INT}$) arriving before the end of the service routine will be ignored and therefore irretrievably lost.

External circuitry normally requests service using TTL-level digital pulses. These are recognized by the CPU provided that their down duration exceeds the ϕ_2 clock period (t_{cyc}) + 250 ns; typically 1.25 μs. HMOS (6805 and 68705) members of

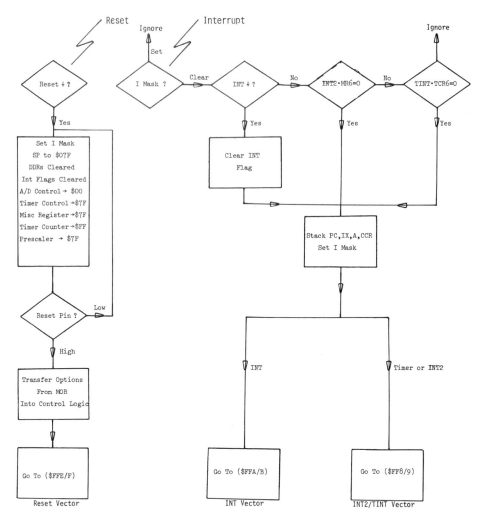

Fig. 7.3 Hardware interrupt recognition

Notes.
INT2 is recognised by the state of MR7
INT2 local mask = MR6 is not automatically cleared
TINT is recognised by the state of TCR7
TINT local mask = TCR7 is not automatically cleared

the family feature a zero-crossing Schmitt trigger $\overline{\text{INT}}$ buffer, which permits sinusoidal interrupt requests. This is frequently a derivative from the mains supply, and can be used for timing information or to synchronize burst firing thyristor circuitry. A typical sinusoidal conditioning circuit is given in Appendix 1, Fig. 16(a).

In Fig. 2.10 we illustrated the technique of wire-ORing multiple sources of interrupt requests to the one $\overline{\text{IRQ}}$ pin. This does not work when the interrupt pin is

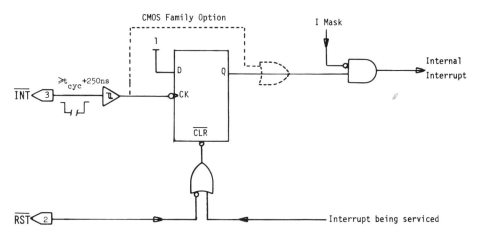

Fig. 7.4   A look at the internal interrupt (INT) flag

edge sensitive, as a second low-going edge ORed with an already low request will not produce a second edge. Thus multiple interrupt sources cannot be supported using the INT input. However, CMOS members of the family (146805/1468705) do have the option of a level-sensitive interrupt pin, labeled $\overline{\text{IRQ}}$ rather than $\overline{\text{INT}}$. In this situation, shown by the hatched line in Fig. 7.4, a bypass link around the interrupt flag is provided for direct access to the internal (level-sensitive) interrupt circuitry. This link is either implemented as a mask option (146805 versions) or can be user-controlled in EPROM devices (1468705 versions) via bit 4 of the mask option register (high for level-sensitive).

Once $\overline{\text{INT}}$ has been recognized, all the internal registers are saved on the stack, as shown in Fig. 7.5. At the end of the interrupt service routine the instruction RTI reverses the process. In a similar manner to the 6802 MPU, a subroutine call (JSR/BSR) saves only the state of the program counter, for later recall on RTS. As the program counter in the 6805 CPU is less than 16 bits wide, some phantom bits

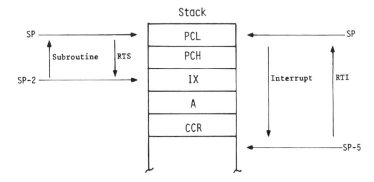

Fig. 7.5   How the CPU state is saved on the stack

will be placed on the stack. Such bits, including the three upper code condition register bits, are saved as logic 1.

The stack/stack pointer combination is much restricted compared with the corresponding setup discussed for the 6802 MPU. Firstly, the 6805's RAM is small, and generally lies between $010 and $07F. In the 68705R3 MCU, the top $20(32) bytes are reserved primarily for the stack, and the stack pointer (SP) is not permitted to drop below $60. This is done by fixing the upper seven SP bits at %0000011 (see Fig. 7.1). Thus the maximum address, i.e., top of stack, is %(0000011)11111 or $07F, while the minimum (bottom of stack) is %(0000011)00000 or $060. Any further interrupt or subroutine call will cause the SP to wrap around through the top of the stack, and this will destroy vital state information. Although the stack is small, up to 16 nested subroutines may be called, or 13 levels and one interrupt. In view of its restricted size, no push or pull operations are implemented in the instruction set, nor are stack pointer manipulations allowed other than reset stack pointer (RSP = $9C), which moves SP to the top of the stack. SP is also set to the top of stack during a reset process.

Once the machine state is saved, the I mask in the CCR is set to prevent interrupts during the service routine. The contents of the INT vector ($FFA/B) are then moved into the program counter, and the INT service routine commences.

The 68705R3 has one more external interrupt, $\overline{INT2}$ (Pin 18). Like INT, this is edge sensitive and therefore cannot be wired for multiple requests. $\overline{INT2}$ also sets the I mask in the CCR, and thus cannot be itself interrupted once underway. However, $\overline{INT2}$ also has a local mask; bit 6 in location $00A, the miscellaneous register (MR) of Fig. 7.6. A negative-going edge on $\overline{INT2}$, of minimum duration t_{cyc} + 250 ns, will set bit MR7; which acts in the capacity of the interrupt flag of Fig. 7.4. Provided that both local (MR6) and master (I bit in the CCR) masks are clear, the CPU will stack the machine state away and set the master I mask, as shown in Fig. 7.3. The INT2 start address is then fetched from $FF8/9, and the service program execution commences.

Unlike the INT interrupt flag of Fig. 7.4, bit MR7 is not cleared automatically on a RTI, but must be specially cleared by writing a 0 to bit 7 of $00A during the interrupt service routine, in the same manner as described in Section 2.3 (see also Listing 9.4). On reset the local mask is set (MR6) and the interrupt flag (MR7) cleared, thereby disabling $\overline{INT2}$. Any $\overline{INT2}$ interrupt which is ignored by the processor will remain latched into bit MR7, and will be recognized as soon as the local and master masks permit, unless MR7 is cleared by software prior to this.

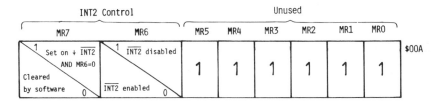

Fig. 7.6   The miscellaneous register

All members of the 6805 family permit the internal timer to interrupt the processor whenever the timer counter decrements down to zero. Although this *timer interrupt* (TINT) is generated internally it is dealt with in a virtually identical way to $\overline{\text{INT2}}$. This time the local mask is bit 6 of the timer control register (TCR), as shown in Fig. 8.5. Bit TCR7 acts as the TINT flag, and like the INT2 flag must be reset by software during the TINT service routine. During reset the TINT flag (TCR7) is cleared and the TINT local mask (TCR6) set to disable interrupts from this source.

The TINT vector is the same as that for INT2, viz., $FF8/9. Thus if the programmer expects interrupts from either source, the common start service routine must examine both the INT2 flag (MR7) and TINT flag (TCR7) to distinguish between sources, and then reset the appropriate flag. The timer section of the 6805 MCU is discussed further in Section 8.3.

8

Watching the World Go by

The personality of a single-chip MCU is primarily a function of its interface capabilities and architecture. In this chapter we specifically examine the 68705R3 device. However, much that we have to say applies to the analogous mask-programmed 6805R2/3 MCUs and, with the exception of the A/D converter, to most of the rest of the family.

8.1   68705R3 ARCHITECTURE

In common with most microprocessors, the 6805 MCU sees memory and interface registers hung on its (internal) data bus as addressable locations. In the MCU device, these registers are an integral part of the chip, and its seems sensible that this should also be the case for the address decoder. The resulting memory map is thus frozen into silicon.

The memory map for the 68705R3 is shown in Fig. 8.1. The CPU sees 4 Kbytes of addressable storage, as delineated by the 12-bit internal address bus of Fig. 7.1. Of this, only the first 128 bytes are alterable by software; the remaining 3,968 bytes are for fixed storage of tabular data and program.

Locations $010–$07F are normal read/write RAM, but the top 32 bytes of this are generally used for stack as regulated by the 5-bit stack pointer of Fig. 7.1. Some of this can be used for scratchpad RAM, but normally this area should be avoided at all cost. The stack pointer is discussed in Section 7.2.

Of greater interest to us here is the register array occupying the lowest 16 locations, of which 13 are implemented in the 68705R3 device. Each of the four PIAs require a data register, although only three data direction registers are provided as Port D is fixed as input only. Both the timer and A/D converter are given two locations. The miscellaneous register, used to service the second interrupt $\overline{INT2}$, has already been described in Fig. 7.5, while the EPROM program control register at $00B is used by the bootstrap program discussed in Chapter 10.

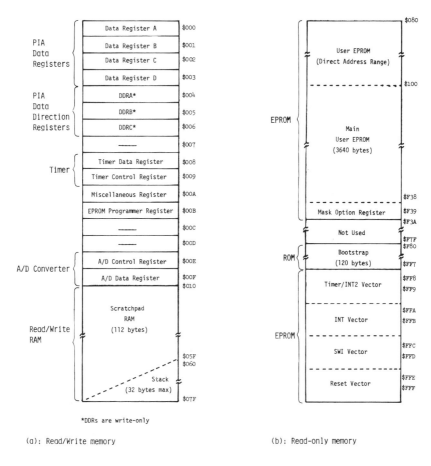

*DDRs are write-only

(a): Read/Write memory   (b): Read-only memory

Fig. 8.1   The universe as seen by the 68705R3/5 MCU

We will take a detailed look at the various I/O facilities available to the 68705R3 in the following three sections. However, it is instructive to take an overall view of the system at this point. As can be seen from Fig. 8.2, the 68705R3 comprises the CPU, together with read-only and read/write memory, address decoder and clock oscillator. The internal data bus services three divisions of peripheral circuitry. These are digital parallel I/O; timing and a 4-channel analog input port.

Of the 40 pins, 33 are used for the peripheral ports. The four parallel PIA ports require 32 lines, seven of which double as inputs for the analog port and an additional interrupt, $\overline{\text{INT2}}$. One pin acts as the timer input. The remaining seven pins are used as $\overline{\text{Reset}}$, $\overline{\text{Interrupt}}$, oscillator (2) and power (3) inputs. The 68705 MCU uses a single 5V supply (at 120 mA) during normal (non-EPROM burn) operation.

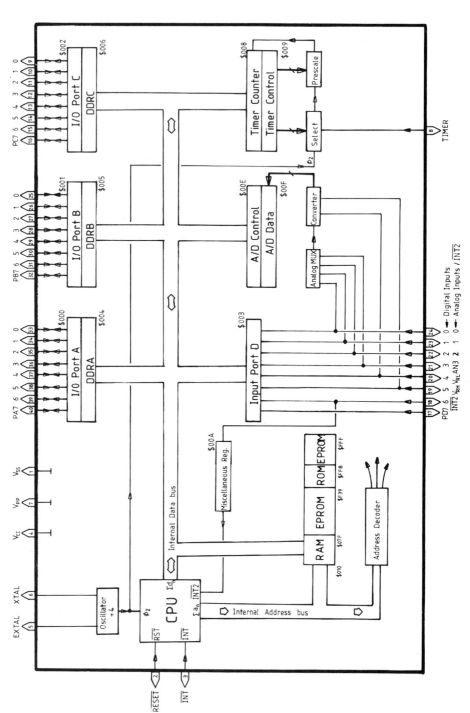

Fig. 8.2 A bird's eye view of the 68705R3/5

8.2   PARALLEL PORTS

All members of the 6805 family make provision for several parallel digital I/O ports. In general each of these ports comprise a data register together with an associated data direction register (DDR). There is no provision for automatic handshaking, so that the PIA control register discussed in Section 3.1 is not required. However, peripheral data lines can be manually wiggled about to create handshake protocols by software: an example of which is given in Section 14.1.

One of the 68705R3's parallel ports (Port D) is permanently configured as input only. Ports A, B and C are fully programmable as bitwise input or output. Figure 8.3 shows an equivalent circuit for any single bit of these three ports. With DDRn = 1, bit n is configured as an output. In this situation, depicted in Figs. 8.3(a) and (b), the I/O pin is simply a buffered version of the bit latch. Writing to that location latches the new data, while reading yields the value of that latch, irrespective of the actual physical state of the I/O pin.

When a bit is set up as input (DDRn = 0), the state of the I/O pin is connected via a buffer to the internal data line. If data is written to such a bit, as shown in Fig. 8.3(c), the bit latch is updated, but this is not reflected at the I/O pin. Being able to set up the latch register while the port is in the input mode is a useful initializing strategy. When the 6805 MCU is reset, all parallel I/O ports are set to input (DDR = $00). Such port bits destined as outputs can be written to their initial value. Only when their direction is altered will these values appear at the I/O pins. As each port bit has its associated DDR bit, I/O direction can be mixed within the one port. Note the DDRs can only be written to; they always read as $FF, irrespective of their true value. Read-modify-write instructions, such as increment, do not operate correctly on these locations.

All peripheral lines are TTL compatible as inputs ($V_{IL} < 0.8$ V; $V_{IH} > 2.0$ V) and outputs ($V_{OL} < 0.4$ V; $V_{OH} > 2.4$ V), but differ somewhat in other electrical respects. We detail the peripheral line properties below.

PERIPHERAL DATA LINES A: PA0 through PA7 (Pins 33–40). All Port A lines are capable of driving four LSTTL loads (sinking 1.6 mA at logic 0). In addition the output buffer (See Fig. 8.3) has an integral pull-up resistor to V_{CC} ($+5$ V). This gives a minimum logic 1 voltage of 3.5 V when driving a high-impedance load (< 10 μA). It is therefore suitable for direct drive of CMOS logic which requires $V_{IL} < 1.5$ V and $V_{IH} > 3.5$ V with a 5 V supply.

Port A lines can be driven by either CMOS or TTL logic. They represent a fan-in of approximately one LSTTL load.

PERIPHERAL DATA LINES B: PB0 through PB7 (Pins 25–32). All Port B lines are capable of driving eight LSTTL loads (sinking 3.2 mA with a logic 0 voltage keeping under 0.4 V). A sink current of 10 mA is available if V_{OL} is allowed to rise to a maximum of 1 V: convenient for driving LEDs. In the high state a minimum of 1 mA can be sourced with V_{OH} keeping above 1.5 V. This is useful for directly

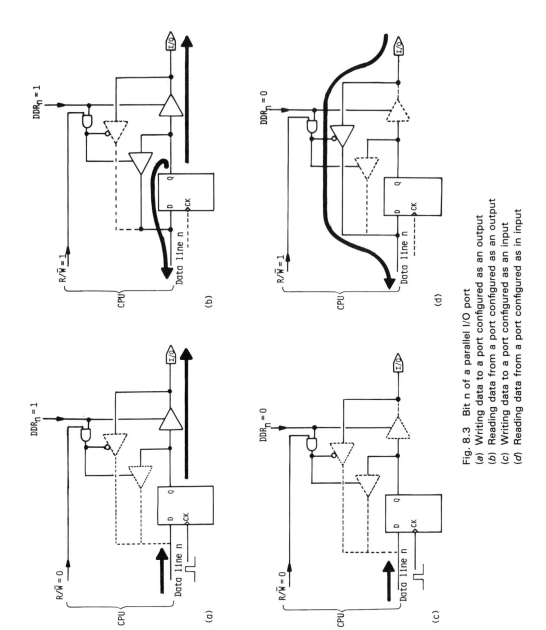

Fig. 8.3 Bit n of a parallel I/O port
(a) Writing data to a port configured as an output
(b) Reading data from a port configured as an output
(c) Writing data to a port configured as an input
(d) Reading data from a port configured as in input

driving Darlington-pair transistor buffers. Output voltages are not CMOS compatible.

As inputs, Port B lines may be driven by either TTL or CMOS logic, with a 1-LSTTL loading.

PERIPHERAL DATA LINES C: PC0 through PC7 (Pins 9–16). Port C lines can drive up to four LSTTL loads. External pull-up resistors are required where CMOS logic is being driven. Both types of logic can drive these lines, which have a 1-LSTTL loading.

PERIPHERAL DATA LINES D: PD0 through PD7 (Pins 17–24). Port D lines are input only, and with the exception of PD7, are shared with the A/D converter and $\overline{INT2}$ (see Fig. 8.2). Logic levels are both TTL and CMOS compatible. Note that a 15 kΩ resistor is internally connected between PD4 and PD5, as shown in Fig. 8.6.

A general overview of the electrical port characteristics is given in Appendix 1, Fig. 19.

8.3   THE TIMER

Most members of the 6805 family possess an 8-bit down counter, which can be clocked by external pulses or the internal ϕ_2 clock. This counter can be read at any time by the CPU, thus determining the number of events since the last read. Furthermore, an automatic interrupt can be generated when the counter decrements to all zeros, i.e., *times out*.

The actual source of timing pulses can be selected by software, and this in turn can be divided selectively in powers of two from direct to $\div 128$ ahead of the timer counter register. The dividing prescaler counter cannot be 'got at' by the CPU; instead its action, together with those of source-select and timer interrupt, is handled by an associated timer control register. As shown in Fig. 8.1, the timer counter (timer data register) and timer control registers live at addresses $008 and $009 respectively.

A highly simplified equivalent for the 6805 family timer is shown in Fig. 8.4. The clocking source for the prescale counter may be either external pulses (Pin 8), the internal clock ϕ_2 or ϕ_2 gated by the timer-pin logic level. This latter mode enables periods to be measured in terms of ϕ_2, typically up to 1 μs resolution. Timer-pin signals must be TTL compatible, and if used as the clock source, have transition times not exceeding 20 ns and a minimum pulse period of half ϕ_2 plus 250 ns; about 400 kHz for a 4 MHz crystal.

The prescale counter comprises seven flip flops sequentially halving the clock frequency. Any one of these flip flops can be connected to the timer counter, or the prescaler may be bypassed. If we take as an example an internal 1 MHz ϕ_2 timer source frequency, then clocking rates of 1,000; 500; 250; 125; 62.5; 31.25; 15.625 and

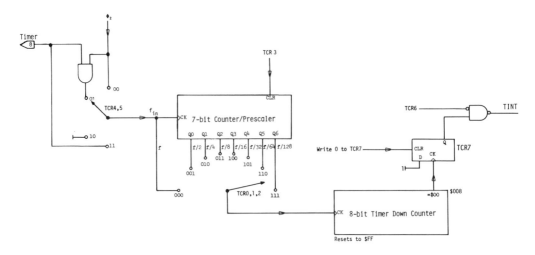

Fig. 8.4   A simplified schematic of the standard 6805 timer under software control

7.8625 kHz are available. As the timer counter has only an 8-bit capacity, the maximum counting period for this situation varies from 256 μs at 1 μs resolution to 32.768 ms at a resolution of 128 μs. Longer periods may be accommodated at the expense of some software overhead. Each time the counter falls through zero, a spare memory location must be incremented. In this way up to 65,536 (2^{16}) periods of the prescale output can be logged. A suitable program is developed in Section 17.1.

The timer counter may be set to any value between $00 and $FF by simply storing to $008. It will then proceed to decrement at the selected rate, and can be read at any time by the CPU without disturbing the count. When it reaches zero the timer interrupt flag (bit 7 of the timer control register) is automatically set, and can be polled in software to determine the instant of time out. If the timer interrupt mask (bit 6 of the timer control register) is clear AND the I mask in the CCR is also clear, a timer interrupt (TINT) will be processed by the CPU, as described in Fig. 7.3. There is no automatic reset of the timer interrupt flag when the timer register is read. Instead bit TC7 must be cleared by software (it cannot be set in this manner) as part of the interrupt service routine (see Listing 17.1).

The timer counter will continue to count down after time out, going from $00 back up to $FF-$FE, etc. If there is a delay in determining time out, then this can be measured by 2s complementing the state of the timer counter; e.g., a read counter state of %11111101 indicates an elapsed time of three ticks, %00000011($03).

The timer control register (TCR) holds the aforesaid timer interrupt flag and mask, as well as the two timer clock-source select bits TCR 5 & 4 and four bits relating to the prescale counter. The division ratio is set as listed in Fig. 8.5 by bits TCR 2, 1 and 0. The division ratio will be altered as soon as these bits are overwrit-

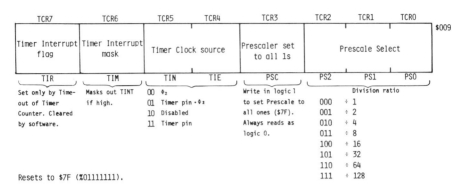

TCR7	TCR6	TCR5	TCR4	TCR3	TCR2	TCR1	TCR0
Timer Interrupt flag	Timer Interrupt mask	Timer Clock source		Prescaler set to all 1s	Prescale Select		
TIR	TIM	TIN	TIE	PSC	PS2	PS1	PS0

Set only by Time-	Masks out TINT	00	ϕ_2	Write in logic 1		Division ratio
out of Timer	if high.	01	Timer pin $\cdot \phi_2$	to set Prescale to	000	÷ 1
Counter. Cleared		10	Disabled	all ones ($7F).	001	÷ 2
by software.		11	Timer pin	Always reads as	010	÷ 4
				logic 0.	011	÷ 8
					100	÷ 16
					101	÷ 32
					110	÷ 64
Resets to $7F (%01111111).					111	÷ 128

Fig. 8.5   The timer control register ($009) in the software programmable mode (MOR6 = 0)

ten, but to ensure a clean start, writing a one into bit TCR 3 at the same time will intialize the prescaler to all ones ($7F). Bit TCR 3 always reads as zero, but pulses the prescaler's clear whenever software attempts to write it to one. A similar consideration exists when the timer control register is set up.

One of the main functions of the EPROM-based 68705 family is to serve in a prototyping role for the corresponding mask-programmed 6805 devices. Thus the 68705R3 device, under the microscope here, mirrors two similar ROM-based equivalents, the 6805R2 and R3. We will discuss these devices in more detail in Chapter 11, but here we note that the timer options of prescale division ratio and clock source are a mask option. As illustrated in Fig. 11.4, the customer must specify the desired configuration prior to manufacture. The CPU clock options of Fig. 7.2 are also frozen into the mask.

As the mask-programmed 6805R, U&P devices do not possess a software alterable timer configuration, some means must be found to simulate this fixed architecture in the inherently more flexible 68705 regime. This is accomplished in the 68705R3 by setting aside an EPROM byte known as the *mask option register* (MOR). This memory byte defines the timer and CPU options as fixed at the time of EPROM programming. An exposition of the MOR was given in Fig. 7.2 where it is seen that if bit MOR6 is zero, then the timer will operate in the software configurable mode of Fig. 8.5. With MOR6 = 1, the fixed option is selected. In this situation bits MOR2, 1, 0 define the frequency division ratio, and MOR5 defines the prescale clock source as either T (the timer pin) or T · ϕ_2. If the designer holds the timer pin permanently high, the prescale is clocked by ϕ_2. There is no inhibit option. Bit MOR4 defines the initial value of the TINT mask (bit TCR6) when the software configurable mode is being used (MOR6 = 0).

Consider as an example that we wish to fix permanently (MOR6 = 1) the timer prescale to divide ϕ_2 (MOR5 = 0) by 128 (MOR2, 1, 0 = 111), and to configure the

MCU oscillator for the crystal mode (MOR7 = 0). The MOR is then set to %01000111($47) during the EPROM burn (see Listing 15.1). In this fixed mode, only timer control bits 7, 6 and 3 are in use. The rest read as logic 1. The TCR still provides the timer interrupt flag (TCR7), the associated local mask (TCR6) and permits the initializing of the prescale counter (TCR3). As the MOR cannot then be altered by software, the timer operation is effectively frozen into the MCU architecture as necessary in the simulation of a mask-programmed part. This is the technique used in Chapter 17. As an unprogrammed EPROM byte is all zeros, a MOR left in this state will result in a timer configured in the software controllable mode, and the CPU clock oscillator in its crystal/external connection.

Note that recent members of the mask-programmed 6805 family do not implement their timer options in the mask. Instead, these are implemented in software in the same manner as described for the 68705 family.

8.4   ANALOG PORT

The 68705R3 MCU (and its mask-programmed 6805R2/3 siblings) has an 8-bit analog-to-digital (A/D) converter implemented on the chip. This uses the successive approximation technique described in Section 6.2 and takes 30 CPU clock cycles to complete a conversion (30 μs with a 4 MHz crystal), see Fig. 8.6.

Directly associated with the A/D converter are two registers. The A/D result register (ARR) living at $00F holds the digital equivalent of the last analog sample. At the end of conversion (EOC) bit 7 of the A/D control register (ACR) goes high, and the digital result is automatically dumped into the ARR for subsequent reading. After this occurs the A/D converter immediately begins the next conversion. In this free-run mode, data in the ARR is always valid. A conversion is also initiated when the CPU writes to the ACR. Thus, e.g., clearing the EOC bit (ACR7) causes the abortion of the current conversion, and the commencement of a new one. When ACR7 goes high this synchronized conversion is complete.

The ACR also holds the channel address, which selects one of eight analog sources through to the A/D converter. Only four of these are accessible to the outside world, channels 4 through 7 being internal calibration levels. Changing a channel number will automatically restart a conversion, but of the newly selected channel.

The analog-input circuitry contains an integral sample-and-hold (S/H) circuit (see Section 6.2). After the A/D converter starts its conversion cycle, an internal 25 pF capacitor is charged to the selected analog input voltage for a period of five clock cycles. For this time the input analog source will 'see' typically the 2.6 kΩ internal multiplexer resistance in series with a 35 pF (25 pF + 10 pF for packaging) capacitor. This sampled voltage is held constant for the remainder of the conversion time (25 clock cycles). If the S/H's aperture time is too long, an external S/H may be used, controlled by one of the parallel port lines.

The conversion result is the digital equivalent of the fraction of V_{IN} within the scale $V_{RL} - V_{RH}$ (i.e., it is radiometric to $V_{RL} - V_{RH}$). The A/D has a built-in $\frac{1}{2}$ least significant bit (LSB) offset, to center the quantizing error to ± 0.5 LSB, rather than $0, -1$ LSB. Thus an analog input between V_{RL} and $V_{RL} + 0.5$ LSB converts to $00; V_{RL} + 0.5$ LSB to $V_{RL} + 1.5$ LSB gives $01 etc. Full scale is reached at 1.5 LSB below V_{RH}.

The radiometric scale should not exceed the logic power supply range $V_{CC} - V_{EE}$ (GND), and neither reference voltage should fall outside these limits. Full linearity of ± 0.5 LSB is maintained for scale lengths down to $0 - 4$ V ($V_{RL} - V_{RH}$). It is preferrable not to use the logic power supply to drive these reference voltages directly, as transients on these lines may result in erroneous conversion values. The reference voltage inputs do not have the same level of protection against static voltage discharge, therefore care must be taken to avoid the application of any voltage outside the maximum ratings.

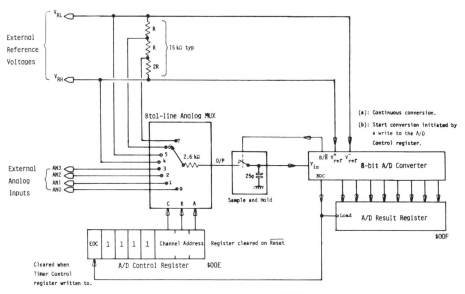

Fig. 8.6 Simplified equivalent of the 6805 family A/D converter

9

Directing the 6805 MCU

The software structure of the 6805 MCU family is directly related to that of its ancestor MPU discussed in Part 1, but modified to take account of differences in the CPU. This necessitates the removal of all operations relating to the B accumulator. Also, the small and fixed location stack has been accounted for by the elimination of all stack-pointer operations except the new instruction reset stack pointer (RSP = $9C) which sets the SP to $07F. Conditional branch operations have been changed owing to the absence of the V flag. Rather more strangely decimal adjust (DAA, Table 1.1) has not been provided, even though the H flag is present. However, its function can be simulated by using two new conditional branches, Branch if Half Carry Clear/Set, BHCC/BHCS (see Table 9.4).

These limitations are more than compensated for by the introduction of a new range of bit-manipulation and conditional branch instructions. Also, the instruction set includes many more index register related operations, which partly ameliorates the reduction of flexibility resulting from the removal of the second accumulator. In all, the 6805 family has a repertoire of 59 instructions with CMOS members (the 146805 branch of the family) being blessed with two additional operations (see Section 11.2).

In Section 9.1 we will examine the 6805 instruction set, together with its address modes. These 'bare bones' will be rounded out in the final section with some illustrative examples of typical program modules.

9.1 THE 6805 INSTRUCTION SET

With the exception of decimal adjust A, the arithmetic operations listed in Table 9.1 are identical to those discussed in Table 1.1. As the index register is only 8 bits wide, the increment and decrement index instructions are placed here, rather than in a separate 16-bit register category. Notice that the assembler recognizes the 6800 mnemonic DEX as equivalent to the official 6805 mnemonic DECX, similarly for Increment.

Instructions such as increment and decrement which can operate on a memory location (as opposed to only an internal register) are classified as *read-modify-write*.

Table 9.1 A summary of the major 6805 arithmetic operations

Operation		Mnemonic	Flags H N Z C	Description
Add				Binary addition
	to A	ADD	✓ ✓ ✓ ✓	A+M → A
with Carry				Includes Carry
	to A	ADC	✓ ✓ ✓ ✓	A+M+C → A
Decrement				Subtract one, no carry
	memory	DEC	• ✓ ✓ •	M-1 → M
	A	DECA	• ✓ ✓ •	A-1 → A
	X	DECX (DEX)	• ✓ ✓ •	X-1 → X
Increment				Add one, no carry
	memory	INC	• ✓ ✓ •	M+1 → M
	A	INCA	• ✓ ✓ •	A+1 → A
	X	INCX (INX)	• ✓ ✓ •	X+1 → X
Subtract				Binary subtraction
	from A	SUB	• ✓ ✓ ✓	A-M → A
with Carry				Includes Carry (borrow)
	from A	SBC	• ✓ ✓ ✓	A-M-C → A

Thus, e.g., the execution of the instruction INC $40 (3C-40) commences by bringing the contents of location $40 down to the CPU; one is then added to this value, and it is sent back up to $40. Obviously the target location must be in read/write memory for this operation to succeed. In the 6805, locations $010-$07F are RAM, and are thus amenable to this type of manipulation. The same is not necessarily true of the bottom 16 locations, which hold the various peripheral data and control registers. For instance, the data direction registers are write-only, always reading as $FF. Thus the operation INC DDRA (INC 04) will result in DDRA clearing, irrespective of its previous state!

Although not shown in Table 9.1, the 6805 has the ability to 2s complement any memory location, A or X. This is useful when the result of arithmetic processing is negative. NEG is of course an example of a read-write-modify instruction.

A comparison of Tables 1.2 and 9.2 shows that with the exception of the two new operations of bit clear/set, the range of data manipulation facilities are the same. With the proviso that the index register replaces the B accumulator, the two tables are virtually identical.

There is, however, one subtle difference between the processors, applying to the clear operation. In the 6802 MPU, clearing a byte always resets the carry flag. This side effect is normally just a nuisance, and can be circumvented only at the expense of loading 00 into a register and storing it at the target address, e.g., LDAB #00; STAB $40 is equivalent to CLR $0040, but leaving C intact. A 6805 clear does not fiddle with the C flag.

One minor change is the alteration of the 6802's mnemonic for arithmetic shift left (ASL) to logic shift left (LSL). Both operations are identical (the former being so called because it can be used to multiply by two). Although LSL is the preferred 6805 mnemonic for this operation, most assemblers permit the use of ASL as an alternative. The 6805 also provides an arithmetic shift right (ASR), not shown in Table 9.2. ASR keeps bit 7 constant, as required when dividing signed 2s complement numbers (see Appendix 2).

Table 9.2   Data manipulation instructions

Operation		Mnemonic	Flags N Z C	Description
Bit Clear				Clears any bit in memory
	memory	BCLR	• • •	
Bit Set				Sets any bit in memory
	memory	BSET	• • •	
Clear				Replaces data by 00
	memory	CLR	R S •	$00 \rightarrow M$
	A	CLRA	R S •	$00 \rightarrow A$
	X	CLRX	R S •	$00 \rightarrow X$
Load				Moves data to
	A	LDA	✓ ✓ •	$M \rightarrow A$
	X	LDX	✓ ✓ •	$X \rightarrow A$
Rotate left				Circular shift through Carry
	memory	ROL	✓ ✓ b_7	M
	A	ROLA	✓ ✓ b_7	A
	X	ROLX	✓ ✓ b_7	X
Rotate right				Circular shift through Carry
	memory	ROR	✓ ✓ b_0	M
	A	RORA	✓ ✓ b_0	A
	X	RORX	✓ ✓ b_0	X
Shift left, logic				Linear shift into Carry
	memory	LSL (ASL)	✓ ✓ b_7	M
	A	LSLA (ASLA)	✓ ✓ b_7	A
	X	LSLX (ASLX)	✓ ✓ b_7	X
Shift right, logic				Linear shift into Carry
	memory	LSR	✓ ✓ b_0	M
	A	LSRA	✓ ✓ b_0	A
	X	LSRX	✓ ✓ b_0	X
Store				Moves data from
	A	STA	✓ ✓ •	$A \rightarrow M$
	X	STX	✓ ✓ •	$X \rightarrow M$
Transfer				Move between A and X
	A to X	TAX	✓ ✓ •	$A \rightarrow X$
	X to A	TXA	✓ ✓ •	$X \rightarrow A$

The 6805 allows the programmer to set or clear any single bit in memory, leaving the other seven bits unchanged. The instructions BSET and BCLR are read-modify-write operations and therefore can only perform on read/write memory. These instructions use the direct address mode to target their data, which restricts their range to the lowest 256 bytes. However, no members of the 6805 MCU family have RAM above this point, and this qualification is therefore of no account.

Source code for these operations specify the bit number N as well as the target address. Thus to set bit 3 of location $40 we have BSET 3,$40. The machine object code for this has only two bytes, viz., $16-40; the bit number being incorporated into the op-code itself. The op-code for BSET N is %0001 nnn0 (or $10 + 2 × N), when nnn is the 3-bit binary code for N. For BCLR N it is %0001 nnn1 or $11 + 2 × N. Thus BCLR 7,$40 (clear bit 7 in location $40) is coded as $1F-40.

The four logic operations of AND, OR, NOT and Exclusive-OR are provided by the 6805. In all cases they operate in a bitwise fashion on the contents of the accumulator. In addition the read-write-modify operation of complementation can be implemented on any data in read/write memory or on the contents of the index register or accumulator, as shown in Table 9.3.

Data comparison and testing instructions are important to a processor designed to operate in a digital control environment. As can be seen from Table 9.4, the 6805 augments the operations listed in Table 1.4 with two bit-oriented conditional branches. This enables the CPU to test any bit in read/write memory and skip based on that decision; all in one instruction! Thus if we wished to skip $20 places forward if bit 3 of memory location $40 is set, then this can be implemented by the instruction BRSET 3,$40,$20. Notice that the operand contains three zones: firstly the bit number, then whence the bit resides and finally the branch offset to be added to the program counter if the test is affirmed.

Table 9.3   The 6805 logic operations

Operation		Mnemonic	Flags N Z C	Description
AND				Logic bitwise AND
	A	AND	✓ ✓ •	$A \cdot M \rightarrow A$
Complement				Logic bitwise NOT
	memory	COM	✓ ✓ S	$\overline{M} \rightarrow M$
	A	COMA	✓ ✓ S	$\overline{A} \rightarrow A$
	X	COMX	✓ ✓ S	$\overline{X} \rightarrow X$
Exclusive-OR				Logic bitwise EX-OR
	A	EOR	✓ ✓ •	$A \oplus M \rightarrow A$
OR				Logic bitwise OR
	A	ORA	✓ ✓ •	$A + M \rightarrow A$

Table 9.4 Data testing and comparison operations

Operation		Mnemonic	Flags N Z C	Description
Bit Test				Non-destructive AND
	A	BITA	✓ ✓ •	A•M ((A) unchanged)
Branch on bit N clear				Branches if bit N=0
	memory	BRCLR N	• • b_N	Skips on b_N = 0, ELSE continue
Branch on bit N set				Branches if bit N=1
	memory	BRSET N	• • b_N	Skips on b_N = 1, ELSE continue
Compare				Non-destructive subtract
	with A	CMP	✓ ✓ ✓	A-M ((A) unchanged)
	with X	CPX	✓ ✓ ✓	X-M ((X) unchanged)
Test for Zero or Minus				Non-destructive subtract zero
	memory	TST	✓ ✓ •	M-00
	A	TSTA	✓ ✓ •	A-00
	X	TSTX	✓ ✓ •	X-00

The machine-code structure of these branch-on-bit instructions comprises three bytes. The op-code incorporates the bit number N, in a similar manner to BSET; being %0000 nnn0 for BRSET and %0000 nnn1 for BRCLR ($2N and $2N + 1). The second byte is the address in the direct mode. The final byte is the normal relative offset, but remembering that the program counter has been incremented three times during the fetch before the sign-extended offset is added (see Section 1.3). The machine code for the preceding example is thus $06-40-20. The alternative procedure using normal 6800-type instructions would be LDA $40; BIT %00001000; BNE $20. Not only does this use twice as many (scarce) memory bytes but it destroys the contents of the accumulator.

The two branch-on-bit instructions perform a further role. After their execution the state of the carry flag is that of the bit under test. Thus BRSET 3,$40,0 is equivalent to load carry with bit 3 of location $40. I have made the relative offset zero in this example so that the program counter will be undisturbed no matter what the bit state is. The operation BRCLR 3,$40,0 has an identical outcome.

As shown in Table 9.5, simple conditional branches are provided for each of the five flags in the CCR, including the half-carry and I mask. As discussed in Section 1.3, the states of the carry and zero flags are used for unsigned magnitude comparisons. To facilitate this aspect, the mnemonics BLO (Branch if LOwer than) and BHS (Branch if Higher or Same as) are used interchangeably with BCS and BCC. Branches on HIgher (BHI) and Lower than or Same (BLS) are based on both the C and Z flags. No 2s complement comparison branches are provided.

Table 9.5   Operations affecting the program counter

Operation	Mnemonic	Description
Branch Always	BRA	Always branches irrespective of flags
Branch Never	BRN	Only increments Program Counter twice
Branch if Higher	BHI	Branches if neither C or Z flag set *
Branch if Lower or Same	BLS	Branches if either C or Z flag set *
Branch if Carry Set	BCS(BLO)	Branches if (A) lower than *
Branch if Carry Clear	BCC(BHS)	Branches if (A) higher or same *
Branch if Not Equal to Zero	BNE	Branches if Z flag not set
Branch if Equal to Zero	BEQ	Branches if Z flag set
Branch if Half-Carry Clear	BHCC	Branches if H flag clear
Branch if Half-Carry Set	BHCS	Branches if H flag set
Branch if Plus	BPL	Branches if N flag clear
Branch if Minus	BMI	Branches if N flag set
Branch if I Mask Clear	BMC	Branches if Interrupt Mask clear
Branch if I Mask Set	BMS	Branches if Interrupt Mask Set
Branch if Interrupt Line Low	BIL	Branches if $\overline{INT}$ pin low
Branch if Interrupt Line High	BIH	Branches if $\overline{INT}$ pin high
Branch to Subroutine	BSR	Always branches to subroutine
Jump	JMP	Jump always, irrespective of flags
Jump to Subroutine	JSR	Jump always to subroutine
No operation	NOP	Only increments Program Counter

* After a subtract or compare

The unconditional BRanch Always (BRA) is complemented by BRanch Never (BRN). The latter has no external effect, but advances the program counter by two and takes 4 cycles (3 for the 146805 CMOS processors) to do it. In essence it is equivalent to a dual NOP (No OPeration).

Somewhat more novel are the pair of instructions branch-on-interrupt line low/high (BIL/BIH). This conditionally skips on the state of the $\overline{INT}$ line (Pin 3 for the 68705R3). The test does not depend on the setting of the I mask bit in the CCR, although it is normally only used when $\overline{INT}$ is not required to perform its legitimate interrupt function. Using BIL/BIH provides a simple means of synchronizing the action of the software by means of an external signal. Thus software containing the instruction LOOP BIH LOOP (2E-FE) will effectively stop any further progression past this point unless the $\overline{INT}$ pin is low.

Like the 6802 MPU, the carry flag and I mask in the CCR can be set or cleared, and in this respect Table 1.6 is applicable also to the 6805 family.

All the address modes discussed in Section 1.3 are available to 6805 instructions. We review them here, commenting on differences in usage where they exist.

Inherent | Op-code |

Single-byte instructions refer to operations on internal registers, such as LSRX (= $54) which shifts the contents of the index register once right.

Immediate | Op-code | Single-byte data |

This address mode applies to constant data of magnitude between 0 and $FF. The data is the second byte of the instruction. For example, LDX #$32 (= $AE-32) results in the constant $32 being placed in the index register. Note that unlike the 6802 MPU all relevent internal registers have a single-byte capacity, thus no double-byte immediate operations exist.

Direct | Op-code | Lower address byte |

This is used for variable data lying out in memory between locations 0 and $FF (page 0). The second byte is this address. For example, LDX $32 (= $BE-32) takes data from location $32 into the index register. In the 6805 MCU family all RAM lies in this area, and for this reason all operations which refer to memory have this address mode available. This differs from the 6802 MPU, which offers only direct addressing for a selection of memory access operations.

Extended | Op-code | Upper address byte | Lower address byte |

This is used for data residing anywhere in memory space. The two bytes following the op-code are the address. Thus, e.g., LDX $0E00 (= $CE-0E-00) takes data from location $0E00 into the index register. In the 6805 MCU family all memory space outside the direct page 0 area is occupied by EPROM/ROM. Data residing in this area can be brought down to the CPU but not returned. Thus the extended address mode is not provided for read-write-modify instructions.

Relative | Op-code | Signed PC offset |

This address mode is identical to that of the 6800 family MPUs. The second byte is treated as a 7-bit signed 2s complement number, which is added to the program counter if the branch condition is fulfilled. Thus BCC $04 (= $24-04) will cause four to be added to (PC) if the carry flag is set. As the normal branch instruction occupies two bytes, the program counter will have already moved on two places before the offset is added.

Relative addressing is also used by the 6805 for its branch-on-bit set/clear instructions. As previously discussed these are 3-byte instructions; thus the Program Counter will have advanced three bytes before the offset is added.

Indexed

This address mode is used when the address (as well as the data) is a variable. However, the single-byte nature of the 6805 index register requires a modified approach to the associated address mode. As this register can no longer point anywhere in memory, three subdivisions of the indexed address mode are provided.

Index Mode 0 | Op-code |

This is a single-byte operation where the effective address is simply the contents of the index register. This if the index register is set at $32 at the time the instruction LDA 0,X ($F6) is executed, data at an effective address of $32 will be loaded into the accumulator. This is a quick and efficient method for dealing with data located between 0 and $FF.

Index Mode 1 | Op-code | Positive IX offset |

The second byte here will be added onto the current contents of the index register to give the effective address. Thus if the index register is set at $32, the instruction LDA $10,X (= $E6-10) will result in data lying at $42 being accessed. This is useful for tables of data located in memory up to $1FE. The fixed offset (part of the permanent program in ROM/EPROM) relates to the table base, while the variable contents of the index register points to the table element.

Index Mode 2 | Op-code | Double-byte positive IX offset |

This is similar to the last mode, but allows access to data anywhere in memory. As an example LDA $0E00,X (= $D6-0E-00) will target data in location $0E32 if (IX) = $32 at this time.

Table 9.6 gives an abbreviated instruction set for the 6805 family, showing the more commonly used instructions, together with their op-codes, effect on the principle CCR flags and operation summary. Notice that read-write-modify instructions (designated † in the table) are not available with extended or index 2 address modes, as these are used only to address ROM/EPROM memory. A detailed description of these instructions is given in Appendix 2.

Table 9.6 An abbreviated 6805 instruction set

Operations	Mnemonic	Immed	Dir	Ext	IX0	IX1	IX2	Inher	Rel	N	Z	C	Operation Summary
Register and Memory													
Add	ADD	AB	BB	CB	FB	EB	DB			✓	✓	✓	Add data to A, result in A
Add with Carry	ADC	A9	B9	C9	F9	E9	D9			✓	✓	✓	Add data plus Carry to A, result in A
And	AND	A4	B4	C4	F4	E4	D4			✓	✓	•	Bitwise AND data to A, result in A
Bit Test	BIT	A5	B5	C5	F5	E5	D5			✓	✓	•	As for AND but A unaltered
	BCLR N		11+2×N							•	•	•	Clears specified bit N in memory
Bit Set	BSET N		10+2×N							•	•	•	Sets specified bit in memory
Clear	CLR	–	3F	–	7F	6F	–			✓	✓	•	Clears memory byte
	CLRA							4F		✓	✓	•	Clears Accumulator
	CLRX							5F		✓	✓	•	Clears Index register
	CLC							98		•	•	R	Clears C flag in CCR
	CLI							9A		•	•	•	Clears I mask in CCR
Compare with	CMP	A1	B1	C1	F1	E1	D1			✓	✓	✓	Subtract data from A, (A) unaltered
	CPX	A3	B3	C3	F3	E3	D3			✓	✓	✓	Subtract data from X, (X) unaltered
Complement, 1's	†COM	–	33	–	73	63	–			✓	✓	S	Bitwise invert memory byte
	COMA							43		✓	✓	S	Bitwise invert (A)
	COMX							53		✓	✓	S	Bitwise invert (X)
Decrement	†DEC	–	3A	–	7A	6A	–			✓	✓	•	M Subtracts one
	DECA							4A		✓	✓	•	A from data
	DECX							5A		✓	✓	•	X Does not produce a carry
Exclusive-OR	EOR	A8	B8	C8	F8	E8	D8			✓	✓	•	Bitwise EX-ORs data to A, result in A
Increment	†INC	–	3C	–	7C	6C	–			✓	✓	•	M Adds one
	INCA							4C		✓	✓	•	A to data
	INCX							5C		✓	✓	•	X Does not produce a carry

Operation	Mnemonic	A6/AE	B6/BE	C6/CE	F6/FE	E6/EE	D6/DE	Inh.	Flags (N Z C)	Description
Load	LDA	AA	BA	CA	FA	EA	DA		✓ ✓ •	Gets data into A
	LDX	AA	BA	CA	FA	EA	DA		✓ ✓ •	Gets data into X
Or	ORA	—	39	—	79	69	—	49 / 59	✓ ✓ •	Bitwise OR data to A, result in A
Rotate Left	‡ROL	—	39	—	79	69	—		M ✓ ✓ b7	(rotate A/M left through C; b7 → C, b0 ← C)
	ROLA							49	A ✓ ✓ b7	
	ROLX							59	X ✓ ✓ b7	
Rotate Right	‡ROR	—	36	—	76	66	—		M ✓ ✓ b0	(rotate A/M right through C; b0 → C, b7 ← C)
	RORA							46	A ✓ ✓ b0	
	RORX							56	X ✓ ✓ b0	
Set	SEC							99	• • S	Sets C flag in CCR
	SEI							9B	• • •	Sets I mask in CCR
Shift Left, Logic	‡LSL	—	38	—	78	68	—		M ✓ ✓ b7	(shift left, 0 → b0, b7 → C)
	LSLA							48	A ✓ ✓ b7	
	LSLX							58	X ✓ ✓ b7	
Shift Right, Logic	‡LSR	—	34	—	74	64	—		M ✓ ✓ b0	(shift right, 0 → b7, b0 → C)
	LSRA							44	A ✓ ✓ b0	
	LSRX							54	X ✓ ✓ b0	
Store	STA	—	B7	C7	F7	E7	D7		A ✓ ✓ •	Register contents to memory
	STX	—	BF	CF	FF	EF	DF		X ✓ ✓ •	Register contents unchanged
Subtract	SUB	A0	B0	C0	F0	E0	D0		✓ ✓ ✓	Sub data from A, result in A
Subtract with Carry	SBC	A2	B2	C2	F2	E2	D2		✓ ✓ ✓	Sub data plus C from A, result in A
Transfer between Registers	TAX							97	• • •	Move (A) to (X). (A) unchanged
	TXA							9F	• • •	Move (X) to (A). (X) unchanged
Test for Zero or Minus	TST	—	3D	—	7D	6D	—		M ✓ ✓ •	Sets Z flag if data is zero
	TSTA							4D	A ✓ ✓ •	Sets N flag if data-bit7 is 1
	TSTX							5D	X ✓ ✓ •	Data unchanged

Table 9.6 An abbreviated 6805 instruction set (continued)

Operation	Mnemonic	Immed	Dir	Ext	IX0	IX1	IX2	Inher	Rel	N	Z	C	Operation Summary
Program Counter													
Branch													Branches where:-
Branch Always	BRA								20	•	•	•	irrespective of flags
Branch Never	BRN								21	•	•	•	never
Branch if Higher than	BHI								22	•	•	•	(A) higher (both C&Z flags not set) *
Branch if Lower or Same	BLS								23	•	•	•	(A) lower or same (C OR Z set)
Branch if Carry Clear	BCC								24	•	•	•	Carry flag clear *
Branch if Higher or Same	EHS								24	•	•	•	(A) higher or same *
Branch if Carry Set	BCS								25	•	•	•	Carry flag set*
Branch if Lower	BLO								25	•	•	•	(A) lower than
Branch if Not Equal	BNE								26	•	•	•	Z flag clear (data not = zero)*
Branch if Equal	BEQ								27	•	•	•	Z flag set (data equal zero)*
Branch if Half Carry Clear	BHCC								28	•	•	•	H flag clear
Branch if Half Carry Set	BHCS								29	•	•	•	H flag set
Branch if Plus	BPL								2A	•	•	•	N flag clear (bit7 zero)
Branch if Minus	BMI								2B	•	•	•	N flag set (bit7 one)
Branch if Int Mask Clear	BMC								2C	•	•	•	Interrupt Mask clear
Branch if Int Mask Set	BMS								2D	•	•	•	Interrupt Mask set
Branch if INT Line Low	BIL								2E	•	•	•	INT pin is low
Branch if INT Line High	BIH								2F	•	•	•	INT pin is high
Branch to Subroutine	BSR								AD	•	•	•	Relative form or JSR
Branch on Bit													
Branch on Bit Clear	†BRCLR N		S						2×N	•	•	b_N	bit N of the specified byte is 0
Branch on Bit Set	†BRSET N		S						1+ 2×N	•	•	b_N	bit N of the specified byte is 1
Jump													
Jump Always	JMP	–	BC	CC	FC	EC	DC			•	•	•	Always goes to specified address
Jump to Subroutine	JSR	–	BD	CD	FD	ED	DD			•	•	↑	As JMP, but PC saced on Stack

		Code		Comments
Return				
Return from Subroutine	RTS	81	· · ·	Restores (PC) from Stack
Return from Interrupt	RTI	80	↑	Retreives all registers from Stack
No Operations				
No Operation	NOP	9D	· · ·	Takes 2 cycles to increment PC
Branch Never	BRN	21	· · ·	Takes 4 cycles to inc PC twice

* After a subtract or compare operation

† Read-Modify-Write instruction

§ Also uses Direct Address mode

Legend
R Reset always
S Set always
✓ Test and set if true, else clear
• Not affected

H Half Carry flag
N Negative (sign) flag
Z Zero flag
C Carry flag

(A) Contents of Accumulator
(X) Contents of Index Register
(M) Contents of Memory
(PC) Contents of Program Counter
CCR Code Condition Register

9.2   SOME SOFTWARE CIRCUITS

The hardware design of a system includes the development of a schematic diagram, prior to construction and test. Not only is this used as a construction plan, and as part of the final documentation, but the logical operation of each circuit can be tested to a limited extent by performing a thought experiment on the schematic. Here operating sequences are developed on paper, with the designer evaluating responses from the depicted interconnections of defined logic elements. In a similar manner schematics may be developed using a computer-aided design (CAD) graphics package, and the resulting circuit simulated in software.

The analogous procedure in software is the production of flow diagrams and associated source code listings. The operations of software modules can be tested in an elementary fashion using thought experiments with typical and extreme input data. Similarly a microprocessor development system can be used to simulate or emulate the 'software circuit' in the same manner as a CAD package is used for hardware.

To give the reader a feeling for 6805 machine-level software, we will develop some typical software circuits in the remainder of this chapter.

Our first example concerns the conversion of an 8-bit binary number to a 3-digit ASCII-coded character string. For instance, binary %11111111 becomes $32 $35 $35 for 255 (see Table 4.1). This format can then be used to transmit to a TTY or electronic aplhanumeric display.

Essentially the process involves subtracting and counting hundreds from the binary number, followed by the same procedure for tens, with the remainder being the units. The transformation between the numbers 0–9 and the corresponding ASCII representation of $30–$39 simply involves the addition of $30. Thus in the flowchart of Fig. 9.1 the character string is set to an initial null state of $30 $30 $30 (or zero). As each successful subtraction is accomplished, the relevent digit is incremented. If we assume that the binary number (BIN) is placed in the accumulator by the calling program, then the subroutine given in Listing 9.1 will perform this algorithmic conversion.

Little more can be said concerning Listing 9.1, except to notice that the hundreds segment (Lines 180–230) and tens segment (Lines 240–290) are identical except for the constant. Indeed the units could also be derived in the same way if desired. Obviously then, a more efficient technique would be to put this procedure inside a loop and store the constants 100, 10, and one in a table, using the index register as a loop pointer. There is little to gain from this approach for single binary bytes, but the saving is considerable for double bytes. Here the constants 10,000; 1,000; 100; 10 and 1 are used, together with double-byte arithmetic operations. Try it!

Our second example is used to illustrate the use of the index register in table access. Consider an extension to the real-time clock software developed in Section 2.3, where a calendar routine is to be entered at midnight (00:00:00). This is to update the array YEAR : MONTH : DAY once each 24 hours.

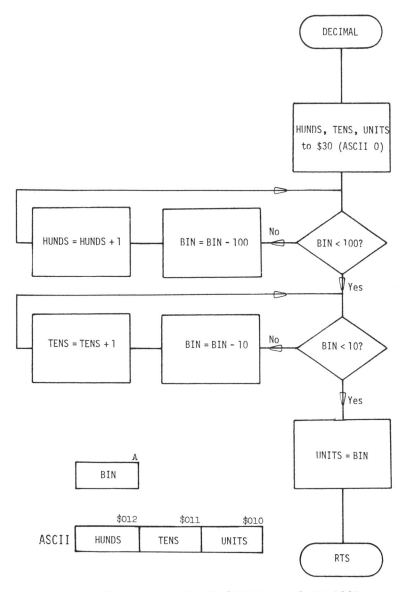

Fig. 9.1   Conversion algorithm for 8-bit binary to 3-digit ASCII

The basic approach illustrated in Fig. 2.9 can be used for this problem, but there are several complications. The major difficulty is the variable month length. As there is no simple mathematical relationship between the month number and length, this information must be stored as a data array in permanent memory. Most of you have this data stored in your memory bank in the form of the alphanumeric

Listing 9.1   Conversion from binary to ASCII

```
Line Machine code       Source code           Comment
10   ****************************************************************************
20   *NAME    : DECIMAL ($E20)
30   *FUNCTION: Converts 8-bit binary to 3-digit ASCII-coded decimal
40   *ENTRY   : Binary byte in A
50   *EXIT    : Hundred's digit in $012; Ten's in $011; Unit's in $010
60   *EXIT    : (A)=Unit's
70   ****************************************************************************
80   *
90        <0012>  HUNDS  EQU   $012         *Hundred's ASCII digit lives here
100       <0011>  TENS   EQU   $011         *Ten's ASCII digit lives here
110       <0010>  UNITS  EQU   $010         *Unit's ASCII digit lives here
120       <0E40>         ORG   $E40         *Subroutine starts here
130  *Initiallisation
140  0E40 AE-30  DECIMAL LDX   #$30         *$30=ASCII for zero
150  0E42 BF-10          STX   UNITS        *Zero character string (000)
160  0E44 BF-11          STX   TENS
170  0E46 BF-12          STX   HUNDS
180  *See how many hundreds there are
190  0E48 A1-64  HUN     CMP   #100         *Is binary less than 100?
200  0E4A 25-06          BLO   TEN          *IF yes THEN go on to try tens
210  0E4C A0-64          SUB   #100         *ELSE subtract 100
220  0E4E 3C-12          INC   HUNDS        *One more hundred
230  0E50 20-F6          BRA   HUN          *and go again
240  *See how many tens there are
250  0E52 A1-0A  TEN     CMP   #10          *Is binary residue less than ten?
260  0E54 25-06          BLO   UNIT         *IF yes THEN remainder is the units
270  0E56 A0-0A          SUB   #10          *ELSE take away 10 from the residue
280  0E58 3C-11          INC   TENS         *and record one more ten
290  0E5A 20-F6          BRA   TEN          *and go again
300  *What's left is the units
310  0E5C BB-10  UNIT    ADD   UNITS        *Remainder (+units), +$30
320  0E5E B7-10          STA   UNITS        *is the ASCII-coded units digit
330  0E60 81             RTS
```

rhyme:

> 30 days hath September; April, June and November.
> All the rest have 31,
> excepting February alone,
> which has but 28 days clear
> and 29 for each leap year.

The rather more prosaic version shown in (b) in fig. 9.2 is in the form of a table stored in 12 successive bytes of EPROM from $080 upwards. The position of a byte relative to the table bottom is a function of the month number, while the content gives that month's length.

To access data from this table, the month number is loaded into the index register, which is then used as a pointer. For example, the length of September (month 9) is accessed by the sequence LDX #9 : LDA BASE-1, X. In this case the

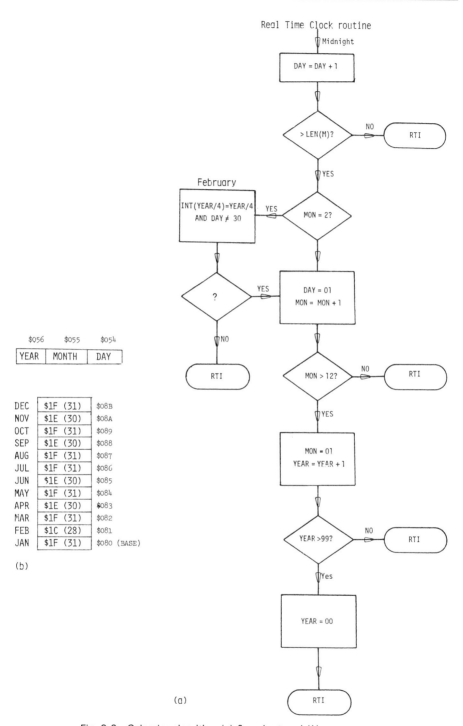

	$056	$055	$054
	YEAR	MONTH	DAY

DEC	$1F (31)	$08B
NOV	$1E (30)	$08A
OCT	$1F (31)	$089
SEP	$1E (30)	$088
AUG	$1F (31)	$087
JUL	$1F (31)	$086
JUN	$1E (30)	$085
MAY	$1F (31)	$084
APR	$1E (30)	$083
MAR	$1F (31)	$082
FEB	$1C (28)	$081
JAN	$1F (31)	$080 (BASE)

(b)

(a)

Fig. 9.2 Calendar algorithm (a) flowchart and (b) memory map

effective address is BASE-1 + (IX) = $07F + 09 = $088 (see (b) in Fig. 9.2). Notice that BASE-1 is used as the table bottom to compensate for the lack of a month 0.

The preceding aide-mémoire verse contained additional information not included in this table. In (b) of Fig. 9.2 February is credited with 28 days. In fact February has 29 days for the year digits which are exactly divisible by four, such as 1988 (exceptions are centennial-year digits not exactly divisible by 400). For all other years the leap day (the twenty-ninth) will have to be included. Checking a binary number for exact (no fraction) divisibility by four is simple. No such number will have a 1 as bit 0 (units) or bit 1 (twos). Thus a leap year is one where the two least significant bits of YEAR are zero (lines 250 and 260 in Listing 9.2). The first exceptional year is 2100, which for all practical purposes may be ignored!

The calendar algorithm is summarized in the flowchart (a) in Fig. 9.2. Apart from the leap-year problem, the main thrust of the flowchart is the straightforward incrementation of the day location ($054) until this rises above the length for that month (LEN(M)). When this happens, the day number is returned to one and the month number incremented. This in turn is returned to one if it exceeds 12, and the year number incremented. A year number exceeding 99 is a new century, and is reset to zero. The implementation for this algorithm is given in Listing 9.2.

Although some of the later 6805 family members support an integral UART (e.g., the 68HC05C4) most mainstream devices do not. However, the serial function can be simulated by software. Our last example is designed as an exercise in the use of the internal timer and PIA to provide this facility.

It is desired to design a subroutine named OUTCH (output character) which will serially transmit a byte in the accumulator to the format shown in Fig. 4.2. Six baud rates are to be selected by switches SW3 SW2 SW1 connected to Port C's PIA lines PC3 PC2 PC1 respectively (see also Fig. 13.1). The relationship between switch settings are:

SW3	SW2	SW1	Baud rate
0	0	0	300 ($\div 32$)
0	0	1	600 ($\div 16$)
0	1	0	1200 ($\div 8$)
0	1	1	2400 ($\div 4$)
1	0	0	4800 ($\div 2$)
1	0	1	9600 ($\div 1$)

Now a baud rate of 9600 has a bit period of 104.1 μs. If we use the internal timer to create a delay of this magnitude, then it will be convenient to utilize the CPU clock ϕ_2 as the counter clock source. Assuming a 4 MHz crystal, which gives $\phi_2 = 1$MHz, and a timer prescale setting of $\div 1$, then a timer counter setting of 104 ($68) will time-out after 104 μs. This accuracy is satisfactory, as the asynchronous transmission, depicted in Fig. 4.2, can tolerate a period variance of $\pm \frac{1}{2}$ bit over the word, or $\pm 5\%$ for a 10-bit word. Prescale values in ascending powers of two up to 32 will then given the slower baud rates tabulated above.

Our solution to this task is in two parts. The first of these is the initialization

Listing 9.2   The calendar routine

```
Line Machine code         Source code           Comment

10   ******************************************************************************
20   *This is the calendar module, extending the RTC routine
30       (0054)  DAY      EQU    $054        *Day number stored here
40       (0055)  MONTH    EQU    $055        *Month number stored here
50       (0056)  YEAR     EQU    $056        *Year number stored here
60   *
70   0000 D1-007F         CMP    BASE-1,X     *Compare DAY with month length
80       (0080)           ORG    $080         *Start of table
90   0080 1F1C1F1E1F1E1F1F1E1F1E1F
                 BASE     FCB    31,28,31,30,31,30,31,31,30,31,30,31
100  *
110  *Now for the program
120      (0E2A)           ORG    $E2A         *Program starts here (see line 350, listing 2.1)
130  0E2A 3C-54           INC    DAY          *One more day gone
140  0E2C B6-54           LDA    DAY          *Examine it
150  *Now check length table for end of month
160  0E2E BE-55           LDX    MONTH
170  0E30 E1-7F           CMP    BASE-1,X     *Compare DAY with month length
180  0E32 23-2A           BLS    CEXIT        *IF Lower or Same THEN exit
190  *Only pass here after the end of the month
200  *Now look for the possibility of February 29th
210  0E34 A3-02           CPX    #2           *Is it month2? (in IX from step 160)
220  0E36 26-0C           BNE    NEWMON       *IF not THEN its a new month
230  0E38 A1-1E           CMP    #30          *IF February 30th THEN definately the end of the month
240  0E3A 27-08           BEQ    NEWMON
250  0E3C 00-5605         BRSET  0,YEAR,NEWMON *Or IF February 29th, but not a leap year
260  0E3F 02-5602         BRSET  1,YEAR,NEWMON *THEN a new month
270  0E42 20-1A           BRA    CEXIT        *ELSE its Feb. 29th (watch out for proposals!)
280  *Pass here if DAY exceeds month length or Feb 30th or 29th on non-leap year
290  0E44 3F-54   NEWMON  CLR    DAY          *Its a new month
300  0E46 3C-54           INC    DAY          *Day one
310  0E48 3C-55           INC    MONTH
320  0E4A B6-55           LDA    MONTH        *Now check for month 13
330  0E4C A1-0D           CMP    #13          *IF it is THEN ring in the new year
340  0E4E 26-0E           BNE    CEXIT        *ELSE exit
350  *Only land here on the stroke of midnight on new year's eve
360  0E50 3F-55           CLR    MONTH        *Its January 1st
370  0E52 3C-55           INC    MONTH        *Month one
380  0E54 3C-56           INC    YEAR         *Happy new year
390  0E56 B6-56           LDA    YEAR         *Can it be the end of the century?
400  0E58 A1-64           CMP    #100
410  0E5A 26-02           BNE    CEXIT        *IF not THEN exit
420  0E5C 3F-56           CLR    YEAR         *ELSE happy new century
430  0E5E 80      CEXIT   RTI                 *and exit
```

software immediately following the external reset condition. We are going to use bit 7 of PIAC as the serial output, and bits 3,2,1 as baud-rate switch inputs. Thus the associated data direction register must be set up accordingly (Steps 110 and 120 in Listing 9.3). The idle state for an asynchronous transmission is logic 1. Thus bit 7

```
10   ************************************************************************
20   *This is the initialisation routine
30       <0002>  SWITCH  EQU   $002       *This is the Switch port and UART output
40       <0006>  DDRC    EQU   $006       *and this is the associated Data Direction register
50       <0008>  TIMER   EQU   $008       *This is the Timer Counter
60       <0009>  TIMCON  EQU   $009       *and the associated Control register
70       <0010>  TEMP    EQU   $010       *Temporary store used by subroutine DELAY
80   ************************************************************************
90       <0100>          ORG   $100       *Initialisation routine starts here
100  0100 1E-02          BSET  7,SWITCH   *Make serial output = 1 behind the scenes
110  0102 A6-80          LDA   #%10000000 *so that it is in the idle state when bit7 is made an output
120  0104 B7-06          STA   DDRC       *The rest of the bits are inputs
130  *Now calculate the Prescale fctor for baudrate
140  0106 AE-20          LDX   #32        *32 is the maximum scale factor (300 baud)
150  0108 B6-02          LDA   SWITCH     *Get baud switch settings
160  010A 44             LSRA             *Align with SW1 in bit0 (right justify)
170  010B A4-07          AND   #%00000111 *Clear all non-switch positions
180  010D 27-04   ILOOP  BEQ   ICONT      *IF zero THEN ratio (in IX) is correct
190  010F 54             LSRX             *ELSE divide ratio by 2
200  0110 4A             DECA             *Decrement switch count
210  0111 20-FA          BRA   ILOOP      *and try again
220  *On passing this point IX holds the division ratio
230  0113 9F      ICONT  TXA              *Move ratio to Accumulator
240  0114 AB-40          ADD   #%01000000 *Set up Timer Control with TINT mask on,
250  0116 B7-09          STA   TIMCON     *internal clock option and prescaler ratio
260  *Other routines follow
270  *
280  *
```

Listing 9.3   Initialization for subroutine OUTCH

of PIAC is set high prior to this action (Step 100). This, together with a pull-up resistor at this point, ensures that no spurious transient occurs on the line whenever the MCU is reset.

The timer control register is also initialized during this preliminary setting-up routine. It inhibits the time-out interrupt (TINT) by setting the local mask (bit TCR6). Also the clock source is set up to internal (i.e. ϕ_2) by clearing bits TCR4&5. The prescale ratio is calculated in Lines 130–210. Essentially the maximum prescale ratio (viz., 32) is successively divided by two as the baud rate switch values (right justified) are decremented to zero. The residue becomes bits TCR2,1,0 in Line 250.

One disadvantage of calculating the prescale ratio during the initialization procedure is that the baud rate cannot be altered after reset. Also the timer cannot be used for other purposes (except perhaps serial input). If this is a problem, then the timer can be set up each time subroutine OUTCH is called. Indeed it can be part of the subroutine itself.

The subroutine algorithm merely sequentially sends out the eight bits in the accumulator, preceded by a start bit (low) and terminated by a stop period (high). As can be seen from Fig. 9.3, the bit period is a function of a separate delay subroutine. This constantly monitors bit TC7 which goes high on time-out. When this occurs the timer is immediately reset and TC7 cleared (Steps 630 and 640 in

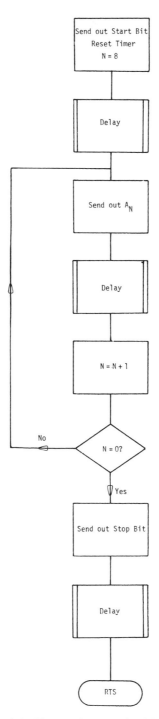

Fig. 9.3   The serial-output algorithm

Listing 9.4). As the timer is obviously not synchronized to the OUTCH call, one of the first tasks initially is to reset the timer (Steps 380–410). Other than this, all timer operations are dealt with in subroutine DELAY.

Notice the sneaky way that OUTCH finally returns to its calling point by simply running on into DELAY from Line 540, and using the latter's return from subroutine in Line 660. If DELAY did not immediately follow OUTCH, a termination of BRA DELAY would have the same effect, and still be more efficient than the conventional BSR DELAY – RTS exit route.

Most of the processor's time will be spent idling in Step 620 (Listing 9.4), and thus an excessive use of OUTCH will severely reduce the MCU's processing time. A timewise more efficient technique could use the timer's interrupt capabilities to

```
300  ********************************************************************
310  *This subroutine sends out one character in series format
320  *ENTRY : 8-bit character in A
330  *EXIT  : (A) & (IX) destroyed
340  *NOTE  : Uses subroutine DELAY
350  ********************************************************************
360       <A050>           ORG   $A050
370  A050 1F-02   OUTCH    BCLR  7,SWITCH    *Clear serial output, PIAC bit7, to start
380  A052 AE-68            LDX   #104        *Set up Timer Counter for the first time
390  A054 BF-08            STX   TIMER
400  A056 17-09            BCLR  3,TIMCON    *Reset Prescale ounter by sending a 1 to TCR3
410  A058 1F-09            BCLR  7,TIMCON    *Clear Time-out flag, bit TCR7
420  A05A AD-12            BSR   DELAY       *and delay one bit period
430  *
440  A05C AE-08            LDX   #8          *Prepare to send out eight data bits, N=8
450  A05E 44      BITN     LSRA              *Move Nth bit into Carry
460  A05F 24-04            BCC   ZERO        *IF C=0 THEN send out a 0
470  A061 1E-02            BSET  7,SWITCH    *ELSE send out a 1
480  A063 20-02            BRA   ONEXT       *and delay
490  A065 1F-02   ZERO     BCLR  7,SWITCH    *Alternatively send out a 0
500  A067 AD-05   ONEXT    BSR   DELAY
510  A069 5A               DEX               *One more bit sent. N=N-1
520  A06A 26-F2            BNE   BITN        *IF not bit8 THEN next bit
530  *
540  A06C 1E-02            BSET  7,SWITCH    *Stop bit = 1. Exit via DELAY
550  ********************************************************************
560  *This is the delay subroutine
570  *ENTRY : Timer Control register already initialised
580  *EXIT  : TEMP (=$010) altered
590  ********************************************************************
600  A06E BF-10   DELAY    STX   TEMP        *Put IX away safely
610  A070 AE-68            LDX   #104        *104 is the Timer Counter's delay constant
620  A072 0F-09FD DWAIT    BRCLR 7,TIMCON,DWAIT *Wait around until TINT flag (bit TCR7) is set
630  A075 BF-08            STX   TIMER       *When it does, set up Timer Counter
640  A077 1F-09            BCLR  7,TIMCON    *and clear the TINT flag
650  A079 BE-10            LDX   TEMP        *Restore the original value of IX
660  A07B 81               RTS               *and exit
```

Listing 9.4 The subroutines OUTCH and DELAY

inform the processor that the delay period has ended. However, this will cause problems due to the fixed time taken to answer an interrupt call, which will have a varying effect on the overall accuracy depending on the chosen baud rate. Also care must be taken to prevent lockout if the regular interrupt faculties are being used simultaneously.

10

Untangling the Bootstrap

Prior to the 1970s, a just switched-on computer was as helpless as a newborn baby. Before any meaningful task could be performed, no matter how small, software had to be loaded into its program memory. This was frequently done by connecting the memory directly to a front panel, where addresses and data were set up on switches by the tame human operator. In such a manner a simple program was laboriously set up a word at a time. The *bootstrap* program was usually a loader routine, which permitted the computer to control a paper-tape reader thereby reading in more sophisticated operating software. The term arose from the saying 'to pick oneself up by one's bootstraps', i.e., to elevate oneself to greater heights from a lowly position.

The development of ROM memory obviated the necessity to key in manually a start-up program, as such a nonvolatile storage medium is ideal for the permanent storage of small-system programs. Nevertheless, the term *bootstrap* is still used to describe a loader program which enables the computer to read in larger programs.

The single-chip microcomputer is in many ways akin to these early computers. On switch-on the virgin MCU is dumb, until code can be got into its program memory. Of course a mask-programmed MCU has the integral ROM configured during manufacture (see Sections 11.1 and 12.1). The problem lies with MCUs designed for prototyping and small- to medium-production runs where the software is carried in EPROM. One approach to this problem, e.g., adopted by the Hitachi 6305 series MCUs, uses a 'piggy-back' EPROM. Here the MCU has no built-in program memory, but the relevant address, data and control lines are made available on a socket mounted on the back of the MCU chip itself. The EPROM is programmed on a regular EPROM programmer, and then plugged into the double-decker MCU.

The Motorola 68705 series uses a rather more sophisticated technique, where the program EPROM is an integral part of the MCU chip. In order to program the internal EPROM, a small mask-programmed ROM contains a bootstrap program which reads code from an external medium and blasts the internal EPROM accordingly. We now proceed to expand this concept in this chapter.

10.1   THE BOOTSTRAP ROM

Figure 8.1 shows that 120 bytes of 68705R3 memory, from $F80 to $FF7, are used for the mask-programmed bootstrap ROM. The actual location may vary between members of the 68705 family but the program function is the same, implementing the following tasks:

> Loads code from external memory
> Programs internal EPROM
> Verifies the state of internal EPROM against external memory.

In order to attain these objectives the bootstrap has been designed to operate within a specific hardware environment. A suitable programming circuit fulfilling these environmental requirements is given in Fig. 10.1, and is suitable for all 68705 family members. The similar circuit shown in Appendix 1, Fig. 21, is suitable only for the 68705R3. In both cases the target (user) code is assumed to have been located previously in an external 2532 (4K × 8) EPROM (2716 EPROM for smaller family members). A regular EPROM programmer can be used for this task. The bootstrap uses Port A to read the contents of this EPROM, which is addressed by the 4040 CMOS 12-bit ripple counter. This is controlled by Port B bits 4 and 3, which respectively clear and increment the counter. The external counter is quickly stepped past any addresses which have no internal EPROM counterpart, such as between $000 and $00F.

Other bits in Port B control additional aspects of the circuit. The bootstrap utilizes bits PB1 and 2 to drive LEDs which indicate that the programming phase has been completed and that verification has been achieved. Bit PB0, in conjunction with transistors Q1 and Q2, is used to apply 21V to the V_{PP} pin during the programming phase and a nominal 5V (via diode D1) during verify. In Fig. 10.1 a 26V main supply is stepped down via zener diode D2 and V_{BE1} to give the 21V V_{PP} programming voltage, and via voltage regulator VR2 to hold the timer pin at 12V. A timer voltage above 9V causes bit 2 of the programming control register (PCR at location $00B) to be set. When the 68705 comes out of reset and bit PCR2 is logic 1, it will vector to the start of the bootstrap ROM via ROM locations $FF6/7. Of course, the normal reset vector of $FFE/F has not by definition been programmed yet. Once the bootstrap has been entered, it will use the various bits in the PCR to program the internal EPROM. However, normally the PCR operation is transparent to the user; more details are given in Appendix 1, Fig. 18.

Programming a 68705 MCU, using Fig. 10.1, involves the following procedure.

I   With switches SW1 and 2 closed and voltage supplies turned off, insert the programmed EPROM and virgin 68705.

II   Apply power.

III   Open SW1. This enables bit PB0 to apply +21V to V_{PP} when the bootstrap desires. At this time pull-up resistor R3 will have Q2 turned on and Q1 off, giving a V_{PP} of nominally 5V.

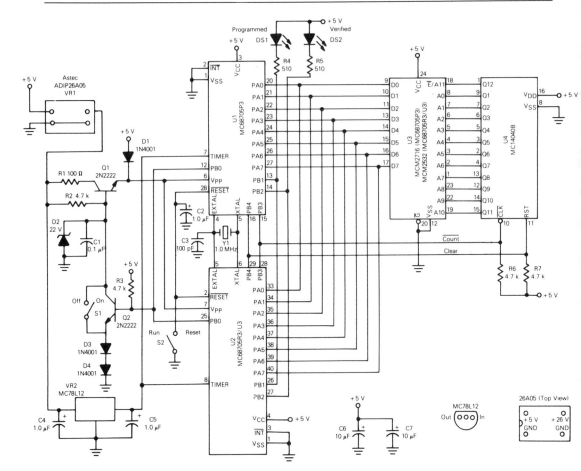

Fig. 10.1 Stand-alone 68705 programming circuit (reproduced by courtesy of Motorola Limited)

IV   Open SW2. This releases reset, and the 68705 senses a high timer pin voltage, which vectors it to the bootstrap.

V   The bootstrap now pulses the clear control line (PB4) and then rapidly clocks the counter to $080, the internal EPROM's start location. At the same time V_{PP} is switched to 21V (PB0). Both program end (DS1) and verify (DS2) LEDs are off.

VI   From $080 to $FFF (except for a burst through $F80–$FF7) the contents of the EPROM are read. If it is not null ($00 is the nonprogrammed state of the internal EPROM), these data are used to blast the internal EPROM. Each step takes approximately 50 ms. The counter is stepped at an enhanced rate where null data is encountered.

VII When the counter reaches $FFF, taking anything between around 20 seconds and 3 minutes depending on the amount of null data, the program end LED illuminates.

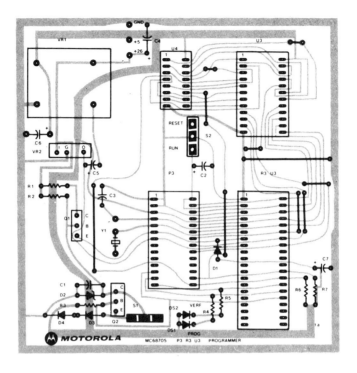

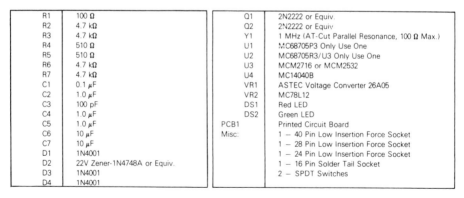

R1	100 Ω		Q1	2N2222 or Equiv.	
R2	4.7 kΩ		Q2	2N2222 or Equiv	
R3	4.7 kΩ		Y1	1 MHz (AT-Cut Parallel Resonance, 100 Ω Max.)	
R4	510 Ω		U1	MC68705P3 Only Use One	
R5	510 Ω		U2	MC68705R3/U3 Only Use One	
R6	4.7 kΩ		U3	MCM2716 or MCM2532	
R7	4.7 kΩ		U4	MC14040B	
C1	0.1 μF		VR1	ASTEC Voltage Converter 26A05	
C2	1.0 μF		VR2	MC78L12	
C3	100 pF		DS1	Red LED	
C4	1.0 μF		DS2	Green LED	
C5	1.0 μF		PCB1	Printed Circuit Board	
C6	10 μF		Misc:	1 – 40 Pin Low Insertion Force Socket	
C7	10 μF			1 – 28 Pin Low Insertion Force Socket	
D1	1N4001			1 – 24 Pin Low Insertion Force Socket	
D2	22V Zener-1N4748A or Equiv.			1 – 16 Pin Solder Tail Socket	
D3	1N4001			2 – SPDT Switches	
D4	1N4001				

Fig. 10.2   Layout and parts list for the programming module (reproduced by courtesy of Motorola Limited)

VIII   The bootstrap then reduces V_{PP} to 5V (PB0 = 0) and quickly increments the counter through its range, comparing external and internal data. After about 15 seconds the verify LED will illuminate if this data comparison is valid.

IX   Close SW2 to reset the MCU.

X   Close SW1 to disable the V_{PP} control.

XI   Turn off the supply and remove the MCU.

A PCB layout for the programming circuit is given in Fig. 10.2, together with a parts list. Although it is shown as a double-sided board, a single-sided version with 10 wire jumpers may be used. The 1:1 artwork for this board is available in Motorola's *M6805 HMOS/M146805 CMOS Family Microcomputer User's Manual* (Prentice-Hall, 2nd Edition, 1983). A commercial programmer based on this principle (the AVPROM 705-SA) is obtainable from: Avocet Systems Inc., P.O. Box 490, Rockport, Maine, 04856, USA.

Most EPROM MCUs are supplied with an integral quartz window. For such devices a normal EPROM eraser may be used to reset all locations to zero.

10.2 USING A PERSONAL COMPUTER FOR ON-CHIP PROGRAMMING

The on-chip EPROM programming procedure discussed in Section 10.1 involves three steps: using an assembler to convert your source to object (machine) code; programming an EPROM; and finally using the circuit of Fig. 10.1 to transfer this code to the 68705. If you are prepared to type the machine code directly into your personal computer, instead of into your EPROM programmer, this procedure may be reduced to two steps. Indeed if you are using a personal computer-based cross-assembler (see Appendix 5) the entire sequence can be run from the one keyboard.

If we are to simulate the specified bootstrap environment, then the 68705 must be duped into thinking that the personal computer is an EPROM. This is essentially done in Fig. 10.3 by replacing EPROM with RAM, which acts as the medium of communication between bootstrap and computer. In the initialize mode, the computer holds the 68705 in its reset state, and downloads machine-code data into the buffer RAM. After this has been accomplished, the RAM is switched to a read-only mode. Thus when the 68705 comes to be released, the bootstrap 'sees' memory which it cannot distingish from the specified EPROM.

The circuitry shown in Fig. 10.3 has been designed to interface to the Apple IIe personal computer, but relatively little alteration is necessary to permit its use with other 8-bit based microcomputers. We will find it easier to expand on this statement if we first discuss the detail operation of the outboard.

The Apple IIe sets aside part of its memory space to service eight peripheral interface slots. Each slot provides buffered versions of the computer's data, address and control buses. In addition, an integral address decoder provides each slot with a select pulse, responding to a slot-dependent location. Specifically, $\overline{\text{Data Select}}$ ($\overline{\text{DS}}$) assigns slot n to the range $C0(8 + n)0$ to $C0(8 + n)F$. Thus $\overline{\text{DS}}$ in slot 4 responds to $C0C0$ to $C0CF$. In Fig. 10.3 a 2 to 4-line decoder (74LS139) qualifies DS with the two lower computer-address lines, and maps the programmer outboard to four locations.

Two 4016 (or 6116) $2K \times 8$ static RAMs are used to emulate a $4K \times 8$ EPROM. These are connected to the computer data bus via a 74LS245 (or 74LS645) octal transceiver, enabled only when the Apple refers to the base address + 2 (e.g., $C0C2$ in slot 4). Otherwise the internal (RAM & MCU) and external (Apple) data buses are isolated from each other. The internal RAM $R/\overline{W}$ control line is also a

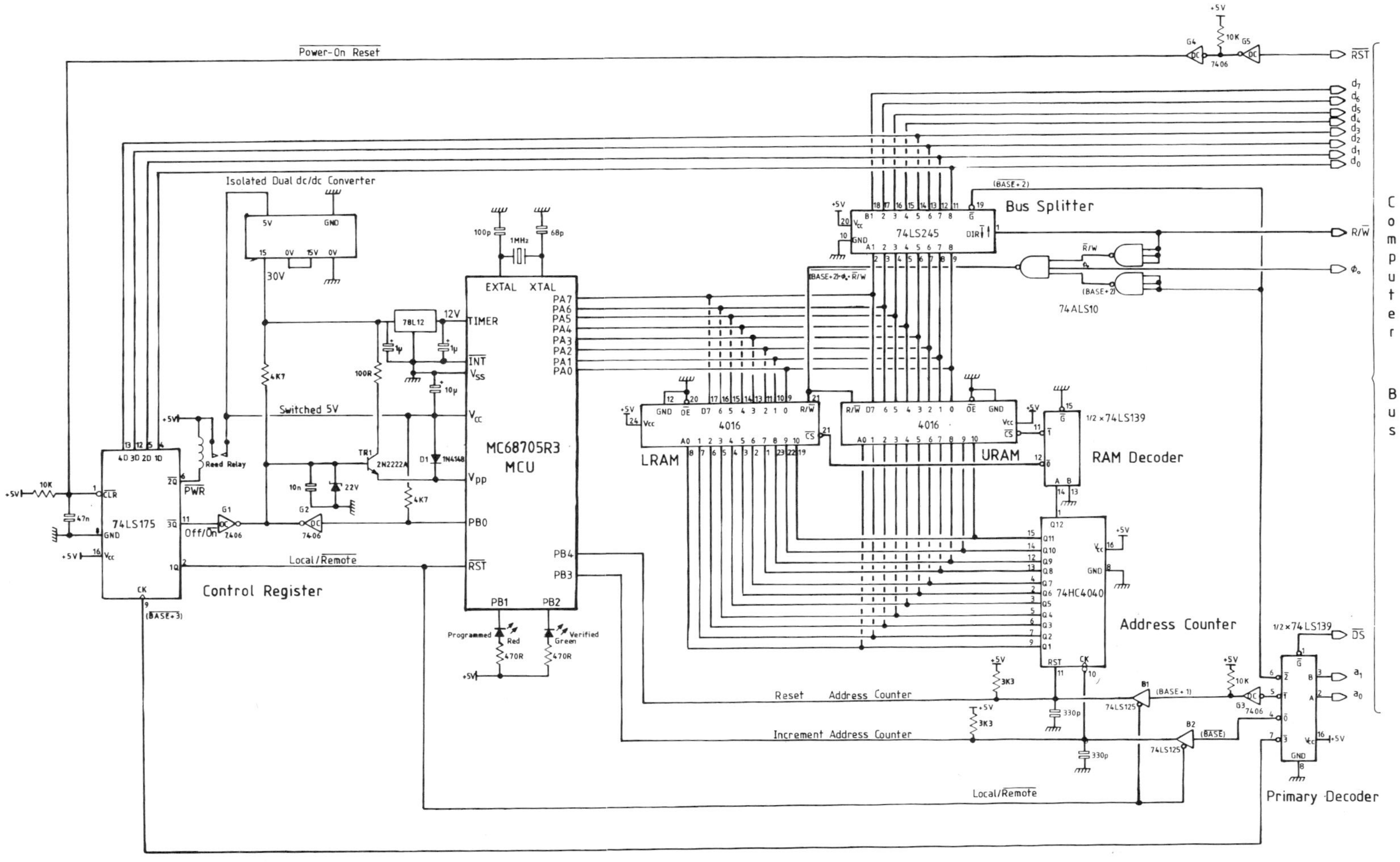

Fig. 10.3 Programming the 68705 MCU from a personal computer

function of address BASE + 2. Normally this internal $R/\overline{W}$ line is high, except when the Apple writes to BASE + 2. In this situation the 74ALS10 detects both $R/\overline{W}$ and BASE + 2 going low, and drives the internal R/W line low. Thus the Apple writes into RAM. The Apple's clock signal (equivalent to ϕ_2) is also used to gate the RAM's $R/\overline{W}$ control to avoid the write-to hazard outlined in Fig. 2.3. A high-speed 74ALS part is specified to avoid the race possibility of the 74LS245 transceiver being disabled before the internal $R/\overline{W}$ goes high at the end of a write cycle. When the Apple reads BASE + 2, the internal $R/\overline{W}$ remains high, and data is read from the RAM via the transceiver.

As in Fig. 10.1, the RAM is addressed via a 4040 12-bit counter. A 74HC part is mandatory here, to permit a response to the submicrosecond pulses emanating from the outboard's primary decoder (the standard part is too slow). This counter is reset whenever the Apple accesses address BASE + 1, while any Apple reference to the BASE address increments the count. Note that the 74HC4040 requires a positive logic level to reset, and a spare 7406 gate (G3) is used to invert the active-low decoder output.

In most multiprocessor systems, one processor is designated the master, having final jurisdiction over the action of one or more slaves. In the situation depicted in Fig. 10.3, the personal computer acts as the master, with the 68705 running under bootstrap, very much the tightly coupled slave. The master controls the slave by means of its $\overline{\text{Reset}}$ and power supply, via a 74LS174 4-bit (control) register. Data on the master's four lower data lines are stored in this register by a write to BASE + 3 action.

Control bit 0 (1Q) directly drives the MCU's $\overline{\text{Reset}}$ input, and is thus equivalent to Switch 2 in Fig. 10.1. It also controls the two 3-state 74HC125 buffers B1 and B2, thus transferring control of the 74HC4040 RAM counter between master (remote control, MCU reset) and slave (local control, MCU running).

Bit 2 (3Q) acts in a comparable way to Switch 1. Transistor Q2 in Fig. 10.1 has been replaced by an open-collector 7406 inverter, G2. This is wire ORed with gate G1 directly driven by the complement of control bit 2. When bit 2 is cleared, the base of transistor TR1 is always low and V_{PP} will be 4.3V (nominally 5V) through D1, irrespective of the state of the MCU's PB0. With bit 2 high, TR1 is controlled from PB0. Under bootstrap control TR1 can be turned off (PB0 = 0) giving $V_{PP} \simeq 5V$ and on (PB0 = 1) to give $V_{PP} \simeq 21V$. The transistor/22V zener diode is equivalent to the Q1/D2 combination of Fig. 10.1.

The outboard of Fig. 10.3 is powered by a single regulated 5V 800 mA supply. This is normally too much to be obtained from the master's own power supply, and an external source should be used. The 5V line should be decoupled to ground by several 1 μF tantalum capacitors distributed throughout the board.

Two nonstandard voltages are required in addition to the normal 5V, viz., $21 \pm 1V$ for V_{PP} and $\simeq 12V$ for the timer pin. In Fig. 10.3 these are derived from a nominal 30V supply, which for convenience is generated by an on-board d.c.-d.c. converter. The author has successfully used a K.E. Developments 5/15D dual 5 to 15V converter wired in series to provide this function. Alternatively the Astec ADIP26A05 single 26V device specified in Fig. 10.1 may be used. If you wish to utilize an alternative converter, this must be able to supply 26–30V at 15 mA. Dual converters must have isolated outputs (i.e., do not share a common 0V) if they are to be wired in series.

The MCU's 5V supply (and all other derived voltages) is switched using a reed relay operated via the control register's bit 1 (2Q). If an off-board separate 30V supply is used, two reed relays (or a single DPST reed) are needed to isolate both supplies.

When the board is powered up, a simple 47nF/10kΩ integrator network provides an automatic reset for the control register. This register is also cleared when the master computer is reset (e.g., when the keyboard reset switch is operated). In the cleared state, the MCU's power is off, the transistor TR1 is off and the board is in its remote mode.

The computer bus signals shown in Figs 10.3 are typical of those available at the parallel-bus expansion port of most personal computers based on the 6502 series (as is the Apple) and 6800/9 range of MPUs. Where an integral address decoder is not provided, you may build your own, based on the principles outlined in Section 2.1. This decoder should be qualified with the clock signal designated ϕ_2, ϕ_0 or E. In 6800-based (not 6809) machines, VMA should also be used as a qualifier (see Figs. 2.2 and 2.3).

Computers based on the 8080/Z80 family of MPUs will have somewhat different control signals. Here the $\overline{\text{Memory Write}}$ ($\overline{\text{MR}}$) status line can be used as a direct replacement for both R/W and ϕ_0 in Fig. 10.1 (ϕ_0 is simply omitted from the circuit). If an external peripheral address decoder is being constructed, any line labeled $\overline{\text{Memory Request}}$ ($\overline{\text{MREQ}}$) or similar should be used as a qualifier, in the same manner as VMA.

Driving software for Fig. 10.3 will depend somewhat on the structure of the data arrays holding the machine code and the master computer actually used. Nevertheless, writing such software is relatively straightforward provided that the following rules and procedures are followed.

I   Machine code may be downloaded from the master computer by clearing the RAM address counter and incrementing to the desired location. The slave MCU must be in its reset state (control register bit 1 = 0) during this process. Once this has been reached, the data byte is stored at BASE + 2. If the software engineer can arrange for this data to be stored in a target-address sequential manner, then the address counter is simply incremented after each store.

The address counter can be cleared by doing a load or store to BASE + 1 (e.g., LDA $C0C1 in Apple slot 4). If BASIC is the chosen program medium, either X = PEEK(BASE + 1) or POKE 0,BASE + 1 (e.g., X = PEEK(49345) in slot 4) will accomplish the same thing. Similarly a counter increment is attained by a load to or store at BASE. Note that POKEing to BASE can cause two increments, as some BASIC interpreters access the specified address twice, therefore PEEK is the preferred instruction in this case (e.g., X = PEEK(49344)).

II Control may be passed to the 68705 slave by first turning on the power (control bit 2 set high) and delaying for a nominal second until this stabilizes. The V_{PP}

1. After this time the master computer must not access the programmer circuitry.

Figure 10.4(a) shows what happens next. The 68705 enters the bootstrap program, which sets up the parallel peripheral ports and timer accordingly. After this, the address counter's reset is pulsed (trace A2) and quickly stepped through the first $80 non-EPROM addresses (the solid blur at the beginning of trace A1). At the same time V_{PP} is upped to 21V by bringing PB0 low, which turns TR1 on (trace A0). At this point the RAM address is stepped at a nominal 50 ms; the resulting data being latched into the 68705 and used to blast the corresponding EPROM byte. In Fig. 10.4(a) the first 15 bytes of Listing 14.4 being transferred into EPROM are shown. The next several thousand bytes are zero here, and as this is the erased state of the MCU's EPROM, the bootstrap quickly steps on the address counter (right-hand side of trace A1).

The programming process is shown more clearly in Fig. 10.4(b), which has an expanded time base. Here the time between the cursor (dotted vertical line C) and Time reference (hatched vertical line Δ) is measured as $\Delta T = 52$ms ($\Delta P = 104$ sample clocks at 500 μs each). This is the time between the end of the initial frenzied burst to $080 and the first address counter increment (trace A1). On the data lines the first three bytes of Listing 14.4, viz., $41;2F;44, are clearly seen. The binary label at the right of the data lines shows the state at the cursor line to be %01000100 or $44. The first non-zero byte ($41 at the Δ line) is only present long enough for the 68705 to save the data in an internal register. The address counter is then incremented, but a nominal 50 ms wait is generated by the bootstrap while the previously grabbed byte is being digested into EPROM.

As the bootstrap ignores zero data bytes, the time to complete the self program varies from around 20 to 200 seconds. Following this, the red LED is illuminated (PB1) and the address counter is quickly stepped through its range again. This time the programming voltage is at 5V (PB0 = 1, TR1 off) and the 68705's EPROM data checked against the corresponding RAM contents. If this check is successful, the green LED then lights (PB2 = 0). Only after this time should the master computer's software resume control of the outboard and perform an orderly shutdown. This is achieved by resetting the MCU and disabling the V_{PP} control transistor (control register bit 3). Finally power is removed.

III A nonblank or improperly erased MCU will usually fail to verify after a programming cycle. This state is readily checked prior to this point by clearing each RAM byte, and going through an EPROM programming cycle. If it fails, the green LED will not light. V_{PP} can be held at +5V for this test, as only the final verify portion of the bootstrap is of interest.

Listing 10.1 gives an example driver software package, based on the hardware described. It is not meant as a definitive program (although it will operate without modification in conjunction with the assembler of Appendix 5), but will be a useful guide for readers writing their own software. The master

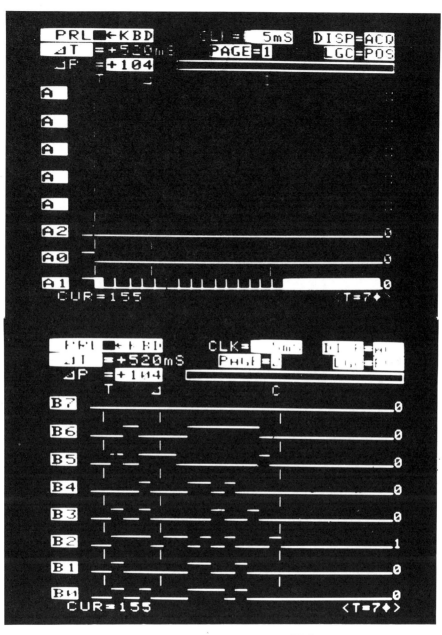

A2	= Address counter reset	(PB4)
A1	= Address counter clock	(PB3)
A0	= V_PP control	(PB0)
B7–B0	= Data lines 0–7	(PA7–PA0)

Fig. 10.4 A logic analyzer's view of events

(a) Programming the first 15 bytes of Listing 14.4 into the 68705. Total time shown = 256 × 5 ms = 1.28 s

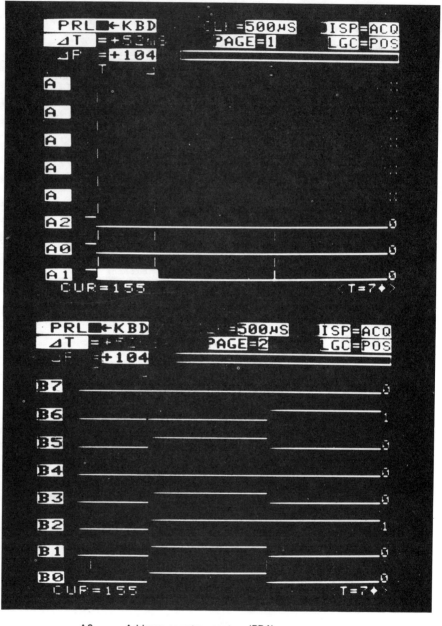

A2	= Address counter reset	(PB4)
A1	= Address counter clock	(PB3)
A0	= V_PP control	(PB0)
B7–B0	= Data lines 7–0	(PA7–PA0)

Fig. 10.4 A logic analyzer's view of events
(*b*) Expansion by 10, showing the first few bytes being grabbed by the bootstrap

computer is an Apple IIe 64K with a single disk drive running under DOS 3.3, an 80-column card and with an optional Epson MX-100 III printer.

The program of listing 10.1 is fully commented, so it is only necessary here to give a background to the major composite routines.

(a) Phase O: Machine code and initialization

```
0  REM ****************************************************
1  REM *S.J.Cahill                                      *
2  REM *University of Ulster                            *
3  REM *Blast 68705 MCU from Hex file                   *
4  REM *1st May, 1985 Version                           *
5  REM ****************************************************
10 BASE = 49344: REM *Apple slot4 ($C0C0=49344)
20 POKE BASE + 3,0: REM *Turn everything off
60 D$ = CHR$ (4): REM  *DOS alert symbol(DOS 3.3)
100 DIM HX$(256): REM *The max number of object code lines is 256
110 PRINT CHR$ (12) CHR$ (21): REM *Turn off 80-column card
200 DATA 173,193,192,173,192,192,32,128,3,208,248,96: REM *Routine to advance RAM counter
210 DATA  141,193,192,169,000,141,194,192,141,192,192,32,128,3,208,243,96: REM *Clear RAM routine
220 DATA 173,189,3,24,233,0,141,189,3,173,190,3,233,0,141,190,3,208,5,173,189,3,201,0,96: REM *Double-byte decrement and
    check for zero subroutine used by routine 200
250 FOR I = 768 TO 779: READ X: POKE I,X: NEXT : REM *Load in machine routine 200
260 FOR I = 784 TO 800: READ X: POKE I,X: NEXT : REM *Load in machine routine 210
270 FOR I = 896 TO 920: READ X: POKE I,X: NEXT : REM *Load in machine routine 220
300 HOME : PRINT "Please insert 68705 MCU into socket"
310 FLASH : PRINT "THE CORRECT WAY UP!": NORMAL
320 PRINT "Any key to continue "
330 GET Z$
```

(b) Phase 1: Test for blank MCU

```
340 REM *****************************************************************
350 REM *Test for blank MCU
360 REM *****************************************************************
400 REM   *First clear RAM contents
410 POKE 957,0: REM   *Set up top of RAM address in $03BE/D (958/957)
420 POKE 958,16
430 CALL 784: REM *Now clear RAM
500 HOME : REM *Clear Apple screen
510 POKE BASE + 3,2: REM *Turn on MCU power supply(Control bit3)
520 PRINT "Checking for blank MCU": PRINT
530 FOR I = 0 TO 3000: NEXT : REM *Delay awhile
560 POKE BASE + 3,3: REM *Release Reset(Control bits 1&3)
600 PRINT "Non-blank if red LED only"
610 PRINT : PRINT "Blank if both red & green LEDs"
620 PRINT : PRINT "Do you wish to ";: INVERSE : PRINT "CONTINUE";: NORMAL : PRINT
625 PRINT : PRINT "Do you wish to ";: INVERSE : PRINT "REPEAT";: NORMAL : PRINT
630 PRINT : PRINT "Do you wish to return to the ";: INVERSE : PRINT "EDITOR";: NORMAL : PRINT
640 INPUT X$
660 POKE BASE + 3,2: REM *Reset MCU(Control bit0 reset)
670 FOR I = 0 TO 1000
680 POKE BASE + 3,0: REM *And remove 5V
690 X$ = LEFT$ (X$,1)
700 IF X$ = "R" THEN 300
710 IF X$ = "E" THEN  PRINT D$"BRUN TEXT EDITOR.OBJ"
720 IF X$ > < "C" THEN 620
```

Listing 10.1   Software package for the 68705 programmer: Phases 0-5

(c) Phase 2: Object code loader

```
1000  REM ***********************************************************************
1010  REM *Now get hex data from disc to RAM
1020  REM ***********************************************************************
1050  HOME
1051  PRINT
1055  PRINT D$"CATALOG"
1060  PRINT : INPUT "Name of HEX file please ";FI$
1070  IF RIGHT$ (FI$,1) = " " THEN FI$ = LEFT$ (FI$, LEN (FI$) - 1): GOTO 1070: REM *Remove leading blanks
1080  IF RIGHT$ (FI$,3) > < "HEX" THEN  VTAB 24: PRINT "Must be ";: FLASH : PRINT "HEX FILE": NORMAL : GOTO 1055
1100  HOME
1120  PRINT "The buffer RAM covers Address map $0000-$0FFF"
1125  PRINT
1130  PRINT "Your 68705 MCU may not allocate all of  this"
1135  PRINT
1140  INPUT "Input 2 or 4 for 2/4K 68705 respectively";K$
1142  K =  VAL (K$)
1144  IF (K > < 2) AND (K > < 4) THEN 1140
1150  RV = 2046 + (K = 4) * 2048: REM *Reset Vector
1160  SV = 2044 + (K = 4) * 2048: REM *SWI Vector
1170  IV = 2042 + (K = 4) * 2048: REM *INT Vector
1180  TV = 2040 + (K = 4) * 2048: REM *Timer INT Vector
1190  MV = 1924 + (K = 4) * 1972: REM *Mask Option Register Location
1200  RST =  - 1:SWI =  - 1:IRQ =  - 1:TIM =  - 1:MO =  - 1: REM    *Null values for Reset;SWI;INTerrupt;Timer INT & Mask Op
      tion Register contents
1599  REM *Then transfer data off disc into computer
1600  PRINT D$"OPEN";FI$: REM *Open hex file (line 1060)
1610  PRINT D$"READ";FI$: REM *and read it
1620  FOR I = 0 TO 256: REM *Up to 256 lines allowed
1630  INPUT HX$(I): REM *Each HX$(n) is one line
1640  IF HX$(I) = "S9" THEN L = I - 1:I = 256: REM  *L=no of lines
1650  NEXT I
1670  PRINT D$"CLOSE";FI$
1680  REM *All L Hex lines now stored in computer as array HX$(n). There are L lines
1685  REM *Now download to RAM
1690  PRINT D$"PR#3": REM *80-column card on
1695  VF =  - 1: REM *Verify correct write to RAM marker
1700  FOR I = 0 TO L: REM *For all lines
1710  HEX$ =  MID$ (HX$(I),3,2): GOSUB 5000: REM *Extract total no. of bytes in line
1720  NB = DE - 3: REM *Number of machine code bytes
1730  HEX$ =  MID$ (HX$(I),5,4): GOSUB 5000: REM *Extract absolute location
1740  PC = DE:PC$ = HEX$: REM  *PC=Program Counter = Absolute location
1810  IF PC > 2047 + (K = 4) * 2048 THEN 2000: REM  *Above memory map
1845  IF NB = 0 THEN 2000: REM *Null line
1850  PRINT "<";PC$;">";
1860  POKE 958,PC / 256: REM    *Prepare to move RAM counter on to Absolute address
1870  POKE 957,(PC -  INT (PC / 256) * 256)
1880  CALL 768
1900  FOR J = 0 TO NB - 1: REM *For all bytes in line
1903  IF PC > RV + 1 THEN  PRINT "?? ";: GOTO 1990: REM *Over the top
1905  IF (PC > MV) AND (PC < TV) THEN  PRINT "ROM";: GOTO 1940: REM *Bootstrap ROM
1907  IF PC < 128 THEN  PRINT "RAM";: GOTO 1940: REM *RAM area
1910  HEX$ =  MID$ (HX$(I),9 + J * 2,2): GOSUB 5000: REM *Get byte
1920 .POKE BASE + 2,DE: REM  *Push out the data
1925  IF  PEEK (BASE + 2) > < DE THEN VF = 1: PRINT "!!":I = L:J = NB: GOTO 1990: REM *Verify sucessful transfer to RAM
1930  PRINT HEX$ + " ";: REM *Print it on the screen
1931  IF PC < MV THEN 1950: REM *Program EPROM
1932  IF PC = MV THEN MO = DE: REM *Mask Option Register contents
1933  IF PC = TV THEN TIM = DE * 256: REM  *Timer/INT2 vector contents, upper byte
1934  IF PC = TV + 1 THEN TIM = TIM + DE: REM *lower byte
1935  IF PC = IV THEN IRQ = DE * 256: REM *INT vector contents, upper byte
1936  IF PC = IV + 1 THEN IRQ = IRQ + DE: REM *lower byte
1937  IF PC = SV THEN SWI = DE * 256: REM *SWI vector contents, upper byte
1938  IF PC = SV + 1 THEN SWI = SWI + DE: REM *lower byte
1939  IF PC = RV THEN RST = DE * 256: REM *RST vector contents, upper byte
```

Listing 10.1   Software package for the 68705 programmer: Phases 0-5 (*continued*)

```
1940  IF PC = RV + 1 THEN RST = RST + DE: REM *lower byte
1950  X =  PEEK (BASE): REM  *Increment RAM Address counter
1970  PC = PC + 1: REM *Next machine location
1990  NEXT J: REM *Next byte
1995  PRINT
2000  NEXT I: REM *Next line
2005  REM *Program now downloaded to RAM
2010  IF VF = 1 THEN  PRINT "Download error, process aborted ": GOTO 3010: REM *See line 1925
2020  IF MO =  - 1 THEN  PRINT "Mask Option Register not programmed";: GOTO 2050
2030  DE = MO: GOSUB 6000: REM  *Prompt user to value of MOR
2040  PRINT "Mask Option Register set to $";HEX$
2050  PRINT
2060  IF TIM =  - 1 THEN  PRINT "Timer/INT2 Interrupt vector not programmed";: GOTO 2090
2070  DE = TIM: GOSUB 6000: REM  *Prompt user to value of Timer/INT2 start address
2080  PRINT "Timer/INT2 vector set to $";HEX$
2090  PRINT
2100  IF IRQ =  - 1 THEN  PRINT "INT vector not programmed";: GOTO 2130
2110  DE = IRQ: GOSUB 6000: REM  *Prompt user to value of INT start address in hex
2120  PRINT "INT vector set to $";HEX$
2130  PRINT
2140  IF SWI =  - 1 THEN  PRINT "SWI vector not programmed";: GOTO 2170
2150  DE = SWI: GOSUB 6000: REM  *Prompt user to value of SWI start address in hex
2160  PRINT "SWI vector set to $";HEX$
2170  PRINT
2180  IF RST =  - 1 THEN  PRINT "Warning! no RESET vector";: GOTO 2210
2190  DE = RST: GOSUB 6000: REM  *Prompt user to Reset address in hex
2200  PRINT "RESET address is $";HEX$
2210  PRINT : PRINT "Any key to continue"
2220  GET X$
2999  REM *Program the 68705 starts here
3000  HOME
3010  PRINT "Do you require a complete ";: INVERSE : PRINT "LISTING";: NORMAL : PRINT : PRINT
3020  PRINT "Do you wish to ";: INVERSE : PRINT "PROGRAM";: NORMAL : PRINT " the 68705": PRINT
3030  PRINT "Do you wish to return to the ";: INVERSE : PRINT "EDITOR";: NORMAL : PRINT : PRINT
3040  INPUT X$
3050  X$ =  LEFT$ (X$,1)
3060  IF X$ = "E" THEN  PRINT D$"BRUN TEXT EDITOR.OBJ"
3070  IF X$ = "L" THEN  GOTO 4000: REM *Operator wants a listing of RAM contents
3080  IF X$ > < "P" THEN 3000: REM *Operator wants to program 68705
```

(d) Phase 3: EPROM programmer routine

```
3097  REM *************************************************************
3098  REM *Program 68705 routine starts here
3099  REM *************************************************************
3100  POKE BASE + 3,2: REM *Turn on 5V supply to MCU
3110  HOME
3120  PRINT "Turning on 5V supply to the 68705"
3130  FOR I = 0 TO 9000: NEXT : REM     *Delay awhile
3140  POKE BASE + 3,6: REM *TURN ON 21V
3150  PRINT : PRINT "Turning on 21V Vpp"
3160  FOR I = 0 TO 1000: NEXT : REM     *Delay awhile
3170  POKE BASE + 3,7: REM *Release Reset
3180  PRINT : PRINT "Programming now commencing"
3190  PRINT "After awhile the red LED will light, indicating programming finished"
3200  PRINT : PRINT "When the green LED is lit the programming is verified"
3210  PRINT : PRINT "Only then key to continue"
3220  GET X$
3230  POKE BASE + 3,3: REM  *Remove 21V
3250  POKE BASE + 3,2: REM *Reset MCU
3260  FOR I = 0 TO 1000: NEXT
3270  POKE BASE + 3,0: REM *And remove 5V
3280  GOTO 3000
```

Listing 10.1   Software package for the 68705 programmer: Phases 0-5 *(continued) (e)* Phase 4: RAM hex dump

```
3997  REM *********************************************************
3998  REM *The formatted list routine starts here
3999  REM *********************************************************
4000  HOME
4005  POKE BASE + 3,0: REM *Reset Option register
4010  INPUT "Hard copy?";PR$
4020  PR$ =  LEFT$ (PR$,1)
4030  IF PR$ = "N" THEN 4200
4035  REM  *Now set up Epson printer
4040  HOME : PRINT "Move paper to top of form, and hit key"
4050  GET X$
4060  PRINT CHR$ (12) CHR$ (21): REM *Turn off 80-column card
4070  PRINT D$;"PR#1": REM *Turn on printer channel
4080  PRINT  CHR$ (27)"Q" CHR$ (80): REM *80 columns
4090  PRINT  CHR$ (27)"C" CHR$ (66): REM *66 lines per page
4100  PRINT  CHR$ (27)"N" CHR$ (4): REM *Skip 4 lines at the perforation
4200  HOME
4205  IF PR$ > < "Y" THEN  PRINT "Key P to Pause, X to eXit"
4210  PRINT  CHR$ (14)FI$;" 68705 listing": PRINT : REM *Heading
4220  POKE 34,2: REM *Leave 2-line window at top of APPLE screen
4230  X =  PEEK (BASE + 1): REM *Reset RAM Address Counter
4240  FOR I = 0 TO 127:X =  PEEK (BASE): NEXT : REM *Move over first 128 68705-RAM bytes
4250  HOME
4260  PRINT "User EPROM:-"
4270  FOR I = 128 TO MV - 1 STEP 24: REM *User EPROM
4280  DE = I: GOSUB 6000: REM *At start of each line print address in hex
4285  PRINT "<";HEX$;"> ";
4290  FOR J = 0 TO 23: REM  *Lines of 24 bytes
4300  DE =  PEEK (BASE + 2): GOSUB 7000: REM *Get byte in hex
4310  PRINT HEX$ + " ";: REM *and print it
4320  X =  PEEK (BASE): REM *Increment RAM Counter
4330  IF I + J = MV - 1 THEN J = 24: REM *Exit if reached Mask Option Register
4340  NEXT J: REM *ELSE next byte
4342  IF  PEEK (49152) = 216 THEN I = MV: GOTO 4700: REM  *Examine APPLE's keyboard buffer for an X for eXit
4345  IF  PEEK (49152) = 208 THEN 4345: REM *Likewise for P, Pause
4348  PRINT
4350  NEXT I: REM *Next line of 24 bytes
4360  DE = MV: GOSUB 6000: REM *We have now arrived at the Mask Option Register
4370  PRINT "<";HEX$;"> ";"Mask Option Register ";
4380  DE =  PEEK (BASE + 2): GOSUB 7000: REM *Get its contents in hex
4390  PRINT HEX$
4400  PRINT "BOOTSTRAP ROM from ";
4410  DE = MV + 1: GOSUB 6000: REM *Loader ROM between MOR and Timer vector
4420  PRINT HEX$" to ";
4430  DE = TV - 1: GOSUB 6000
4440  PRINT HEX$
4450  FOR I = MV + 1 TO TV:X =  PEEK (BASE): NEXT : REM  *Step Address register on past BOOTSTRAP
4460  DE = TV: GOSUB 6000: REM *Now prepare to display Timer/INT2 vector
4470  PRINT "<";HEX$;"> Timer/INT2 vector ";
4485  DE =  PEEK (BASE + 2) * 256: REM *Upper byte
4495  X =  PEEK (BASE):DE = DE +  PEEK (BASE + 2): GOSUB 6000: REM *Lower byte
4500  PRINT HEX$
4510  X =  PEEK (BASE): REM *and the same for the INT vector
4520  DE = IV: GOSUB 6000: REM *Now prepare to display INT vector
4530  PRINT "<";HEX$;"> INT vector ";
4535  DE =  PEEK (BASE + 2) * 256: REM *Upper byte
4545  X =  PEEK (BASE):DE = DE +  PEEK (BASE + 2): GOSUB 6000: REM *Lower byte
4550  PRINT HEX$
4560  X =  PEEK (BASE): REM *and the same for the SWI vector
4570  DE = SV: GOSUB 6000:  REM *Now prepare to display SWI vector
4580  PRINT "<";HEX$;"> SWI vector ";
4585  DE =  PEEK (BASE + 2) * 256: REM *Upper byte
4595  X =  PEEK (BASE):DE = DE +  PEEK (BASE + 2): GOSUB 6000: REM *Lower byte
4600  PRINT HEX$
4610  X =  PEEK (BASE): REM  *and the same for the RESET vector
```

Listing 10.1   Software package for the 68705 programmer: Phases 0-5 *(continued)*

```
4620 DE = RV: GOSUB 6000: REM   *Now prepare to display RESET vector
4630 PRINT "<";HEX$;"> RESET vector ";
4635 DE = PEEK (BASE + 2) * 256: REM *Lower byte
4645 X = PEEK (BASE):DE = DE + PEEK (BASE + 2): GOSUB 6000
4650 PRINT HEX$
4700 X = PEEK (49168): REM  *Clear APPLES's keyboard buffer
4710 IF PR$ = "Y" THEN  PRINT : PRINT D$"PR#3": REM  *IF in printer mode THEN go back to 80-column VDU card
4720 PRINT : PRINT "Any key to continue"
4730 GET X$
4740 X = PEEK (49168): REM  *Clear APPLE's keyboard buffer
4750 POKE 34,0: REM *Remove screen window, see line 4220
4760 HOME
4770 GOTO 3000: REM *Return
```

(f) Phase 5: Utility subroutines

```
4810 REM *System subroutines
4820 REM *********************************************************
4900 :
4996 REM *Converts HEX string of any length to decimal
4997 REM *ENTRY:HEX$, format $NNN or NNN
4998 REM *EXIT :DE=decimal
4999 REM *Variables used: I9;AS
5000 DE = 0
5005 IF LEFT$ (HEX$,1) = "$" THEN HEX$ = RIGHT$ (HEX$, LEN (HEX$) - 1)
5010 FOR I9 = 1 TO LEN (HEX$)
5020 AS = ASC ( MID$ (HEX$,I9,1))
5030 IF AS < 48 OR (AS > 57 AND AS < 65) OR AS > 70 THEN PRINT "Illegal Hex digit, try again! ": INPUT HEX$: GOTO 5000
5040 DE = DE * 16 + (AS > 64) * (AS - 55) + (AS < 58) * (AS - 48)
5050 NEXT
5060 RETURN
5995 REM *********************************************************
5996 REM *Subroutine converts decimal to hexadecimal
5997 REM *ENTRY:DE, any +ve integer up to 4097
5998 REM *EXIT: HEX$, three digit
5999 REM *:Variables used are I9,H(2)
6000 HEX$ = ""
6005 IF DE > 4097 THEN  PRINT "Illegal address > $FFF ":HEX$ = "***": RETURN
6010 FOR I9 = 2 TO 0 STEP  - 1
6020 H(I9) =  INT (DE / 16 ^ I9):DE = DE - H(I9) * 16 ^ I9
6030 HEX$ = HEX$ +  CHR$ ((H(I9) + (H(I9) > 9) * 7) + 48)
6040 NEXT I9
6050 RETURN
6900 REM *********************************************************
6996 REM *Subroutine converts decimal to hexadecimal
6997 REM *ENTRY:DE, any +ve integer up to 255
6998 REM *EXIT: HEX$, two digit
6999 REM *:Variables used are I9,H1,H2
7000 H1 =  INT (DE / 16):H2 = DE - H1 * 16
7010 HEX$ =  CHR$ (H1 + (H1 > 9) * 7 + 48) +  CHR$ (H2 + (H2 > 9) * 7 + 48)
7020 RETURN
7030 REM ***********************************************************
```

Listing 10.1   Software package for the 68705 programmer: Phases 0-5 (*continued*)

PHASE 0: LINES 10–330

This sector is primarily concerned with loading the various machine-level programs described in Listing 10.2. Two processes are implemented at this level. The first subroutine CTRINC increments the RAM Address counter up to the value prestored in locations $03BD/E by the calling program. The second clears each location in the buffer RAM.

```
0000:         1 *This is the machine code used by the 68705 programmer software of listing 10.1
0000:         2 *
03BD:         3 TARGET  EQU  $03BD    ;Target number held here & $03BE
C0C0:         4 CLOCK   EQU  $C0C0    ;Address counter's clock pin
C0C1:         5 RESET   EQU  $C0C1    ;Address counter's reset pin
C0C2:         6 RAM     EQU  $C0C2    ;Buffer RAM entry

0000:         8 *****************************************************************
0000:         9 *This subroutine increments Address counter by number stored in TARGET/TARGET+1
0000:        10 *ENTRY : Number of increments in TARGET/TARGET+1
0000:        11 *EXIT  : TARGET/TARGET+1 = 0000
0000:        12 *EXIT  : (A)&(CCR) destroyed
0000:        13 *****************************************************************

0300:        14         ORG  $0300    ;Increment subroutine lives here
0300:AD C1 C0 15 CTRINC LDA  RESET    ;Pulse counter's reset pin
0303:AD C0 C0 16 ILOOP  LDA  CLOCK    ;Increment counter
0306:20 80 03 17        JSR  DPDEC    ;Decrement tally
0309:D0 F8   18         BNE  ILOOP    ;IF not yet zero THEN again
030B:60      19         RTS           ;ELSE exit

030C:        21 *****************************************************************
030C:        22 *This subroutine clears all buffer RAM
030C:        23 *ENTRY : Number of RAM locations in TARGET/TARGET+1
030C:        24 *EXIT  : TARGET/TARGET+1 = 0000
030C:        25 *EXIT  : (A)&(CCR) destroyed
030C:        26 *****************************************************************

0310:        27         ORG  $0310    ;Clear subroutine lives here
0310:8D C1 C0 28 CLEAR  STA  RESET    ;Pulse counter's reset pin
0313:A9 00   29         LDA  #00      ;Zero data
0315:8D C2 C0 30 CLOOP  STA  RAM      ;To RAM
0318:8D C0 C0 31        STA  CLOCK    ;Increment RAM counter
031B:20 80 03 32        JSR  DPDEC    ;Decrement tally
031E:D0 F5   33         BNE  CLOOP    ;IF not yet completed THEN again
0320:60      34         RTS           ;ELSE exit

0321:        36 *****************************************************************
0321:        37 *This subroutine decrements ($03BD/E) by one
0321:        38 *ENTRY : None
0321:        39 *EXIT  : ($03BD/E) becomes ($03BD/E)-1
0321:        40 *EXIT  : Z flag set if ($03BD/E)=zero
0321:        41 *EXIT  : (A)&(CCR) destroyed
0321:        42 *****************************************************************

0380:        43         ORG  $0380    ;Double precision decrement lives here
0380:AD BD 03 44 DPDEC  LDA  TARGET   ;Get lsb
0383:18      45         CLC
0384:E9 00   46         SBC  #0       ;Subtract one
0386:8D BD 03 47        STA  TARGET   ;and restore
0389:AD BE 03 48        LDA  TARGET+1 ;Get msb
038C:E9 00   49         SBC  #0       ;Subtract carry
038E:8D BE 03 50        STA  TARGET+1 ;and restore
0391:D0 05   51         BNE  DEXIT    ;IF msb not zero THEN exit
0393:AD BD 03 52        LDA  TARGET   ;ELSE check lsb
0396:C9 00   53         CMP  #0       ;for zero
0398:60      54 DEXIT   RTS           :and return
```

Listing 10.2   Machine-level software used by the programmer package

Both these subroutines use a double-precision decrement utility subroutine stored at $038). The machine code of Listing 10.2 is of course pertinent only to the 6502 processor used by the Apple computer. If desired both processes can be implemented in BASIC, but will take a considerably longer time to run.

PHASE 1: LINES 410–720

This checks for a blank MCU by clearing all buffer RAM locations before applying power and lifting the 68705's reset. As only the verify portion of the bootstrap is being utilized, the V_{PP} control transistor is kept off by leaving bit 3 low. If the internal EPROM is all blank, the bootstrap will illuminate both red and green LEDs after a pause of around 10 seconds. The operator can then choose to go on (if perhaps an additional routine is being added to existing firmware) or try again with another MCU.

PHASE 2: LINES 1050–3080

Machine code targeted to the MCU's EPROM must be downloaded into buffer RAM. In the situation depicted in Listing 10.1, this data is stored in a sequential access disk file, whose name is given by the operator in Line 1060. This file has been created by the 6805 assembler program which actually produces the machine code from the original source input.

The extraction of the relevant data from a hex file obviously depends on the structure of these files. An example file using the standard Motorola S-record format is shown in Listing 10.3. Here it is seen that a file consists of several short records structured as S1 NB AAAA HHHH – – – – HHHH CS, where S1 is the header, NB is the number of following bytes, AAAA is the address of the first machine code byte and HHHH – – – – HHHH is the machine code. Each record is terminated by

Listing 10.3   Motorola S-format machine file structure

a checksum byte (the inverse of the modulo-8 sum of the data), used for error check-ing (CS). For example, record 1 has $23 bytes following NB, the first location is $0A00 in which the machine code is $A6. The last machine byte is $01, and the checksum is $49. A record header S9 indicates end of file.

Most Motorola compatible assemblers produce machine code files (sometimes called MIKBUG or MINIBUG format) of this form. The file shown in Listing 10.3 has been produced by the assembler of Appendix 5, and is in fact the machine file generated from the diagnostic program developed in Section 14.

In Listing 10.1, lines 1600–2000 bring in the complete S-format machine file and extracts machine code, location and number of bytes from each record. As each line is processed, it is output to the screen (see Listing 14.4) and sent down to the buffer RAM. Values pertaining to the various interrupt vectors and mask option register are noted, and output for information. The program caters for both 2K (e.g., 68705P3) and 4K (e.g., 68705R3) sized MCUs. If the hex file contains data outside of the relevent memory maps then the operator is prompted (Line 1903).

PHASE 3: LINES 3100–3280

This short routine actually programs the MCU. It is similar to phase 1, but the V_{PP} control (bit 3) is set high to permit the application of 21V to the V_{PP} pin as dictated by the bootstrap during the EPROM programming phase.

PHASE 4: LINES 4000–4770

A complete printout of the contents of the buffer RAM (and by implication in 68705 EPROM memory if successfully programmed) is produced in this sector. This is accomplished by incrementing the RAM address counter through valid areas, and reading the consequent data. A typical printout is shown in Listing 14.4.

PHASE 5: LINES 4900–7020

These are utility subroutines used to convert between decimal and hexadecimal word formats.

11

All in the Family

Through most of this part of the book we have focused on the 68705R3 member of the family, although other related MCUs have been occasionally alluded to. This single-minded approach has been adopted partly because this is the MCU used in the project (to be introduced in Section 12.2), but also to avoid cluttering the text with too many variations on a theme. Fortunately the software and CPU are virtually the same throughout the family, with changes mainly in peripheral interface and memory size. In this section we round off Part 2 by examining a representative selection of 6805 variants.

The common 6805 family core is emphasized in Fig. 11.1, where a spectrum of Motorola 6805 devices is illustrated. Although in the main we will use members from this range to illustrate this chapter, note that Motorola has licensed the 6805 core to several other manufacturers, including RCA, Thompson-CSF and Hitachi (who also manufacture the allied 6305 family of CMOS MCUs). However, the peripheral and memory arrangements often differ from the parent range.

11.1 MASKED-ROM 6805 MCUs

The star of this book, the 68705R3, is an EPROM version of the 6805R2/3 masked ROM MCU. We will discuss the economics of EPROM versus ROM-based devices in Section 11.2; it is sufficient here to say that the former is primarily designed to form the basis of prototype development, as a debug aid and for small- to medium-production runs. The relatively high tooling-up charges incurred with mask-ROM devices, coupled with their lower unit cost, make these types the natural choice for larger volume production.

Figure 11.2 shows the block diagram of the 6805R2 masked-ROM MCU. A comparison between this and the EPROM 68705R3 version of Fig. 8.2 shows that they are virtually identical barring the replacement of EPROM by ROM. The 6805R2 has 2,048 bytes of user ROM and 64 bytes of RAM, while the 6805R3 has 3,776 and 112 bytes respectively.

The bootstrap ROM of the EPROM MCU is redundant in mask-programmed parts, which sport an integral diagnostic program, the self-test ROM ($F38-$FF7

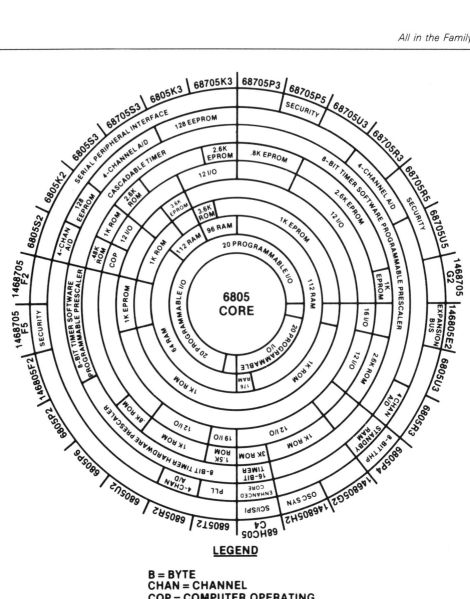

LEGEND

B = BYTE
CHAN = CHANNEL
COP = COMPUTER OPERATING
            PROPERLY
I/O = INPUT OUTPUT
OSC SYN = OSCILLATOR
                  SYNTHESIZER
PLL = PHASE LOCK LOOP
SCI = SERIAL COMMUNICATION
          INTERFACE
SPI = SERIAL PERIPHERAL
          INTERFACE

8-BIT THP = 8-BIT TIMER HARDWARE
                    PRESCALER

Fig. 11.1   M6805 family spectrum (reproduced by courtesy of Motorola Limited)

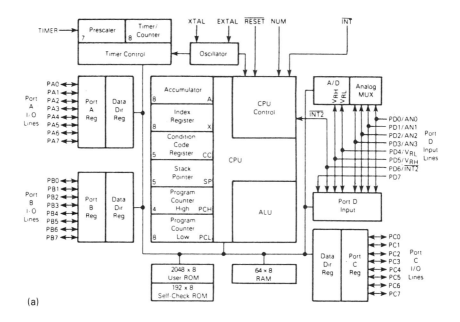

(a)

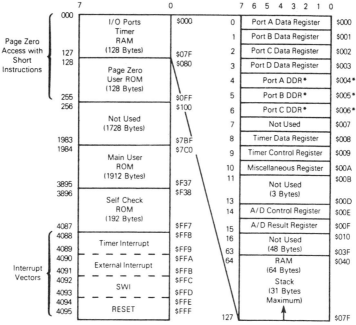

*Caution: Data direction registers (DDRs) are write-only; they read as $FF.

(b)

Fig. 11.2   The MC6805R2 MCU (reproduced by courtesy of Motorola Limited)
(a) Block diagram   (b) Memory map

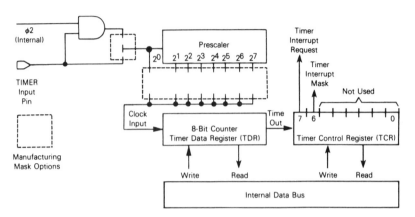

Fig. 11.3   The 6805R2/U2/P2-4-6's mask-configured timer (reproduced by courtesy of Motorola Limited)

in Fig. 11.2). This assumes that the MCU, like the bootstrap ROM, is placed in a specific hardware environment. When the MCU is reset with the timer pin held above 9V, the MCU vectors to the start of the self-test routine. This exercises RAM (walking test), ROM (checksum), timer, interrupts, parallel ports and A/D converter. The results are displayed on an array of four LEDs. Of course, this is only an internal check, suitable for an incoming part functional test, and does not apply to the final (target) system (see Chapter 14).

When the manufacturer creates the ROM mask to implement the customer's specification, various options are enabled by the mask at the same time. An example of a mask-configured timer is shown in Fig. 11.3. Here the requested timer prescale ratio is selected by linking the appropriate prescale counter output through to the timer counter's clock input. Similarly, the prescale counter clock can be linked either to the MCU internal clock (ϕ_2) gated by the timer pin level or to the timer pin itself. These links are defined by the mask during the metalization fabrication stage.

Figure 11.4 shows a 6805P2 custom-ordering form, which lists the various mask options. In addition to the timer links specified in Fig. 11.3, the integral clock oscillator can be set to either the crystal or resistor mode (see Fig. 7.2); and an internal pull-up resistor can be linked to parallel Port A's outputs (to give the higher logic 1 voltage necessary to drive CMOS parts). The low-voltage inhibit (LVI) option listed in Fig. 11.4 causes an automatic reset of the MCU if the power supply falls below a certain level (typically 3.75V). The reset is not released until the supply rises again to near normal (typically 4.7V). Figure 7.4 shows another example of a mask option, relevant to CMOS 6805s. Other than LVI, the corresponding EPROM MCU (the 68705P3 in this case) can emulate the various mask options by using the mask option register, as summarized in Fig. 7.2. Later members of the mask-ROM 6805 family feature a software programmable timer, described in Section 8.3, rather than the fixed configuration of Fig. 11.3.

The 6805S2 lies at the more sophisticated end of the family. This MCU features a 4- or 5-channel 8-bit analog-to-digital converter (A/D), three timers and

MC6805P2 MCU CUSTOM ORDERING INFORMATION

Date _____ Customer PO Number _____

Customer Company _____

Motorola Part Numbers

MC _____

SC _____

Address _____

City _____ State _____ Zip _____

Country _____

Phone _____ Extension _____

Customer Contact Person _____

Customer Part Number _____

OPTION LIST
Select the options for your MCU from the following list. A
manufacturing mask will be generated from this information.

Timer Clock Source
☐ Internal φ2 clock
☐ TIMER input pin

Internal Oscillator Input
☐ Crystal
☐ Resistor

Timer Prescaler
☐ 2^0 (divide by 1)
☐ 2^1 (divide by 2)
☐ 2^2 (divide by 4)
☐ 2^3 (divide by 8)
☐ 2^4 (divide by 16)
☐ 2^5 (divide by 32)
☐ 2^6 (divide by 64)
☐ 2^7 (divide by 128)

Low Voltage Inhibit
☐ Disable
☐ Enable

Port A Output Drive
☐ CMOS and TTL
☐ TTL Only

Pattern Media (All other media requires prior factory approval.)
☐ EPROMs (MCM2716 or MCM2532)
☐ EPROM MCU (MC68705P3)
☐ Floppy Disk
☐ Other _____

Clock Freq. _____

Temp. Range _____ ☐ 0° to +70°C (Standard)   ☐ −40° to +85°C

Marking Information (12 Characters Maximum)

Title _____

Signature _____

Fig. 11.4   Custom MCU ordering form for the MC6805P2 (reproduced courtesy of
Motorola Limited)

a serial interface port. The A/D converter is identical to that described in Section
8.4, but with a mask option of a fifth input channel replacing the $\overline{\text{INT2}}$/PD2 input.
However, the timers are a much enhanced version of the standard circuit supported
by the 68(7)05R3, and provide facilities approaching those of the programmable
interval timer of Chapter 5.

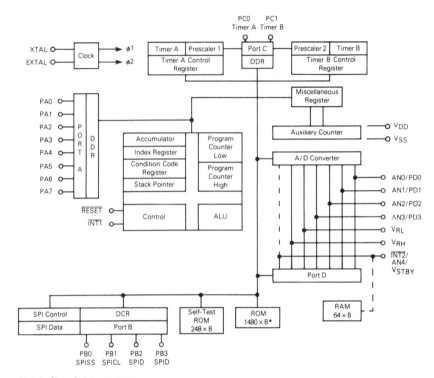

Fig. 11.5 MC6805S2 architecture (reproduced by courtesy of Motorola Limited)

Timer A in Fig. 11.5, like the standard 6805 timer, comprises an 8-bit down counter with an associated 7-bit programmable prescaler driven from either an external source (PC0) or the internal clock (ϕ_2) or the logic product of the two. This basic configuration is enhanced by coupling the counter with a latch register. On time out, the counter reloads with the contents of this latch, rather than always with $FF. A TINT interrupt can be set or/and a timer output pin toggled (PB0 or PB1) at this instant.

Timer B is a 16-bit counter with an associated 16-bit buffer latch register. Like the 6840 PIT, the full 16 bits can be transferred via this latch simultaneously. Time-out B can also request a TINT and can toggle a timer output (PB1 or PB0). The B prescaler has a 15-bit capacity allowing divison ratios of up to 32,768 (2^{15}), and can be clocked by an external signal at PC1 or ϕ_2 or the product of these.

Many MCU applications lie in the embedded control field, where noise or mechanical disruption are a frequently encountered hazard. For example, cardiac defibrillators often employ MPU/MCU control, and it is difficult to prevent the 5 kV pulses (discharged through the fibrillating heart) from influencing the electronics. In this case any loss of control will be catastrophic One technique to prevent runaway uses the concept of a 'watchdog timer'. Here a counter decrements to zero and resets the MCU on time-out. In the normal course of events this is undesirable, and the target software should arrange continually to present this counter at a rate sufficient to prevent time-out. Should the MCU (or MPU) run wild, this pumping-up procedure will not occur and a reset action will follow.

The auxiliary counter shown in Fig. 11.5 is the 6805's third timer and is designed for use primarily as watchdog timer. It is clocked by ϕ_2 and has a 12-bit capacity. Thus for a 4 MHz crystal the maximum duration from disruption to recovery is around 4 ms. The auxiliary counter is automatically preset to $FFF on reset, and can be set back to this value by program through the miscellaneous register.

The 6805S2 MCU sports an integral series communication interface (SCI). This is a sophisticated serial port primarily aimed at supporting multiple processor arrangements, where the various MCUs and peripheral devices communicate through a single serial data link. Over this line the master MCU transmits the address of the slave it wishes to communicate with, followed by one or more serialized data bytes. When the address byte is sent, following a start bit, all slaves are interrupted to consider the address field. If this is recognized as being its own personal identification number, then a communication link is established, otherwise the slave goes about its own business.

The SCI is not primarily concerned with communication with a serial terminal, as described in Section 4. Some MCUs have an integral UART for this purpose, e.g., the 68HC05C4, which has both a SCI and serial peripheral interface (SPI).

11.2 CMOS MPUs AND MCUs

Many embedded control applications involve operation independent of mains supplies. When such operation is other than intermittent, the associated battery gives rise to serious design problems. In remote areas, it may even be necessary to use solar cells as the prime energy source. The MCUs described up to now require around 100 mA at a 5 V supply (500 mW), which taken together with the requirements of the supporting circuitry poses a next to impossible burden on the battery.

The normal solution to this problem is to replace the logic and memory circuits by their CMOS counterparts. Figure 11.6 shows the mechanism for this improvement, using a simple inverter as an example. The standard MOS (metal oxide semiconductor) technology uses N-channel transistors (NMOS) with resistive loads (actually the resistor is normally a biased NMOS transistor). When the transistor is on (output low) a current flows from V_{DD} through R_L; ignoring the resistance of the on transistor. Using a high-value load resistor reduces dissipation but tends to slow down operating frequency due to the increased CR time constant. When the transistor is off (output high) there is no standing power dissipation, just that occasioned by load-drive current.

Replacing the passive load resistor by a P-channel MOS transistor gives the 'totem-pole' structure of Fig. 11.6(b). The two transistors always work in antiphase;

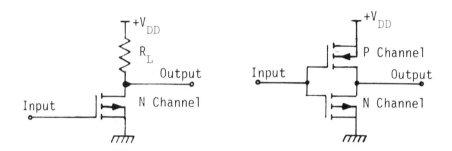

Fig. 11.6 MOS Technologies
(a) NMOS/HMOS inverter
(b) CMOS/HCMOS inverter

thus when the lower N-channel transistor is off the upper P-channel device is on (logic 1) and vice versa. Other than a short current spike during switching, due to nonbalanced transistor characteristics (known as *overlap conduction*) there is no power dissipation other than that demanded by the load.

The price to pay for this increase in performance is the additional complexity of the CMOS cell as compared with its NMOS equivalent. This leads to a larger silicon die size and a corresponding reduction in yield (and increase in expense). In the case of microprocessors and MCUs, the integration density is of a high order, and this problem has meant that in the main CMOS MPU/MCUs were not generally available until the middle 1980s. The 6802 MPU discussed in Part 1 uses NMOS technology, while the 6805 MCUs scrutinized up to this point use a high-density version (HMOS). Similarly, fabrication densities in CMOS have been increased with new device introductions, which use the HCMOS technology to cram more onto the one chip.

The 146805E2 was the the first introduction to the CMOS branch of the family. As you can see from Fig. 11.7(a) the internal structure of this device is typical of the 6805 family, but there is no on-board ROM/EPROM. Instead the (normally) internal address, data and control buses are brought out at the expense of two of the parallel ports, C & D. To avoid too high an attrition rate of port lines, the lower eight address lines (a_0-a_7) and the data bus are multiplexed. The address lines appear during the first half of the clock cycle ϕ_2 (designated here $\overline{\text{Data Strobe}}$, Pin 4) and an $\overline{\text{Address Strobe}}$ ($\overline{\text{AS}}$, Pin 6) is used to clock an external CMOS octal latch (e.g., a 74HC373) at this point. The data bus is then exerted and is stable as usual at the end of the cycle, which also sees the stable address $a_{12}-a_8$ on Pins 15–19 and a_7-a_0 provided by the external demultiplexer latch. An external R/$\overline{\text{W}}$ signal is also supplied (Pin 5).

Use of an external EPROM (CMOS or otherwise) reduces the die complexity of the device to an economic level, but also has certain advantages to the user. A standard EPROM programmer may be used to set up prototype programs. The emergence of three buses to the outside world permits easier debugging, especially when the 146805E2 is being used to emulate other members of the family. The 146805E2 is cataloged as a MPU rather than MCU, because of the lack of on-board

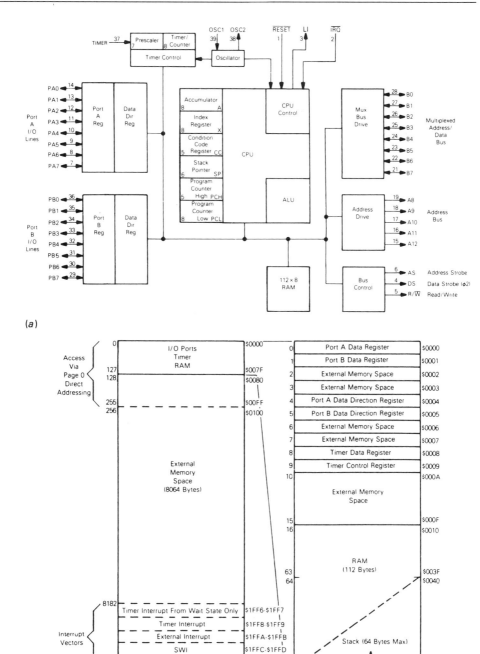

(a)

(b)

Fig. 11.7   The MC146805E2 CMOS MPU (reproduced by courtesy of Motorola Limited)
(a) Block schematic
(b) Memory map

ROM/EPROM. Later CMOS introductions, such as the 146805F2 and 146805G2, have integral ROM/EPROM and are therefore true MCUs. The 68HC805C4 is unusual in that it uses an integral EEPROM (electrically erasible PROM) as the prototyping equivalent of the ROMed 68HC05C4.

The 146805E2 MPU has a worst case unloaded supply current demand of 10 mA at 5 V (50 mW) running at a clock frequency of 1 MHz. However, the flexibility of CMOS MCUs is such that performance can be traded off against power dissipation using both hardware and software techniques. The specified power supply range for these devices is typically 3 V–6 V (compared to the HMOS range of 5.25 ± 0.5 V), which in itself is a bonus for battery powered applications. Moreover power consumption considerably reduces with supply voltage, as does (unfortunately) the maximum possible clocking rate. Thus the 146805E2 has a maximum unloaded supply current demand of only 1.3 mA at a 3 V supply (3.9 mW) and clock rate of 200 kHz.

Power dissipation shows an almost linear relationship with clock frequency. This is because in going through one cycle, each internal switch must charge and discharge the following MOS transistor gate capacitance, C. These charge and discharge currents dissipate CV^2 Joules per cycle, or CV^2f Watts at a cycle frequency of f Hertz. Reducing both supply voltage (V) and clock rate (f) will considerably lower the power dissipation. CMOS MPU/MCUs, unlike their HMOS siblings, are completely static and therefore the clock rate can be reduced to (a useless) zero. As an example, the 1468705G2 MCU (with integral 2106-byte EPROM) shows a typical operating current at 5 V 1 MHz to be 2.75 mA declining to 0.3 mA at 100 kHz and 0.15 mA at zero Hertz.

To take advantage of this frequency dependent dissipation reduction, CMOS MCUs have two software operations not available to their HMOS counterparts. The first of these is WAIT ($8F), which disconnects the clock from all internal circuitry except the timer. During the WAIT execution the I mask in the CCR is cleared. This state of inanimate suspension is only broken when the 'princess is kissed' or, in MCU terms, when an interrupt arrives. This may be external or internal from the timer (which is still running). When this occurs, the MCU awakens and fetches the contents of the appropriate interrupt vector into the program counter. The 146805E2 has a maximum waiting current demand of 1.5 mA at 5 V.

STOP ($8E) is similar to WAIT (wait for interrupt) in that the oscillator is turned off, causing all processing (including the timer) to cease. A MCU thus hibernating can be wakened only by either resetting or interrupting. When this occurs, the oscillator is turned back on and a period of 1920 cycles is allowed for stabilization, before the reset or interrupt is vectored to. While stopped, the 146805E2 requires no more than 200 μA at 5 V (1 mW) and 100 μA at 3 V (300 μW).

Besides WAIT and STOP, CMOS 6805 software is virtually identical to the HMOS equivalent, although execution is a little faster for some instructions. Some of the most recent introductions (e.g., the 68HC05C4 and 63705Z) have an unsigned multiply instruction (MUL = $42), which multiplies the contents of the accumulator and index registers to give a 16-bit product in the concatenated index and accumulator registers, i.e., $X \times A \rightarrow X:A$.

PART THREE

The Project

Now that we have been acquainted with the single-chip microcomputer, let us attempt to put our new-found knowledge to some practical use. In this part, we will follow through a MCU-based product from inception through to the construction of a functional prototype.

12

The Broad Scenario

At the starting line the customer will specify the system in a global sense; essentially what goes in and what comes out. The 'black box' implementing this macro transfer function is likely to be mentioned, if at all, *en passant*. Of course, there will be technical constraints imposed by this specification, such as size, speed and power supply, but these will rarely do more than point the finger towards a likely implementation strategy. The final hardware (and software if applicable) configuration will be dictated by a myriad of considerations including financial targets, marketing, available development equipment and expertise.

So, under what situations will it be advisable to use a single-chip microcomputer? Indeed, extending this line of thought somewhat, overall what choices does the designer have? A good choice between alternatives during the various stages of product design involves awareness of more than technical matters. We will look at some of the possibilities in this chapter, before beginning the project proper.

12.1   SYSTEM DESIGN

There are several critical steps between agreeing a specification (see Section 12.2) and actually getting down to the nitty gritty of hardware/software design. One of the more important of these involves the selection of the system transducers, since these form the interface between the electronics and the real world. These will be chosen on the basis of an analysis of the parameters involved, together with their measurement and interconversion to an analagous electrical quantity.

The choice of transducer is not unduly influenced by the technology which is to be used for the central processing electronics, but their selection at this time, coupled with a system-task analysis, will permit a rough block diagram to be made of the system. In Fig. 12.1 this is indicated under the heading of System Formulation.

With a functional outline of the system selected, some thought can be given to the technology of the central electronics. At the macro level this will involve a partition between analog and digital processes. For example, should an input signal

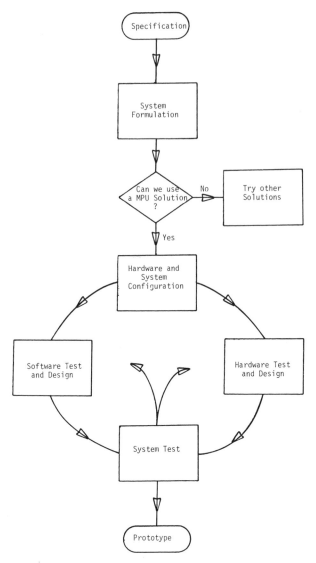

Fig. 12.1   A broad outline of circuit development

be filtered before the A/D conversion (analog filter) or after (a digital software filter)? Most current implementations rely on a mixture of both types of processing.

At the digital end of things the choice lies between random logic (i.e., hardwired digital combinational and sequential circuitry) and programmable logic (microprocessor and microcomputer software-directed hardware). Conventional logic is usually best for small systems with few functions, which are unlikely to require expansion. In larger systems, this type of logic may appear in the guise of programmable arrays or even custom-designed integrated circuits where numbers warrant.

In general microprocessors do everything sequentially, one thing at a time, while random logic can process in parallel. Thus where nanosecond speed is important, conventional logic is indicated (but note that analog electronics is even faster). It is possible to run several microprocessor/microcomputer chips in parallel to increase the throughput, but frequently a mixed logic approach is used when a microprocessor is used in a supervisory role to control the action of supporting random logic and analog circuitry.

Assuming that a microprocessor-based solution is decided upon, the processing tasks must be partitioned between hardware and software. If we take an alphanumeric readout as an illustrative example; then the choice is between an expensive intelligent display which incorporates integral ASCII decoder hardware and a cheaper dumb display where the segment patterns are picked out by software. The former will cost more on a unit basis, but the latter will require money before the product is launched to design the software-driver package. This of course is at a fairly trivial level, but in general hardware is available off the shelf and therefore has a low initial design cost and takes the load off the central processor. Software is rarely obtainable ready-made and requires initial investment in a (highly paid) software engineer, but is usually more flexible than a hardware-only solution. Thus, when technically feasible, a software-oriented solution is indicated for large production runs, where the initial investment is amortized by a lower unit cost.

With the tasks allocated (at least initially) between hardware and software, what choices has the designer available to him/her in implementing the hardware? There are three main approaches to the problem.

In situations when the ratio of design cost to production numbers is poor, a systems implementation should be considered. This entails using a commercial microcomputer as the processor. Such instruments are normally sold with keyboard, VDU and sufficient memory to handle most tasks. Generally the hardware engineer will be concerned only to customize the system by designing specialist supporting hardware and interface circuitry. The software engineer will create a software package based on this microcomputer, which will drive the hardware. Frequently the microcomputer will support commercially available software-development packages, such as monitor, assembler and compilers, which facilitates the software design process at low cost.

Tailoring a general-purpose machine to a *semidedicated* role requires a relatively low investment 'up-front' and low production expenses. Furthermore, documentation and the provision of service facilities are eased, as a preexisting commercial product is used. Technically, this type of implementation is bulky, but where facilities such as a VDU or disc drive are needed, the size is not necessarily greater than a custom-designed product. The same applies to unit cost. Sometimes the customer may already possess the microcomputer, the vendor simply selling the hardware plug-in interface and software package. For the end user, this can be an attractive proposition.

Thus a system-level implementation is indicated when low-to medium-production runs are in prospect and the system complexity is high; e.g., computerized laboratory equipment. For one-offs this approach is the only economic proposition, provided that such a system will fit into the technical boundary constraints. For example, it would obviously be ridiculous (but technically feasible) to employ this technique for, say, a washing-machine controller.

At the middle range of complexity, a system may be constructed using a bought-in single-board computer (SBC). Sometimes several modules are used (e.g., MPU, memory, analog conversion), and these are plugged into a motherboard carrying the processor buses. If necessary these may be augmented with in-house designed boards to complete the configuration.

Although the cost of these bought-in cards may be up to ten times the material cost of the self-produced equivalent, they are likely to be competitive in production runs of up to several thousand. Like system-level implemented systems, they considerably reduce the up-front hardware expenses and do not require elaborate production and test facilities. By shortening the design time, the product can be marketed earlier, and later (if successful) the economics improved by substitution of in-house boards. Although often more expensive than a system based on a commercial microcomputer, a board-level implementation gives greater flexibility to configure the hardware to the specific product needs. Furthermore, in a multiple-card configuration, at least some of the standard modules can be used for more than one product (e.g., a memory card), thus gaining the cost benefits of larger purchase volumes.

Neither the system or board-level approach provides an economical means of production for volumes much in excess of a thousand, with the exception of high value-complexity products. In many cases technical demands, such as size or speed, preclude these techniques even for small production runs. In such situations, a fundamental chip-level design is indicated.

Chip-level involves implementation at the component level. In this situation, the circuitry is fabricated from scratch, giving a configuration *dedicated* to the specific application. Given that the designers require an intimate knowledge of a spectrum of integrated circuits and timing relationships and they must keep their eye on the eventual production process, the cost of developing, testing and production of such systems is large. Furthermore, the upfront expenses are high and may cause cash-flow problems. However, the cost of materials is low, and this approach often leads to the best technical solution to the problem. For most dedicated microprocessor systems, software is developed in a similar way to chip-level hardware, as illustrated in Fig. 12.2. There is little in the way of off-the-shelf packages which can be used in an analogous way to system and board-level hardware. For this reason software design is always an expensive proposition, and is difficult to amortize in small production runs.

Given that we have opted for a microprocessor-oriented fundamental-level implementation, what are the indications for the use of a single-chip MCU? MCUs require more expensive development equipment and therefore increase up-front costs. Although the MCU chip itself is rather more expensive than a comparable MPU, this is offset by a reduction in size and power consumption and an increase in reliability. Microprocessors are however frequently more powerful and flexible than their MCU cousins. Being more standardized means that they can be bought

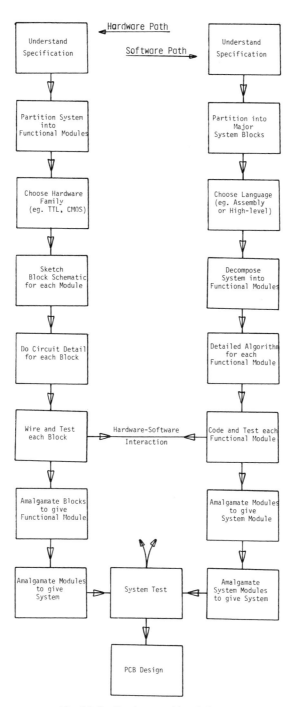

Fig. 12.2 Fundamental-level design

in from a variety of manufacturers (second-sourced). This also means that expertise is more likely to be readily available than for MCUs, which come in the proverbial 57 varieties.

We have already seen in Section 11, that most MCUs are produced with EPROM program memory to facilitate prototype evaluation. Simplistically, once the veracity of the program has been established, production should use the equivalent ROMed MCU. In reality the choice of action is not so clearly defined as this. In evaluating factors beyond that of a straight cost comparison between the EPROM and ROM equivalent MCUs, it may well be that production levels of up to 25,000 should be undertaken using the more expensive device!

On a unit basis EPROM MCUs are normally between 3 and 5 times the price of their ROM partners. This is due to not only the expense of an EPROM structure as opposed to the mask ROM equivalent but the necessity to use a windowed ceramic package. ROM MCUs can use a much cheaper plastic package. The same package consideration applies to a piggy-back arrangement, where a ROM-less MCU carries a socket on top to accept a standard EPROM chip.

With this disparity in mind, why use EPROM MCUs in production? Well, one major reason is the high initial costs incurred with ROM MCUs. This is due primarily to the tooling-up charges by the manufacturer for the ROM mask, and the minimum purchase order of several thousand. It is difficult to quote actual prices, as these vary considerably between device and manufacturer, but the following quotation from Motorola in 1986 will give the reader a feeling for the sums involved.

Device type	MC6805R3 (ROM)	MC68705R3 (EPROM)
Set up charge	$3,500	– – –
Minimum quantity	5,000	1
Unit cost/100	– – –	$12
Unit cost/1,000	– – –	$10
Unit cost/50,000	$3.60	$ 8.50

Taking the above quotation as an example it is likely that even at the minimum of 5,000, the ROMed version will be cheaper. However, an average product will require between one and two mask changes in its lifetime, each incurring a new mask charge. Furthermore, it is likely that ROMed MCUs will take several months to produce, and certainly will not be available off-the-shelf. This order latency, coupled with a minimum quantity requirement, means that money must be paid up-front of production, and creates inventory problems.

A recent development is the introduction of once-only programmable MCUs by Hitachi. They use EPROM as fixed memory in the normal way, except that the chip is buried in a low-cost plastic package. As there is no window, no erasure is possible. These ZTAT (zero turn around time) MCUs (e.g., the HD63705VOP 4K-byte CMOS device) are around 30–50 % of the cost of a reprogrammable equivalent.

With the preceding discussion in mind, it is certain that production quantities of below 1,000 should be undertaken using EPROMed MCUs. Between this level and 10,000 the decision could go either way, and (unless flexibility is the overriding consideration) above this quantity a ROMed MCU is indicated.

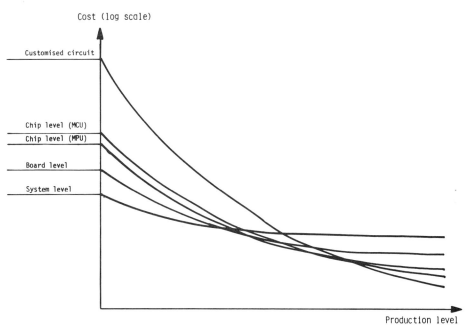

Fig. 12.3   A cost-versus-production comparison

12.2   SPECIFICATION

The project specification is the rock on which the enterprise is built. As such it should be treated with the same respect afforded to the foundation of any building.

The product request will normally originate either from the customer or as a projected need from marketing personnel. Unless the objective is the exact replacement of a product already on the market, such a request is likely to be couched in vague generalities, with little beyond a list of desirable functions and constraints. The obvious boundary constraints will be financial as well as technical, but other concerns may well involve complying with legal requirements, e.g., safety regulations, and dealing with outside bodies, such as telecommunications utilities.

In essence, the design team must tease as much information as possible from the originator, take away the request and return with a set of proposals. This will involve consideration of the following questions:

What is it to do?
Is it possible?
How is it to be done?
Can the request be modified?

The outcome of this soul-searching is communicated to the customer, and after several iterations through the loop a concrete system specification will emerge, provided that the project is thought to be viable. It is important that the specification be decided at this point, not least to avoid the phenomena of 'creeping featurism'. This document will be used as the basis of a detailed hardware and software development; culminating in a full working prototype.

With this discussion in mind, let us begin the process with the specification on which our project is to be based. The customer has asked us to construct an annunciator displaying both time and temperature. This is to be a desk-top version of the giant display time/temperature annunciators seen at shopping malls in USA.

After some debate, the following prototype specification was settled.

I	Facilities	: Display of either time only or time alternating with temperature at regular intervals
II	Temperature range	: $-10°C$ to $+50°C$
III	Temperature accuracy	: $\pm 2\%$ of reading or $\pm 1°C$, whichever is the larger
IV	Temperature resolution	: Whole degrees
V	Temperature format	: Degrees Fahrenheit or Celsius (Centigrade)
VI	Time accuracy	: ± 1 minute per month
VII	Time resolution	: Whole seconds
VIII	Time format	: 12- and 24-hour
IX	Power	: Mains 110 Vac 60 Hz/240 Vac 50 Hz
X	Ergonomics	: Front panel switch selection of time and temperature formats and time-set; readout to be capable of being read in poor light
XI	Production	: Large scale

We are going to design and construct a full working implementation of this specification in the remainder of the book. Such a functional prototype is necessary to enable hardware and software action to be monitored, to deal with any residual design malfunction and, just as importantly, to demonstrate a working system to the customer. With customer approval, and this may involve several major design modifications, the design for production can commence.

Setting up an electronic production line is expensive, and the alternative of subcontracting all or part of this activity is one of the major design decisions which will be taken at this point. With the assumption of in-house manufacture, the next stage is the construction of several preproduction prototypes. In making a few units, as if for sale, the production team will be verifying that the system can be economically built on an assembly line. Electronic devices are relatively standard, but mechanical components such as printed-circuit boards, switches, connectors, case and artwork are somewhat variable. Decisions must be made regarding method of construction, second-sourcing of components, stock levels and even down to whether to use sockets for the integrated circuits. Just as important, but often overlooked, is how and when to test components, subsystems and the final product.

Setting up a production line will involve extensive documentation, following on from the paperwork produced by the design team. Initially a preproduction schedule will be prepared, which will include component lists, circuit diagrams, physical and interconnection specifications and printed-circuit board details.

The production literature covers assembly details and wiring patterns. In some cases programs for computer-aided manufacture (CAM) facilities will be covered under this heading. Included in this category is the testing documentation. This may be either a tester's manual or software for automatic test equipment (ATE).

Postproduction documentation covers service manuals and of course the user's handbook. The quality of this material will often add considerably to the satisfaction of the customer, which (hopefully) will eventually increase the reputation of the manufacturer and further sales.

But enough of this background, let us get stuck into the design of our MCU-based annunciator!

13

The Hard Reality

The underlying reality of a microprocessor-oriented system is its hardware infrastructure. This will normally consist of address-decoding, memory, interface and peripheral circuitry. Although the high level of function integration exhibited by the MCU somewhat reduces the hardware engineer's burden, the problem of peripheral design and matching still remains.

In this chapter we develop the hardware necessary to implement the specification outlined in Section 12.2, based on the 68705R3 MCU.

13.1   THE MCU SYSTEM

The integration of the 68705R3 MCU with its supporting hardware, excluding the temperature transducer, is shown in Fig. 13.1. The system is powered from a single 5 V supply rated at 200 mA. Of this, the unloaded MCU takes approximately 120 mA.

The MCU's internal oscillator is regulated by a 3.2768 MHz crystal, giving a CPU clock frequency of 819.2 kHz. This seemingly odd value when divided by 2^{15} gives a period of 10 ms, which is used in Section 17.1 as the fundamental period for the real-time clock.

An automatic power-on reset is provided by tying $\overline{\text{Reset}}$ (Pin 2) to ground with a 2.2 μF capacitor, as described in Section 7.2. A manual reset is obtained by paralleling this capacitor with a switch.

As the timer and two interrupt inputs are not used in this application, they are disabled by being pulled up to 5 V. Analog channels AN1,2,3 are similarly unused, and they are connected to zero potential.

From the specification outlined in Section 12.2, it is possible to isolate 12 distinct submodes of operation thus:

I   Time only; 24-hour format
II   Time only; 12-hour format
III   Time/temperature alternate; 24-hour/°C formats
IV   Time/temperature alternate; 12-hour/°C formats

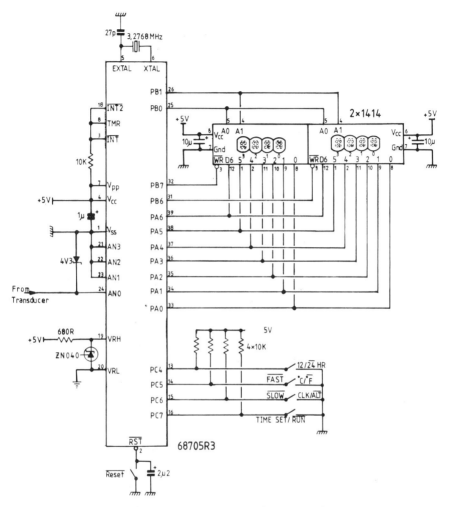

Fig. 13.1   The annunciator, excluding transducer

V	Time/temperature alternate; 24-hour/°F formats
VI	Time/temperature alternate; 12-hour/°F formats
VII	Time-set, normal; 12-hour format
VIII	Time-set, normal; 24-hour format
IX	Time-set, slow; 12-hour format
X	Time-set, slow; 24-hour format
XI	Time-set, fast; 12-hour format
XII	Time-set, fast; 24-hour format

The actual submode is chosen by setting the appropriate pattern of four switches driving the upper bits of Port C. Switch 7 (i.e., connected to PC7) selects between the two major operating modes viz., normal (I to VI) and time-set. Switch 4

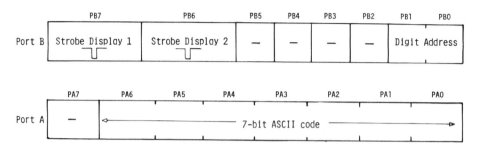

Fig. 13.2   How Ports A and B relate to the 8-digit readout

always chooses between the 24-hour and 12-hour time formats. The function of switches 6 and 5 depends on the major mode selected. Switch 6 selects between either the alternate or time-only routines when normally running and slow ($\times 25$) increment in the time-set modes. Similarly Switch 5 provides choice between Celsius and Fahrenheit temperature scales, or gives a fast ($\times 1{,}500$) time increment.

One of the distinctive attributes of MCU-based systems, is the reduction in chip count. To complement this property, two 4-digit intelligent displays have been

5314
ZN REF 040 (283-520)
Temperature dependant electrical characteristics

Parameter	Symbol	Min.	Max.	Units
Output voltage change over operating temperature range (see note 1)	ΔV_{OT}	4.2	14	mV
Output voltage temperature coefficient (see note 2)	TCV_O	15	50	ppm/°C

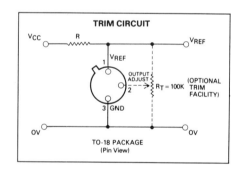

Electrical characteristics

$T_A = 25°C$ and pin 2 open circuit unless otherwise stated (Load should be less than 220pF or greater than 22nF).

Parameter	Symbol	Conditions	Min.	Typ.	Max.	Units
Output voltage	V_O	$I_{REF} = 500\mu A$	3.970	4.010	4.050	V
Output voltage adjustment range	V_{OR}	$R_T = 100k\Omega$	—	±5	—	%
Change in TCV_O with output adjustment	TCV_{OR}		—	0.8	—	ppm/°C/%
Turn on or 'Knee' current	I_{ON}	Over full temperature range	—	120	150	μA
Operating current range	I_{REF}	See note 3	0.15	—	75	mA
Turn on settling time to within 0.1% of V_O	t_{ON}	Overshoot typically less than 1%	—	5.0	—	$\mu sec.$
Output voltage noise (over the range 0.1Hz-10Hz)	e_{np-p}	Peak to peak measurement	—	50	—	μV
Dynamic impedance	R_D	I_{REF} 0.5mA-5mA See note 4 and 5	—	2.0	3.0	Ω

Fig. 13.3   The ZN REF040 voltage reference (reproduced by courtesy of RS Components Limited and Ferranti Electronics plc)

chosen as the output peripheral (Hewlett Packard HPDL1414 or Intersil ICL1414). This gives the eight digits necessary to display hours, minutes and seconds, together with their separators. Each 1414 display comprises four 16-segment LED digits, with integral RAM, ASCII to 16-segment decoder and drivers, all in a 17.5×20 mm (0.7×0.8 inch) 12-pin DIL package. To write data into digit RAM, a 2-bit digit address is presented to A_0A_1 together with the 6-bit ASCII code to the data inputs D_0-D_6. This data code is latched in to the addressed RAM area by pulsing $\overline{\text{Write}}$ ($\overline{\text{WR}}$, Pin 3) low. Thus to display the character A at digit 3 we place the ASCII code for A (%1000001) on the data bus, %11 on the address bus, and pulse $\overline{\text{WR}}$ low. Full details, together with the character set are given in Appendix 3. Note especially the recommended 5 V decoupling requirement, also shown in Fig. 13.1.

In our configuration of Fig. 13.1, we have used six lines from Port A (PA0–PA6) to provide the ASCII code for the two paralleled 1414 displays. The 2-bit digit address is likewise provided by the two lower Port B bits PB0 and PB1. Port B line 6 is used to pulse the least significant 1414 display's $\overline{\text{Write}}$, while line 7 carries out the same function for the most significant group of four digits. This arrangement is summarized in Fig. 13.2.

The temperature transducer provides an analog voltage which is a linear function of that variable. Connected to analog channel 0 (Pin 24), the MCU will see this voltage as zero if it is at the lower reference potential (V_{RL}, Pin 20) and full scale ($FF) if at the higher reference (V_{RH}, Pin 19). A 4.3 V zener diode at this point provides some over- and reverse-voltage protection. V_{RH} should preferably not be

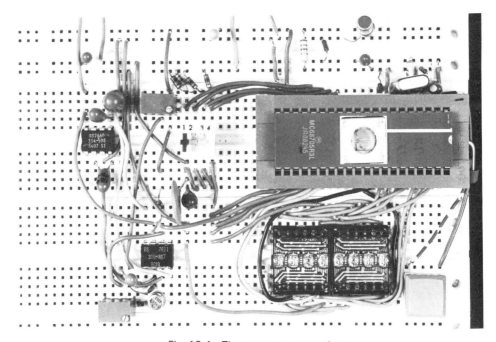

Fig. 13.4 The prototype annunciator

the 5 V logic supply: neither V_{RH} nor V_{RL} should lie outside the range V_{CC} to V_{SS}, and $V_{RH}-V_{RL}$ should not be less than $+4$ V.

In Fig. 13.1 a precision reference ZN040 IC is used to derive an accurate low-noise 4 V source for V_{RH}. As can be seen from Fig. 13.3, a series limiter resistor is interposed between the unregulated supply (5 V in this case) and the ZN040. This must limit the current to around 1 mA (0.5 mA bias for the ZN040, 0.25 mA for V_{RH} and 0.25 mA to the transducer). A 680Ω resistor provides approximately 1.5 mA, which gives some safety margin against V_{CC} fluctuations. A full scale voltage range of 4 volts gives an equivalence of $4/255 = 15.686$ mV for the least significant bit (LSB). If a 4 V reference IC is not available, a 3.9 V 300 mW zener diode is an acceptable alternative. A 180Ω series resistor should be used in this case.

We do a detail design exercise for the temperature transducer in Section 13.2, and Fig. 13.4 shows the complete prototype circuit.

13.2   MEASURING TEMPERATURE

There are several electrical properties of materials which are affected by temperature and are, therefore, useful in the measurement of that quantity. For example, the thermistor depends on resistance variation. Probably the most common phenomenon used for this purpose is the variation of the contact potential between dissimilar metals. However, such thermocouples require considerable coaxing to yield a linear analog signal suitable for further processing. Within a limited temperature range of typically $-50°C$ to $+150°C$ ($-60°F$ to $+300°F$), silicon sensors have many advantages. These devices are usually based on the temperature dependence of the leakage current across the junction of two differently doped semiconductor regions. The Intersil AD590 sensor, shown in Fig. 13.5, gives a current output scaled to 1 μA per degree absolute (Kelvin). The absolute scale is zero at $-273°C$ but has an incremental value of $1°C$. Thus a current of 273 μA indicates $0°C$; and our specified range of $-10°C$ to $+50°C$ equates to $263°K-323°K$ (μA).

The AD590 is available in several packages and accuracy selections. The AD590KH is linear to $±2°C$ (if trimmed to zero error at $25°C$) over the range $-55°C$ to $150°C$ and has a $±2.5°C$ calibration error. As can be seen from Fig. 13.5, the sensor is typically housed in a metal-can transistor package, of 5 mm diameter. To external circuitry the AD590 behaves like a 2-lead current source, provided that a potential difference of between 4 and 30 V is applied across the device. The third leg of a TO-52 packaged device is part of the metal case. Connecting this to local ground reduces noise pickup, but at the expense of an increased thermal mass.

An examination of the RS/AD590 data sheet of Appendix 4, especially Figs. 2, 3 and 4B, shows that over the restricted temperature range of $-10°C$ to $+50°C$, the specified error of $±1°C$ is readily achievable. However, some scale and offset adjustment will be required.

As we have seen in Section 13.1, the analog port accepts a voltage range from 0 to 4 V only. Given that our sensor provides an output from 263 to 323 μA, it is obvious that some analog processing is necessary. Two tasks need implementing.

AD590
Temperature Transducer

FEATURES

- **Linear current output: 1 µA/°K**
- **Wide range: −55°C to +150°C**
- **Two-terminal device: Voltage in/current out**
- **Laser trimmed to ±0.5°C calibration accuracy (AD590M)**
- **Excellent linearity: ±0.5°C over full range (AD590M)**
- **Wide power supply range: +4V to +30V**
- **Sensor isolation from case**
- **Low cost**

GENERAL DESCRIPTION

The AD590 is an integrated-circuit temperature transducer which produces an output current proportional to absolute temperature. The device acts as a high impedance constant current regulator, passing $1 \mu A/°K$ for supply voltages between +4V and +30V. Laser trimming of the chip's thin film resistors is used to calibrate the device to $298.2 \mu A$ output at $298.2°K$ (+25°C).

The AD590 should be used in any temperature-sensing application between −55°C and +150°C (0°C and 70°C for TO-92).

in which conventional electrical temperature sensors are currently employed. The inherent low cost of a monolithic integrated circuit combined with the elimination of support circuitry makes the AD590 an attractive alternative for many temperature measurement situations. Linearization circuitry, precision voltage amplifiers, resistance-measuring circuitry and cold-junction compensation are not needed in applying the AD590. In the simplest application, a resistor, a power source and any voltmeter can be used to measure temperature.

In addition to temperature measurement, applications include temperature compensation or correction of discrete components, and biasing proportional to absolute temperature. The AD590 is available in chip form making it suitable for hybrid circuits and fast temperature measurements in protected environments.

The AD590 is particularly useful in remote sensing applications. The device is insensitive to voltage drops over long lines due to its high-impedance current output. Any well-insulated twisted pair is sufficient for operation hundreds of feet from the receiving circuitry. The output characteristics also make the AD590 easy to multiplex: the current can be switched by a CMOS multiplexer or the supply voltage can be switched by a logic gate output.

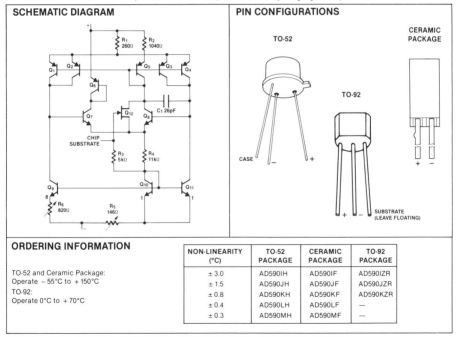

SCHEMATIC DIAGRAM

PIN CONFIGURATIONS

ORDERING INFORMATION

TO-52 and Ceramic Package:
Operate −55°C to +150°C
TO-92:
Operate 0°C to +70°C

NON-LINEARITY (°C)	TO-52 PACKAGE	CERAMIC PACKAGE	TO-92 PACKAGE
±3.0	AD590IH	AD590IF	AD590IZR
±1.5	AD590JH	AD590JF	AD590JZR
±0.8	AD590KH	AD590KF	AD590KZR
±0.4	AD590LH	AD590LF	—
±0.3	AD590MH	AD590MF	—

Fig. 13.5   The AD590 silicon temperature sensor (reproduced by courtesy of Intersil Inc.)

Firstly, the range of 60 μA must be scaled to a voltage range of 4 V. Secondly, 0 V must represent the bottom of the temperature range, which implies that an offset of −263 μA must be added to the sensor output.

Both offset and scaling functions are performed by the circuit shown in Fig. 13.6 (see also Appendix 4, Fig. 4A). This is based around an operational amplifier connected in a standard summing mode. With the noninverting input (Pin 3) connected to ground, the inverting mode will be at 0 V potential (virtual earth). If we assume a constant offset current i_0, then it is clear that any change in sensor current Δi_T will be reflected through the scale (feedback) resistor R_S; thus:

$$\Delta i_T = \Delta i_S$$

As the summing end of R_S is at zero potential, this change in current gives a corresponding change in output voltage (Pin 6) of:

$$\Delta v_T = \Delta i_S R_S = \Delta i_T R_S$$

Now our temperature range covers a span of 60°C, and with a resolution of one part in 255 (for an 8-bit converter), we can for convenience equate the least significant bit to $\frac{1}{4}$°C. As the LSB is worth 15.686 mV (see Section 13.1), 1 μA must scale to 4×15.686 mV (62.75 mV). This gives:

$$R_S = \frac{\Delta v_T}{\Delta i_T} = \frac{62.75 \times 10^{-3}}{10^{-6}} \simeq 62 \text{ k}\Omega$$

Choosing a fixed 56 kΩ resistor with a 10 kΩ potentiometer gives sufficient adjustment to trim out sensor error and resistor tolerances. For best results a multiturn trimming potentiometer should be used.

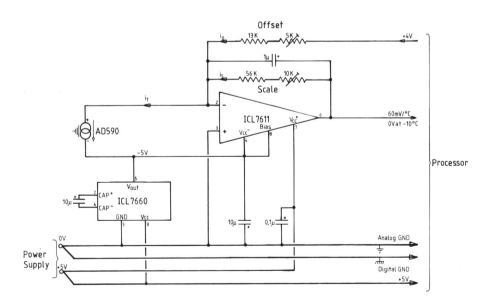

Fig. 13.6   The temperature transducer

At $-10°C$ we require v_T to be zero. As the sensor will be sinking approximately 263 μA from the summing node at this temperature, the offset resistor must supply the same current to the node, in order to balance this out. Making use of the fixed 4 V reference source of Fig. 13.1 gives a value for R_0 thus:

$$R_0 = \frac{4}{263 \times 10^{-6}} \approx 15 \text{ k}\Omega$$

This we implement with a 13 kΩ resistor in series with a 5 kΩ multiturn potentiometer.

Both the operational amplifier and temperature source require a negative bias voltage. This is conveniently generated using an Intersil ICL7660 d.c. inverter chip to provide a nominal -5 V from the $+5$ V logic supply. This latter is also used as the positive supply for the operational amplifier. To reduce noise, both the positive and ground rails should be kept separate from the digital circuitry, returning to common points at the power supply. The resulting digital and analog grounds are distinguished in Figs. 13.1 and 13.6 by the symbols $\frac{\text{\tiny I}}{\text{\tiny /////}}$ and $\frac{\text{\tiny I}}{=}$ respectively. Also the positive and negative rails should be decoupled with tantalum capacitors as near to the operational amplifier as possible.

Most bipolar or FET operational amplifiers powered from ± 5 V rails can produce only a swing of approximately ± 3.5 V before saturating. As the A/D converter range is 0 to 4 V, corresponding with $-10°C$ to $+63.75°C$, we have specified a CMOS operational amplifier in Fig. 13.6. The Intersil ICL7611 can swing to within millivolts of the supply. The Texas Instruments TLC271 is a pin-compatible alternative.

When the circuit is constructed, the output voltage should lie between one and two volts, and should rise when the sensor is warmed (e.g., with your finger). There is little point in calibrating the transducer at this point in the development cycle; it is best left until the system is complete (see Section 18.1).

If the transducer output is saturated positively, you can suspect the R_0 circuit, and if negatively the sensor (check the polarity connections of the latter). An amplifier problem is indicated if the inverting node is not at zero potential. Assuming that this is not the case, a microammeter connected in series with the sensor or R_0 will quickly isolate the problem. Both power rails should be investigated, particularly the -5 V supply derived from the 7660 inverter, which acts as an excellent oscillator if not decoupled as shown!

14

We Go Looking for Trouble

We are approaching microprocessor design in this text as a serial hardware and software exercise, whereas they are normally parallel tasks undertaken as a team effort. The software 'circuits' will usually have been put together on a microprocessor development system (MDS), where at least a partial verification of correct operation has taken place. Hardware circuitry may have been simulated using a computer-aided (CAD) package, but will in any case probably have ended up as prototype on a breadboard. System integration involves the bringing together of these two separate components with the aim of checking for a successful hardware/software interaction.

It is possible to identify two phases in the system integration process. The first of these involves the verification of the hardware integrity. Without the reassurance of a fully working hardware environment, the second phase of this process, viz., the testing of the system software, cannot be undertaken with any degree of confidence.

In practice very little more than d.c. and continuity tests can be performed on hardware as it stands. Thus without software the only significant check that can be carried out on the MCU of Fig. 13.1 is the action of the reset switch, continuity between ports and peripherals, and the operation of the internal oscillator (using an oscilloscope EXTAL should exhibit a distorted sinusoid of between approximately 0.2 and 1.2 V, and XTAL between 0.4 and 1.6 V, both at the ϕ_2 frequency).

In order to isolate the testing of the hardware and the system software, it is necessary to introduce a package of programs specifically designed to exercise fully the various modules. This diagnostic package should be kept as simple as possible to eliminate the possibility of software errors masking hardware problems. Such a package is primarily aimed at checking the surrounding support circuitry, and not the MCU's component parts, although by implication this must partially be the case. The self-test ROM, which replaces the bootstrap ROM in mask-programmed 6805s (see Section 11.1) is an example of an internal-check diagnostic package.

The question remains of how to transport the diagnostic software to the hardware environment. If you have access to a suitable in-circuit emulator (ICE), then the software will run in RAM on your MDS, and the target hardware will be simply treated as an adjunct to the development system. If you are designing your own software, rather than using an already verified package (as you are doing here), then this approach permits you to use the full armory of debugging facilities of the MDS on your target hardware. Nevertheless, in the last analysis the ICE is never quite the same as the real thing. Thus burning the software into the MCU's EPROM should always be the final test (and is of course the only way if an ICE is not available). This procedure also implicitly checks the veracity of your MCU EPROM programmer. Once successfully programmed, the diagnostic 68705 may be kept, and inserted in place of the system 6805 any subsequent time the integrity of the hardware is to be confirmed.

In the context of Fig. 13.1, we primarily require to test the display peripheral devices, and both switch and analog ports. The system flowchart of Fig. 14.1 outlines the tasks which must be undertaken by the package. Two routines are shown, as selected by the switch connected to PC7, where either the switch or analog ports are exercised. Both routines make use of, and thus implicitly test, the

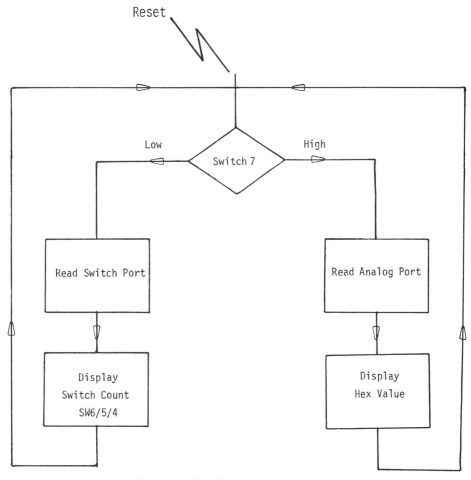

Fig. 14.1   The diagnostic system flowchart

display devices. The rest of the chapter develops the implementing software, and looks at the results.

14.1   DISPLAY HANDLER

The 8-digit display peripheral is our only window into the MCU. Therefore the software interaction to this port is of prime importance. The simplest action targets a single character to one display digit. Referring back to Fig. 13.2, we see that this is accomplished by placing the relevant ASCII code in Port A, digit address 0 to 3 in Port B's lower two bits, and pulsing either bit PB6 for digits 0 to 3 or PB7 for digits 4 to 7. Thus, e.g., to place the character 9 in digit 5 involves the following steps:

```
LDA    #$39          : ASCII for 9 is $39
STA    00            : Send it to Port A (the display port) at $00
LDA    #%11000001    : Address 01 is digit 5 in the upper display
STA    01            : Send it to Port B (the digit port) at $01
BCLR   7,01          : Force bit PB7 low
BSET   7,01          : and then high, to strobe the upper display
```

Clearly the foregoing procedure can be used as many times as necessary to build up any message of not more than eight digits. However, this strategy is wasteful of scarce EPROM space. A more efficient approach uses a display handler subroutine which can be called up at any time by the main program. Such a subroutine should be capable of handling strings of ASCII-coded characters stored either in EPROM for fixed messages (see Listing 14.1(c)) or RAM for variable messages. The calling program need only tell the subroutine where the string is stored.

In the algorithm illustrated in Fig. 14.2, the calling program passes the start address of the string to the subroutine in the 8-bit index register. This means that the string must either be in RAM ($010–$05F) or in EPROM between $080 and $0FF. The subroutine (named PDATA for Print DATA) simply extracts each digit in turn from the string and sends it to the display, moving from left to right. The digit address N is decremented on each pass of the loop. Two ASCII codes are used as nonprintable control characters. The null code ($00) signifies a one-digit skip (decrement address only), and the end-of-transmission (EOT) code ($04) is used to terminate the message prematurely. Normally the subroutine automatically exits after the eighth digit.

As an example, consider displaying the left justified message SWITCH . This is represented by the ASCII-coded string $53; 57; 49; 54; 43; 48; 20; 04, which is stored in EPROM as constant data pertinent to the program. If the first character of the string (S = $53) is located at $087, then the index register must be set to $87 prior to jumping to PDATA.

Listing 14.1(b) shows the minutiae of the subroutine. This closely follows the algorithm outlined in Fig. 14.2, and the line numbers on that diagram refer to this

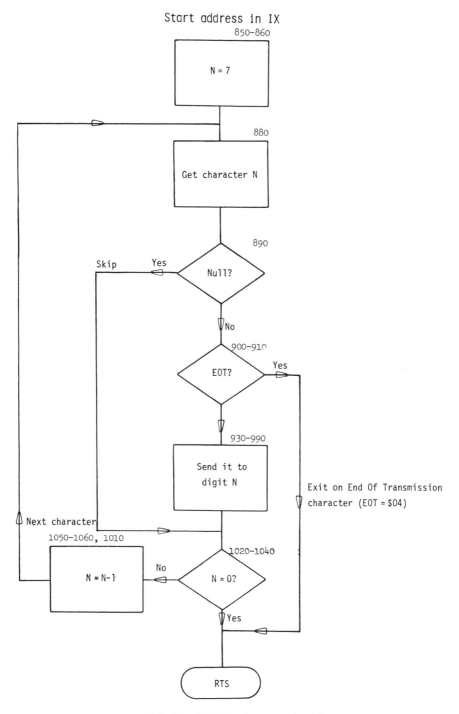

Fig. 14.2   The PDATA subroutine algorithm

(*a*) Peripheral map

```
10      <0000>  DISPLAY EQU   $000      *Port A = Display port
20      <0001>  DIGIT   EQU   $001      *Port B addresses 4 digits in each of 2 nybbles n2n1xxxd4d2d1
30      <0002>  SWITCH  EQU   $002      *Port C = Switch port
40      <0004>  DDRA    EQU   $004      *Data Direction register A
50      <0005>  DDRB    EQU   $005      *Data Direction register B
60      <0008>  TIMER   EQU   $008      *Timer Data Counter
70      <0009>  TIMCTRL EQU   $009      *Timer Control register
80      <000E>  ANCTRL  EQU   $00E      *Analog Control register
90      <000F>  ANALOG  EQU   $00F      *Analog Data register
```

(*b*) PDATA subroutine

```
740  *************************************************************************
750  *Name      : PDATA ($E00)
760  *Function  : Prints out string of up to 8 characters
770  *Entry     : IX points to 1st character
780  *Exit      : IX points to last character; A destroyed
790  *Note 1    : String must be terminated by EOT (=4)
800  *Note 2    : NULL (=0) leaves existing character unchanged
810  *Note 3    : String starts at leftmost digit (digit 7)
820  *************************************************************************
830  *
840      <0E00>          ORG    $E00
850  0E00 A6-C7   PDATA   LDA    #%11000111    *Address MSD digit (7=111)
860  0E02 B7-01           STA    DIGIT
870  *
880  0E04 F6      GETIT   LDA    0,X           *Get character from string
890  0E05 27-13           BEQ    NEXTDIG       *IF a null THEN move on
900  0E07 A1-04           CMP    #4            *IF EOT THEN end of string
910  0E09 27-1A           BEQ    XPDATA
920  *Enter this segment only if a printable character
930  0E0B B7-00           STA    DISPLAY       *Send it to the Display port
940  0E0D 05-0106         BRCLR  2,DIGIT,LSDISP *IF digit address <4 THEN lower digit
950  0E10 1F-01           BCLR   7,DIGIT       *ELSE pulse upper display's Strobe
960  0E12 1E-01           BSET   7,DIGIT       *(ie bit7 of port B)
970  0E14 20-04           BRA    NEXTDIG       *and so to the next character
980  0E16 1D-01   LSDISP  BCLR   6,DIGIT       *Pulse lower display
990  0E18 1C-01           BSET   6,DIGIT       *(ie bit6 of port B)
1000 *
1010 0E1A 5C      NEXTDIG INCX                 *Move on character pointer
1020 0E1B B6-01           LDA    DIGIT         *Now check for an overlong string
1030 0E1D A1-C0           CMP    #%11000000    *ie have we just printed to digit0?
1040 0E1F 27-04           BEQ    XPDATA        *IF so THEN time to go
1050 0E21 3A-01           DEC    DIGIT         *ELSE decrement digit address
1060 0E23 20-DF           BRA    GETIT         *and go again
1070 0E25 81      XPDATA  RTS                  *Subroutine exit
1080 *
```

Listing 14.1   Display interface software

(c) Program constants

```
1100 *
1110 *Strings
1120 *
1130      (0080)          ORG    $080
1140 0080 412F443D2024
                 STRG1    FCC    'A/D= $'
1150 0086 04
                          FCB    4
1160 0087 53574954434820
                 STRG2    FCC    'SWITCH '
1170 008E 04
                          FCB    4
1180 *
1190 *Reset vector
1200 *
1210      (0FFE)          ORG    $FFE
1220 0FFE 0A00
                 RESET    FDB    $A00         *Program starts at $A00
1230 *
```

Listing 14.1   Display interface software   (*continued*)

listing. The character subscript N is conveniently stored as the three lower bits in Port B, and in Lines 850 and 860 is set to 7. Only bits PB1 and 0 physically address digits in the display (see Fig. 13.2), but bit PB2 can be tested (branch if bit 2 of Port B is 0, Line 940) to decide which group of four digits is to be accessed. Lines 950 and 960 strobe the upper group (PB2 = 1), while 980 and 990 operate on the lower group (PB2 = 0).

On each pass through the loop the index register is incremented (Line 1010), and N decremented (Line 1050). The subroutine terminates when N reaches zero (Lines 1030 and 1040) or the character EOT is picked out of the string (Lines 900 and 910). A NULL character causes a jump over the display-strobe routine (Line 890).

Listing 14.1(c) defines the constants used by the diagnostic software and stored in EPROM. These are chiefly two strings of alpha characters located from $080 to $08F. These strings are compatible with subroutines PDATA. Notice how the pseudo operator *form constant character* (FCC) is used to locate and define printable ASCII characters. This is more convenient than using FCB (see Listing 9.2) which necessitates the manual looking up of character codes. FCC requires that the string be delimited at start and finish by identical characters (single quotes in Lines 1140 and 1160). The EOT control character is nonprintable, and is therefore added to the strings using FCB in Lines 1150 and 1170. Two strings (STRG1 at $080 and STRG2 at $087) are defined, and these are used in the routines described in the following sections.

Also defined in Listing 14.1(c) is the contents of the reset vector, $FFE/F. These two locations at the top of EPROM must be programmed to reflect the entry point of the program $0A00 (see Listing 14.2(a), Line 130). This is done on Lines 1210 and 1220, where the pseudo operator *form double byte* (FDB) conveniently defines the two-byte address. FDB is simply the dual-byte version of FCB.

14.2   CHECKING THE SWITCHES

The main program commences by configuring Ports A and B as outputs (the display ports), Lines 160–180 of Listing 14.2(a). The switch port (Port C) is not specifically set up as all parallel ports are initialized as input at reset. The state of switch PC7 is then used to determine which of the two test routines is to be executed, Line 200. With the assumption that switch PC7 is logic 1, the switch-test module of Listing 14.2(b) is entered. The objective of this routine is to display the message SWITCH n, where n is a decimal digit representing the state of the switches PC6 PC5 PC4. The state of PC7 has been implicitly tested in Line 200. This is done by first printing the message SWITCH (Lines 230 and 240) and then reading the switch port in Line 250. As the switches are physically connected to the upper four bits of Port C (see Fig. 13.1), we shift this data four times right and clear the five leftmost bits (Lines 260–300).

With the right-justified binary number n representing the state of the three lower switches in the accumulator, we next need to convert to its ASCII equivalent. This is done in Line 310 by making the upper nybble three, e.g., $07 (%00000111) becomes $37 (%00110111). The actual display of n is accomplished by sending the contents of the accumulator to the display port (Line 320), addressing digit 0 (Lines 330 and 340) and then strobing the lower group of three digits (Lines 350 and 360).

(a) Peripheral initialization

```
110  *This is the diagnostic software, consisting of two modules
120  *
130      <0A00>        ORG    $A00
140  *First set up the PIAs
150  *
160  0A00 A6-FF        LDA    #%11111111
170  0A02 B7-04        STA    DDRA         *Ports A & B are to be outputs
180  0A04 B7-05        STA    DDRB
190  *
200  0A06 0F-021B ROUTE BRCLR 7,SWITCH,ANTEST *IF switch7 = 0 THEN analog test module
```

(b) Switch-test module

```
220  *The first module checks the switches and display hardware
230  0A09 AE-87        LDX    #STRG2        *Prepare to print out the message 'Switch'
240  0A0B CD-0E00      JSR    PDATA
250  0A0E B6-02        LDA    SWITCH        *Get settings SW7 SW6 SW5 SW4
260  0A10 44           LSRA                 *Align to
270  0A11 44           LSRA                 *0000SW7 SW6 SW5 SW4
280  0A12 44           LSRA
290  0A13 44           LSRA                 *Prepare to clear bit3
300  0A14 A4-F7        AND    #%11110111    *giving 00000SW6 SW5 SW4
310  0A16 AB-30        ADD    #$30          *and convert to ASCII
320  0A18 B7-00        STA    DISPLAY       *Send out to Display port
330  0A1A A6-C0        LDA    #%11000000    *Address digit 00
340  0A1C B7-01        STA    DIGIT
350  0A1E 1D-01        BCLR   6,DIGIT       *and pulse bit6
360  0A20 1C-01        BSET   6,DIGIT       *ie the lower display strobe
370  0A22 20-E2        BRA    ROUTE         *Start all over again
```

Listing 14.2   Checking out the switches

14.3   AND THE ANALOG PORT

When switch PC7 is zero, the analog-port test routine will be exercised, Lines 410–710 in Listing 14.3. The objective of this module is to print out the message A/D = $hh, where hh is the 2-digit hexadecimal equivalent of the analog signal present at AN0, see Fig. 14.3(b).

Listing 14.3 shows the implementation of this objective. Essentially two subtasks can be identified. The first of these reads the analog port. During reset the A/D control register at $00E (see Fig. 8.6) is cleared. This points the analog multiplexer to input channel 0, which is the channel of interest here. In its normal mode of operation, the A/D converter will free-run, and the digital equivalent can be read at any time at $00F. With this in mind, the A/D control register does not require any manipulation after reset, and Line 430 simply brings the analog equivalent down into the accumulator for processing. As the free-running nature of the A/D converter will lead to a continually changing value in the A/D result register ($00F), the value at this point is kept conveniently in the index register (Line 440), from which it can be retrieved at any time subsequently.

```
390  *The second module checks the analog port
400  *
410  0A24 AE-80   ANTEST  LDX   #STRG1        *Prepare to print out
420  0A26 CD-0E00         JSR   PDATA         *message 'A/D= $'
430  0A29 B6-0F           LDA   ANALOG        *Get analog data
440  0A2B 97              TAX                 *Put it in IX for safekeeping
450  0A2C 44              LSRA                *Move upper nybble
460  0A2D 44              LSRA                *over to lower nybble position
470  0A2E 44              LSRA                *(eg F3 becomes 03)
480  0A2F 44              LSRA                *Lower digit lost
490  0A30 AB-30           ADD   #$30          *Start conversion to ASCII
500  0A32 A1-39           CMP   #$39          Is it >9? (eg 0F becomes 3F)
510  0A34 23-02           BLS   DISMSB        IF not THEN display it
520  0A36 AB-07           ADD   #7            *ELSE correct ASCII conversion
530  *(eg 3F becomes 46 = ASCII for F)
540  0A38 B7-00   DISMSB  STA   DISPLAY       *Send out ASCII MSB
550  0A3A A6-C1           LDA   #%11000001    *Address digit 1
560  0A3C B7-01           STA   DIGIT
570  0A3E 1D-01           BCLR  6,DIGIT       *Pulse upper digit
580  0A40 1C-01           BSET  6,DIGIT
590  *Now process lower nybble
600  0A42 9F              TXA                 *Retreive data from IX (see line 290)
610  0A43 A4-0F           AND   #%00001111    *Null upper byte
620  0A45 AB-30           ADD   #$30          *Start to convert to ASCII
630  0A47 A1-39           CMP   #$39          *Is it >9?
640  0A49 23-02           BLS   DISLSB        *IF not THEN OK
650  0A4B AB-07           ADD   #7            *ELSE correct
660  0A4D B7-00   DISLSB  STA   DISPLAY       *Send out ASCII LSB
670  0A4F A6-C0           LDA   #%11000000    *Address digit0
680  0A51 B7-01           STA   DIGIT
690  0A53 1D-01           BCLR  6,DIGIT       *Pulse upper digit
700  0A55 1C-01           BSET  6,DIGIT
710  0A57 20-AD           BRA   ROUTE
```

Listing 14.3   Checking the analog port

The second task involves the dismemberment of the 8-bit binary value in the accumulator into two 7-bit ASCII characters. Thus %11100110 ($E6) must be transformed into %1000101 + %0110110 ($45 + $36). The transformation algorithm mapping a single nybble to a ASCII-coded digit is:

For nybble values 0−9 (%0000−1001) add $30.
For nybble values A−F (%1010−1111) add $37.

We have already met the $30 conversion factor for decimal digits in Listing 14.2. The hexadecimal alpha digits A−F must transform to $41−46 for ASCII. As for decimal-digit conversion, the factor is linear, but this time is $37.

In Listing 14.3, this transformation is carried out twice. Initially the upper nybble is isolated by shifting the data four time right, Lines 450−480. The conversion factor $30 is then added, Line 490. If the nybble was above 9, then the value at this point will be above $39, and a further correction of seven is added, Lines 500−520. The resulting ASCII code is then sent to digit 1 in display 0, Lines 540−580.

Finally the transformation is repeated on the the lower nybble of the data, which is retrieved from the index register in Line 600. This nybble is isolated by clearing the upper four bits, Line 610. Thereafter the correction and display is carried out in an identical fashion, except that digit 0 in display 0 is the target, Lines 620−700.

14.4   ALL TOGETHER

Given the software developed in this section, we will of course need to program a blank 68705R3 MCU in the manner described in Chapter 10. In fact the example illustrated in Listing 10.3 gives a complete machine code compilation for this diagnostic package. However, the hexadecimal dump of Listing 14.4 gives a more graphic relationship of the machine code to the memory structure of the MCU. This was generated using a slightly modified version of Listing 10.1, Lines 4000−4770.

Noting that the erased MCU EPROM state is $00 (normal EPROMS erase to $FF), we can see that the diagnostic package occupies only a tiny proportion of available program memory. Because of this, we are going to include this code along with the system-proper software; which in any case uses the subroutine PDATA. We will evoke this resident diagnostic facility by using some unspecified combination of the option switches of Fig. 13.1; but more of this later.

One final point for discussion concerning Listing 14.4 relates to the mask option register (MOR). You will remember (Fig. 7.2) that the MOR deals with the clock oscillator configuration and timer control. We have not made use of the timer for the diagnostic package, but the oscillator must be set up in the crystal mode, i.e., bit MOR7 = 0. In this situation we have simply left MOR ($F38) in its erased state, and this is recorded in Listing 14.4 as unprogrammed. None of the interrupt vectors has been programmed, except reset (($FFE/F) = $0A00).

Once the 68705R3 has been programmed, it should be inserted into its socket (Fig. 13.1) and power applied. Both (a) and (b) of Fig. 14.3 show typical displays,

```
User EPROM:-
<080> 41 2F 44 3D 20 24 04 53 57 49 54 43 48 20 04 00 00 00 00 00 00 00 00 00 00 00 00 00 00 00 00 00    ← Strings
<0A0> 00 00 00 00 00 00 00 00 00 00 00 00 00 00 00 00 00 00 00 00 00 00 00 00 00 00 00 00 00 00 00 00
<0C0> 00 00 00 00 00 00 00 00 00 00 00 00 00 00 00 00 00 00 00 00 00 00 00 00 00 00 00 00 00 00 00 00
<0E0> 00 00 00 00 00 00 00 00 00 00 00 00 00 00 00 00 00 00 00 00 00 00 00 00 00 00 00 00 00 00 00 00
<100> 00 00 00 00 00 00 00 00 00 00 00 00 00 00 00 00 00 00 00 00 00 00 00 00 00 00 00 00 00 00 00 00
<120> 00 00 00 00 00 00 00 00 00 00 00 00 00 00 00 00 00 00 00 00 00 00 00 00 00 00 00 00 00 00 00 00
<140> 00 00 00 00 00 00 00 00 00 00 00 00 00 00 00 00 00 00 00 00 00 00 00 00 00 00 00 00 00 00 00 00
<160> 00 00 00 00 00 00 00 00 00 00 00 00 00 00 00 00 00 00 00 00 00 00 00 00 00 00 00 00 00 00 00 00
<180> 00 00 00 00 00 00 00 00 00 00 00 00 00 00 00 00 00 00 00 00 00 00 00 00 00 00 00 00 00 00 00 00
<1A0> 00 00 00 00 00 00 00 00 00 00 00 00 00 00 00 00 00 00 00 00 00 00 00 00 00 00 00 00 00 00 00 00
<1C0> 00 00 00 00 00 00 00 00 00 00 00 00 00 00 00 00 00 00 00 00 00 00 00 00 00 00 00 00 00 00 00 00
<1E0> 00 00 00 00 00 00 00 00 00 00 00 00 00 00 00 00 00 00 00 00 00 00 00 00 00 00 00 00 00 00 00 00
<200> 00 00 00 00 00 00 00 00 00 00 00 00 00 00 00 00 00 00 00 00 00 00 00 00 00 00 00 00 00 00 00 00
<220> 00 00 00 00 00 00 00 00 00 00 00 00 00 00 00 00 00 00 00 00 00 00 00 00 00 00 00 00 00 00 00 00
<240> 00 00 00 00 00 00 00 00 00 00 00 00 00 00 00 00 00 00 00 00 00 00 00 00 00 00 00 00 00 00 00 00
<260> 00 00 00 00 00 00 00 00 00 00 00 00 00 00 00 00 00 00 00 00 00 00 00 00 00 00 00 00 00 00 00 00
<280> 00 00 00 00 00 00 00 00 00 00 00 00 00 00 00 00 00 00 00 00 00 00 00 00 00 00 00 00 00 00 00 00
<2A0> 00 00 00 00 00 00 00 00 00 00 00 00 00 00 00 00 00 00 00 00 00 00 00 00 00 00 00 00 00 00 00 00
<2C0> 00 00 00 00 00 00 00 00 00 00 00 00 00 00 00 00 00 00 00 00 00 00 00 00 00 00 00 00 00 00 00 00
<2E0> 00 00 00 00 00 00 00 00 00 00 00 00 00 00 00 00 00 00 00 00 00 00 00 00 00 00 00 00 00 00 00 00
<300> 00 00 00 00 00 00 00 00 00 00 00 00 00 00 00 00 00 00 00 00 00 00 00 00 00 00 00 00 00 00 00 00
<320> 00 00 00 00 00 00 00 00 00 00 00 00 00 00 00 00 00 00 00 00 00 00 00 00 00 00 00 00 00 00 00 00
<340> 00 00 00 00 00 00 00 00 00 00 00 00 00 00 00 00 00 00 00 00 00 00 00 00 00 00 00 00 00 00 00 00
<360> 00 00 00 00 00 00 00 00 00 00 00 00 00 00 00 00 00 00 00 00 00 00 00 00 00 00 00 00 00 00 00 00
<380> 00 00 00 00 00 00 00 00 00 00 00 00 00 00 00 00 00 00 00 00 00 00 00 00 00 00 00 00 00 00 00 00
<3A0> 00 00 00 00 00 00 00 00 00 00 00 00 00 00 00 00 00 00 00 00 00 00 00 00 00 00 00 00 00 00 00 00
<3C0> 00 00 00 00 00 00 00 00 00 00 00 00 00 00 00 00 00 00 00 00 00 00 00 00 00 00 00 00 00 00 00 00
<3E0> 00 00 00 00 00 00 00 00 00 00 00 00 00 00 00 00 00 00 00 00 00 00 00 00 00 00 00 00 00 00 00 00
<400> 00 00 00 00 00 00 00 00 00 00 00 00 00 00 00 00 00 00 00 00 00 00 00 00 00 00 00 00 00 00 00 00
<420> 00 00 00 00 00 00 00 00 00 00 00 00 00 00 00 00 00 00 00 00 00 00 00 00 00 00 00 00 00 00 00 00
<440> 00 00 00 00 00 00 00 00 00 00 00 00 00 00 00 00 00 00 00 00 00 00 00 00 00 00 00 00 00 00 00 00
<460> 00 00 00 00 00 00 00 00 00 00 00 00 00 00 00 00 00 00 00 00 00 00 00 00 00 00 00 00 00 00 00 00
<480> 00 00 00 00 00 00 00 00 00 00 00 00 00 00 00 00 00 00 00 00 00 00 00 00 00 00 00 00 00 00 00 00
<4A0> 00 00 00 00 00 00 00 00 00 00 00 00 00 00 00 00 00 00 00 00 00 00 00 00 00 00 00 00 00 00 00 00
<4C0> 00 00 00 00 00 00 00 00 00 00 00 00 00 00 00 00 00 00 00 00 00 00 00 00 00 00 00 00 00 00 00 00
<4E0> 00 00 00 00 00 00 00 00 00 00 00 00 00 00 00 00 00 00 00 00 00 00 00 00 00 00 00 00 00 00 00 00
<500> 00 00 00 00 00 00 00 00 00 00 00 00 00 00 00 00 00 00 00 00 00 00 00 00 00 00 00 00 00 00 00 00
<520> 00 00 00 00 00 00 00 00 00 00 00 00 00 00 00 00 00 00 00 00 00 00 00 00 00 00 00 00 00 00 00 00
<540> 00 00 00 00 00 00 00 00 00 00 00 00 00 00 00 00 00 00 00.00 00 00 00 00 00 00 00 00 00 00 00 00
<560> 00 00 00 00 00 00 00 00 00 00 00 00 00 00 00 00 00 00 00 00 00 00 00 00 00 00 00 00 00 00 00 00
<580> 00 00 00 00 00 00 00 00 00 00 00 00 00 00 00 00 00 00 00 00 00 00 00 00 00 00 00 00 00 00 00 00
<5A0> 00 00 00 00 00 00 00 00 00 00 00 00 00 00 00 00 00 00 00 00 00 00 00 00 00 00 00 00 00 00 00 00
<5C0> 00 00 00 00 00 00 00 00 00 00 00 00 00 00 00 00 00 00 00 00 00 00 00 00 00 00 00 00 00 00 00 00
<5E0> 00 00 00 00 00 00 00 00 00 00 00 00 00 00 00 00 00 00 00 00 00 00 00 00 00 00 00 00 00 00 00 00
<600> 00 00 00 00 00 00 00 00 00 00 00 00 00 00 00 00 00 00 00 00 00 00 00 00 00 00 00 00 00 00 00 00
<620> 00 00 00 00 00 00 00 00 00 00 00 00 00 00 00 00 00 00 00 00 00 00 00 00 00 00 00 00 00 00 00 00
<640> 00 00 00 00 00 00 00 00 00 00 00 00 00 00 00 00 00 00 00 00 00 00 00 00 00 00 00 00 00 00 00 00
<660> 00 00 00 00 00 00 00 00 00 00 00 00 00 00 00 00 00 00 00 00 00 00 00 00 00 00 00 00 00 00 00 00
<680> 00 00 00 00 00 00 00 00 00 00 00 00 00 00 00 00 00 00 00 00 00 00 00 00 00 00 00 00 00 00 00 00
<6A0> 00 00 00 00 00 00 00 00 00 00 00 00 00 00 00 00 00 00 00 00 00 00 00 00 00 00 00 00 00 00 00 00
<6C0> 00 00 00 00 00 00 00 00 00 00 00 00 00 00 00 00 00 00 00 00 00 00 00 00 00 00 00 00 00 00 00 00
<6E0> 00 00 00 00 00 00 00 00 00 00 00 00 00 00 00 00 00 00 00 00 00 00 00 00 00 00 00 00 00 00 00 00
<700> 00 00 00 00 00 00 00 00 00 00 00 00 00 00 00 00 00 00 00 00 00 00 00 00 00 00 00 00 00 00 00 00
<720> 00 00 00 00 00 00 00 00 00 00 00 00 00 00 00 00 00 00 00 00 00 00 00 00 00 00 00 00 00 00 00 00
<740> 00 00 00 00 00 00 00 00 00 00 00 00 00 00 00 00 00 00 00 00 00 00 00 00 00 00 00 00 00 00 00 00
<760> 00 00 00 00 00 00 00 00 00 00 00 00 00 00 00 00 00 00 00 00 00 00 00 00 00 00 00 00 00 00 00 00
<780> 00 00 00 00 00 00 00 00 00 00 00 00 00 00 00 00 00 00 00 00 00 00 00 00 00 00 00 00 00 00 00 00
<7A0> 00 00 00 00 00 00 00 00 00 00 00 00 00 00 00 00 00 00 00 00 00 00 00 00 00 00 00 00 00 00 00 00
```

Listing 14.4   View of the programmed diagnostic MCU

```
<7E0> 00 00 00 00.00 00 00 00 00 00 00 00 00 00 00 00 00 00 00 00 00 00 00 00 00 00 00 00 00 00 00 00
<800> 00 00 00 00 00 00 00 00 00 00 00 00 00 00 00 00 00 00 00 00 00 00 00 00 00 00 00 00 00 00 00 00
<820> 00 00 00 00 00 00 00 00 00 00 00 00 00 00 00 00 00 00 00 00 00 00 00 00 00 00 00 00 00 00 00 00
<840> 00 00 00 00 00 00 00 00 00 00 00 00 00 00 00 00 00 00 00 00 00 00 00 00 00 00 00 00 00 00 00 00
<860> 00 00 00 00 00 00 00 00 00 00 00 00 00 00 00 00 00 00 00 00 00 00 00 00 00 00 00 00 00 00 00 00
<880> 00 00 00 00 00 00 00 00 00 00 00 00 00 00 00 00 00 00 00 00 00 00 00 00 00 90 00 00 00 00 00 00
<8A0> 00 00 00 00 00 00 00 00 00 00 00 00 00 00 00 00 00 00 00 00 00 00 00 00 00 00 00 00 00 00 00 00
<8C0> 00 00 00 00 00 00 00 00 00 00 00 00 00 00 00 00 00 00 00 00 00 00 00 00 00 00 00 00 00 00 00 00
<8E0> 00 00 00 00 00 00 00 00 00 00 00 00 00 00 00 00 00 00 00 00 00 00 00 00 00 00 00 00 00 00 00 00
<900> 00 00 00 00 00 00 00 00 00 00 00 00 00 00 00 00 00 00 00 00 00 00 00 00 00 00 00 00 00 00 00 00
<920> 00 00 00 00 00 00 00 00 00 00 00 00 00 00 00 00 00 00 00 00 00 00 00 00 00 00 00 00 00 00 00 00
<940> 00 00 00 00 00 00 00 00 00 00 00 00 00 00 00 00 00 00 00 00 00 00 00 00 00 00 00 00 00 00 00 00
<960> 00 00 00 00 00 00 00 00 00 00 00 00 00 00 00 00 00 00 00 00 00 00 00 00 00 00 00 00 00 00 00 00
<980> 00 00 00 00 00 00 00 00 00 00 00 00 00 00 00 00 00 00 00 00 00 00 00 00 00 00 00 00 00 00 00 00
<9A0> 00 00 00 00 00 00 00 00 00 00 00 00 00 00 00 00 00 00 00 00 00 00 00 00 00 00 00 00 00 00 00 00
<9C0> 00 00 00 00 00 00 00 00 00 00 00 00 00 00 00 00 00 00 00 00 00 00 00 00 00 00 00 00 00 00 00 00
<9E0> 00 00 00 00 00 00 00 00 00 00 00 00 00 00 00 00 00 00 00 00 00 00 00 00 00 00 00 00 00 00 00 00
<A00> A6 FF B7 04 B7 05 0F 02 1B AE B7 CD 0E 00 B6 02 44 44 44 44 A4 F7 AB 30 B7 00 A6 C0 B7 01 1D 01   ← Main
<A20> 1C 01 20 E2 AE 80 CD 0E 00 B6 0F 97 44 44 44 44 AB 30 A1 39 23 02 AB 07 B7 00 A6 C1 B7 01 1D 01   ← Diagnostic
<A40> 1C 01 9F A4 0F AB 30 A1 39 23 02 AB 07 B7 00 A6 C0 B7 01 1D 01 1C 01 20 AD 00 00 00 00 00 00 00   ← Program
<A60> 00 00 00 00 00 00 00 00 00 00 00 00 00 00 00 00 00 00 00 00 00 00 00 00 00 00 00 00 00 00 00 00
<A80> 00 00 00 00 00 00 00 00 00 00 00 00 00 00 00 00 00 00 00 00 00 00 00 00 00 00 00 00 00 00 00 00
<AA0> 00 00 00 00 00 00 00 00 00 00 00 00 00 00 00 00 00 00 00 00 00 00 00 00 00 00 00 00 00 00 00 00
<AC0> 00 00 00 00 00 00 00 00 00 00 00 00 00 00 00 00 00 00 00 00 00 00 00 00 00 00 00 00 00 00 00 00
<AE0> 00 00 00 00 00 00 00 00 00 00 00 00 00 00 00 00 00 00 00 00 00 00 00 00 00 00 00 00 00 00 00 00
<B00> 00 00 00 00 00 00 00 00 00 00 00 00 00 00 00 00 00 00 00 00 00 00 00 00 00 00 00 00 00 00 00 00
<B20> 00 00 00 00 00 00 00 00 00 00 00 00 00 00 00 00 00 00 00 00 00 00 00 00 00 00 00 00 00 00 00 00
<B40> 00 00 00 00 00 00 00 00 00 00 00 00 00 00 00 00 00 00 00 00 00 00 00 00 00 00 00 00 00 00 00 00
<B60> 00 00 00 00 00 00 00 00 00 00 00 00 00 00 00 00 00 00 00 00 00 00 00 00 00 00 00 00 00 00 00 00
<B80> 00 00 00 00 00 00 00 00 00 00 00 00 00 00 00 00 00 00 00 00 00 00 00 00 00 00 00 00 00 00 00 00
<BA0> 00 00 00 00 00 00 00 00 00 00 00 00 00 00 00 00 00 00 00 00 00 00 00 00 00 00 00 00 00 00 00 00
<BC0> 00 00 00 00 00 00 00 00 00 00 00 00 00 00 00 00 00 00 00 00 00 00 00 00 00 00 00 00 00 00 00 00
<BE0> 00 00 00 00 00 00 00 00 00 00 00 00 00 00 00 00 00 00 00 00 00 00 00 00 00 00 00 00 00 00 00 00
<C00> 00 00 00 00 00 00 00 00 00 00 00 00 00 00 00 00 00 00 00 00 00 00 00 00 00 00 00 00 00 00 00 00
<C20> 00 00 00 00 00 00 00 00 00 00 00 00 00 00 00 00 00 00 00 00 00 00 00 00 00 00 00 00 00 00 00 00
<C40> 00 00 00 00 00 00 00 00 00 00 00 00 00 00 00 00 00 00 00 00 00 00 00 00 00 00 00 00 00 00 00 00
<C60> 00 00 00 00 00 00 00 00 00 00 00 00 00 00 00 00 00 00 00 00 00 00 00 00 00 00 00 00 00 00 00 00
<C80> 00 00 00 00 00 00 00 00 00 00 00 00 00 00 00 00 00 00 00 00 00 00 00 00 00 00 00 00 00 00 00 00
<CA0> 00 00 00 00 00 00 00 00 00 00 00 00 00 00 00 00 00 00 00 00 00 00 00 00 00 00 00 00 00 00 00 00
<CC0> 00 00 00 00 00 00 00 00 00 00 00 00 00 00 00 00 00 00 00 00 00 00 00 00 00 00 00 00 00 00 00 00
<CE0> 00 00 00 00 00 00 00 00 00 00 00 00 00 00 00 00 00 00 00 00 00 00 00 00 00 00 00 00 00 00 00 00
<D00> 00 00 00 00 00 00 00 00 00 00 00 00 00 00 00 00 00 00 00 00 00 00 00 00 00 00 00 00 00 00 00 00
<D20> 00 00 00 00 00 00 00 00 00 00 00 00 00 00 00 00 00 00 00 00 00 00 00 00 00 00 00 00 00 00 00 00
<D40> 00 00 00 00 00 00 00 00 00 00 00 00 00 00 00 00 00 00 00 00 00 00 00 00 00 00 00 00 00 00 00 00
<D60> 00 00 00 00 00 00 00 00 00 00 00 00 00 00 00 00 00 00 00 00 00 00 00 00 00 00 00 00 00 00 00 00
<D80> 00 00 00 00 00 00 00 00 00 00 00 00 00 00 00 00 00 00 00 00 00 00 00 00 00 00 00 00 00 00 00 00
<DA0> 00 00 00 00 00 00 00 00 00 00 00 00 00 00 00 00 00 00 00 00 00 00 00 00 00 00 00 00 00 00 00 00
<DC0> 00 00 00 00 00 00 00 00 00 00 00 00 00 00 00 00 00 00 00 00 00 00 00 00 00 00 00 00 00 00 00 00
<DE0> 00 00 00 00 00 00 00 00 00 00 00 00 00 00 00 00 00 00 00 00 00 00 00 00 00 00 00 00 00 00 00 00
<E00> A6 C7 B7 01 F6 27 13 A1 04 27 1A B7 00 05 01 06 1F 01 1E 01 20 04 1D 01 1C 01 5C B6 01 A1 C0 27   ← Subroutine
<E20> 04 3A 01 20 DF 81 00 00 00 00 00 00 00 00 00 00 00 00 00 00 00 00 00 00 00 00 00 00 00 00 00 00   ← PDATA
<E40> 00 00 00 00 00 00 00 00 00 00 00 00 00 00 00 00 00 00 00 00 00 00 00 00 00 00 00 00 00 00 00 00
<E60> 00 00 00 00 00 00 00 00 00 00 00 00 00 00 00 00 00 00 00 00 00 00 00 00 00 00 00 00 00 00 00 00
<E80> 00 00 00 00 00 00 00 00 00 00 00 00 00 00 00 00 00 00 00 00 00 00 00 00 00 00 00 00 00 00 00 00
<EA0> 00 00 00 00 00 00 00 00 00 00 00 00 00 00 00 00 00 00 00 00 00 00 00 00 00 00 00 00 00 00 00 00
<EC0> 00 00 00 00 00 00 00 00 00 00 00 00 00 00 00 00 00 00 00 00 00 00 00 00 00 00 00 00 00 00 00 00
<EE0> 00 00 00 00 00 00 00 00 00 00 00 00 00 00 00 00 00 00 00 00 00 00 00 00 00 00 00 00 00 00 00 00
<F00> 00 00 00 00 00 00 00 00 00 00 00 00 00 00 00 00 00 00 00 00 00 00 00 00 00 00 00 00 00 00 00 00
<F20> 00 00 00 00 00 00 00 00 00 00 00 00 00 00 00 00 00 00 00 00 00 00 00 00
<F38> Mask Option Register 00
BOOTSTRAP ROM from F39 to FF7
<FF8> Timer/INT2 vector 000
<FFA> INT vector 000
<FFC> SWI vector 000
<FFE> RESET vector A00
```

Listing 14.4   View of the programmed diagnostic MCU (*continued*)

(a)

(b)

Fig. 14.3   Typical diagnostic displays
(a) SW7 = 0
(b) SW7 = 1

as they relate to the state of switch PC7. In the analog test mode, the reading should change as the temperature of the sensor is raised, or as the calibrate or gain potentiometers of Fig. 13.5 are altered. Alternatively the temperature transducer could be temporarily replaced by a 10 kΩ potentiometer between 4 V and analog ground. Connecting the center tap to analog channel 0 should give a display which can be altered from \$00 to \$FF. Some jitter in the LSB is quite normal, and can be ignored for the purposes of this test.

Should the test fail, some elementary detective work will quickly isolate the problem. Failing any coherent display, check port bits PB7 and PB6. These should be pulsing low at a regular rate of several kHz as the displays are strobed. Also pulsing should be bits PA0–6 and PB0 and 1. If these are pulsing, then either the displays are defective or, more likely, their interconnection to the MCU is.

If Ports A and B are still, then suspect either the MCU or the EPROM programming circuit. Check the XTAL and EXTAL pins with an oscilloscope for parasinusoidal waveforms at around 800 kHz. The presence of these signals are an indicator of a functional MCU. Also inspect the operation of the reset circuitry and polarity of the associated capacitor.

If all checks tally, then suspect the programmer circuitry; although if the verify LED illuminates, then this is unlikely. However, in this situation it is possible that the MCU is not reading the correct data from external memory, and is thus verifying against an erroneous base. This might be due to incorrect connections between memory and MCU, e.g., most significant and least significant transposition. And, of course, it is just conceivable that you have made an error in typing in your source code, a meticulous scrutinization of that data will unearth any problem in this respect.

A failure in only one of the two test modules indicates a poor connection between switches or transducer to the appropriate MCU pins. A simple voltage check will pick this up. Assuming no connection problem or software error, then there is a chance that damage has occurred to the pertinent input port. The analog port in particular is susceptible to damage by static electricity, but all MCU inputs, and for that matter 1414 display inputs, are easily damaged by this means. You have been warned!

15

The Soft Option

The division of labor between the hardware and software camps in MCU-based systems is usually biased towards the latter. This project is no exception to the rule. Therefore this chapter and Chapters 16 and 17 examine the software aspects of our annunciator.

Specifically in this chapter we perform a macro-task analysis for the specification of Section 12.2. We also look at the behind-the-scenes setting up of the several peripheral control registers and the initialization of the variable strings used to display temperature and time.

15.1 THE MACRO ANALYSIS

In applying a top-down strategy to software design we begin by isolating the main system structure. Four major tasks may be identified, as shown in Fig. 15.1. The first of these is the diagnostic package developed in Chapter 14. As it seems likely at this juncture that there will be spare EPROM capacity after the system software has been accommodated, we make the decision here to take this package on-board to give resident diagnostics.

The three remaining tasks are involved in generating the annunciator parameters of temperature and time. Of these, temperature is the easiest to process, involving only the reading of the analog transducer, conversion to the °F or °C scale as appropriate and the display of the same.

Processing the time parameter is more complex, as by definition this is critically dependent on the instant of occurrence of an external event; oscillations of a quartz crystal in this case. Thus, although displaying this information to the nearest second can be a relatively leisurely affair, the updating of the time array must be made promptly in order not to miss a tick of the clock.

The task analysis of Fig. 15.1 separates the time problem into two routines. The simplest of these merely formats and displays the time, to either a 12-hour or 24-hour scale, whenever the time-mode path is chosen. The critical update-procedure is implemented by an interrupt service routine. The internal timer is used to count the crystal oscillations (ϕ_2) and automatically create an interrupt request

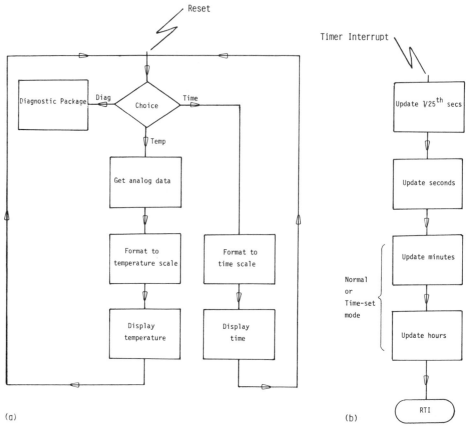

Fig. 15.1   Macro flowchart for the annunciator
(a)   Background routines
(b)   Time update foreground routine

(TINT) after 2^{15} 'ticks' of the oscillator. As we have chosen a crystal resonating at 3.2768 MHz, this gives a 819.2 kHz ($=2^{15} \times 25$) tick rate. Thus this internal interrupt will be generated each one twenty-fifth of a second (a *jiffy*), at which time the hours, minutes, seconds and jiffies are updated. The increment rate of minutes and hours may be further modified if the operator desires a time-set operation.

The decision as to which background module is to be run is a function of the 'choice' box in Fig. 15.1. This in turn is a function of the settings at the switch port of Fig. 13.1. As the resident diagnostics are an unscheduled extra, some unused combination of these switches must be used to signal the operator's desire. Having all switches at logic 1 is a convenient setting, and is not listed as a legitimate combination in Section 13.1.

Assuming that the diagnostics are not requested, then the decision tree illustrated in Fig. 15.2 looks first at switch 7. A logic 1 in this position signifies the time set mode, and passes operation to the time-display module. If this is not the case

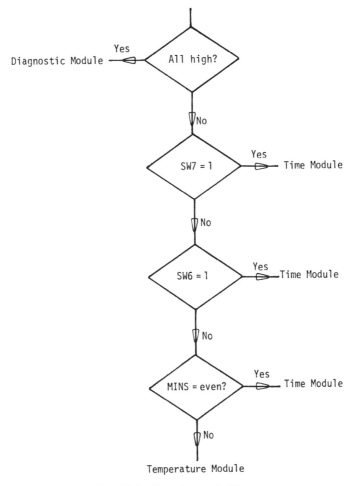

Fig. 15.2 The primary decision tree

a high switch 6 (clock mode) similarly points to the time-display module. If neither of these decisions are true then the alternate-mode is indicated. In this mode the time-display module must be exercised at every other minute. Thus the state of the minute content in the time array (MINS = ($015)) can be tested for, say, evenness, to fulfill this criterion. If all this fails then the temperature module is entered.

There are of course other relevant combinations of these switches, such as clock format (12- or 24-hour). However, these are of a secondary nature, and only influence events within the appropriate module.

All the while the MCU is 'sweating' over these tasks, the foreground time-update module is periodically entered 25 times each second. This must be true even if the time module is not running. The observer standing well back will appear to see this happen in parallel with the chosen background module, although the MCU of course can run only in a serial manner.

15.2 IN THE BEGINNING

It is necessary to set up variables and constants to their starting values before letting the MCU loose into the main routines. This normally involves three distinct phases; viz., configuring peripheral registers, defining constants in EPROM and initializing variables in RAM. Listing 15.1 shows the setting-up procedure for our specific project.

Besides the two fixed character strings required for the diagnostic package (see Listing 14.1(c)) in Lines 300–340, only reset/interrupt vectors and the mask option register (MOR) require definition. As we will see in Section 17.1 the timer will be operated in its fixed (ROM emulation) mode, and will consequently be configured by means of the MOR at $F38 (see Section 8.3). Lines 380–390 define the constant to be programmed into this EPROM byte, according to the specification established in Section 17.1. Likewise the timer interrupt (TINT) vector content at $FF8/9 is defined in Lines 430–440 to point to $0B00, which is to be used as the beginning of the TINT service routine (see Listing 17.1).

The main background program originates at $0100 (as defined in Lines 480 and 490). This begins by setting up Ports A and B as outputs (Lines 560–580 of Listing 15.2), as required by Fig. 13.1; see also Listing 14.1(a). All data direction registers are cleared on reset, and thus port C will already be configured as input. As already observed, the timer is to be controlled by the MOR; however, the local timer-interrupt mask (bit 6 of the timer control register (TCR)) must be cleared in order to pass on TINT requests to the processor, see Fig. 8.5. Clearing TCR in Line 590 accomplishes this task. The state of the other TCR bits need not be considered in the fixed mode. Notwithstanding the local timer flag, the I mask in the CCR must be cleared before an interrupt from any source can be accepted. As this bit is always set on reset, it must be cleared by software but only at the end of the initialization module, Line 780 in Listing 15.2, by which time all parameters are in their correct state.

The A/D control register (ACR) is cleared on reset, and this targets channel 0 for the analog input. As our temperature transducer drives this channel, no explicit initialization is required for the ACR.

In Section 14.1, we designed subroutine PDATA as a software interface to the display. PDATA expected to find a string of up to eight ASCII-coded characters in memory, the start address of which was placed in the index register prior to the subroutine call.

The two messages used as part of the diagnostic module were essentially fixed, with only the last one or two places filled by variables. PDATA was used to display the constant part of the string, while the variables were sent directly to the readout digit. These fixed strings are stored in EPROM (Lines 300–340).

The messages displayed during execution of the time-and-temperature modules are illustrated in Fig. 15.3. An examination of this diagram shows that these messages are mainly comprised as variables. For example, only the colons in the 24-hour time message in (a) of Fig. 15.3 remain fixed. If we wish to use PDATA to interface to this type of message, rather than directly targeting to individual

```
10      <0038>  CSTRG   EQU  $038          *Celsius string
20      <0000>  DISPLAY EQU  $000          *Port A = Display port
30      <0001>  DIGIT   EQU  $001          *Port B addresses 4 digits in each of 2 nybbles n2n1xxxd4d2d1
40      <0002>  SWITCH  EQU  $002          *Port C = Switch port
50      <0004>  DDRA    EQU  $004          *Data Direction register A
60      <0005>  DDRB    EQU  $005          *Data Direction register B
70      <0008>  TIMER   EQU  $008          *Timer Data Counter
80      <0009>  TIMCTRL EQU  $009          *Timer Control register
90      <000E>  ANCTRL  EQU  $00E          *Analog Control register
100     <000F>  ANALOG  EQU  $00F          *Analog Data register
110     <0010>  UNITS   EQU  $010          *Subroutine DECIMAL places it's ASCII-coded unit's digit here
120     <0011>  TENS    EQU  $011          *and the ten's digit here
130     <0012>  HUNDS   EQU  $012          *and the hundreds digit here
140     <0013>  JIFFIES EQU  $013          *Hundreths of second ticks here
150     <0014>  SECS    EQU  $014          *and seconds
160     <0015>  MINS    EQU  $015          *and minutes
170     <0016>  HOURS   EQU  $016          *and hours
180     <0020>  TSTRG24 EQU  $020          *24-hour Time string
190     <0028>  TSTRG12 EQU  $028          *12-hour Time string
200     <0030>  FSTRG   EQU  $030          *Fahrenheit string
210     <0038>  CSTRG   EQU  $038          *Celsius string
220     <0040>  LBYTE   EQU  $040          *LBYTE/UBYTE = double-byte workspace
230     <0041>  UBYTE   EQU  $041
240     <0050>  QUOT    EQU  $050          *Quotient for division routine
250     ****************************************************************
260     *Module defines constants in EPROM
270     *
280     *Strings
290     *
300     <0080>          ORG  $080
310 0080 412F443D2024
                STRG1   FCC  'A/D= $'
320 0086 04
                        FCB  4
330 0087 53574954434820
                STRG2   FCC  'SWITCH '
340 008E 04
                        FCB  4
350     *
360     *Mask Option Register
370     *
380     <0F38>          ORG  $F38
390 0F38 47
                        FCB  %01000111    *Xtal; Fixed Timer; Internal Clock; /128
400     *
410     *Timer Interrupt Vector
420     *
430     <0FF8>          ORG  $FF8
440 0FF8 0B00
                        FDB  $B00         *Timer service starts at $B00
450     *
460     *Reset Vector
470     *
480     <0FFE>          ORG  $FFE
490 0FFE 0100
                        FDB  $100         *Background program starts at $100
```

Listing 15.1 Defining constants in EPROM

```
510  *Now follows the main body of routines
520    <0100>      ORG   $100          *Starts at $100
530  ****************************************************************************
540  *Module initialises peripheral registers and RAM-based strings
550  *
560  0100 A6-FF     LDA   #%11111111
570  0102 B7-04     STA   DDRA          *Port A as output
580  0104 B7-05     STA   DDRB          *Port B as output
590  0106 3F-09     CLR   TIMCTRL       *Clear Timer Interrupt Mask
600  *
610  *Strings
620  *
630  0108 AE-20     LDX   #TSTRG24      *Point Index to start of RAM strings
640  010A A6-20 CLOOP LDA  #$20         *#$20 = ASCII for Space
650  010C F7        STA   0,X           *which is put in all string characters
660  010D 5C        INCX
670  010E A3-40     CPX   #CSTRG+8      *up to $03E
680  0110 25-F8     BLO   CLOOP
690  0112 A6-3A     LDA   #':           *Now put colons into 24-hour string
700  0114 B7-22     STA   TSTRG24+2
710  0116 B7-25     STA   TSTRG24+5
720  0118 A6-4D     LDA   #'M           *Terminate 12-hour string with M (ie AM/PM)
730  011A B7-2F     STA   TSTRG12+7
740  011C A6-46     LDA   #'F           *Terminate Fahrenheit string with F
750  011E B7-37     STA   FSTRG+7
760  0120 A6-43     LDA   #'C           *Terminate Celsius string with C
770  0122 B7-3F     STA   CSTRG+7
780  0124 9A        CLI                 *Enable all interrupts
```

Listing 15.2   Setting up constants in RAM

	$20	$21	$22	$23	$24	$25	$26	$27	
TSTRG24	Tens hours	Units hours	: † $3A	Tens minutes	Units minutes	: † $3A	Tens seconds	Units seconds	(a)

	$28	$29	$2A	$2B	$2C	$2D	$2E	$2F	
TSTRG12	Tens hours	Units hours	Flashing seconds colon $3A/$20	Tens minutes	Units minutes	† $20	A or P $41/$52	M † $4F	(b)

	$30	$31	$32	$33	$34	$35	$36	$37	
FSTRG	† $20	† $20	† $20	† $20	Hunds °F	Tens °F	Units °F	F † $46	(c)

	$38	$39	$3A	$3B	$3C	$3D	$3E	$3F	
CSTRG	† $20	† $20	† $20	† $20	Sign $20/$2D	Tens °C	Units °C	C † $43	(d)

† Constants

Fig. 15.3   Variable string format
(a) 24-hour string
(b) 12-hour string
(c) °F string
(d) °C string

```
800  *Module selects which background program
810  *
820  0125 B6-02   CHOICE  LDA  SWITCH          *Get option switches
830  0127 A4-F0           AND  #%11110000      *Clear all nonused bits
840  0129 A1-F0           CMP  #%11110000      *Are all switches open?
850  012B 26-03           BNE  NEXTC           *IF not THEN next choice
860  012D CC-0A00         JMP  DIAG            *ELSE do the Diagnostic routine
870  0130 0E-0208 NEXTC   BRSET 7,SWITCH,TIME  *IF Switch7 open THEN display Time
880  0133 0C-0205         BRSET 6,SWITCH,TIME  *or IF CLK/ALT Switch open THEN display Time
890  0136 00-1502         BRSET 0,MINS,TIME    *or IF this is closed and an even minute THEN display Time
900  0139 20-03           BRA  GET             *ELSE Temperature
910  013B CC-01DA TIME    JMP  CLOCK           *Go to clock display module
920  ******************************************************************
930  *This is the Temperature module
```

Listing 15.3   Testing the option switches

digits, then we must build up the relevant strings in RAM. Variables are entered into the string just prior to the appropriate module display routine (see, e.g., Lines 1330–1430 in Listing 16.2). Here, in the initialization portion of the program, we blank (ASCII = $20) all character locations in the four variable strings (Lines 630–680), and insert any constants, viz., colons in the 24-hour string, the trailing M for the AM/PM 12-hour string, and the trailing C and F identifiers on the temperature strings (Lines 690–770).

Returning now to the main program flow, the decision logic implementing the algorithm of Fig. 15.2 is executed in Lines 820–890 of Listing 15.3. Firstly, the lower four (undefined) switch port settings are zeroed (Lines 820 and 830), and the result tested for all switches high (Lines 840–860). An affirmative forces a jump to the diagnostic module of Listing 14.1(b). Otherwise a set switch at position 7 or 6 forces a branch to the time-display module (Lines 870 and 880). If neither of the conditions exist, the annunciator is in the time/temperature mode, where the data is alternated on consecutive minutes. Thus Line 890 checks the least significant bit of the minute location, and if logic 0 (even minutes) causes a time display.

If all this fails, then temperature is to be evaluated and displayed. This is the subject of Chapter 16.

16

What Temperature Is It?

Temperature is one of the two parameters which are to be annunciated. We have already discussed the hardware implementing the transducer in Section 13.2; here, we evolve the software circuits needed to read, process and display the temperature in the chosen scale.

Before delving into this detail, we require to review the supporting cast of two subroutines. PDATA (at $E00) is the first of these, and was developed for the diagnostic package in Section 14.1. This sends a string of ASCII-coded characters stored in EPROM or RAM to the display. The index register must be pointed to the first of these characters prior to calling up the subroutine. The program is given in Listing 14.1(b).

The second subroutine converts a binary byte in the accumulator to three ASCII-coded decimal digits. Thus, e.g., %11111010 ($FA) becomes $32–$35–$30 for 250. These digits are respectively stored at HUNDS ($012), TENS ($011) and UNITS ($010) prior to return. Subroutine DECIMAL (at $E40) is discussed in Section 9.2, and appears in Listing 9.1.

16.1   TALKING TO THE TRANSDUCER

Interrogating the analog port is simply a matter of reading the contents of the analog result register (ARR) at $00F. The ARR always holds the result of the last complete conversion. Because of the free-running nature of the A/D converter, it is unnecessary to take any specific action to initiate a new conversion.

We have already shown in Section 13.2 that the transducer output voltage is directly proportional to the temperature in degrees Celsius, with an offset of $10°C$. The scaling is such that a change of one least significant bit in the ARR is worth $0.25°C$. Thus the temperature data is given as

$$T = (°C + 10) \times 4$$

Rather than using the raw data T directly in our computations, it is preferable to read several samples and apply a low-pass filtering algorithm to reduce the effects

```
930  *This is the Temperature module
940  *
950  *Acquire the average of 256 readings
960  *
970  013E 3F-40    GET    CLR    LBYTE         *Clear space for double-byte sum
980  0140 3F-41           CLR    UBYTE
990  0142 5F             CLRX                  *Index used as loop counter
1000 *Add Nth sample to sum total
1010 0143 B6-0F    GTLOOP LDA    ANALOG        *Get latest analog sample
1020 0145 BB-40           ADD    LBYTE         *Add it to lower byte
1030 0147 B7-40           STA    LBYTE
1040 0149 B6-41           LDA    UBYTE         *Now get upper byte of sum
1050 014B A9-00           ADC    #00           *Add carry only
1060 014D B7-41           STA    UBYTE
1070 *256 times yet?
1080 014F 5C              INCX                  *One more time
1090 0150 26-F1           BNE    GTLOOP        *IF not finished THEN again
1100 *Divide by 256 and round off
1110 0152 B6-41           LDA    UBYTE         *ELSE get upper sum byte
1120 0154 0F-4001         BRCLR 7,LBYTE,SCALE *Only roundup if remainder bit7 is set
1130 0157 4C              INCA
1140 *
1150 *Now check which temperature scale is required
1160 0158 0B-022B SCALE   BRCLR 5,SWITCH,FAHREN *IF C/F switch is low THEN Fahrenheit
1170 *ELSE Celsius scale
```

Listing 16.1   Low-pass filtering temperature data

of noise. This is justified in this situation, as speed of response is not a parameter of great importance.

A simple (but not terribly efficient) filtering algorithm was used in the program example of Fig. 1.8. There, 256 samples were added together to give a double-byte sum. The upper byte only of that sum represents a division by 256, which is the average over the sampling period. Lines 930–1130 of Listing 16.1 closely follow the coding of that developed in Section 1.4. Line 1010 reads the ARR, the result of which is added to the double-byte sum in $040/1 (LBYTE/UBYTE) in Lines 1020–1060. The index register is used as a loop counter, and when this overflows back to zero (i.e., 256) the upper byte is brought down to the accumulator (Lines 1080–1110). This average is then incremented as a rounding-up operation if bit 7 of the lower byte is logic 1, i.e., if the remainder $\geqslant \frac{1}{2}$ (Lines 1120 and 1130).

Finally in Listing 16.1, Line 1160 branches to the Fahrenheit-scale module if switch 5 is low, otherwise the Celsius-scale module is directly entered by default.

16.2   DEGREES CELSIUS

The result of the filter module leaves the average temperature data

$$T = (^{\circ}C + 10) \times 4$$

in the accumulator. The choice of a Celsius display will then only involve subtracting the $10°C$ offset and dividing by four. However, life is a little more complicated than this, since our specified range includes negative temperatures down to $-10°C$. Detecting a negative result is easy, since after the subtraction the carry flag will be set if this is the case. Of course, the $10°C$ offset is represented by 40 quarter degrees, and this is the argument used in Line 1240 of Listing 16.2. The following branch-if-higher or same (BHS) is an alternative mnemonic for branch-if-carry clear (BCC), and is affirmed if $T \geqslant 40$, i.e., a temperature of zero or more.

For positive temperatures the only action that needs to be taken is to blank out the sign digit in the Celsius display string (CSTRG), Line 1230, and divide by four. In the case of a subzero temperature, the result of the subtraction will be a 2s complement negative number. This can be brought back to positive by 2s complementing again (double negative gives positive), and this is done with the negate operation, of Line 1260. We also need to send out the ASCII code for $-$ to the sign location in CSTRG, Lines 1270 and 1280.

With the modulus of the temperature in quarter degrees now in the accumulator, we shift right twice to divide by four. This leaves the most significant bit of the remainder in the carry flag, which is added to the Celsuis temperature in Line 1320 to round up.

Now with the temperature in whole degrees Celsius, we can convert to decimal (subroutine DECIMAL) and place the resulting ASCII-coded tens and units digits

```
1190 *This is the Celsius scale module
1200 *
1210 *Temperature data in Accumulator = Degrees (C+10)*4
1220 015B AE-20        LDX    #$20        *Character4 of C string is the sign
1230 015D BF-3C        STX    CSTRG+4     *Blank it out
1240 015F A0-28        SUB    #40         *Take away 10C (40=10*4)
1250 0161 24-05        BHS    MODLUS      *IF above zero THEN positive temperature
1260 0163 40           NEGA               *ELSE 2's complement to get temperature modulus
1270 0164 AE-2D        LDX    #'-         *and make sign of celsius string minus
1280 0166 BF-3C        STX    CSTRG+4
1290 *Temperature data in A = modulus of degrees C*4
1300 0168 44    MODLUS LSRA               *Divide by 4
1310 0169 44           LSRA               *by shifting right twice
1320 016A A9-00        ADC    #0          *and round off by adding the carry
1330 016C CD-0E40      JSR    DECIMAL     *Convert to BCD string
1340 *Now create Celsius string
1350 016F AE-20        LDX    #$20
1360 0171 BF-3D        STX    CSTRG+5     *Blank out tens of centigrade
1370 0173 B6-11        LDA    TENS        *Get actual digit
1380 0175 A1-30        CMP    #'0         *IF zero THEN leave blank
1390 0177 27-02        BEQ    CUNIT
1400 0179 B7-3D        STA    CSTRG+5     *ELSE send out digit to string
1410 017B B6-10  CUNIT LDA    UNITS       *Get units digit
1420 017D B7-3E        STA    CSTRG+6     *and put in celsius string
1430 017F AE-38        LDX    #CSTRG      *Now display string
1440 0181 CD-0E00      JSR    PDATA
1450 0184 20-AA        BRA    NEXTC       *and return
1460
```

Listing 16.2   Celsius option

into the Celsius string, Lines 1330–1420. Rather than putting zero into the tens digit, it is aesthetically preferable to replace it with the code for blank ($20). Thus Lines 1350 and 1360 blank the ten's digit, which is only updated in Line 1400 if the test for zero in Lines 1380 and 1390 fails. The unit digit is always displayed, even if zero.

Once the Celsius string has been updated, it only remains to point the index register to the beginning of the string ($038) and call up subroutine PDATA. The module then terminates with a return to the choice module.

16.3   DEGREES FAHRENHEIT

Conversion of the temperature data T to degrees Fahrenheit is intrinsically more difficult. The relationship between the Celsius and Fahrenheit scales is given as:

$$°F = (°C \times 9/5) + 32$$

But

$$T = (°C + 10) \times 4$$

giving

$$°C = T/4 - 10$$

Thus

$$°F = ((T/4 - 10) \times 9/5) + 32$$

or

$$°F = ((T \times 9)/20) + 14$$

and this is the relationship between the T data in the accumulator and the Fahrenheit scale that must be implemented in software.

The main mathematical operations in this transform are those of multiplication and division. We have already designed general purpose subroutines to implement these functions in Listings 1.2 and 1.3, and it is tempting to use these. However, neither operation is used more than once by the system software; furthermore the operands are constants (i.e., $\times 9$ and $\div 20$). Thus it will be memory efficient to simplify the general purpose routines and implement them as in-line code.

Multiplication by nine using the shift and add algorithm simply involves shifting the multiplicand left three times and adding the unshifted multiplicand to this subproduct ($\times 8 + \times 1 = \times 9$). It is convenient to use locations $040/041 (UBYTE/LBYTE), just vacated by the filter module, for the product. Initially the product space is set up to a 16-bit version of T, the multiplicand, and Lines 1540–1590 of Listing 16.3 constitute three double-precision shift-left operations ($= 8T$). After adding T (still in the accumulator) the resulting product will have a maximum value of $255 \times 9 = 2,095$ or %1000 00101111, and this occupies 12 of the available 16 bits.

```
1470 *This is the Fahrenheit scale module
1480 *
1490 *Temperature data in A = (C+10)*4 =T
1500 *Degrees Fahrenheit = ((9*T)/20)+14
1510 *First multiply by 9, ie *8+*1
1520 0186 3F-41    FAHREN  CLR   UBYTE        *Clear Upper byte of Product (to be)
1530 0188 B7-40            STA   LBYTE        *Move T to Lower byte of Product
1540 018A 38-40            LSL   LBYTE        *Shift three times
1550 018C 39-41            ROL   UBYTE
1560 018E 38-40            LSL   LBYTE
1570 0190 39-41            ROL   UBYTE
1580 0192 38-40            LSL   LBYTE        *To give T*8
1590 0194 39-41            ROL   UBYTE
1600 0196 BB-40            ADD   LBYTE        *Then add T
1610 0198 B7-40            STA   LBYTE
1620 019A B6-41            LDA   UBYTE
1630 019C A9-00            ADC   #00
1640 019E B7-41            STA   UBYTE        *to give T*9 in UBYTE/LBYTE
1650 *Now divide by 20
1660 01A0 3F-50            CLR   QUOT         *Quotient byte zero
1670 01A2 AE-08            LDX   #8           *Divide to a resolution of 8 bits
1680 01A4 B6-41    SUBT    LDA   UBYTE        *Get Dividend
1690 01A6 A0-05            SUB   #5           *Compare with upper byte of 20*2^6
1700 01A8 25-02            BCS   UPDATEQ      *IF a carry THEN Divisor is less than Dividend: dont subtract
1710 01AA B7-41            STA   UBYTE        *ELSE subtract to give the new Dividend
1720 01AC 39-50    UPDATEQ ROL   QUOT         *Shift carry bit (0 for sucess; 1 for fail) into Quotient
1730 01AE 38-40            LSL   LBYTE        *Shift Dividend once left
1740 01B0 39-41            ROL   UBYTE
1750 01B2 5A               DECX               *One more pass
1760 01B3 26-EF            BNE   SUBT         *Eight times yet?
1770 01B5 B6-50            LDA   QUOT         *Get Quotient
1780 01B7 43               COMA               *Invert to correct for line UPDATEQ
1790 01B8 44               LSRA               *Reject 2^1/2 digit
1800 01B9 A9-0E            ADC   #14          *Round off and add correction factor of 14
1810 *Now prepare to display
1820 01BB CD-0E40          JSR   DECIMAL      *First convert to BCD
1830 01BE AE-20            LDX   #$20
1840 01C0 BF-34            STX   FSTRG+4      *Blank out hundreds
1850 01C2 B6-12            LDA   HUNDS        *Get hundreds digit
1860 01C4 A1-30            CMP   #'0          *Is it zero?
1870 01C6 27-02            BEQ   DISPTEN      *IF so THEN leave blank
1880 01C8 B7-34            STA   FSTRG+4      *ELSE put in string
1890 01CA B6-11    DISPTEN LDA   TENS         *Get tens digit
1900 01CC B7-35            STA   FSTRG+5      *and put in string
1910 01CE B6-10            LDA   UNITS        *Get units digit
1920 01D0 B7-36            STA   FSTRG+6      *and throw it in
1930 01D2 AE-30            LDX   #FSTRG       *Now display the whole Fahrenheit string
1940 01D4 CD-0E00          JSR   PDATA
1950 01D7 CC-0130          JMP   NEXTC        *and again
```

Listing 16.3   The Fahrenheit software

The shift and subtract division algorithm is shown in Fig. 1.10. In the context of our need to divide the 12-bit product 9T by 20, this involves successive subtraction by 20×2^N. As $20 \times 2^7 = 2,560$ is greater than the largest possible value of dividend (9T), the first subtraction will be 20×2^6 (%0101 00000000). If this is successful, the remainder replaces the dividend and $Q_6 = 1$ (where Q is the quotient bit). If unsuccessful, the dividend remains intact, and $Q_6 = 0$. The procedure is then repeated for 20×2^5 to give Q_5. After seven subtractions Q_0 is evaluated.

Each subtraction requires the movement of the subtrahend once right, thus 20×2^6 becomes 20×2^5 etc. An alternative strategy involves leaving the subtrahend fixed and moving the dividend left once after each operation. Relatively this is indistinguishable from the first process, but in this case is easier to implement in software.

Observe the last two rows in Fig. 16.1. The upper of these shows the 12-bit product 9T, which is now the dividend. The lower row shows 20×2^6 aligned with the dividend. As the lower byte of the subtrahend happens to be zero in this case, the first subtraction is simply implemented by taking %00000101 (5) from the upper byte of the dividend (Lines 1680 and 1690 in Listing 16.3). If this is unsuccessful, the carry bit will be set and the difference is not put back into the dividend (Line 1700). On the other hand a successful subtraction yields a zero C bit, and the dividend is updated (Line 1710), becoming the remainder. The normal procedure would be to shift the subtrahend right once and repeat. However, the second time around would involve a double-precision subtract, as the subtrahend would now be %00000010 10000000 (20×2^5). Rather, moving the dividend/remainder once left will enable us still to implement the subtraction by taking away 5 from the upper byte, no matter how many times we go around the loop.

How many times need we go round the loop? Well eight times is a convenient number for an 8-bit CPU, and this will give us resolution down to Q_{-1}, or $\frac{1}{2}°F$. Thus the 8-bit quotient need only be shifted right once and rounded to give whole

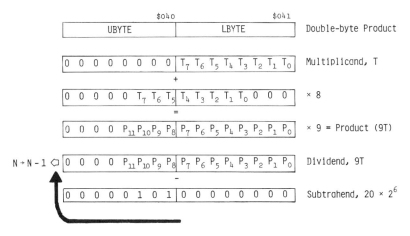

Fig. 16.1   Multiplying by 9/20

°F resolution (Line 1790). It has already been noted that a successful subtraction of 20×2^N gives a 0 carry bit, else $C = 1$. Also the corresponding Q is 1 else 0. Thus using a previously cleared byte (QUOT = \$050), we need only shift left each time round the loop to build up eight successive carry bits (1720). The final quotient in Line 1770 will of course be the inverse of the actual value, but this is easily rectified in Line 1780. Finally to obtain Fahrenheit degrees, the constant 14 is added to the quotient divided by two. Line 1800 uses an add-with-carry operation to add not only the 14 but the carry ejected during the previous shift ($\div 2$). This is the $\frac{1}{2}$°F bit, and rounds off the final value.

Displaying the Fahrenheit temperature involves conversion to decimal (Line 1820) and the placing of the resulting ASCII-coded digits for hundreds, tens and units into their allotted places in the Fahrenheit string (\$30–37). Like the Celsius display, it is aesthetically preferable to blank out the leftmost digit if this is a zero, Lines 1830–1870. In this case this is the hundreds digit. The lowest Fahrenheit temperature specified is 14°F (-10°C), so it is never necessary to blank the tens digit. Finally, subroutine PDATA is invoked to move the string to the display.

17

Just in Time

Any timepiece can be regarded as comprising three subsystems. The primary of these is the exploitation of some time-dependent physical process to create a train of 'ticks'. These must be totalized in some way to mark the passage of time and finally displayed to the curious onlooker. Thus a simple hourglass exploits the movement of grains of sand through a narrow orifice totalizing as a column and measured against gradations on the glass.

At a rather more sophisticated level a mechanical clock uses the oscillations of a balance-wheel hairspring (literally) to produce ticks, the energy for which comes from the mainspring. These are totalized by a train of gearwheels and eventually drive hands around a graded scale. The electronic counterpart uses a quartz crystal-controlled oscillator to provide the ticks and either a stepper motor to drive hands (the so-called *analog display*) or a binary counter to totalize and drive a digital display.

In Section 17.1, we look at how to use our MCU to generate ticks and to accumulate these in a relevant way. Section 17.2 develops the software to convert the totalized tick count to either a 12- or 24-hour display format.

17.1 HANDLING THE INTERRUPTS

Given that the 6805 MCU family have integral oscillators which are capable of being governed by an external crystal, it seems reasonable to use the derived CPU clock ϕ_2 as the input to the counting chain, rather than to utilize an external oscillator. Since this 'tick-rate' is too fast to totalize by software, we can arrange for the internal timer to divide this frequency down to a more manageable rate. From Fig. 8.4 we see that the 8-bit timer taken together with the 7-bit prescale counter gives a total division capacity of 2^{15}. Remembering that the oscillator adds a further $\div 4$ scale to the crystal, this gives a crystal frequency of $2^{17} = 131.072$ kHz to provide a 1-second tick. As the allowed crystal frequency range for the 6805 is 400 kHz–4 MHz, we need to choose some convenient multiple of 2^{17} lying in this range. Crystals of 3.2768 MHz are readily obtainable, giving a tick rate of 40 ms ($2^{17} \times 25$). This is the crystal frequency illustrated in Fig. 13.1.

Our next problem is deciding on the crystal specification to meet the proposed accuracy of ±1 minute per month (Section 12.2). There are around 43,000 minutes in an average month, which translates to a crystal tolerance of 23 parts in a million. The crystal used by the author (RS Components Limited, PO Box 99, Corby, Northants NN17 9RS, UK; stock no. 307–777) is specified as having an initial tolerance of 10 parts per million (ppm) and a temperature stability of 12.5 ppm over the range −20°C to +70°C. Therefore even a worst case addition of tolerances is within our determined limits. In practice most 3.2768 MHz crystals should prove satisfactory.

If the enthusiastic predictions of the marketing personnel come to fruition, the annunciator will eventually be implemented in a masked-ROM MCU, likely the 6805R2 device, see Section 12.2. Thus, it seems sensible to operate the timer in the fixed mode, with the mask option register (MOR) holding the mask options. Using Fig. 7.2 as our reference, we must set bit 7 to 0 to choose the crystal mode for the clock oscillator, MOR6 = 1 for timer mode; MOR5 = 0 defines ϕ_2 as the prescaler source. Bits MOR2,1,0 should be %111 to give a prescale factor of ÷128 (2^7). The resulting MOR EPROM byte %01000111 ($47) is defined as a constant in Line 390 of Listing 15.1.

In the fixed timer mode, the timer control register (TCR) of Fig. 8.5 has, in this context, only two relevant bits. TCR7 is set on each pass of the timer counter through all zero. A timer interrupt (TINT) will be simultaneously generated, provided that the local interrupt mask at TCR6 is clear. Thus zeroing TCR in Line 590 of Listing 15.2 clears the decks for the prescale-timer counter to create a TINT each $2^{15} \phi_2$ pulses, or 25 times a second, with a 3.2768 MHz crystal. The only effort the MCU need make to facilitate this regular tick rate is to ensure that the interrupt flag, TCR7, is cleared by software during the interrupt service routine.

On receipt of a TINT, the MCU will jump to the start of the relevant service routine, which is ordained in this case to be $0B00. Thus the contents of the TINT vector $FF8/9 are defined in Lines 430 and 440 of Listing 15.1 to be $0B–00.

We have now arranged matters so that at 25 times a second the MCU will jump to $0B00. Whenever this happens we must add one event to the total, which indicates time past. There are 2,160,000 such events in each day, which is the total time span that we wish to record. Thus we could use three bytes in RAM for the count (2^{24} = 16,777,216). However, a format more amenable to the organization of the final display utilizes four bytes to represent hours (maximum 23), minutes and seconds (maximum 59) and ticks or jiffies (maximum 24). Although this requires an extra byte of very scarce RAM, processing by the display routine is very considerably reduced; the trade-off being between RAM and ROM. Lines 140–170 in Listing 15.1 name the four RAM bytes $013–017 as storage areas for JIFFIES, SECS, MINS and HOURS.

Essentially all we need to do during each service is to add one to the jiffy count. If the resulting total is greater than the maximum (24) then this is cleared and one is added to the seconds total. And so on up the array, as shown in Fig. 2.9. Somehow this array has to be intialized after power-up or to correct an existing time. The most efficient way of doing this is to speed up the incrementation process during a time-set mode. We have already discussed this in Section 13.1, where it was

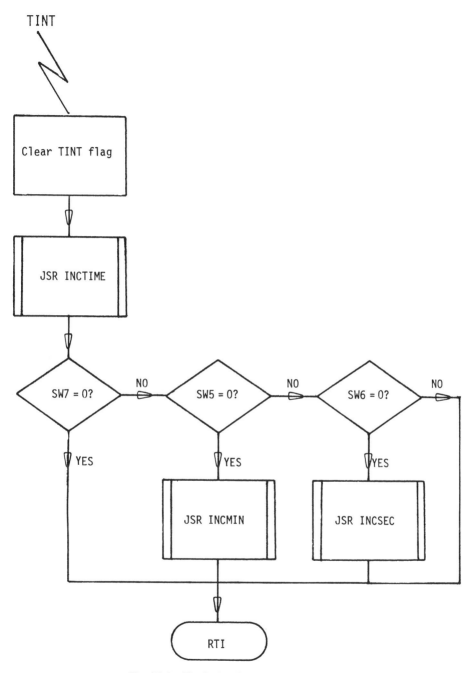

Fig. 17.1 The logic of the TINT service routine

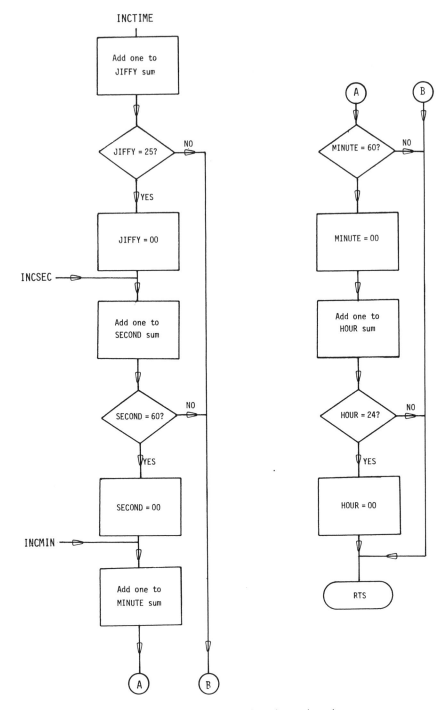

Fig. 17.2   The composite update-time subroutine

determined that switch PC7 = logic 1 would act as a changeover from normal to fast time. If PC7 = 1 then we can use PC6 = 0 to add one second to the array every interrupt (slow-set = × 25 real time) and PC5 = 0 to add one minute every interrupt (fast-set = 1,500 × real time).

This stratagem is shown in Fig. 17.1. On entry to the TINT service routine, the TINT flag (TCR7) is cleared irrespectively, and one jiffy is added to the 4-wide

```
3210 ***********************************************************************
3220 *This is the Timer Interrupt Service routine
3230 *It adds a Jiffy to the Time array 25 times per second
3240 *It adds 1 sec to the Time array 25 times per sec in the Slow Time-set mode
3250 *It adds 1 min to the Time array 25 times per sec in the Fast Time-set mode
3260 ***********************************************************************
3270 *
3280 *Main TINT Service routine
3290 *
3300      <0B00>           ORG   $B00
3310 0B00 1F-09            BCLR  7,TIMCTRL      *Reset TINT flag
3320 0B02 CD-0B20          JSR   INCTIME        *Add a Jiffy to the Time array
3330 0B05 0F-020E          BRCLR 7,SWITCH,TEXIT *IF not in Time-set mode THEN exit
3340 *Following services Time-set operations
3350 0B08 0A-0205          BRSET 5,SWITCH,TNEXT *Check Fast-set switch
3360 0B0B CD-0B34          JSR   INCMIN         *IF active THEN add a minute to total
3370 0B0E 20-06            BRA   TEXIT          *and exit
3380 0B10 0C-0203 TNEXT    BRSET 6,SWITCH,TEXIT *Check Slow-set switch
3390 0B13 CD-0B2A          JSR   INCSEC         *IF active THEN add a second to the total
3400 0B16 B0      TEXIT RTI                     *End of Service routine
3410 *
3420 *This local subroutine provides the mechanism for updating the Time array
3430 *
3440      <0B20>           ORG   $B20
3450 0B20 3C-13  INCTIME INC   JIFFIES          *One more 25th of a second gone
3460 0B22 B6-13          LDA   JIFFIES          *Now check for overflow (>24)
3470 0B24 A1-19          CMP   #25
3480 0B26 25-20          BLO   TIEXIT           *IF none THEN done
3490 0B28 3F-13          CLR   JIFFIES          *ELSE reset JIFFIES to zero
3500 *
3510 0B2A 3C-14  INCSEC  INC   SECS             *Entry point for Slow Time-set mode
3520 0B2C B6-14          LDA   SECS             *Now check for overflow (>59)
3530 0B2E A1-3C          CMP   #60
3540 0B30 25-16          BLO   TIEXIT           *IF none THEN done
3550 0B32 3F-14          CLR   SECS             *ELSE reset Seconds to zero
3560 *
3570 0B34 3C-15  INCMIN  INC   MINS             *Entry point for Fast Time-set mode
3580 0B36 B6-15          LDA   MINS             *Now check for overflow (>59)
3590 0B38 A1-3C          CMP   #60
3600 0B3A 25-0C          BLO   TIEXIT           *IF not THEN done
3610 0B3C 3F-15          CLR   MINS             *ELSE reset Minutes to zero
3620 *
3630 0B3E 3C-16          INC   HOURS
3640 0B40 B6-16          LDA   HOURS            *Now check for overflow (>23)
3650 0B42 A1-18          CMP   #24
3660 0B44 25-02          BLO   TIEXIT           *IF not THEN done
3670 0B46 3F-16          CLR   HOURS            *ELSE reset Hours to zero
3680 0B48 81     TIEXIT RTS                     *Return to TINT main routine
```

Listing 17.1   Servicing the timer

time array. If switch PC7 = 0 (as it normally is) nothing more is done and the routine terminates. During a time-set operation (PC7 = 1), a set PC5 forces an extra minute into the array, or a set PC6 forces an additional second. If neither switch is clear, the array is not altered further.

Now, the process of adding a jiffy onto the array involves the conditional addition of a second (on a JIFFY overflow) and minute (on a SECOND overflow). Thus it should be possible to construct the 'add a jiffy' routine in such a way as to provide an entry point directly into the increment second and increment minute sectors. Such a composite routine is going to be called from three separate points in the main TINT service routine, and is therefore best treated as a subroutine. As this subroutine is never called from outside the service routine, it is known as a local subroutine. Thus the subroutines INCTIME, INCMIN and INCSEC in Fig. 17.1 actually refer to the same subroutine, but with three separate entry points. This approach, shown in Fig. 17.2, is rather unstructured but is very efficient.

The implementation of the composite TINT service routine is shown in Listing 17.1. Lines 3310–3400 implement Fig. 17.1. Line 3310 clears bit 7 of the timer control register (the TINT flag), and Line 3320 jumps into the time-array update subroutine at the 'add-a-jiffy' point. After this, the service routine exits if bit 7 of the switch port is clear (normal mode). If this is not the case, Lines 3350–3370 cause a minute to be added if bit 5 is clear and exit. Likewise Lines 3380–3400 test bit 6 clear and, if affirmative, add a second to the array.

The actual time-update subroutine is implemented in Lines 3450–3680. This follows the flow of Fig. 17.2 closely, and is similar to the real-time clock code of Listing 2.1. Notice the two additional entry points at Lines 3510 (add-a-second) and 3570 (add-a-minute).

17.2   TELLING THE TIME

The interrupt service routine is invisible to the main (background) program; as far as it is concerned the time-array is always (magically!) up to date. Its job is to translate this array to fit into the display formats specified in (a) and (b) of Fig. 15.3.

There is an exact correspondence between the time-array and 24-hour string. Thus translation simply involves converting hours (Lines 2210–2260), minutes (Lines 2000–2070) and seconds (Lines 2110–2160) into ASCII-coded decimal and storing them in the correct part of the 24-hour string.

The correlation between the time-array and 12-hour format is somewhat more complex. Comparing (a) and (b) in Fig. 15.3 shows that the minutes display is the same. Thus Lines 2030 and 2060 are carbon copies of 2040 and 2070 respectively. Seconds are not directly displayed in this format, but the colon between hours and minutes flashes at a 1-second rate. This is implemented in Listing 17.2 by initially blanking out the colon, Lines 2090 and 2100, which is only restored on odd seconds (bit 0 of SECS = 1), Lines 2170–2190.

```
1970 *This is the Time Display routine
1980 *
1990 *First see to the Minutes
2000 01DA B6-15   CLOCK   LDA    MINS       *Get Minutes
2010 01DC CD-0E40         JSR    DECIMAL    *and convert to ASCII coded decimal
2020 01DF B6-11           LDA    TENS       *Tens of minutes
2030 01E1 B7-2B           STA    TSTRG12+3  *update 12-hour string
2040 01E3 B7-23           STA    TSTRG24+3  *and 24-hour string
2050 01E5 B6-10           LDA    UNITS      *Do the same for units of minutes
2060 01E7 B7-2C           STA    TSTRG12+4
2070 01E9 B7-24           STA    TSTRG24+4
2080 *Now see to the Seconds
2090 01EB A6-20           LDA    #$20       *Blank out flashing flashing 12-hour colon
2100 01ED B7-2A           STA    TSTRG12+2
2110 01EF B6-14           LDA    SECS       *Get Seconds
2120 01F1 CD-0E40         JSR    DECIMAL    *Convert to ASCII decimal
2130 01F4 B6-11           LDA    TENS       *Tens of seconds
2140 01F6 B7-26           STA    TSTRG24+6  *to 24-hour string
2150 01F8 B6-10           LDA    UNITS      *Same for units of seconds
2160 01FA B7-27           STA    TSTRG24+7
2170 01FC 01-1404         BRCLR  0,SECS,NOWHOUR *On odd seconds leave 12-hour colon blanked
2180 01FF A6-3A           LDA    #':        *ELSE colon on
2190 0201 B7-2A           STA    TSTRG12+2
2200 *Finally the Hours
2210 0203 B6-16   NOWHOUR LDA    HOURS      *Get Hours
2220 0205 CD-0E40         JSR    DECIMAL    *Into decimal
2230 0208 B6-11           LDA    TENS       *Tens of hours
2240 020A B7-20           STA    TSTRG24    *to the 24-hour string
2250 020C B6-10           LDA    UNITS      *Same for units
2260 020E B7-21           STA    TSTRG24+1
2270 *Now we have the problem of converting to a 12-hour format
2280 0210 AE-41           LDX    #'A        *First assume its AM
2290 0212 BF-2E           STX    TSTRG12+6
2300 0214 B6-16           LDA    HOURS      *Now test hours value
2310 0216 A1-0C           CMP    #12        *Check : Is it midday or later?
2320 0218 25-04           BLO    HCONVERT   *IF not THEN leave as AM
2330 021A AE-50           LDX    #'P        *ELSE PM
2340 021C BF-2E           STX    TSTRG12+6
2350 021E 4D      HCONVERTTSTA              *Check : Is it zero hour (midnight)?
2360 021F 26-04           BNE    ONEPM?     *IF not THEN try for 1PM plus
2370 0221 AB-0C           ADD    #12        *ELSE convert 0 to 12 oclock
2380 0223 20-06           BRA    HR12       *Conversion done
2390 0225 A1-0D   ONEPM?  CMP    #13        *Check : Is it 13 or more hours?
2400 0227 25-02           BLO    HR12       *IF not THEN no conversion needed
2410 0229 A0-0C           SUB    #12        *ELSE take away 12
2420 022B CD-0E40 HR12    JSR    DECIMAL    *Convert to decimal
2430 022E B6-11           LDA    TENS       *Get tens of hours
2440 0230 A1-30           CMP    #'0        *Blank it out if zero
2450 0232 26-02           BNE    TCONT      *IF not THEN dont
2460 0234 A6-20           LDA    #$20       *Blank code
2470 0236 B7-28   TCONT   STA    TSTRG12
2480 0238 B6-10           LDA    UNITS      *Update units of hours
2490 023A B7-29           STA    TSTRG12+1
2500 *At last display one of these strings
2510 023C 08-0204         BRSET  4,SWITCH,DISP12 *Based on the state of Switch4
2520 023F AE-20           LDX    #TSTRG24   *IF zero THEN point to 24-hour string
2530 0241 20-02           BRA    TOUTPUT
2540 0243 AE-28   DISP12  LDX    #TSTRG12   *ELSE do a 12-hour display
2550 0245 CD-0E00 TOUTPUT JSR    PDATA      *Send it to the display device
2560 0248 CC-0130         JMP    NEXTC
```

Listing 17.2 Displaying the time

The conversion of hours between the formats is given as:

24-hour	→	*12-hour*

00 hours (00 : 00-00 : 59) → 12 hours AM (12 : 00-12 : 59, Lines 2350/70)
One hour to 12 hours   → No change
13 hours to 23 hours   → 1 hour to 12 hours PM (Lines 2390–2410)
00 hours to 11 hours   → AM (Lines 2280–2320)
12 hours to 23 hours   → PM (Lines 2330–2340)

Once the hour has been transformed (add 12 if zero hours; subtract 12 if 13 to 23 hours) then it is changed to decimal in the normal way, Line 2420. If the tens-of-hours digit is zero, a blank is sent in its place to the top of the 12-hour string, Lines 2440–2470. Otherwise the top two characters represent the hour digits, Lines 2470–2490.

With the time strings updated, the relevant one is sent to the display, depending on the state of switch PC4 (Line 2510), by simply pointing the index register to the appropriate string. An example of both these display formats is shown in Fig. 18.1.

18

Grand Finale

Now that both hardware and software aspects of our project are covered, it only remains to program the 68705R3's EPROM, plug in and switch on. Although it is unlikely that malfunction will occur at this point in the proceedings, the first part of this chapter gives advice on possible problems, and some guidance on calibrating the annunciator.

While the study and construction of a system to somebody else's design criterion is a valuable educational experience, this should only be regarded as a steppingstone to the objective of the reader acquiring the ability to complete his or her own project successfully. With a view to easing the transition across the not inconsiderable gap between these two accomplishments, Section 18.2 suggests some extensions to our project which can be undertaken by the reader.

18.1 COMMISSIONING THE ANNUNCIATOR

We spent some considerable time in Chapter 14 detailing a test procedure for the hardware annunciator circuit. With the assumption that the diagnostic software ran as specified in Section 14.4, then it is likely that any malfunction at this stage will originate in the software aspects of the circuit. The original diagnostic software has been incorporated with the annunciator, however, and can be called up at any time by opening all four option switches and pressing reset. Therefore, follow the instructions in Section 14.4 to checkout the hardware.

Listing 18.1 shows a complete hex dump of the contents of the 68705's program EPROM. In the advent that the diagnostic checkout fails, a careful comparison between this and your own code should be made. Code corruption is even more likely when the diagnostics pass and the main annunciator functions fail. The fault is unlikely to lie with the 68705's EPROM programmer of Fig. 10.1 or 10.3 if the verify LED is lit after a program pass. Rather an error in your source code (probably typing) is the likely culprit.

To recover from the diagnostic mode, set the option switches to the desired configuration and press $\overline{\text{Reset}}$. Typically after a power-down situation the time will have to be set. This can be accomplished by setting switches SW7,6,5,4 to 1010 (see

ANNUNCIATOR-HEX 68705 listing

User EPROM:-

```
⟨080⟩ 41 2F 44 3D 20 24 04 53 57 49 54 43 4B 20 04 00 00 00 00 00 00 00 00 00 00 00 00 00 00 00 00 00    ← Diagnostic strings
⟨0A0⟩ 00 00 00 00 00 00 00 00 00 00 00 00 00 00 00 00 00 00 00 00 00 00 00 00 00 00 00 00 00 00 00 00
⟨0C0⟩ 00 00 00 00 00 00 00 00 00 00 00 00 00 00 00 00 00 00 00 00 00 00 00 00 00 00 00 00 00 00 00 00
⟨0E0⟩ 00 00 00 00 00 00 00 00 00 00 00 00 00 00 00 00 00 00 00 00 00 00 00 00 00 00 00 00 00 00 00 00    Main routine
⟨100⟩ A6 FF B7 04 B7 05 3F 09 AE 20 A6 20 F7 5C A3 40 25 FB A6 3A B7 22 B7 25 A6 4D B7 2F A6 46 B7 37    ← Initialisation
⟨120⟩ A6 43 B7 3F 9A B6 02 A4 F0 A1 F0 26 03 CC 0A 00 0E 02 0B 0C 02 05 00 15 02 20 03 CC 01 DA 3F 40    ← & Choice
⟨140⟩ 3F 41 5F B6 0F BB 40 B7 40 B6 41 A9 00 B7 41 5C 26 F1 B6 41 0F 40 01 4C 0B 02 2B AE 20 BF 3C A0    ← Temperature
⟨160⟩ 2B 24 05 40 AE 2D BF 3C 44 44 A9 00 CD 0E 40 AE 20 BF 3D B6 11 A1 30 27 02 B7 3D B6 10 B7 3E AE
⟨180⟩ 38 CD 0E 00 20 AA 3F 41 B7 40 38 40 39 41 38 40 39 41 38 40 39 41 BB 40 B7 40 B6 41 A9 00 B7 41
⟨1A0⟩ 3F 50 AE 08 B6 41 A0 05 25 02 B7 41 39 50 38 40 39 41 5A 26 EF B6 50 43 44 A9 0E CD 0E 40 AE 20
⟨1C0⟩ BF 34 B6 12 A1 30 27 02 B7 34 B6 11 B7 35 B6 10 B7 36 AE 30 CD 0E 00 CC 01 30 B6 15 CD 0E 40 B6    ← Time display
⟨1E0⟩ 11 B7 2B B7 23 B6 10 B7 2C B7 24 A6 20 B7 2A B6 14 CD 0E 40 B6 11 B7 26 B6 10 B7 27 01 14 04 A6
⟨200⟩ 3A B7 2A B6 16 CD 0E 40 B6 11 B7 20 B6 10 B7 21 AE 41 BF 2E B6 16 A1 0C 25 04 AE 50 BF 2E 4D 26
⟨220⟩ 04 AB 0C 20 06 A1 0D 25 02 A0 0C CD 0E 40 B6 11 A1 30 26 02 A6 20 B7 2B B6 10 B7 29 0B 02 04 AE
⟨240⟩ 20 20 02 AE 2B CD 0E 00 CC 01 30 00 00 00 00 00 00 00 00 00 00 00 00 00 00 00 00 00 00 00 00 00
⟨260⟩ 00 00 00 00 00 00 00 00 00 00 00 00 00 00 00 00 00 00 00 00 00 00 00 00 00 00 00 00 00 00 00 00
⟨280⟩ 00 00 00 00 00 00 00 00 00 00 00 00 00 00 00 00 00 00 00 00 00 00 00 00 00 00 00 00 00 00 00 00
⟨2A0⟩ 00 00 00 00 00 00 00 00 00 00 00 00 00 00 00 00 00 00 00 00 00 00 00 00 00 00 00 00 00 00 00 00
⟨2C0⟩ 00 00 00 00 00 00 00 00 00 00 00 00 00 00 00 00 00 00 00 00 00 00 00 00 00 00 00 00 00 00 00 00
⟨2E0⟩ 00 00 00 00 00 00 00 00 00 00 00 00 00 00 00 00 00 00 00 00 00 00 00 00 00 00 00 00 00 00 00 00
⟨300⟩ 00 00 00 00 00 00 00 00 00 00 00 00 00 00 00 00 00 00 00 00 00 00 00 00 00 00 00 00 00 00 00 00
⟨320⟩ 00 00 00 00 00 00 00 00 00 00 00 00 00 00 00 00 00 00 00 00 00 00 00 00 00 00 00 00 00 00 00 00
⟨340⟩ 00 00 00 00 00 00 00 00 00 00 00 00 00 00 00 00 00 00 00 00 00 00 00 00 00 00 00 00 00 00 00 00
⟨360⟩ 00 00 00 00 00 00 00 00 00 00 00 00 00 00 00 00 00 00 00 00 00 00 00 00 00 00 00 00 00 00 00 00
⟨380⟩ 00 00 00 00 00 00 00 00 00 00 00 00 00 00 00 00 00 00 00 00 00 00 00 00 00 00 00 00 00 00 00 00
⟨3A0⟩ 00 00 00 00 00 00 00 00 00 00 00 00 00 00 00 00 00 00 00 00 00 00 00 00 00 00 00 00 00 00 00 00
⟨3C0⟩ 00 00 00 00 00 00 00 00 00 00 00 00 00 00 00 00 00 00 00 00 00 00 00 00 00 00 00 00 00 00 00 00
⟨3E0⟩ 00 00 00 00 00 00 00 00 00 00 00 00 00 00 00 00 00 00 00 00 00 00 00 00 00 00 00 00 00 00 00 00
⟨400⟩ 00 00 00 00 00 00 00 00 00 00 00 00 00 00 00 00 00 00 00 00 00 00 00 00 00 00 00 00 00 00 00 00
⟨420⟩ 00 00 00 00 00 00 00 00 00 00 00 00 00 00 00 00 00 00 00 00 00 00 00 00 00 00 00 00 00 00 00 00
⟨440⟩ 00 00 00 00 00 00 00 00 00 00 00 00 00 00 00 00 00 00 00 00 00 00 00 00 00 00 00 00 00 00 00 00
⟨460⟩ 00 00 00 00 00 00 00 00 00 00 00 00 00 00 00 00 00 00 00 00 00 00 00 00 00 00 00 00 00 00 00 00
⟨480⟩ 00 00 00 00 00 00 00 00 00 00 00 00 00 00 00 00 00 00 00 00 00 00 00 00 00 00 00 00 00 00 00 00
⟨4A0⟩ 00 00 00 00 00 00 00 00 00 00 00 00 00 00 00 00 00 00 00 00 00 00 00 00 00 00 00 00 00 00 00 00
⟨4C0⟩ 00 00 00 00 00 00 00 00 00 00 00 00 00 00 00 00 00 00 00 00 00 00 00 00 00 00 00 00 00 00 00 00
⟨4E0⟩ 00 00 00 00 00 00 00 00 00 00 00 00 00 00 00 00 00 00 00 00 00 00 00 00 00 00 00 00 00 00 00 00
⟨500⟩ 00 00 00 00 00 00 00 00 00 00 00 00 00 00 00 00 00 00 00 00 00 00 00 00 00 00 00 00 00 00 00 00
⟨520⟩ 00 00 00 00 00 00 00 00 00 00 00 00 00 00 00 00 00 00 00 00 00 00 00 00 00 00 00 00 00 00 00 00
⟨540⟩ 00 00 00 00 00 00 00 00 00 00 00 00 00 00 00 00 00 00 00 00 00 00 00 00 00 00 00 00 00 00 00 00
⟨560⟩ 00 00 00 00 00 00 00 00 00 00 00 00 00 00 00 00 00 00 00 00 A6 00 00 00 00 00 00 00 00 00 00 00
⟨580⟩ 00 00 00 00 00 00 00 00 00 00 00 00 00 00 00 00 00 00 00 00 00 00 00 00 00 00 00 00 00 00 00 00
⟨5A0⟩ 00 00 00 00 00 00 00 00 00 00 00 00 00 00 0E 00 00 00 00 00 00 00 00 00 00 00 00 00 00 00 00 00
⟨5C0⟩ 00 00 00 00 00 00 00 00 00 00 00 00 00 00 00 00 00 00 00 00 00 00 00 00 00 00 00 00 00 00 00 00
⟨5E0⟩ 00 00 00 00 AE 00 00 00 00 00 00 00 00 00 00 00 00 00 00 00 00 00 00 00 00 00 00 00 00 00 00 00
⟨600⟩ 00 00 00 00 00 00 00 00 00 00 00 00 00 00 00 00 00 00 00 00 00 00 00 00 00 00 00 00 00 00 00 00
⟨620⟩ 00 00 00 00 00 00 00 00 00 00 00 00 00 00 00 00 00 00 00 00 00 00 00 00 00 00 00 00 00 00 00 00
⟨640⟩ 00 00 00 00 00 00 00 00 00 00 00 00 00 00 00 00 00 00 00 00 00 00 00 00 00 00 00 00 00 00 00 00
⟨660⟩ 00 00 2B 00 00 B6 00 00 00 00 00 00 00 00 00 00 00 00 00 2A 00 00 00 00 14 00 0E 40 00 00 27 00
⟨680⟩ 00 00 00 00 00 00 00 00 00 00 00 00 00 00 00 00 00 00 00 00 00 00 00 00 00 00 2E 00 00 00 00 00
⟨6A0⟩ 00 00 00 00 00 00 00 00 00 00 00 00 00 00 00 00 00 00 00 00 00 0C 00 00 00 00 00 00 00 00 00 00
⟨6C0⟩ 00 00 00 00 00 00 00 00 00 00 00 00 00 00 00 00 00 00 00 00 00 00 00 00 00 00 00 00 00 00 00 00
⟨6E0⟩ 00 00 00 00 00 00 00 00 00 00 00 00 00 00 00 00 00 00 00 00 00 00 00 00 00 00 00 00 00 00 00 00
⟨700⟩ 00 00 00 00 00 00 00 00 00 00 00 00 00 00 00 00 00 00 00 00 00 00 00 00 00 00 00 00 00 00 00 00
⟨720⟩ 00 00 00 00 00 00 00 00 00 00 00 00 00 00 00 00 00 00 00 00 00 00 00 00 00 00 00 00 00 00 00 00
⟨740⟩ 00 00 00 00 00 00 00 00 00 00 00 00 00 00 00 00 00 00 00 00 00 00 00 00 00 00 00 00 00 00 00 00
⟨760⟩ 00 00 00 00 00 00 00 00 00 00 00 00 00 00 00 00 00 00 00 00 00 00 00 00 00 00 00 00 00 00 00 00
⟨780⟩ 00 00 00 00 00 00 00 00 00 00 00 00 00 00 00 00 00 00 00 00 00 00 00 00 00 00 00 00 00 00 00 00
⟨7A0⟩ 00 00 00 00 00 00 00 00 00 00 00 00 00 00 00 00 00 00 00 00 00 00 00 00 00 00 00 00 00 00 00 00
⟨7C0⟩ 00 00 00 00 00 00 00 00 00 00 00 00 00 00 00 00 00 00 00 00 00 00 00 00 00 00 00 00 00 00 00 00
⟨7E0⟩ 00 00 00 00 00 00 00 00 00 00 00 00 00 00 00 00 00 00 00 00 00 00 00 00 00 00 00 00 00 00 00 00
⟨800⟩ 00 00 00 00 00 00 00 00 00 00 00 00 00 00 00 00 00 00 00 00 00 00 00 00 00 00 00 00 00 00 00 00
⟨820⟩ 00 00 00 00 00 00 00 00 00 00 00 00 00 00 00 00 00 00 00 00 00 00 00 00 00 00 00 00 00 00 00 00
```

Listing 18.1   The programmed annunciator 68705 EPROM

```
<B40> 00 00 00 00 00 00 00 00 00 00 00 00 00 00 00 00 00 00 00 00 00 00 00 00 00 00 00 00 00 00 00 00
<B60> 00 00 00 00 00 00 00 00 00 00 00 00 00 00 00 00 00 00 00 00 00 00 00 00 00 00 00 00 00 00 00 00
<B80> 00 00 00 00 00 00 00 00 00 00 00 00 00 00 00 00 00 00 00 00 00 00 00 00 00 00 00 00 00 00 00 00
<BA0> 00 00 00 00 00 00 00 00 00 00 00 00 00 00 00 00 00 00 00 00 00 00 00 00 00 00 00 00 00 00 00 00
<BC0> 00 00 00 00 00 00 00 00 00 00 00 00 00 00 00 00 00 00 00 00 00 00 00 00 00 00 00 00 00 00 00 00
<BE0> 00 00 00 00 00 00 00 00 00 00 00 00 00 00 00 00 00 00 00 00 00 00 00 00 00 00 00 00 00 00 00 00
<900> 00 00 00 00 00 00 00 00 00 00 00 00 00 00 00 00 00 00 00 00 00 00 00 00 00 00 00 00 00 00 00 00
<920> 00 00 00 00 00 00 00 00 00 00 00 00 00 00 00 00 00 00 00 00 00 00 00 00 00 00 00 00 00 00 00 00
<940> 00 00 00 00 00 00 00 00 00 00 00 00 00 00 00 00 00 00 00 00 00 00 00 00 00 00 00 00 00 00 00 00
<960> 00 00 00 00 00 00 00 00 00 00 00 00 00 00 00 00 00 00 00 00 00 00 00 00 00 00 00 00 00 00 00 00
<9B0> 00 00 00 00 00 00 00 00 00 00 00 00 00 00 00 00 00 00 00 00 00 00 00 00 00 00 00 00 00 00 00 00
<9A0> 00 00 00 00 00 00 00 00 00 00 00 00 00 00 00 00 00 00 00 00 00 00 00 00 00 00 00 00 00 00 00 00
<9C0> 00 00 00 00 00 00 00 00 00 00 00 00 00 00 00 00 00 00 00 00 00 00 00 00 00 00 00 00 00 00 00 00
<9E0> 00 00 00 00 00 00 00 00 00 00 00 00 00 00 00 00 00 00 00 00 00 00 00 00 00 00 00 00 00 00 00 00    Diagnostic routine
<A00> A6 FF B7 04 B7 05 0F 02 1B AE 87 CD 0E 00 B6 02 44 44 44 44 A4 F7 AB 30 B7 00 A6 C0 B7 01 1D 01  ← Switch test
<A20> 1C 01 20 E2 AE B0 CD 0E 00 B6 0F 97 44 44 44 44 AB 30 A1 39 23 02 AB 07 B7 00 A6 C1 B7 01 1D 01  ← Analog test
<A40> 1C 01 9F A4 0F AB 30 A1 39 23 02 AB 07 B7 00 A6 C0 B7 01 1D 01 1C 01 20 AD 00 00 00 00 00 00 00
<A60> 00 00 00 00 00 00 00 00 00 00 00 00 00 00 00 00 00 00 00 00 00 00 00 00 00 00 00 00 00 00 00 00
<AB0> 00 00 00 00 00 00 00 00 00 00 00 00 00 00 00 00 00 00 00 00 00 00 00 00 00 00 00 00 00 00 00 00
<AA0> 00 00 00 00 00 00 00 00 00 00 00 00 00 00 00 00 00 00 00 00 00 00 00 00 00 00 00 00 00 00 00 00
<AC0> 00 00 00 00 00 00 00 00 00 00 00 00 00 00 00 00 00 00 00 00 00 00 00 00 00 00 00 00 00 00 00 00
<AE0> 00 00 00 00 00 00 00 00 00 00 00 00 00 00 00 00 00 00 00 00 00 00 00 00 00 00 00 00 00 00 00 00    Timer Service routine
<B00> 1F 09 CD 0B 20 0F 02 0E 0A 02 05 CD 0B 34 20 06 0C 02 03 CD 0B 2A B0 00 00 00 00 00 00 00 00 00  ← Decision routine
<B20> 3C 13 B6 13 A1 19 25 20 3F 13 3C 14 B6 14 A1 3C 25 16 3F 14 3C 15 B6 15 A1 3C 25 0C 3F 15 3C 16  ← Update array subroutine
<B40> B6 16 A1 1B 25 02 3F 16 81 00 00 00 00 00 00 00 00 00 00 00 00 00 00 00 00 00 00 00 00 00 00 00
<B60> 00 00 00 00 00 00 00 00 00 00 00 00 00 00 00 00 00 00 00 00 00 00 00 00 00 00 00 00 00 00 00 00
<BB0> 00 00 00 00 00 00 00 00 00 00 00 00 00 00 00 00 00 00 00 00 00 00 00 00 00 00 00 00 00 00 00 00
<BA0> 00 00 00 00 00 00 00 00 00 00 00 00 00 00 00 00 00 00 00 00 00 00 00 00 00 00 00 00 00 00 00 00
<BC0> 00 00 00 00 00 00 00 00 00 00 00 00 00 00 00 00 00 00 00 00 00 00 00 00 00 00 00 00 00 00 00 00
<BE0> 00 00 00 00 00 00 00 00 00 00 00 00 00 00 00 00 00 00 00 00 00 00 00 00 00 00 00 00 00 00 00 00
<C00> 00 00 00.00 00 00 00 00 00 00 00 00 00 00 00 00 00 00 00 00 00 00 00 00 00 00 00 00 00 00 00 00
<C20> 00 00 00 00 00 00 00 00 00 00 00 00 00 00 00 00 00 00 00 00 00 00 00 00 00 00 00 00 00 00 00 00
<C40> 00 00 00 00 00 00 00 00 00 00 00 00 00 00 00 00 00 00 00 00 00 00 00 00 00 00 00 00 00 00 00 00
<C60> 00 00 00 00 00 00 00 00 00 00 00 00 00 00 00 00 00 00 00 00 00 00 00 00 00 00 00 00 00 00 00 00
<C80> 00 00 00 00 00 00 00 00 00 00 00 00 00 00 00 00 00 00 00 00 00 00 00 00 00 00 00 00 00 00 00 00
<CA0> 00 00 00 00 00 00 00 00 00 00 00 00 00 00 00 00 00 00 00 00 00 00 00 00 00 00 00 00 00 00 00 00
<CC0> 00 00 00 00 00 00 00 00 00 00 00 00 00 00 00 00 00 00 00 00 00 00 00 00 00 00 00 00 00 00 00 00
<CE0> 00 00 00 00 00 00 00 00 00 00 00 00 00 00 00 00 00 00 00 00 00 00 00 00 00 00 00 00 00 00 00 00
<D00> 00 00 00 00 00 00 00 00 00 00 00 00 00 00 00 00 00 00 00 00 00 00 00 00 00 00 00 00 00 00 00 00
<D20> 00 00 00 00 00 00 00 00 00 00 00 00 00 00 00 00 00 00 00 00 00 00 00 00 00 00 00 00 00 00 00 00
<D40> 00 00 00 00 00 00 00 00 00 00 00 00 00 00 00 00 00 00 00 00 00 00 00 00 00 00 00 00 00 00 00 00
<D60> 00 00 00 00 00 00 00 00 00 00 00 00 00 00 00 00 00 00 00 00 00 00 00 00 00 00 00 00 00 00 00 00
<D80> 00 00 00 00 00 00 00 00 00 00 00 00 00 00 00 00 00 00 00 00 00 00 00 00 00 00 00 00 00 00 00 00
<DA0> 00 00 00 00 00 00 00 00 00 00 00 00 00 00 00 00 00 00 00 00 00 00 00 00 00 00 00 00 00 00 00 00
<DC0> 00 00 00 00 00 00 00 00 00 00 00 00 00 00 00 00 00 00 00 00 00 00 00 00 00 00 00 00 00 00 00 00    Subroutines
<DE0> 00 00 00 00 00 00 00 00 00 00 00 00 00 00 00 00 00 00 00 00 00 00 00 00 00 00 00 00 00 00 00 00
<E00> A6 C7 B7 01 F6 27 13 A1 04 27 1A B7 00 05 01 06 1F 01 1E 01 20 04 1D 01 1C 01 5C B6 01 A1 C0 27  ← PDATA
<E20> 04 3A 01 20 DF B1 00 00 00 00 00 00 00 00 00 00 00 00 00 00 00 00 00 00 00 00 00 00 00 00 00 00  ← DECIMAL
<E40> AE 30 BF 10 BF 11 BF 12 A1 64 25 06 A0 64 3C 12 20 F6 A1 0A 25 06 A0 0A 3C 11 20 F6 BB 10 B7 10
<E60> 81 00 00 00 00 00 00 00 00 00 00 00 00 00 00 00 00 00 00 00 00 00 00 00 00 00 00 00 00 00 00 00
<E80> 00 00 00 00 00 00 00 00 00 00 00 00 00 00 00 00 00 00 00 00 00 00 00 00 00 00 00 00 00 00 00 00
<EA0> 00 00 00 00 00 00 00 00 00 00 00 00 00 00 00 00 00 00 00 00 00 00 00 00 00 00 00 00 00 00 00 00
<EC0> 00 00 00 00 00 00 00 00 00 00 00 00 00 00 00 00 00 00 00 00 00 00 00 00 00 00 00 00 00 00 00 00
<EE0> 00 00 00 00 00 00 00 00 00 00 00 00 00 00 00 00 00 00 00 00 00 00 00 00 00 00 00 00 00 00 00 00
<F00> 00 00 00 00 00 00 00 00 00 00 00 00 00 00 00 00 00 00 00 00 00 00 00 00 00 00 00 00 00 00 00 00
<F20> 00 00 00 00 00 00 00 00 00 00 00 00 00 00 00 00 00 00 00 00 00 00
<F38> Mask Option Register 47
BOOTSTRAP ROM from F39 to FF7
<FF8> Timer/INT2 vector B00
<FFA> INT vector 000
<FFC> SWI vector 000
<FFE> RESET vector 100
```

Listing 18.1   The programmed annunciator 68705 EPROM (*continued*)

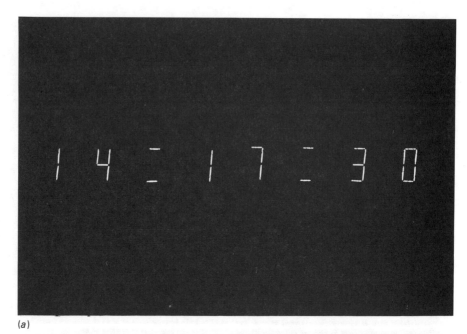

(a)

(b)

Fig. 18.1 Typical displays
(a) 24-hour time
(b) 12-hour time

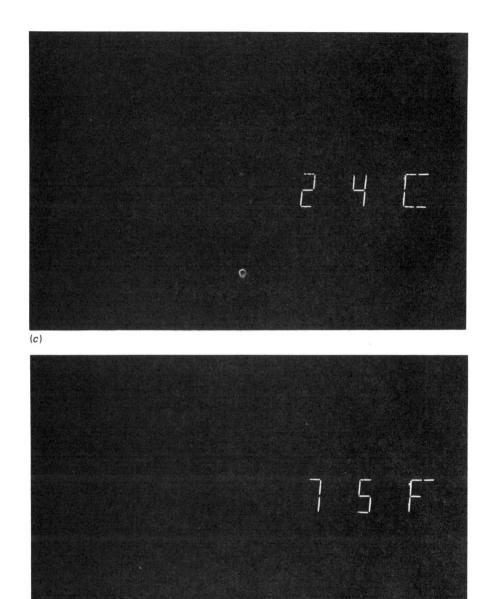

Fig. 18.1 Typical displays (continued)
(c) °C temperature
(d) °F temperature

Fig. 13.1) to give a slow ($\times 25$) time set in the 24-hour mode. At switch-on it is possible that a nonlegitimate time will appear (i.e., an hour display >23 or second/minute reading > 59), as the relevent RAM locations are not reset during the initialization phase of the software. Changing SW5 to logic 0 (fast set $\times 1,500$) will quickly speed the display through this erroneous range. Both fast and slow switches (SW5 and 6) can then be used to bring the time up to the correct point. With both these switches open, time will advance at the normal rate.

Should the time display refuse to advance, check that the timer input (Pin 8) is logic 1. In Section 17.1 we choose the internal clock ϕ_2 as the timer source (MOR5 $= 0$). This option actually selects ϕ_2 gated by the timer pin level, i.e., $T \cdot \phi_2$. Thus if T is low, we have effectively inhibited the count (and in fact you can make use of this as a time-freeze input).

Once the time is correct then SW7 can be closed, and this will place the annunciator in the normal run-mode. In this situation SW5 selects either the 24- or 12-hour display formats (see Figs. 18.1(a) and (b)), while SW6 selects either a continuous time display or alternating between a time and temperature output on a 1-minute each basis. Figures 18.1(c) and (d) show typical temperature displays.

It should be necessary to calibrate the temperature transducer only once. As there are two interdependent variable parameters, viz., scale-gain and zero point (see Fig. 13.6), a 2-point iterative procedure should be used. This involves two known temperatures, which for convenience can be melting ice and room temperature. The melting ice can be in a plastic bag to avoid contact with the sensor, but beware of condensation which can still cause water damage. Remember that the density of water peaks at $+4°C$, and water at this temperature will lie at the bottom of the bag, giving a lower reference at this temperature rather than $0°C$. Warm water with an accurate mercury thermometer, or failing this a known room-temperature, may be used for the second reference.

With switches SW7 and 6 closed (logic 0) the temperature display will alternate with time. Place the ice-water mixture in good contact with the sensor, and after stabilization adjust R_o (see Fig. 13.6) to give $4°C$. Repeat this procedure at the higher reference, but this time adjusting R_s. Iteratively repeat the complete procedure until no further adjustment is required.

18.2   SOME IDEAS FOR EXPANSION

The annunciator used as an example in this text is a relatively simple application of single-chip microcomputers in digital instrumentation. At this level of complexity the effectiveness of such an approach scores little over a wholly random logic-based implementation. However, the MCU-based product can readily be changed or extended with relatively little alteration to the hardware circuitry. Flexible personality is the chief asset of this type of implementation.

EVENT TIMER

The clock section of our project annunciator is essentially an elapsed time counter, totalizing 40 ms ticks since reset (or setting up). These ticks are in turn generated by counting 2^{15} 819.2 kHz oscillator cycles. The 15-bit counter chain comprises the 7-bit prescaler register and 8-bit timer. The MOR is set to drive this chain by ϕ_2 gated with the logic level of the timer pin (Pin 9). In Fig. 13.1 we showed this pin pulled up to logic 1.

With this discussion in mind, it is a simple matter to measure the period of an external event, provided that the event detector provides an active-high logic level for its duration. If this drives the timer pin, then only logic 1 duration will be measured. This signal *must* be clean as any noise spikes, e.g., bounce from a limit switch, will create erroneous counts. As an example, an event with a beginning and end detector, perhaps a falling weight passing two photo transistors, could use a simple cross-coupled NAND latch to buffer (and debounce) the event to the microcomputer.

Some software changes will be necessary. At the very least this will involve the inclusion of code to zero the time array during reset initialization. As the software stands, the resolution is one twenty-fifth of a second, and this can be utilized by changing the display software. An alternative format is mm:ss.1/10 1/100, giving a maximum elapsed time of 99 minutes 59.99 seconds to a resolution of 0.01 second. To achieve this, a division ratio of 2^{13} (prescale $= 2^5$) must be used to give the 10 ms tick rate.

MAXIMUM-MINIMUM THERMOMETER

The thermometer section of the annunciator displays the current temperature. Only a simple software change is necessary to record the maximum and minimum temperature since last reset. The function of the switches at Port C will of course have to be reassigned to reflect the changed options. If it is desired to display this new data in addition to the original annunciator information, then two extra switches, connected perhaps to PC2 and 3, will be required to reflect the new options.

As a maximum-minimum thermometer, the MCU hardware and software can readily be extended to encompass the control function. Typically used in a greenhouse environment, a temperature below a predetermined limit (set in the same manner as we developed for the annunciator clock) can be used to sound an alarm. More ambitiously, a heater can be switched on in this event using a spare parallel port line, e.g., PB7. Either a buffered electromechanical relay can be used as the power switch, or a solid-state relay. A typical example of the latter can switch up to 25A at 280 Vac – e.g., the International Rectifier D2425-1 on a 1°C/W heatsink – and is directly controllable with an unbuffered logic-level signal. Various control strategies can be devised to keep the temperature constant or to follow a time-of-day related pattern. This can encompass solenoid control of window shades or refrigeration plant, to avoid overheating in the sun.

Up to this point we have talked about using one of the analog channels. There is no problem in extending this to four channels. In the context of a greenhouse, this could encompass three additional temperatures at various points inside and outside the house or different parameters such as humidity and external wind speed.

Channel capacity may be expanded by using external analog multiplexers controlled by spare parallel port lines. Thus four 16- to 1-line analog multiplexers addressed by four parallel lines would give an overall 64-channel capacity.

DATA LOGGING

The systems discussed in this section give information concerning events at only one instant in time. A natural extension to this is the logging of a series of data values over a period of time. Thus, e.g., a data logger could be used to acquire the temperature at every five minutes over a period of 24 hours.

Two problems arise in extending our annunciator to act as a *data logger*. Firstly, memory capacity to store the data array and, secondly, display. In general the additional memory is required only where the data logger is situated in a remote site. Then data must be stored for collection (or interrogation, say by telephone line) at a future time. Although the 6805 series has severely limited RAM capacities, RAM chips may be interfaced as external peripheral devices. A typical interface technique giving sequential access (which is suitable for this application) is shown in Fig. 10.3.

Where long-term monitoring is envisaged, nonvolatile RAM obviates the necessity for periodically changing the logger. The RAM is simply removed, and returned to base for examination. For example, the Mostek MK48Z02 has an in-

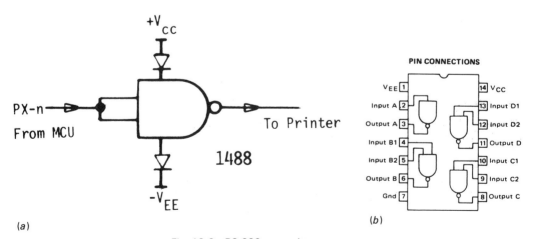

Fig. 18.2 RS-232 transmitter
(*a*) Transmitter
(*b*) MC1488 pinout (reproduced by courtesy of Motorola Limited)

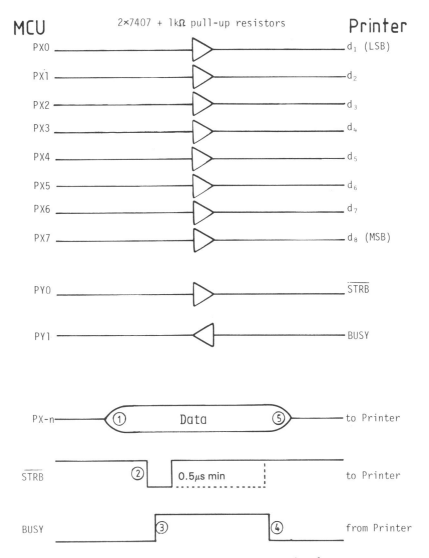

MCU   2×7407 + 1kΩ pull-up resistors   Printer

PX0 d_1 (LSB)

PX1 d_2

PX2 d_3

PX3 d_4

PX4 d_5

PX5 d_6

PX6 d_7

PX7 d_8 (MSB)

PY0 $\overline{STRB}$

PY1   BUSY

PX-n   ①   Data   ⑤   to Printer

$\overline{STRB}$ ②   0.5µs min   to Printer

BUSY   ③   ④   from Printer

Fig. 18.3   A bare-bones parallel-printer interface

tegral lithium cell, giving a ten-year data retention. The MK48Z02's capacity is 2,048 bytes. Because of its low-active current drain it is especially useful, in conjunction with CMOS MCUs, for battery or solar power operation.

With the logger in a more local site, it may be interfaced to a printer, which will give a hard copy display of the data profile. Most serial printers accept data in the RS-232 format discussed in Section 5.2. A practical interface between the 6805 MCU and a RS-232 printer is given in Fig. 18.2. Note that as the 1488 line driver has an inverting action, the polarity of the serial OUTCH transmission software of

Section 9.2 must be reversed. Remember also that OUTCH presupposes the use of a 4 MHz crystal.

Many printers, especially those oriented towards personal computer terminals, use a parallel 'Centronics' type interface. Essentially this comprises an 8-bit data bus, together with several handshake lines. A minimum configuration is shown in Fig. 18.2, and the corresponding 6805 driver subroutine must provide for the following sequence.

1. If BUSY is passive THEN put data out on parallel port, ELSE repeat 1.
2. Allowing a few microseconds for stabilization, bring $\overline{\text{STROBE}}$ ($\overline{\text{STRB}}$) low for a minimum of 0.5 μs.
3. The printer responds by activating its BUSY line.
4. When the printer has digested the data and is ready for some more, it will deactivate BUSY.
5. Transmitter can now remove its data. Go to 1.

Most printers will have additional handshake lines. The most common of these are $\overline{\text{ACK}}$, PE and SLCT. $\overline{\text{ACK}}$ is a nominal 10 μs pulse produced by the printer to acknowledge that data has been received, and that it is ready for the next byte. BUSY goes low after this event. $\overline{\text{ACK}}$ is normally used to interrupt the MCU/MPU. PE indicates end of paper and SLCT is active when the printer is powered up.

Annotated Reading List

Boney, J., 'The Design of the M6805: A Controller Optimised 8-bit Architecture', *Proc. Electro/81*, Session 11/5, 1982. (The evolution of the 6805 architecture, by one of the original designers.)

Cahill, S. J., *Designing microprocessor-based digital circuitry*, Prentice-Hall, 1985. (A good background to the hardware and software aspects of microprocessor systems!)

Coates, R. F., 'Picotutor Assembly-language Trainer', Parts I and II, *Wireless World* (UK), vol 88 (Dec 1982) pp 52–4; vol 89 (Jan 1983) pp 70–2. (A simple monitor-based development system based on the 68705R3 MCU.)

Coates, R. F., 'Assembly Language Programming', Parts I to VIII, *Wireless World* (UK), vol 89 (1983) : (Mar) pp 33–5; (Apr) pp 63–6; (May) pp 51–2; (June) pp 59–61; (Aug) pp 68–9; (Sept) pp 45–9; (Oct) pp 71–2; vol 90 (Apr 1984) pp 36–41. (Assembly language tutorials for the 6805, Z80 and 6809 processors plus hardware interface for the Picotutor.)

Gonzales, D. R., 'The Versatile MC6805S2 Peripheral Circuitry Allows a Variety of Applications', *Proc MINI/MICRO Midwest 83*, Session 1/2, 1984. (Looks at one of the 6805 MCU family with onboard serial interface.)

Gonzales, D. R., 'Data Security Using Single-chip Micros with On-board EEPROM', *Electronic Engineering* (UK), vol 57 (Jan 1985) pp 75–80. (Data and software security problems in single-chip MCUs)

Huston, W, 'Self-programmed Single-chips . . . The MC68705s', *Proc Electro/82*, Session 29/1, 1983. (A useful discussion on the economics of EPROM vers ROMed MCUs.)

Lagan, J. A., 'The Programming Ease of the M6805 Family', *Proc Electro/82*, Session 25/1, 1983. (A software review of the 6805 MCU family.)

Lister, P. F. (ed), *Single-chip Microcomputers*, Granada, 1984. (Contributed chapters by representatives of all the major MCU manufacturers. Includes details on the MK68200 16-bit MCU.)

Lockerbie, N. A., 'Sampling Frequency Meter', *Wireless World* (UK), vol 90 (Jan 1984) pp 37–40. (Application of the 146805E2 CMOS MPU as a windspeed monitor in remote areas for periods of up to 12 months.)

'Microprocessors and Microcomputers - CMOS challenges on speed and power', *Electronics Industry* (UK) vol 12 (Oct 1986) pp 19–31. (A useful review of available MCUs.)

Motorola, '*M6805 HMOS M146805 CMOS Family User's Manual,* 2nd ed, Prentice-Hall, 1983. (Hardware, software and programming details for the commoner 6805 MCU devices; includes a monitor listing.)

Motorola, *MCU/MPU Applications Manual*, Motorola, vol 2, 1984. (A compilation of 30 application notes, many of which cover MCUs.)

Stechahn, A. D & Den Otter, J., *Industrial Applications for Microprocessors*, Reston Publishing Company, 1982. (A useful book on interfacing, and as a bonus Chapter 6 looks at the 6805E2 MPU.)

Whitlock, R., 'Single Chip Microcontroller', Parts 1, 2 and 3, *Electronics & Computing Monthly* (UK) (1983): (Oct) pp 35–7; (Nov) pp 28–30; (Dec) pp 89–90. (Introduction to the 68705 processor including self-programming.)

Whitlock, R., 'A Cross-assembler for the MC68705s', *Electronics & Computing Monthly* (UK) (Jan 1984) pp 53–7. (A simple cross-assembler in BASIC to run on your home computer.)

Appendix 1

The 68705R3 Data Sheet

Reproduced by courtesy of Motorola Limited

MOTOROLA SEMICONDUCTORS

Colvilles Road, Kelvin Estate-East Kilbridge/Glasgow-SCOTLAND

MC68705R3

Advance Information

8-BIT EPROM MICROCOMPUTER UNIT WITH A/D

The MC68705R3 Microcomputer Unit (MCU) is an EPROM member of the M6805 Family of low-cost single-chip microcomputers. The user programmable EPROM allows program changes and lower volume applications in comparison to the factory mask programmable versions. The EPROM versions also reduce the development costs and turn-around time for prototype evaluation of the mask ROM versions. This 8-bit microcomputer contains a CPU, on-chip CLOCK, EPROM, boot-strap ROM, RAM, I/O, A/D Converter, and a TIMER.

Because of these features, the MC68705R3 offers the user an economical means of designing an M6805 Family MCU into his system, either as a prototype evaluation, as a low-volume production run, or a pilot production run.

A comparison table of the key features for several members of the M6805 Family is shown on the last page of this data sheet.

HARDWARE FEATURES
- 8-Bit Architecture
- 112 Bytes of RAM
- Memory Mapped I/O
- 3776 Bytes of User EPROM
- Internal 8-Bit Timer with 7-Bit Prescaler
  - Programmable Prescaler
  - Programmable Timer Input Modes
- 4 Vectored Interrupts — External (2), Timer (1), and Software (1)
- Zero-Cross Detection on $\overline{INT}$ Input
- 24 TTL/CMOS Compatible Bidirectional I/O Lines (8 Lines are LED Compatible)
- 8 Digital Input Lines
- A/D Converter
  - 8-Bit Conversion, Monotonic
  - 4 Multiplexed Analog Inputs
  - $\pm \frac{1}{2}$ LSB Quantitizing Error
  - $\pm \frac{1}{2}$ LSB All Other Errors
  - ± 1 LSB Total Error (Max)
  - Ratiometric Conversion
- On-Chip Clock Generator
- Master Reset
- Complete Development System Support on EXORciser
- 5 V Single Supply
- Emulates the MC6805R2
- Bootstrap Program in ROM Simplifies EPROM Programming

SOFTWARE FEATURES
- Similar to M6800 Family
- Byte Efficient Instruction Set
- Easy to Program
- True Bit Manipulation
- Bit Test and Branch Instructions
- Versatile Interrupt Handling
- Versatile Index Registers
- Powerful Indexed Addressing for Tables
- Full Set of Conditional Branches
- Memory Usable as Registers/Flags
- Single Instruction Memory Examine/Change
- 10 Powerful Addressing Modes
- All Addressing Modes Apply to EPROM, RAM, and I/O

HMOS
(HIGH-DENSITY, N-CHANNEL DEPLETION LOAD, 5 V EPROM PROCESS)

8-BIT EPROM MICROCOMPUTER WITH A/D

L SUFFIX
CERAMIC PACKAGE
CASE 715

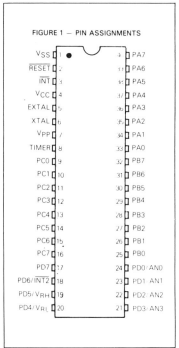

FIGURE 1 — PIN ASSIGNMENTS

VSS ☐ 1	40 ☐ PA7
RESET ☐ 2	39 ☐ PA6
$\overline{INT}$ ☐ 3	38 ☐ PA5
VCC ☐ 4	37 ☐ PA4
EXTAL ☐ 5	36 ☐ PA3
XTAL ☐ 6	35 ☐ PA2
VPP ☐ 7	34 ☐ PA1
TIMER ☐ 8	33 ☐ PA0
PC0 ☐ 9	32 ☐ PB7
PC1 ☐ 10	31 ☐ PB6
PC2 ☐ 11	30 ☐ PB5
PC3 ☐ 12	29 ☐ PB4
PC4 ☐ 13	28 ☐ PB3
PC5 ☐ 14	27 ☐ PB2
PC6 ☐ 15	26 ☐ PB1
PC7 ☐ 16	25 ☐ PB0
PD7 ☐ 17	24 ☐ PD0/AN0
PD6/$\overline{INT2}$ ☐ 18	23 ☐ PD1/AN1
PD5/V_{RH} ☐ 19	22 ☐ PD2/AN2
PD4/V_{RL} ☐ 20	21 ☐ PD3/AN3

©MOTOROLA INC., 1982   ADI-858-R1

MC68705R3

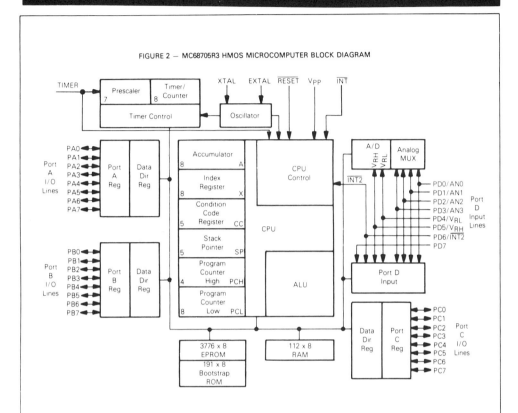

FIGURE 2 — MC68705R3 HMOS MICROCOMPUTER BLOCK DIAGRAM

MAXIMUM RATINGS

Rating	Symbol	Value	Unit
Supply Voltage	V_{CC}	−0.3 to +7.0	V
Input Voltage			
EPROM Programming Voltage (Vpp Pin)	V_{PP}	−0.3 to +22.0	V
TIMER Pin			
Normal Mode	V_{in}	−0.3 to +7.0	V
Bootstrap Programming Mode	V_{in}	−0.3 to +15.0	V
All Others	V_{in}	−0.3 to +7.0	V
Operating Temperature Range	T_A	0 to +70	°C
Storage Temperature Range	T_{stg}	−55 to +150	°C
Junction Temperature	T_J	+150	°C

This device contains circuitry to protect the inputs against damage due to high static voltages or electric fields; however, it is advised that normal precautions be taken to avoid application of any voltage higher than maximum rated voltages to this high-impedance circuit. For proper operation it is recommended that V_{in} and V_{out} be constrained to the range $V_{SS} \leq (V_{in}$ or $V_{out}) \leq V_{CC}$. Reliability of operation is enhanced if unused inputs are tied to an appropriate logic voltage level (e.g., either V_{SS} or V_{CC}).

THERMAL CHARACTERISTICS

Characteristic	Symbol	Value	Unit
Thermal Resistance			
Ceramic Package	θ_{JA}	50	°C/W

 MOTOROLA *Semiconductor Products Inc.*

MC68705R3

POWER CONSIDERATIONS

The average chip-junction temperature, T_J, in °C can be obtained from:

$$T_J = T_A + (P_D \cdot \theta_{JA}) \qquad (1)$$

Where:

$T_A \equiv$ Ambient Temperature, °C

$\theta_{JA} \equiv$ Package Thermal Resistance, Junction-to-Ambient, °C/W

$P_D \equiv P_{INT} + P_{PORT}$

$P_{INT} \equiv I_{CC} \times V_{CC}$, Watts — Chip Internal Power

$P_{PORT} \equiv$ Port Power Dissipation, Watts — User Determined

For most applications $P_{PORT} \blacktriangleleft P_{INT}$ and can be neglected. P_{PORT} may become significant if the device is configured to drive Darlington bases or sink LED loads.

An approximate relationship between P_D and T_J (if P_{PORT} is neglected) is:

$$P_D = K \div (T_J + 273°C) \qquad (2)$$

Solving equations 1 and 2 for K gives:

$$K = P_D \bullet (T_A + 273°C) + \theta_{JA} \bullet P_D{}^2 \qquad (3)$$

Where K is a constant pertaining to the particular part. K can be determined from equation 3 by measuring P_D (at equilibrium) for a known T_A. Using this value of K the values of P_D and T_J can be obtained by solving equations (1) and (2) iteratively for any value of T_A.

PROGRAMMING OPERATION ELECTRICAL CHARACTERISTICS ($V_{CC} = 5.25$ Vdc ± 0.5, $V_{SS} = 0$ Vdc, $T_A = 20°$ to 30°C unless otherwise noted)

Characteristic	Symbol	Min	Typ	Max	Unit
Programming Voltage	V_{PP}	20.0	21.0	22.0	V
Vpp Supply Current Vpp = 5.25 V Vpp = 21.0 V	I_{PP}	— —	— —	8 30	mA
Oscillator Frequency	$f_{osc(p)}$	0.9	1.0	1.1	MHz
Bootstrap Programming Mode Voltage (TIMER Pin) @ $I_{IHTP} = 100\,\mu A$ Max	V_{IHTP}	9.0	12.0	15.0	V

A/D CONVERTER CHARACTERISTICS ($V_{CC} = +5.25$ V ± 0.5 Vdc, $V_{SS} = 0$ Vdc, $T_A = 0°$ to 70°C unless otherwise noted)

Characteristic	Min	Typ	Max	Unit	Comments
Resolution	8	8	8	Bits	
Non-Linearity	—	—	$\pm 1/2$	LSB	For $V_{RH} = 4.0$ to 5.0 V and $V_{RL} = 0$ V.
Quantitizing Error	—	—	$\pm 1/2$	LSB	
Conversion Range	V_{RL}	—	V_{RH}	V	
V_{RH}	—	—	5.0	V	A/D accuracy may decrease proportionately as
V_{RL}	V_{SS}	—	0.2	V	V_{RH} is reduced below 4.0 V. The sum of V_{RH} and V_{RL} must not exceed V_{CC}.
Conversion Time	30	30	30	t_{cyc}	Includes sampling time
Monotonicity		Inherent (within total error)			
Zero Input Reading	00	00	01	hexadecimal	$V_{in} = 0$
Ratiometric Reading	FF	FF	FF	hexadecimal	$V_{in} = V_{RH}$
Sample Time	5	5	5	t_{cyc}	
Sample/Hold Capacitance, Input	—	—	25	pF	
Analog Input Voltage	V_{RL}	—	V_{RH}	V	Negative transients on any analog lines (pins 19-24) are not allowed at any time during conversion.

Ⓜ **MOTOROLA** *Semiconductor Products Inc.*

MC68705R3

SWITCHING CHARACTERISTICS (V_{CC} = +5.25 Vdc ±0.5 Vdc, V_{SS} = 0 Vdc, T_A = 0° to 70°C unless otherwise noted)

Characteristic	Symbol	Min	Typ	Max	Unit
Oscillator Frequency Normal	f_{osc}	0.4	—	4.2	MHz
Instruction Cycle Time (4/f_{osc})	t_{cyc}	0.950	—	10	μs
INT, INT2, or Timer Pulse Width (See Interrupt Section)	t_{WL}, t_{WH}	t_{cyc} + 250	—	—	ns
RESET Pulse Width	t_{RWL}	t_{cyc} + 250	—	—	ns
RESET Delay Time (External Cap = 1.0 μF)	t_{RHL}	100	—	—	ms
INT Zero Crossing Detection Input Frequency (for ±5° Accuracy)	f_{INT}	0.03	—	1.0	kHz
External Clock Duty Cycle (EXTAL) (See Figure 12)	—	40	50	60	%

ELECTRICAL CHARACTERISTICS (V_{CC} = +5.25 Vdc ±0.5 Vdc, V_{SS} = 0 Vdc, T_A = 0° to 70°C unless otherwise noted)

Characteristic	Symbol	Min	Typ	Max	Unit
Input High Voltage RESET (4.75≤V_{CC}≤5.75) (V_{CC}<4.75) INT (4.75≤V_{CC}≤5.75) (V_{CC}<4.75) All Other	V_{IH}	4.0 V_{CC}−0.5 4.0 V_{CC}−0.5 2.0	— — ** ** —	V_{CC} V_{CC} V_{CC} V_{CC} V_{CC}	V V V
Input High Voltage (TIMER Pin) Timer Mode Bootstrap Programming Mode	V_{IH}	2.0 9.0	— 12.0	V_{CC} 15.0	V V
Input Low Voltage RESET INT All Other	V_{IL}	−0.3 −0.3 −0.3	— ** —	0.8 1.5 0.8	V V V
INT Zero-Crossing Input Voltage — Through a Capacitor	V_{INT}	2.0	—	4.0	$V_{ac\ p-p}$
Internal Power Dissipation (No Port Loading, V_{CC}=5.25 V, T_A=0°C)	P_{INT}	—	600	TBD	mW
Input Capacitance EXTAL All Other (See Note)	C_{in}	— —	25 10	— —	pF pF
RESET Hysteresis Voltage (See Figure 11) Out of Reset Voltage Into Reset Voltage	V_{IRES+} V_{IRES-}	2.1 0.8	— —	4.0 2.0	V V
Programming Voltage (Vpp Pin) Programming EPROM Operating Mode	V_{PP}*	20.0 4.0	21.0 V_{CC}	22.0 5.75	V V
Input Current TIMER (V_{in}=0.4 V) INT (V_{in}=0.4 V) EXTAL (V_{in}=2.4 V to V_{CC}) (V_{in}=0.4 V) RESET (V_{in}=0.8 V) (External Capacitor Changing Current)	I_{in}	— — — — −4.0	— 20 — — —	20 50 10 −1600 −50	μA

* V_{PP} is pin 7 on the MC68705R3 and is connected to V_{CC} in the normal operating mode. In the MC6805R2, pin 7 is NUM and is connected to V_{SS} in the normal operating mode. The user must allow for this difference when emulating the MC6805R2 ROM-based MCU.
** Due to internal biasing, this input (when not used) floats to approximately 2.0 V.

NOTE: Port D analog inputs, when selected, C_{in} = 25 pF for the first 5 out of 30 cycles.

(M) MOTOROLA *Semiconductor Products Inc.*
4

MC68705R3

PORT ELECTRICAL CHARACTERISTICS (V_{CC} = +5.25 Vdc ±0.5 Vdc, V_{SS} = 0 Vdc, T_A = 0° to 70°C unless otherwise noted)

Characteristic	Symbol	Min	Typ	Max	Unit
Port A					
Output Low Voltage, I_{Load} = 1.6 mA	V_{OL}	—	—	0.4	V
Output High Voltage, I_{Load} = −100 μA	V_{OH}	2.4	—	—	V
Output High Voltage, I_{Load} = −10 μA	V_{OH}	3.5	—	—	V
Input High Voltage, I_{Load} = −300 μA (Max)	V_{IH}	2.0	—	V_{CC}	V
Input Low Voltage, I_{Load} = −500 μA (Max)	V_{IL}	−0.3	—	0.8	V
Hi-Z State Input Current (V_{in} = 2.0 V to V_{CC})	I_{IH}	—	—	−300	μA
Hi-Z State Input Current (V_{in} = 0.4 V)	I_{IL}	—	—	−500	μA
Port B					
Output Low Voltage, I_{Load} = 3.2 mA	V_{OL}	—	—	0.4	V
Output Low Voltage, I_{Load} = 10 mA (Sink)	V_{OL}	—	—	1.0	V
Output High Voltage, I_{Load} = −200 μA	V_{OH}	2.4	—	—	V
Darlington Current Drive (Source), V_O = 1.5 V	I_{OH}	−1.0	—	−10	mA
Input High Voltage	V_{IH}	2.0	—	V_{CC}	V
Input Low Voltage	V_{IL}	−0.3	—	0.8	V
Hi-Z State Input Current	I_{TSI}	—	2	20	μA
Port C					
Output Low Voltage, I_{Load} = 1.6 mA	V_{OL}	—	—	0.4	V
Output High Voltage, I_{Load} = −100 μA	V_{OH}	2.4	—	—	V
Input High Voltage	V_{IH}	2.0	—	V_{CC}	V
Input Low Voltage	V_{IL}	−0.3	—	0.8	V
Hi-Z State Input Current	I_{TSI}	—	2	20	μA
Port D (Input Only)					
Input High Voltage	V_{IH}	2.0	—	V_{CC}	V
Input Low Voltage	V_{IL}	−0.3	—	0.8	V
Input Current*	I_{in}	—	—	20	μA

*The A/D conversion resistor (15 kΩ typical) is connected internally between PD5/V_{RH} and PD4/V_{RL}.

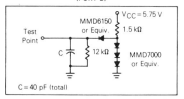

FIGURE 3 — TTL EQUIVALENT TEST LOAD
(PORT B)

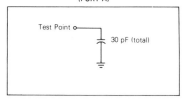

FIGURE 4 — CMOS EQUIVALENT TEST LOAD
(PORT A)

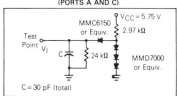

FIGURE 5 — TTL EQUIVALENT TEST LOAD
(PORTS A AND C)

 MOTOROLA *Semiconductor Products Inc.*

SIGNAL DESCRIPTION

The input and output signals for the MCU, shown in Figure 1, are described in the following paragraphs.

V$_{CC}$ AND V$_{SS}$

Power is supplied to the MCU using two pins. V$_{CC}$ is power and V$_{SS}$ is the ground connection.

$\overline{INT}$

This pin allows an external event to asynchronously interrupt the processor. It can also be used as a polled input using the BIL and BIH instructions. Refer to Interrupts section for additional information.

XTAL AND EXTAL

These pins provide connections to the on-chip clock oscillator circuit. A crystal, a resistor, or an external signal, depending on the CLK bit (see Mask Options section), is connected to these pins to provide a system clock source with various stability/cost tradeoffs. Lead lengths and stray capacitance on these two pins should be minimized. Refer to Internal Clock Generator Options section for recommendations about these inputs.

TIMER

This pin is used as an external input to control the internal timer/counter circuitry. This pin also detects a higher voltage level used to initiate the bootstrap program (see Programming Firmware section). Refer to Timer section for additional information about the timer circuitry.

RESET

This pin has a Schmitt trigger input and an on-chip pullup. The MCU can be reset by pulling $\overline{RESET}$ low. Refer to Resets section for additional information.

VPP

This pin is used when programming the EPROM. By applying the programming voltage to this pin, one of the requirements is met for programming the EPROM. In normal operation, this pin is connected to V$_{CC}$. Refer to Programming Firmware section and Electrical Characteristics section.

INPUT/OUTPUT LINES
(PA0-PA7, PB0-PB7, PC0-PC7, PD0-PD7)

These 32 lines are arranged into four 8-bit ports (A, B, C, and D). Ports A, B, and C are programmable as either inputs or outputs under software control of the data direction register (DDRs). Port D has up to four analog inputs, plus two voltage reference inputs when the A/D is used (PD5/V$_{RH}$, PD4/V$_{RL}$), an $\overline{INT2}$ input, and from one to eight digital inputs. All port D lines can be directly read and used as binary inputs. If any analog input is used, then the voltage reference pins (PD5/V$_{RH}$, PD4/V$_{RL}$) must be used in the analog mode. Refer to Input/Output, A/D Converter, and Interrupts sections for additional information.

MEMORY

As shown in Figure 6, the MCU is capable of addressing 4096 bytes of memory and I/O registers with its program

FIGURE 6 — MCU MEMORY MAP

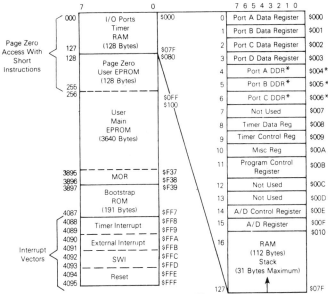

*Caution: Data direction registers (DDRs) are write-only; they read as $FF.

MOTOROLA *Semiconductor Products Inc.*

MC68705R3

counter. The MCU has implemented 4093 bytes of these locations. This consists of: 3776 bytes of user EPROM, 191 bytes of bootstrap ROM, 112 bytes of user RAM, an EPROM mask option register (MOR), a program control register (PCR), seven bytes of I/O, two timer registers, a miscellaneous register, and two A/D registers. The user EPROM is located in two areas. The main EPROM area is memory locations $080 to $F37. The second area is reserved for eight interrupt/reset vector bytes at memory locations $FF8 to $FFF. The MCU uses 13 of the lowest 16 memory locations for program control and I/O features such as ports, the port DDRs, the timer, and A/D registers. The mask option register at memory location $F38 completes the total. The 112 bytes of user RAM include up to 31 bytes for the stack.

The shared stack area is used during the processing of interrupt and subroutine calls. The contents of the CPU registers are pushed onto the stack in the order shown in Figure 7. Since the stack pointer decrements during pushes, the low order byte (PCL) of the program counter is stacked first; then the higher order four bits (PCH) are stacked. This ensures that the program counter is loaded correctly as the stack pointer increments when it pulls data from the stack. A subroutine call causes only the program counter (PCL, PCH) contents to be pushed onto the stack; the remaining CPU registers are not pushed.

FIGURE 7 — INTERRUPT STACKING ORDER

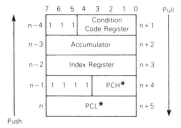

*For subroutine calls, only PCL and PCH are stacked.

CENTRAL PROCESSING UNIT

The CPU of the M6805 Family is implemented independently from the I/O or memory configuration. Consequently, it can be treated as an independent central processor communicating with I/O and memory via internal address, data, and control buses.

REGISTERS

The CPU has five registers available to the programmer. They are shown in Figure 8 and are explained in the following paragraphs.

ACCUMULATOR (A)

The accumulator is a general purpose 8-bit register used to hold operands and results of the arithmetic calculations or data manipulations.

INDEX REGISTER (X)

The index register is an 8-bit register used for the indexed addressing mode. It contains an 8-bit value that may be added to an instruction value to create an effective address. The index register can also be used for data manipulations using read-modify-write instructions. The index register may also be used as a temporary storage area.

PROGRAM COUNTER (PC)

The program counter is a 12-bit register that contains the address of the next instruction to be executed.

STACK POINTER (SP)

The stack pointer is a 12-bit register that contains the address of the next free location on the stack. During an MCU reset or the reset stack pointer (RSP) instruction, the stack pointer is set to location $07F. The stack pointer is then decremented as data is pushed onto the stack and incremented as data is then pulled from the stack. The seven most significant bits of the stack point are permanently set to 0000011. Subroutines and interrupts may be nested down to location $061 (31 bytes maximum), which allows the programmer to use up to 15 levels of subroutine calls (less if interrupts are allowed).

CONDITION CODE REGISTER (CC)

The condition code register is a 5-bit register in which four bits are used to indicate the results of the instruction just executed. These bits can be individually tested by a program and specific action taken as a result of their state. Each of the five bits is explained below.

HALF CARRY (H) — Set during ADD and ADC operations to indicate that a carry occurred between bits 3 and 4.

FIGURE 8 — PROGRAMMING MODEL

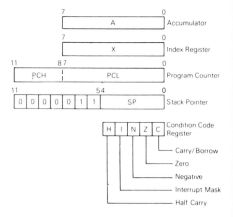

 MOTOROLA *Semiconductor Products Inc.*

INTERRUPT (I) — When this bit is set the timer and exter-nal interrupt ($\overline{INT}$) are masked (disabled). If an interrupt occurs while this bit is set, the interrupt is latched and is pro-cessed as soon as the interrupt bit is cleared.

NEGATIVE (N) — When set, this bit indicates that the result of the last arithmetic, logical, or data manipulation was negative (bit 7 in the result is a logical "1").

ZERO (Z) — When set, this bit indicates that the result of the last arithmetic, logical, or data manipulation was zero.

CARRY/BORROW (C) — When set, this bit indicates that a carry or borrow out of the arithmetic logic unit (ALU) occurred during the last arithmetic operation. This bit is also affected during bit test and branch instructions plus shifts and rotates.

TIMER

The MCU timer consists of an 8-bit software program-mable counter which is driven by a 7-bit prescaler with 1-of-8 selectable outputs. Various timer clock sources may be selected ahead of the prescaler and counter. The timer selec-tions are made via the timer control register (TCR) and/or the mask option register (MOR). The TCR also contains the interrupt control bits. The sections elsewhere entitled Timer Control Register and Mask Options include additional details on controlling this timer.

The MCU timer circuitry is shown in Figure 9. The 8-bit counter may be loaded under program control and is decre-mented toward zero by the f_{CIN} counter input (output of the prescaler selector). Once the 8-bit counter has decremented to zero, it sets the TIR (timer interrupt request) bit 7 (b7 of TCR). The TIM (timer interrupt mask) bit (b6) can be soft-ware set to inhibit the interrupt request, or software cleared to pass the interrupt request to the processor. When the I bit in the condition code register is cleared, the processor receives the timer interrupt. The MCU responds to this inter-rupt by saving the present CPU state on the stack, fetching the timer interrupt vector from locations $FF8 and $FF9, and executing the interrupt routine. The processor is sensitive to the level of the timer interrupt request line; therefore if the interrupt is masked, the TIR bit may be cleared by software (e.g., BCLR) without generating an interrupt. The TIR bit MUST be cleared, by the timer interrupt service routine, to clear the timer interrupt register.

The timer interrupt and $\overline{INT2}$ share the same interrupt vec-tor. The interrupt routine thus must check the two request bits to determine the source of the interrupt.

The counter continues to count (decrement) after falling through to $FF from zero. Thus, the counter can be read at any time by the processor without disturbing the count. This allows a program to determine the length of time since the occurrence of a timer interrupt and does not disturb the counting process.

The clock input to the timer can be from an external source (decrementing the counter occurs on a positive tran-sition of the external source) applied to the TIMER input pin, or it can be the internal $\phi2$ signal. The maximum frequency of a signal that can be recognized by the TIMER or $\overline{INT}$ pin logic is dependent on the parameter labeled t_{WL}, t_{WH}. The pin logic that recognizes the high (or low) state on the pin must also recognize the low (or high) state on the pin in order to "re-arm" the internal logic. Therefore, the period can be calculated as follows: (assumes 50/50 duty cycle for a given period)

$$t_{cyc} \times 2 + 250 \text{ ns} = \text{period} = \frac{1}{\text{freq}}$$

The period is not simply $t_{WL} + t_{WH}$. This computation is allowable, but it does reduce the maximum allowable fre-quency by defining an unnecessarily longer period (250 ns twice).

When the $\phi2$ signal is used as the source, it can be gated by an input applied to the TIMER pin allowing the user to easily perform pulse-width measurements. (Note: When the MOR TOPT bit is set and the CLS bit is clear, an ungated $\phi2$ clock input is obtained by tying the TIMER pin to V_{CC}.) The source of the clock input is selected via the TCR or the MOR as described later.

A prescaler option can be applied to the clock input that extends the timing interval up to a maximum of 128 counts before decrementing the counter. This prescaling TCR or MOR option selects one of eight outputs on the 7-bit binary divider; one output bypasses prescaling. To avoid truncation errors, the prescaler is cleared when bit b3 of the TCR is written to a logic "1"; however, TCR bit b3 always reads as a logic "0" to ensure proper operation with read-modify-write instructions (bit set and clear for example).

At reset, the prescaler and counter are initialized to an all "1s" condition; the timer interrupt request bit (TCR, b7) is cleared and the timer interrupt request mask (TCR, b6) is set. TCR bits b0, b1, b2, b4, and b5 are initialized by the corres-ponding mask option register (MOR) bits at reset. They are then software selectable after reset.

Note that the timer block diagram in Figure 9 reflects two separate timer control configurations: a) software controlled mode via the timer control register (TCR), and b) MOR con-trolled mode to emulate a mask ROM version with the mask option register. In the software controlled mode, all TCR bits are read/write, except bit b3 which is write-only (always reads as a logic "0"). In the MOR controlled mode, TCR bits b7 and b6 are read/write, bit b3 is write-only (reads as logic "0"), and the other five have no effect on a write and read as logic "1s". The two configurations provide the user with the capability to freely select timer options as well as accurately emulate the MC6805R2 mask ROM version. In the following paragraphs refer to Figure 9 as well as the Timer Control Register and Mask Options sections.

The TOPT (time option) bit (b6) in the mask option register is EPROM programmed to a logical "0" to select the soft-ware controlled mode, which is described first. TCR bits b5, b4, b3, b2, b1, and b0 give the program direct control of the prescaler and input selection options.

The timer prescaler input (f_{PIN}) can be configured for three different operating modes plus a disable mode, de-pending upon the value written to TCR control bits b4 and b5 (TIE and TIN). Refer to Timer Control Register section.

When the TIE and TIN bits are programmed to "0", the timer input is from the internal clock ($\phi2$) and TIMER input pin is disabled. The internal clock mode can be used for periodic interrupt generation as well as a reference for fre-quency and event measurement.

When TIE = 1 and TIN = 0, the internal clock and the TIMER input pin signals are ANDed to form the timer input. This mode can be used to measure external pulse widths. The external pulse simply gates in the internal clock for the duration of the pulse. The accuracy of the count in this mode is ± one count.

When TIE = 0 and TIN = 1, no f_{PIN} input is applied to the prescaler and the timer is disabled.

When TIE and TIN are both programmed to a "1", the timer is from the external clock. The external clock can be used to count external events as well as provide an external frequency for generating periodic interrupts.

 MOTOROLA *Semiconductor Products Inc.*

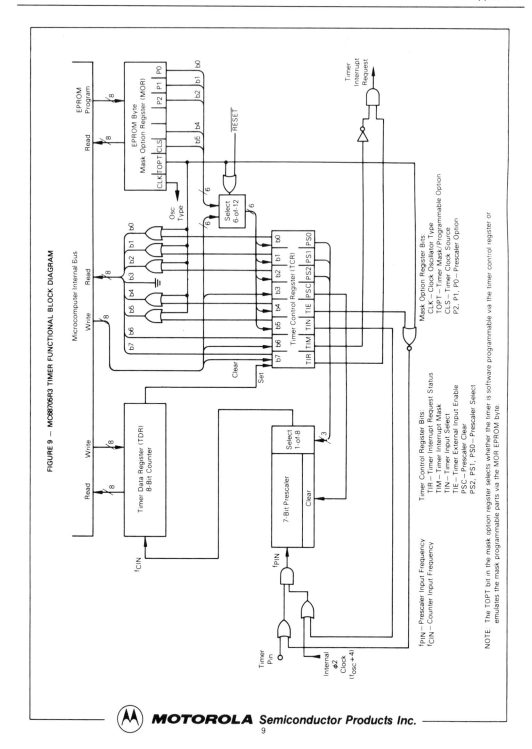

FIGURE 9 — MC68705R3 TIMER FUNCTIONAL BLOCK DIAGRAM

Mask Option Register Bits:
CLK — Clock Oscillator Type
TOPT — Timer Mask/Programmable Option
CLS — Timer Clock Source
P2, P1, P0 — Prescaler Option

Timer Control Register Bits:
TIR — Timer Interrupt Request Status
TIM — Timer Interrupt Mask
TIN — Timer Input Select
TIE — Timer External Input Enable
PSC — Prescaler Clear
PS2, PS1, PS0 — Prescaler Select

f_{PIN} — Prescaler Input Frequency
f_{CIN} — Counter Input Frequency

NOTE: The TOPT bit in the mask option register selects whether the timer is software programmable via the timer control register or emulates the mask programmable parts via the MOR EPROM byte.

9

MC68705R3

Bits b0, b1, and b2 in the TCR are program controlled to choose the appropriate prescaler output. The prescaling divides the f_{PIN} frequency by 1, 2, 4, etc. in binary multiples to 128 producing f_{CIN} frequency to the counter. The processor cannot write into or read from the prescaler; however, the prescaler is set to all "1s" by a write operation to TCR, b3 (when bit 3 of the written data equals "1"), which allows for truncation-free counting.

The MOR controlled mode of the timer is selected when the TOPT (timer option) bit (b6) in the MOR is programmed to a logical "1" to emulate the MC6805R2 mask-programmable prescaler. The timer circuits are the same as described above, however, the timer control register (TCR) is configured differently, as discussed below.

The logical level for the functions of bits b0, b1, b2, and b5 in the TCR are all determined at the time of EPROM programming. They are controlled by corresponding bits within the mask option register (MOR, $F38). The value programmed into MOR bits b0, b1, b2, and b5 controls the prescaler division and the timer clock selection. Bit b4 (TIE) is set to a logical "1" in the MOR controlled mode. (When read by software, these five TCR bits always read as logical "1s".) As in the software programmable configuration, the TIM (b6) and TIR (b7) bits of the TCR are controlled by the counter and software as described above and in the Timer Control Register section. Bit b3 of the TCR, in the MOR controlled mode, always reads as a logical "0" and can be written to a logical "1" to clear the prescaler. The MOR controlled mode is designed to exactly emulate the MC6805R2 which has only TIM, TIR, and PSC in the TCR and has the prescaler options defined as manufacturing mask options.

RESETS

The MCU can be reset in two ways: by initial power-up, and by the external reset input ($\overline{RESET}$). Upon power-up, a delay of t_{RHL} is needed before allowing the $\overline{RESET}$ input to go high. This time allows the internal clock generator to stabilize. Connecting a capacitor to the $\overline{RESET}$ input, as shown in Figure 10, typically provides sufficient delay.

The internal circuit connected to the $\overline{RESET}$ pin consists of a Schmitt trigger which senses the $\overline{RESET}$ line logic level. The Schmitt trigger provides an internal reset voltage when it senses logical "0" on the $\overline{RESET}$ pin. During power-up, the Schmitt trigger switches on (removes reset) when the $\overline{RESET}$ pin voltage rises to V_{IRES+}. When the $\overline{RESET}$ pin voltage falls to a logical "0" for a period longer than one

t_{CYC}, the Schmitt trigger switches off to provide an internal reset voltage. The "switch off" voltage occurs at V_{IRES-}. A typical reset Schmitt trigger hysteresis curve is shown in Figure 11. See Figure 15 under Interrupts section for the complete reset sequence.

FIGURE 11 — TYPICAL RESET SCHMITT TRIGGER HYSTERESIS

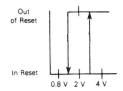

INTERNAL CLOCK GENERATOR OPTIONS

The internal clock generator circuit is designed to require a minimum of external components. A crystal, a resistor, a jumper wire, or an external signal may be used to generate a system clock with various stability/cost tradeoffs. The mask option register (EPROM) is programmed to select crystal or resistor operation. The oscillator frequency is internally divided by four to produce the internal system clocks.

The different connection methods are shown in Figure 12. Crystal specifications and suggested PC board layouts are given in Figure 13. A resistor selection graph is given in Figure 14.

The crystal oscillator start-up time is a function of many variables: crystal parameters (especially R_S), oscillator load capacitances, IC parameters, ambient temperature, and supply voltage. To ensure rapid oscillator start-up, neither the crystal characteristics nor the load capacitances should exceed recommendations.

BOOTSTRAP ROM

The bootstrap ROM contains a factory program which allows the MCU to fetch data from an external device and transfer it into the MC68705R3 EPROM. The bootstrap program provides: timing of programming pulses, timing of V_{PP} input, and verification after programming. See Programming Firmware section.

MASK OPTION REGISTER (MOR)

The mask option register is an 8-bit user programmed (EPROM) register in which six of the bits are used. Bits in this register are used to select the type of system clock, the timer option, the timer/prescaler clock source, and the prescaler option. It is fully described in the Mask Options section.

FIGURE 10 — POWER-UP RESET DELAY CIRCUIT

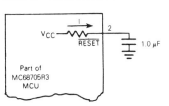

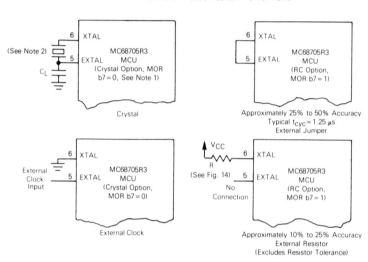

FIGURE 12 — CLOCK GENERATOR OPTIONS

NOTE: 1. When the TIMER input pin is in the V_{IHTP} range (in the bootstrap EPROM programming mode), the crystal option is forced. When the TIMER input is at or below V_{CC}, the clock generator option is determined by bit 7 of the mask option register (CLK).

2. The recommended C_L value with a 4.0 MHz crystal is 27 pF maximum, including system distributed capacitance. There is an internal capacitance of approximately 25 pF on the XTAL pin. For crystal frequencies other than 4 MHz, the total capacitance on each pin should be scaled as the inverse of the frequency ratio. For example, with a 2 MHz crystal, use approximately 50 pF on EXTAL and approximately 25 pF on XTAL. The exact value depends on the Motional-Arm parameters of the crystal used.

FIGURE 13 — CRYSTAL MOTIONAL-ARM
PARAMETERS AND SUGGESTED PC BOARD LAYOUT

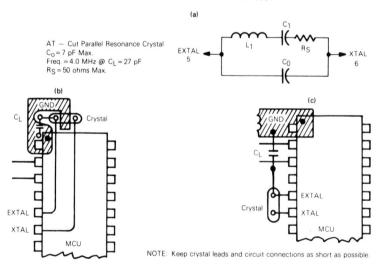

NOTE: Keep crystal leads and circuit connections as short as possible.

 MOTOROLA *Semiconductor Products Inc.*

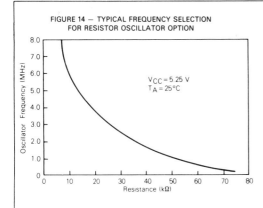

FIGURE 14 — TYPICAL FREQUENCY SELECTION
FOR RESISTOR OSCILLATOR OPTION

$V_{CC} = 5.25$ V
$T_A = 25°C$

INTERRUPTS

The MCU can be interrupted four different ways: through the external interrupt ($\overline{INT}$) input pin, the internal timer interrupt request, the external port D bit 6 ($\overline{INT2}$) input pin, or the software interrupt instruction (SWI). When any interrupt occurs: the current instruction (including SWI) is completed, processing is suspended, the present CPU state is pushed onto the stack, the interrupt bit (I) in the condition code register is set, the address of the interrupt routine is obtained from the appropriate interrupt vector address, and the interrupt routine is executed. Stacking the CPU register, setting the I bit, and vector fetching require a total of 11 t_{CYC} periods for completion. A flowchart of the interrupt sequence is shown in Figure 15. The interrupt service routine must end with a return from interrupt (RTI) instruction which allows the MCU to resume processing of the program prior to the interrupt (by unstacking the previous CPU state). Unlike

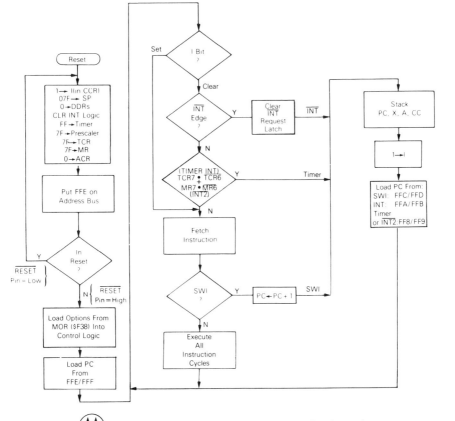

FIGURE 15 — RESET AND INTERRUPT PROCESSING
FLOWCHART

MOTOROLA *Semiconductor Products Inc.*

MC68705R3

RESET, hardware interrupts do not cause the current instruction execution to be halted, but are considered pending until the current instruction execution is complete.

When the current instruction is complete, the processor checks all pending hardware interrupts and if unmasked, proceeds with interrupt processing; otherwise, the next instruction is fetched and executed. Note that masked interrupts are latched for later interrupt service.

If both an external interrupt and a timer interrupt are pending at the end of an instruction execution, the external interrupt is serviced first. The SWI is executed as any other instruction.

Note

The timer and $\overline{INT2}$ interrupts share the same vector address. The interrupt routine must determine the source by examining the interrupt request bits (TCR b7 and MR b7). Both TCR b7 and MR b7 can only be written to "0" by software.

The external interrupt, $\overline{INT}$ and $\overline{INT2}$, are synchronized and then latched on the falling edge of the input signal. The $\overline{INT2}$ interrupt has an interrupt request bit (bit 7) and a mask bit (bit 6) located in the miscellaneous register (MR); refer to Figure 18. The $\overline{INT2}$ interrupt is inhibited when the mask bit is set. The $\overline{INT2}$ is always read as a digital input on Port D. The $\overline{INT2}$ and timer interrupt request bits, if set, cause the MCU to process an interrupt when the condition code I bit is clear.

A sinusoidal input signal (f_{INT} maximum) can be used to generate an external interrupt, as shown in Figure 16(a), for use as a zero-crossing detector. This allows applications such as servicing time-of-day routines and engaging/disengaging ac power control devices. Off-chip full wave rectification provides an interrupt at every zero crossing of the ac signal and thereby provide a 2f clock. For digital applications the $\overline{INT}$ pin can be driven by a digital signal. The maximum frequency of a signal that can be recognized by the TIMER or $\overline{INT}$ pin logic is dependent on the parameter labeled t_{WL}, t_{WH}. The pin logic that recognizes the high (or low) state on the pin must also recognize the low (or high) state on the pin in order to "re-arm" the internal logic. Therefore, the period can be calculated as follows: (assumes 50/50 duty cycle for a given period)

$$t_{cyc} \times 2 + 250 \text{ ns} = \frac{1}{\text{freq}}$$

The period is not simply $t_{WL} + t_{WH}$. This computation is allowable, but it does reduce the maximum allowable frequency by defining an unnecessarily longer period (250 ns twice). See Figure 16(b).

FIGURE 16 — TYPICAL INTERRUPT CIRCUITS

(a) Zero-Crossing Interrupt

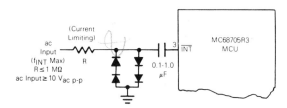

(b) Digital-Signal Interrupt

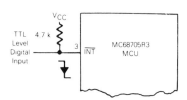

A software interrupt (SWI) is an executable instruction which is executed regardless of the state of the I bit in the condition code register. SWIs are usually used as breakpoints for debugging or as system calls.

INPUT/OUTPUT

There are 32 input/output pins. The $\overline{INT}$ pin may be polled with branch instructions to provide an additional input pin. All pins on ports A, B, and C are programmable as either inputs or outputs under software control of the corresponding data direction register (DDR). The port I/O programming is accomplished by writing the corresponding bit in the port DDR to a logic "1" for output or a logic "0" for input. On reset all the DDRs are initialized to a logic "0" state, placing the ports in the input mode. The port output registers are not initialized on reset and should be initialized by software before changing the DDRs from input to output. When programmed as outputs, all output ports read latched output data, regardless of the logic levels at the output pin, due to output loading; refer to Figure 17.

All input/output lines are TTL compatible as both inputs and outputs. Port A lines are CMOS compatible as outputs while port B, C, and D lines are CMOS compatible as inputs. Port D lines are input only; thus, there is no corresponding DDR. When programmed as outputs, port B is capable of sinking 10 milliamperes and sourcing 1 milliampere on each pin.

Port D provides the multiplexed analog inputs, reference voltage, and $\overline{INT2}$. All of these lines are shared with the port D digital inputs. Port D may always be used as digital inputs and may also be used as analog inputs. The V_{RL} and V_{RH} lines (PD4 and PD5) are internally connected to the A/D resistor. Analog inputs may be prescaled to attain the V_{RL} to V_{RH} recommended input voltage range.

The memory map in Figure 6 gives the addresses of data registers and DDRs. The register configuration is provided in Figure 18. Figure 19 provides some example of port connections.

Caution

The corresponding DDRs for ports A, B, and C are write-only registers (registers at $004, $005, and $006). A read operation on these registers is undefined. Since BSET and BCLR are read-modify-write in function, they cannot be used to set or clear a single DDR bit (all "unaffected" bits would be set). It is recommended that all DDR bits in a port must be written using a single-store instruction.

The latched output data bit (see Figure 17) may always be written. Therefore, any write to a port writes all of its data bits even though the port DDR is set to input. This may be used to initialize the data register and avoid undefined outputs; however, care must be exercised when using read-modify-write instructions since the data read corresponds to the pin level if the DDR is an input ("0") and corresponds to the latched output data when the DDR is an output ("1").

FIGURE 17 — TYPICAL PORT I/O CIRCUITRY

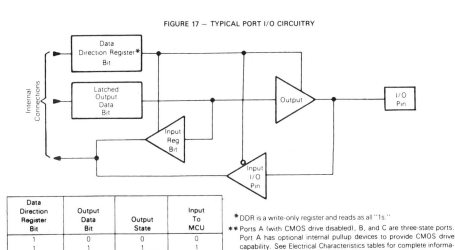

Data Direction Register Bit	Output Data Bit	Output State	Input To MCU
1	0	0	0
1	1	1	1
0	X	Hi-Z **	Pin

*DDR is a write-only register and reads as all "1s."

**Ports A (with CMOS drive disabled), B, and C are three-state ports. Port A has optional internal pullup devices to provide CMOS drive capability. See Electrical Characteristics tables for complete information.

MC68705R3

FIGURE 18 — MCU REGISTER CONFIGURATION

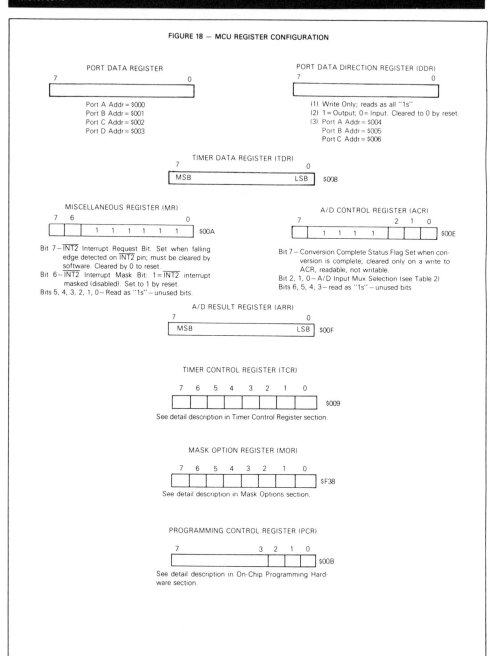

PORT DATA REGISTER

Port A Addr = $000
Port B Addr = $001
Port C Addr = $002
Port D Addr = $003

PORT DATA DIRECTION REGISTER (DDR)

(1) Write Only; reads as all "1s"
(2) 1 = Output; 0 = Input. Cleared to 0 by reset.
(3) Port A Addr = $004
    Port B Addr = $005
    Port C Addr = $006

TIMER DATA REGISTER (TDR)

MSB   LSB $008

MISCELLANEOUS REGISTER (MR)

1 1 1 1 1 1 $00A

Bit 7 — $\overline{INT2}$ Interrupt Request Bit: Set when falling
edge detected on $\overline{INT2}$ pin; must be cleared by
software. Cleared by 0 to reset.
Bit 6 — $\overline{INT2}$ Interrupt Mask Bit: 1 = $\overline{INT2}$ interrupt
masked (disabled). Set to 1 by reset.
Bits 5, 4, 3, 2, 1, 0 — Read as "1s" — unused bits.

A/D CONTROL REGISTER (ACR)

1 1 1 1 $00E

Bit 7 — Conversion Complete Status Flag Set when con-
version is complete; cleared only on a write to
ACR, readable, not writable.
Bit 2, 1, 0 — A/D Input Mux Selection (see Table 2)
Bits 6, 5, 4, 3 — read as "1s" — unused bits

A/D RESULT REGISTER (ARR)

MSB   LSB $00F

TIMER CONTROL REGISTER (TCR)

7 6 5 4 3 2 1 0 $009

See detail description in Timer Control Register section.

MASK OPTION REGISTER (MOR)

7 6 5 4 3 2 1 0 $F38

See detail description in Mask Options section.

PROGRAMMING CONTROL REGISTER (PCR)

7   3 2 1 0 $00B

See detail description in On-Chip Programming Hardware section.

(M) MOTOROLA *Semiconductor Products Inc.*

MC68705R3

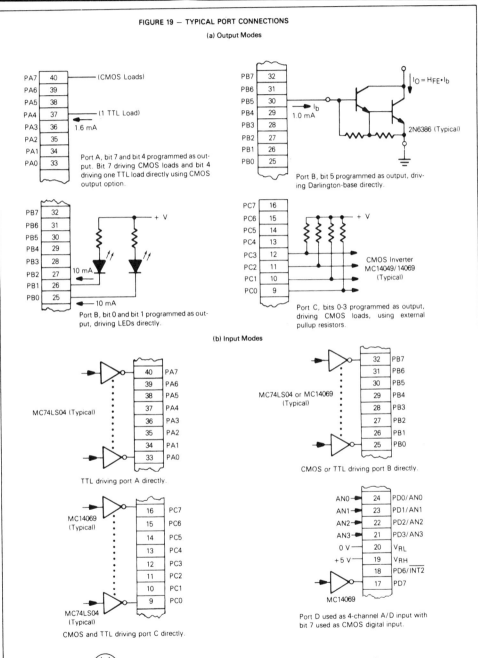

FIGURE 19 — TYPICAL PORT CONNECTIONS

(a) Output Modes

Port A, bit 7 and bit 4 programmed as output. Bit 7 driving CMOS loads and bit 4 driving one TTL load directly using CMOS output option.

Port B, bit 5 programmed as output, driving Darlington-base directly.

Port B, bit 0 and bit 1 programmed as output, driving LEDs directly.

Port C, bits 0-3 programmed as output, driving CMOS loads, using external pullup resistors.

(b) Input Modes

TTL driving port A directly.

CMOS or TTL driving port B directly.

CMOS and TTL driving port C directly.

Port D used as 4-channel A/D input with bit 7 used as CMOS digital input.

MOTOROLA *Semiconductor Products Inc.*

16

MC68705R3

ANALOG-TO-DIGITAL CONVERTER (A/D)

The MCU has an 8-bit A/D converter implemented on the chip using a successive approximation technique, as shown in Figure 20. Up to four external analog inputs, via port D, are connected to the A/D through a multiplexer. Four internal analog channels may be selected for calibration purposes (V_{RH}, $V_{RH}/2$, $V_{RH}/4$, and V_{RL}). The accuracy of these internal channels will not necessarily meet the accuracy specifications of the external channels.

The multiplexer selection is controlled by the A/D control register (ACR) bits 0, 1, and 2; see Table 1. This register is cleared during any reset condition. Refer to Figure 18 for register configuration.

Whenever the ACR is written, the conversion in progress is aborted, the conversion complete flag (ACR bit 7) is cleared, and the selected input is sampled and held internally.

The converter operates continuously using 30 machine cycles to complete a conversion of the sampled analog input. When conversion is complete, the digitized sample or digital value is placed in the A/D result register (ARR), the conversion complete flag is set, the selected input is sampled again, and a new conversion is started.

The A/D is ratiometric. Two reference voltages (V_{RH} and V_{RL}) are supplied to the converter via port D pins. An input voltage equal to V_{RH} converts to $FF (full scale) and an input voltage equal to V_{RL} converts to $00. An input voltage greater than V_{RH} converts to $FF and no overflow indication is provided. For ratiometric conversions, the source of each analog input should use V_{RH} as the supply voltage and be referenced to V_{RL}.

TIMER CONTROL REGISTER (TCR)

The configuration of the TCR is determined by the logic level of bit 6 (timer option, TOPT) in the mask option register (MOR). Two configurations of the TCR are shown below, one for TOPT = 1 and the other for TOPT = 0. TOPT = 1 configures the TCR to emulate the MC6805R2. When TOPT = 0,

FIGURE 20 — A/D BLOCK DIAGRAM

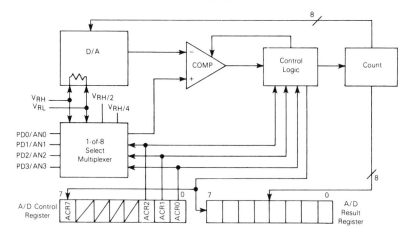

TABLE 1 — A/D INPUT MUX SELECTION

A/D Control Register				A/D Output (Hex)		
ACR2	ACR1	ACR0	Input Selected	Min	Typ	Max
0	0	0	AN0			
0	0	1	AN1			
0	1	0	AN2			
0	1	1	AN3			
1	0	0	V_{RH}*	FE	FF	FF
1	0	1	V_{RL}*	00	00	00
1	1	0	$V_{RH}/4$*	3F	40	41
1	1	1	$V_{RH}/2$*	7F	80	81

*Internal (Calibration) levels

 MOTOROLA *Semiconductor Products Inc.*

it provides software control of the TCR. When TOPT = 1, the prescaler "mask" options are user programmable via the MOR. A description of each TCR bit is provided below (also see Figure 9 and Timer section).

b7	b6	b5	b4	b3	b2	b1	b0	
TIR	TIM	1	1	PSC*	1	1	1	Timer Control Register $009

TCR with MOR TOPT = 1 (MC6805R2 Emulation)

b7	b6	b5	b4	b3	b2	b1	b0	
TIR	TIM	TIN	TIE	PSC*	PS2	PS1	PS0	Timer Control Register $009

TCR with MOR TOPT = 0 (Software Programmable Timer)

* = write only, reads as a zero

b7, TIR   Timer Interrupt Request — Used to initiate the timer interrupt or signal a timer data register underflow when it is a logical "1".
   1 = Set when the timer data register changes to all zeros.
   0 = Cleared by external reset or under program control.

b6, TIM   Timer Interrupt Mask — Used to inhibit the timer interrupt to the processor when it is a logical "1".
   1 = Set by an external reset or under program control.
   0 = Cleared under program control.

b5, TIN   External or Internal — Selects the input clock source to be either the external TIMER pin (8) or the internal $\phi2$.
   1 = Selects the external clock source.
   0 = Selects the internal $\phi2$ ($f_{OSC} \div 4$) clock source.

b4, TIE   External Enable — Used to enable the external TIMER pin (8) or to enable the internal clock (if TIN = 0) regardless of the external TIMER pin state (disables gated clock feature). When TOPT = 1, TIE is always a logical "1".
   1 = Enables external TIMER pin.
   0 = Disables external TIMER pin.

TIN-TIE Modes

TIN	TIE	Clock
0	0	Internal Clock ($\phi2$)
0	1	Gated (AND) of External and Internal Clocks
1	0	No Clock
1	1	External Clock

b3, PSC   Prescaler Clear — This a write-only bit. It reads as a logical zero so the BSET and BCLR on the TCR function correctly. Writing a "1" into PSC generates a pulse which clears the prescaler.

b2, PS2   Prescaler Select — These bits are decoded to
b1, PS1   select one of eight outputs on the timer
b0, PS0   prescaler. The table below shows the prescaler division resulting from decoding these bits.

PS2	PS1	PS0	Prescaler Division
0	0	0	1 (Bypass Prescaler)
0	0	1	2
0	1	0	4
0	1	1	8
1	0	0	16
1	0	1	32
1	1	0	64
1	1	1	128

Note

When changing the PS2-0 bits in software, the PSC bit should be written to a "1" in the same write cycle to clear the prescaler. Changing the PS bits without clearing the prescaler may cause an extraneous toggle of the timer data register.

MASK OPTIONS

The MC68705R3 mask option register is implemented in EPROM. Like all other EPROM bytes, the MOR contains all zeros prior to programming.

When used to emulate the MC6805R2, five of the eight MOR bits are used in conjunction with the prescaler. Of the remaining, the b7 bit is used to select the type of clock oscillator and bits b3 and b4 are not used. Bits b0, b1, and b2 determine the division of the timer prescaler. Bit b5 determines the timer clock source. The value of the TOPT bit (b6) is programmed to configure the TCR (a logic "1" for MC6805R2 emulation).

If the MOR timer option (TOPT) bit is a 0, bits b5, b4, b2, b1, and b0 set the initial value of their respective TCR bits during reset. After initialization the TCR is software controllable.

A description of the MOR bits is as follows:

b7	b6	b5	b4	b3	b2	b1	b0	
CLK	TOPT	CLS			P2	P1	P0	Mask Option Register $F38

b7, CLK   Clock Oscillator Type
   1 = RC
   0 = Crystal

Note

V_{IHTP} on the TIMER pin (8) forces the crystal mode.

b6, TOPT   Timer Option
   1 = MC6805R2 type timer/prescaler. All bits, except 3, 6, and 7, of the timer control register (TCR) are invisible to the user. Bits 5, 2, 1, and 0 of the mask option register determine the equivalent MC6805R2 mask options.
   0 = All TCR bits are implemented as a software programmable timer. The state of bits 5, 4, 2, 1, and 0 set the initial values of their respective TCR bits (TCR is then software controlled after initialization).

 MOTOROLA *Semiconductor Products Inc.*

b5, CLS   Timer/Prescaler Clock Source
1 = External TIMER pin.
0 = Internal $\phi2$

b4   Not used if MOR TOPT = 1 (MC6805R2 emulation). Sets initial value of TCR TIE if MOR TOPT = 0.

b3   Not used.

b2, P2
b1, P1   Prescaler Option—the logical levels of these
b0, P0   bits, when decoded, select one of eight outputs on the timer prescaler. The table below shows the division resulting from decoding combinations of these three bits.

P2	P1	P0	Prescaler Division
0	0	0	1 (Bypass Prescaler)
0	0	1	2
0	1	0	4
0	1	1	8
1	0	0	16
1	0	1	32
1	1	0	64
1	1	1	128

Two examples for programming the MOR are discussed below.

Example 1   To emulate an MC6805R2 to verify your program with an RC oscillator and an event count input for the timer with no prescaling, the MOR would be set to "11111000". To write the MOR, it is simply programmed as any other EPROM byte.

Example 2   Suppose you wish to use the MC68705R3 programmable prescaler functions, and you wish the initial condition of the prescaler to be divided by 64, with the input disabled and an internal clock source. If the clock oscillator was to be in the crystal mode, the MOR would be set to "00001110".

ON-CHIP PROGRAMMING HARDWARE

The programming control register (PCR) at location $00B is an 8-bit register which utilizes the three LSBs (the five MSBs are set to logic "1s"). This register provides the necessary control bits to allow programming the MC68705R3 EPROM. The bootstrap program manipulates the PCR when programming so that users need not be concerned with the PCR in most applications. A description of each bit follows.

b7	b6	b5	b4	b3	b2	b1	b0	
1	1	1	1	1	VPON	PGE	PLE	Programming Control Register $00B

b0, $\overline{\text{PLE}}$ Programming Latch Enable—When cleared, this bit allows the address and data to be latched into the EPROM. When this bit is set, data can be read from the EPROM.
1 = (set) read EPROM
0 = (clear) latch address and data into EPROM (read disabled)
$\overline{\text{PLE}}$ is set during a reset, but may be cleared any time. However, its effect on the EPROM is inhibited if $\overline{\text{VPON}}$ is a logic "1".

b1, $\overline{\text{PGE}}$ Program Enable—When cleared, $\overline{\text{PGE}}$ enables programming of the EPROM. $\overline{\text{PGE}}$ can only be cleared if $\overline{\text{PLE}}$ is cleared. $\overline{\text{PGE}}$ must be set when changing the address and data; i.e., setting up the byte to be programmed.
1 = (set) inhibit EPROM programming
0 = (clear) enable EPROM programming (if $\overline{\text{PLE}}$ is low)
$\overline{\text{PGE}}$ is set during a reset; however, it has no effect on EPROM circuits if $\overline{\text{VPON}}$ is a logic "1".

b2, $\overline{\text{VPON}}$ (Vpp ON) — $\overline{\text{VPON}}$ is a read-only bit and when at a logic "0" it indicates that a "high voltage" is present at the Vpp pin.
1 = no "high voltage" on Vpp pin
0 = "high voltage" on Vpp pin
$\overline{\text{VPON}}$ being "1" "disconnects" $\overline{\text{PGE}}$ and $\overline{\text{PLE}}$ from the rest of the chip, preventing accidental clearing of these bits from affecting the normal operating mode.

Note
$\overline{\text{VPON}}$ being "0" does not indicate that the Vpp level is correct for programming. It is used as a safety interlock for the user in the normal operating mode.

The programming control register functions are shown below.

VPON	PGE	PLE	Programming Conditions
0	0	0	Programming mode (program EPROM byte)
1	0	0	$\overline{\text{PGE}}$ and $\overline{\text{PLE}}$ disabled from system
0	1	0	Programming disabled (latch address and data in EPROM)
1	1	0	$\overline{\text{PGE}}$ and $\overline{\text{PLE}}$ disabled from system
0	0	1	Invalid state; $\overline{\text{PGE}}$ = 0 iff $\overline{\text{PLE}}$ = 0
1	0	1	Invalid state; $\overline{\text{PGE}}$ = 0 iff $\overline{\text{PLE}}$ = 0
0	1	1	"High voltage" on Vpp
1	1	1	$\overline{\text{PGE}}$ and $\overline{\text{PLE}}$ disabled from system (operating mode)

ERASING THE EPROM

The MC68705R3 EPROM can be erased by exposure to high-intensity ultraviolet (UV) light with a wavelength of 2537 Å. The recommended integrated dose (UV intensity x exposure time) is 15 Ws/cm^2. The lamps should be used without shortwave filters and the MC68705R3 should be positioned about one inch from the UV tubes. Ultraviolet erasure clears all bits of the MC68705R3 EPROM to the "0" state. Data is then entered by programming "1s" into the desired bit locations.

Caution

Be sure that the EPROM window is shielded from light except when erasing. This protects both the EPROM and light-sensitive nodes.

PROGRAMMING FIRMWARE

The MC68705R3 has 191 bytes of mask ROM containing a bootstrap program which can be used to program the MC68705R3 EPROM. The vector at addresses $FF6 and $FF7 is used to start executing the program. This vector is fetched when V_{IHTP} is applied to pin 8 (TIMER pin) of the MC68705R3 and the $\overline{RESET}$ pin is allowed to rise above V_{IRES+}. Figure 21 provides a schematic diagram of a circuit and a summary of programming steps which can be used to program the EPROM in the MC68705R3.

PROGRAMMING STEPS

The MCM2532 UV EPROM must first be programmed with an exact duplicate of the information that is to be transferred to the MC68705R3. Non-EPROM addresses are ignored by the bootstrap. Since the MC68705R3 and the MCM2532 are to be inserted and removed from the circuit, they should be mounted in sockets. In addition, the precaution below must be observed (refer to Figure 21):

Caution

Be sure S1 and S2 are closed and V_{CC} and +26 V are not applied when inserting the MC68705R3 and MCM2532 into their respective sockets. This ensures that $\overline{RESET}$ is held low while inserting the devices.

FIGURE 21 — PROGRAMMING CONNECTIONS SCHEMATIC DIAGRAM

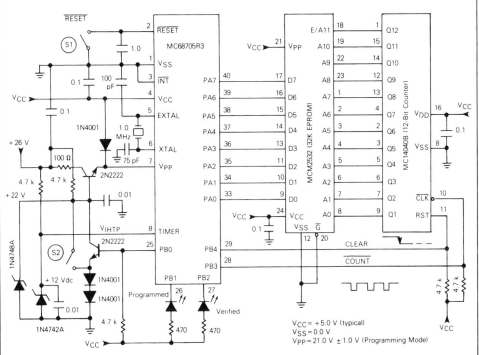

Summary of Programming Steps:
1. When plugging in the MC68705R3 or the MCM2532 be sure that S1 and S2 are closed and that V_{CC} and +26 V are not applied.
2. To initiate programming, be sure S1 is closed, S2 is closed, and V_{CC} and +26 V are applied. Then open S2, followed by S1.
3. Before removing the MC68705R3, first close S2 and then close S1. Disconnect V_{CC} and +26 V then remove the MC68705R3.

 MOTOROLA *Semiconductor Products Inc.*

When ready to program the MC68705R3 it is only necessary to provide V_CC and +26 V, open switch S2 (to apply V_PP and V_IHTP), and then open S1 (to remove reset). Once the voltages are applied and both S2 and S1 are open, the CLEAR output control line (PB4) goes high and then low, then the 12-bit counter (MC14040B) is clocked by the PB3 output (COUNT). The counter selects the MCM2532 EPROM byte which is to load the equivalent MC68705R3 EPROM byte selected by the bootstrap program. Once the EPROM location is loaded, COUNT clocks the counter to the next EPROM location. This continues until the MC68705R3 is completely programmed at which time the programmed indicator LED is lit. The counter is cleared and the loop is repeated to verify the programmed data. The verified indicator LED lights if the programming is correct.

Once the MC68705R3 has been programmed and verified, close switch S2 (to remove V_PP and V_IHTP) and close switch S1 (to reset). Disconnect +26 V and V_CC, then remove the MC68705R3 from its socket.

MC6805R2 EMULATION

The MC68705R3 emulates the MC6805R2 "exactly." MC6805R2 mask features are implemented in the mask option register (MOR) EPROM byte on the MC68705R3. There are a few minor exceptions to the exactness of emulation which are listed below.

1. The MC6805R2 "future ROM" area is implemented in the MC68705R3 and these 1728 bytes must be left unprogrammed to accurately simulate the MC6805R2. (The MC6805R2 reads all zeros from this area.)
2. The reserved ROM areas in the MC6805R2 and MC68705R3 have different data stored in them and this data is subject to change without notice. The MC6805R2 uses the reserved ROM for the self-check feature and the MC68705R3 uses this area for the bootstrap program.
3. The MC6805R2 reads all ones in its 48 byte "future RAM" area. This RAM is not implemented in the MC6805R2 mask ROM version, but is implemented in the MC68705R3.
4. The V_PP line (pin 7) in the MC68705R3 must be tied to V_CC for normal operation. In the MC6805R2, pin 7 is the NUM pin and is grounded in normal operation.
5. The LVI feature is not available in the MC68705R3. Processing differences are not presently compatible with proper design of this feature in the EPROM version.
6. The function in the non-user mode is not identical to the MC6805R2 version. Therefore, the MC68705R3 does not function in the MEX6805 Support System. In normal operation, all pin functions are the same as on the MC6805R2 version, except for pin 7 as previously noted.

The operation of all other circuitry has been exactly duplicated or designed to function exactly the same way in both devices including interrupts, timer, data ports, and data direction registers (DDRs). A stated design goal has been to provide the user with a safe inexpensive way to verify his program and system design before committing to a factory programmed ROM.

SOFTWARE

BIT MANIPULATION

The MCU has the ability to set or clear any single random-access memory or input/output bit (except the data direction register; see Caution under Input/Output section) with a single instruction (BSET, BCLR). Any bit in the page zero memory can be tested, using the BRSET and BRCLR instructions, and the program branches as a result of its state. The carry bit equals the value of the bit referenced by BRSET and BRCLR. A rotate instruction may then be used to accumulate serial input data in a RAM location or register. This capability to work with any bit in RAM, ROM, or I/O allows the user to have individual flags in RAM or to handle I/O bits as control lines. The coding example in Figure 22 illustrates the usefulness of the bit manipulation and test instructions. Assume that the MCU is to communicate with an external serial device. The external device has a data ready signal, a data output line, and a clock line to clock data one bit at a time, LSB first, out of the device. The MCU waits until the data is ready, clocks the external device, picks up the data in the carry flag (C bit), clears the clock line, and finally accumulates the data bit in a RAM location.

ADDRESSING MODES

The MCU has 10 addressing modes which are explained briefly in the following paragraphs. For additional details and graphical illustrations, refer to the M6805 Family User Manual.

The term "effective address" (EA) is used in describing the addressing modes. EA is defined as the address from which the argument for an instruction is fetched or stored.

IMMEDIATE — In the immediate addressing mode, the operand is contained in the byte immediately following the opcode. The immediate addressing mode is used to access constants which do not change during program execution (e.g., a constant used to initialize a loop counter).

FIGURE 22 — BIT MANIPULATION EXAMPLE

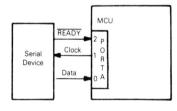

```
              .
              .
              .
SELF   BRSET  2, PORTA, SELF
              .
              .
              .
       BSET   1, PORTA
       BRCLR  0, PORTA, CONT
CONT   BCLR   1, PORTA
       ASR    RAMLOC
              .
              .
              .
```

 MOTOROLA *Semiconductor Products Inc.*

DIRECT — In the direct addressing mode, the effective address of the argument is contained in a single byte following the opcode byte. Direct addressing allows the user to directly address the lowest 256 bytes in memory with a single 2-byte instruction. This address area includes all on-chip RAM, I/O registers, and 128 bytes of EPROM. Direct addressing is an effective use of both memory and time.

EXTENDED — In the extended addressing mode, the effective address of the argument is contained in the two bytes following the opcode. Instructions using extended addressing are capable of referencing arguments anywhere in memory with a single 3-byte instruction. When using the Motorola assembler, the programmer need not specify whether an instruction uses direct or extended addressing. The assembler automatically selects the shortest form of the instruction.

RELATIVE — The relative addressing mode is only used in branch instructions. In relative addressing, the contents of the 8-bit signed byte following the opcode (the offset) is added to the PC, if and only if, the branch condition is true. Otherwise, control proceeds to the next instruction. The span of relative addressing is from −126 to +129 from the opcode address. The programmer need not worry about calculating the correct offset when using the Motorola assembler, since it calculates the proper offset and checks to see if it is within the span of the branch.

INDEXED, NO OFFSET — In the indexed, no offset addressing mode, the effective address of the argument is contained in the 8-bit index register. Thus, this addressing mode can access the first 256 memory locations. These instructions are only one byte long. This mode is often used to move a pointer through a table or to hold the address of a frequently referenced RAM or I/O location.

INDEXED, 8-BIT OFFSET — In the indexed, 8-bit offset addressing mode, the effective address is the sum of the contents of the unsigned 8-bit index register and unsigned byte following the opcode. This addressing mode is useful in selecting the kth element in an n element table. With this 2-byte instruction, k would typically be in X with the address of the beginning of the table in the instruction. As such, tables may begin anywhere within the first 256 addressable locations and could extend as far as location 510 ($1FE is the last location at which the instruction may begin).

INDEXED, 16-BIT OFFSET — In the indexed, 16-bit offset addressing mode, the effective address is the sum of the contents of the unsigned 8-bit index register and the two unsigned bytes following the opcode. This address mode can be used in a manner similar to indexed, 8-bit offset, except that this 3-byte instruction allows tables to be anywhere in memory. As with direct and extended addressing, the Motorola assembler determines the shortest form of indexed addressing.

BIT SET/CLEAR — In the bit set/clear addressing mode, the bit to be set or cleared is part of the opcode and the byte following the opcode specifies the direct address of the byte in which the specified bit is to be set or cleared. Thus, any read/write bit in the first 256 locations of memory, including I/O, can be selectively set or cleared with a single 2-byte instruction. See Caution under the Input/Output section.

BIT TEST AND BRANCH — The bit test and branch addressing mode is a combination of direct addressing and relative addressing. The bit which is to be tested and the condition (set or clear) is included in the opcode, and the address of the byte to be tested is in the single byte immediately following the opcode byte. The signed relative 8-bit offset is in the third byte and is added to the value of the PC if the branch condition is true. This single 3-byte instruction allows the program to branch based on the condition of any readable bit in the first 256 locations of memory. The span of branching is from −125 to +130 from the opcode address. The state of the tested bit is also transferred to the carry bit of the condition code register. See Caution under the Input/Output section.

INHERENT — In the inherent addressing mode, all the information necessary to execute the instruction is contained in the opcode. Operations specifying only the index register or accumulator, as well as control instruction with no other arguments, are included in this mode. These instructions are one byte long.

INSTRUCTION SET

The MCU has a set of 59 basic instructions, which when combined with the 10 addressing modes produce 207 usable opcodes. They can be divided into five different types: register/memory, read-modify-write, branch, bit manipulation, and control. The following paragraphs briefly explain each type. All the instructions within a given type are presented in individual tables.

REGISTERS/MEMORY INSTRUCTIONS — Most of these instructions use two operands. One operand is either the accumulator or the index register. The other operand is obtained from memory using one of the addressing modes. The jump unconditional (JMP) and jump to subroutine (JSR) instructions have no register operand. Refer to Table 2.

READ-MODIFY-WRITE INSTRUCTIONS — These instructions read a memory location or a register, modify or test its contents, and write the modified value back to memory or to the register (see Caution under Input/Output section). The test for negative or zero (TST) instruction is included in the read-modify-write instructions, though it does not perform the write. Refer to Table 3.

BRANCH INSTRUCTIONS — The branch instructions cause a branch from the program when a certain condition is met. Refer to Table 4.

BIT MANIPULATION INSTRUCTIONS — These instructions are used on any bit in the first 256 bytes of the memory (see Caution under Input/Output section). One group either sets or clears. The other group performs the bit test and branch operations. Refer to Table 5.

CONTROL INSTRUCTIONS — The control instructions control the MCU operations during program execution. Refer to Table 6.

ALPHABETICAL LISTING — The complete instruction set is given in alphabetical order in Table 7.

OPCODE MAP SUMMARY — Table 8 is an opcode map for the instructions used on the MCU.

 MOTOROLA *Semiconductor Products Inc.*

MC68705R3

TABLE 2 — REGISTER/MEMORY INSTRUCTIONS

Function	Mnemonic	Immediate Op Code	# Bytes	Cycles	Direct Op Code	# Bytes	Cycles	Extended Op Code	# Bytes	Cycles	Indexed (No Offset) Op Code	# Bytes	Cycles	Indexed (8 Bit Offset) Op Code	# Bytes	Cycles	Indexed (16 Bit Offset) Op Code	# Bytes	Cycles
Load A from Memory	LDA	A6	2	2	B6	2	4	C6	3	5	F6	1	4	E6	2	5	D6	3	6
Load X from Memory	LDX	AE	2	2	BE	2	4	CE	3	5	FE	1	4	EE	2	5	DE	3	6
Store A in Memory	STA	—			B7	2	5	C7	3	6	F7	1	5	E7	2	6	D7	3	7
Store X in Memory	STX	—			BF	2	5	CF	3	6	FF	1	5	EF	2	6	DF	3	7
Add Memory to A	ADD	AB	2	2	BB	2	4	CB	3	5	FB	1	4	EB	2	5	DB	3	6
Add Memory and Carry to A	ADC	A9	2	2	B9	2	4	C9	3	5	F9	1	4	E9	2	5	D9	3	6
Subtract Memory	SUB	A0	2	2	B0	2	4	C0	3	5	F0	1	4	E0	2	5	D0	3	6
Subtract Memory from A with Borrow	SBC	A2	2	2	B2	2	4	C2	3	5	F2	1	4	E2	2	5	D2	3	6
AND Memory to A	AND	A4	2	2	B4	2	4	C4	3	5	F4	1	4	E4	2	5	D4	3	6
OR Memory with A	ORA	AA	2	2	BA	2	4	CA	3	5	FA	1	4	EA	2	5	DA	3	6
Exclusive OR Memory with A	EOR	A8	2	2	B8	2	4	C8	3	5	F8	1	4	E8	2	5	D8	3	6
Arithmetic Compare A with Memory	CMP	A1	2	2	B1	2	4	C1	3	5	F1	1	4	E1	2	5	D1	3	6
Arithmetic Compare X with Memory	CPX	A3	2	2	B3	2	4	C3	3	5	F3	1	4	E3	2	5	D3	3	6
Bit Test Memory with A (Logical Compare)	BIT	A5	2	2	B5	2	4	C5	3	5	F5	1	4	E5	2	5	D5	3	6
Jump Unconditional	JMP	—			BC	2	3	CC	3	4	FC	1	3	EC	2	4	DC	3	5
Jump to Subroutine	JSR	—			BD	2	7	CD	3	8	FD	1	7	ED	2	8	DD	3	9

TABLE 3 — READ-MODIFY-WRITE INSTRUCTION

Function	Mnemonic	Inherent (A) Op Code	# Bytes	Cycles	Inherent (X) Op Code	# Bytes	Cycles	Direct Op Code	# Bytes	Cycles	Indexed (No Offset) Op Code	# Bytes	Cycles	Indexed (8 Bit Offset) Op Code	# Bytes	Cycles
Increment	INC	4C	1	4	5C	1	4	3C	2	6	7C	1	6	6C	2	7
Decrement	DEC	4A	1	4	5A	1	4	3A	2	6	7A	1	6	6A	2	7
Clear	CLR	4F	1	4	5F	1	4	3F	2	6	7F	1	6	6F	2	7
Complement	COM	43	1	4	53	1	4	33	2	6	73	1	6	63	2	7
Negate (2's Complement)	NEG	40	1	4	50	1	4	30	2	6	70	1	6	60	2	7
Rotate Left Thru Carry	ROL	49	1	4	59	1	4	39	2	6	79	1	6	69	2	7
Rotate Right Thru Carry	ROR	46	1	4	56	1	4	36	2	6	76	1	6	66	2	7
Logical Shift Left	LSL	48	1	4	58	1	4	38	2	6	78	1	6	68	2	7
Logical Shift Right	LSR	44	1	4	54	1	4	34	2	6	74	1	6	64	2	7
Arithmetic Shift Right	ASR	47	1	4	57	1	4	37	2	6	77	1	6	67	2	7
Test for Negative or Zero	TST	4D	1	4	5D	1	4	3D	2	6	7D	1	6	6D	2	7

 MOTOROLA *Semiconductor Products Inc.*

23

TABLE 4 — BRANCH INSTRUCTIONS

Function	Mnemonic	Relative Addressing Mode		
		Op Code	# Bytes	# Cycles
Branch Always	BRA	20	2	4
Branch Never	BRN	21	2	4
Branch IFF Higher	BHI	22	2	4
Branch IFF Lower or Same	BLS	23	2	4
Branch IFF Carry Clear	BCC	24	2	4
(Branch IFF Higher or Same)	(BHS)	24	2	4
Branch IFF Carry Set	BCS	25	2	4
(Branch IFF Lower)	(BLO)	25	2	4
Branch IFF Not Equal	BNE	26	2	4
Branch IFF Equal	BEQ	27	2	4
Branch IFF Half Carry Clear	BHCC	28	2	4
Branch IFF Half Carry Set	BHCS	29	2	4
Branch IFF Plus	BPL	2A	2	4
Branch IFF Minus	BMI	2B	2	4
Branch IFF Interrupt Mask Bit is Clear	BMC	2C	2	4
Branch IFF Interrupt Mask Bit is Set	BMS	2D	2	4
Branch IFF Interrupt Line is Low	BIL	2E	2	4
Branch IFF Interrupt Line is High	BIH	2F	2	4
Branch to Subroutine	BSR	AD	2	8

TABLE 5 — BIT MANIPULATION INSTRUCTIONS

Function	Mnemonic	Addressing Modes					
		Bit Set/Clear			Bit Test and Branch		
		Op Code	# Bytes	# Cycles	Op Code	# Bytes	# Cycles
Branch IFF Bit n is set	BRSET n (n = 0 7)	—	—	—	$2 \bullet n$	3	10
Branch IFF Bit n is clear	BRCLR n (n = 0 7)	—	—	—	$01 + 2 \bullet n$	3	10
Set Bit n	BSET n (n = 0 7)	$10 + 2 \bullet n$	2	7	—	—	—
Clear bit n	BCLR n (n = 0 7)	$11 + 2 \bullet n$	2	7	—	—	—

TABLE 6 — CONTROL INSTRUCTIONS

Function	Mnemonic	Inherent		
		Op Code	# Bytes	# Cycles
Transfer A to X	TAX	97	1	2
Transfer X to A	TXA	9F	1	2
Set Carry Bit	SEC	99	1	2
Clear Carry Bit	CLC	98	1	2
Set Interrupt Mask Bit	SEI	9B	1	2
Clear Interrupt Mask Bit	CLI	9A	1	2
Software Interrupt	SWI	83	1	11
Return from Subroutine	RTS	81	1	6
Return from Interrupt	RTI	80	1	9
Reset Stack Pointer	RSP	9C	1	2
No-Operation	NOP	9D	1	2

MOTOROLA *Semiconductor Products Inc.*

MC68705R3

TABLE 7 — INSTRUCTION SET

Mnemonic	Addressing Modes										Condition Codes				
	Inherent	Immediate	Direct	Extended	Relative	Indexed (No Offset)	Indexed (8 Bits)	Indexed (16 Bits)	Bit Set/ Clear	Bit Test & Branch	H	I	N	Z	C
ADC		X	X	X		X	X	X			Λ	•	Λ	Λ	Λ
ADD		X	X	X		X	X	X			Λ	•	Λ	Λ	Λ
AND		X	X	X		X	X	X			•	•	Λ	Λ	•
ASL	X		X			X	X				•	•	Λ	Λ	Λ
ASR	X		X			X	X				•	•	Λ	Λ	Λ
BCC					X						•	•	•	•	•
BCLR									X		•	•	•	•	•
BCS					X						•	•	•	•	•
BEQ					X						•	•	•	•	•
BHCC					X						•	•	•	•	•
BHCS					X						•	•	•	•	•
BHI					X						•	•	•	•	•
BHS					X						•	•	•	•	•
BIH					X						•	•	•	•	•
BIL					X						•	•	•	•	•
BIT		X	X	X		X	X	X			•	•	Λ	Λ	•
BLO					X						•	•	•	•	•
BLS					X						•	•	•	•	•
BMC					X						•	•	•	•	•
BMI					X						•	•	•	•	•
BMS					X						•	•	•	•	•
BNE					X						•	•	•	•	•
BPL					X						•	•	•	•	•
BRA					X						•	•	•	•	•
BRN					X						•	•	•	•	•
BRCLR										X	•	•	•	•	Λ
BRSET										X	•	•	•	•	Λ
BSET									X		•	•	•	•	•
BSR					X						•	•	•	•	•
CLC	X										•	•	•	•	0
CLI	X										•	0	•	•	•
CLR	X		X			X	X				•	•	0	1	•
CMP		X	X	X		X	X	X			•	•	Λ	Λ	Λ
COM	X		X			X	X				•	•	Λ	Λ	1
CPX		X	X	X		X	X	X			•	•	Λ	Λ	Λ

Condition Code Symbols

H   Half Carry (From Bit 3)
I   Interrupt Mask
N   Negative (Sign Bit)
Z   Zero
C   Carry/Borrow
Λ   Test and Set if True, Cleared Otherwise
•   Not Affected
?   Load CC Register From Stack
1   Set
0   Clear

 MOTOROLA *Semiconductor Products Inc.*

MC68705R3

TABLE 7 — INSTRUCTION SET (CONTINUED)

Mnemonic	Addressing Modes										Condition Codes				
	Inherent	Immediate	Direct	Extended	Relative	Indexed (No Offset)	Indexed (8 Bits)	Indexed (16 Bits)	Bit Set/ Clear	Bit Test & Branch	H	I	N	Z	C
DEC	X		X			X	X				•	•	Λ	Λ	•
EOR		X	X	X		X	X	X			•	•	Λ	Λ	•
INC	X		X			X	X				•	•	Λ	Λ	•
JMP			X	X		X	X	X			•	•	•	•	•
JSR			X	X		X	X	X			•	•	•	•	•
LDA		X	X	X		X	X	X			•	•	Λ	Λ	•
LDX		X	X	X		X	X	X			•	•	Λ	Λ	•
LSL	X		X			X	X				•	•	Λ	Λ	Λ
LSR	X		X			X	X				•	•	0	Λ	Λ
NEQ	X		X			X	X				•	•	Λ	Λ	Λ
NOP	X										•	•	•	•	•
ORA		X	X	X		X	X	X			•	•	Λ	Λ	•
ROL	X		X			X	X				•	•	Λ	Λ	Λ
RSP	X										•	•	•	•	•
RTI	X										?	?	?	?	?
RTS	X										•	•	•	•	•
SBC		X	X	X		X	X	X			•	•	Λ	Λ	Λ
SEC	X										•	•	•	•	1
SEI	X										•	1	•	•	•
STA			X	X		X	X	X			•	•	Λ	Λ	•
STX			X	X		X	X	X			•	•	Λ	Λ	•
SUB		X	X	X		X	X	X			•	•	Λ	Λ	Λ
SWI	X										•	1	•	•	•
TAX	X										•	•	•	•	•
TST	X		X			X	X				•	•	Λ	Λ	•
TXA	X										•	•	•	•	•

Condition Code Symbols

H	Half Carry (From Bit 3)
I	Interrupt Mask
N	Negative (Sign Bit)
Z	Zero
C	Carry/Borrow
Λ	Test and Set if True, Cleared Otherwise
•	Not Affected
?	Load CC Register From Stack
1	Set
0	Clear

MOTOROLA *Semiconductor Products Inc.*

26

TABLE 8 — M68705 HMOS FAMILY INSTRUCTION SET OPCODE MAP

Cell format: MNEMONIC (cycles, bytes). Address mode is given by the column header.

Low \ Hi	0 BTB (Bit Manip.)	1 BSC (Bit Manip.)	2 REL (Branch)	3 DIR (Read-Modify-Write)	4 INH (RMW)	5 INH (RMW)	6 IX1 (RMW)	7 IX (RMW)	8 INH (Control)	9 INH (Control)	A IMM (Reg/Mem)	B DIR (Reg/Mem)	C EXT (Reg/Mem)	D IX2 (Reg/Mem)	E IX1 (Reg/Mem)	F IX (Reg/Mem)
0	BRSET0 (10,3)	BSET0 (7,2)	BRA (4,2)	NEG (6,2)	NEGA (4,1)	NEGX (4,1)	NEG (7,2)	NEG (6,1)	RTI (9,1)		SUB (2,2)	SUB (4,2)	SUB (5,3)	SUB (6,3)	SUB (5,2)	SUB (4,1)
1	BRCLR0 (10,3)	BCLR0 (7,2)	BRN (4,2)						RTS (6,1)		CMP (2,2)	CMP (4,2)	CMP (5,3)	CMP (6,3)	CMP (5,2)	CMP (4,1)
2	BRSET1 (10,3)	BSET1 (7,2)	BHI (4,2)								SBC (2,2)	SBC (4,2)	SBC (5,3)	SBC (6,3)	SBC (5,2)	SBC (4,1)
3	BRCLR1 (10,3)	BCLR1 (7,2)	BLS (4,2)	COM (6,2)	COMA (4,1)	COMX (4,1)	COM (7,2)	COM (6,1)	SWI (11,1)		CPX (2,2)	CPX (4,2)	CPX (5,3)	CPX (6,3)	CPX (5,2)	CPX (4,1)
4	BRSET2 (10,3)	BSET2 (7,2)	BCC (4,2)	LSR (6,2)	LSRA (4,1)	LSRX (4,1)	LSR (7,2)	LSR (6,1)			AND (2,2)	AND (4,2)	AND (5,3)	AND (6,3)	AND (5,2)	AND (4,1)
5	BRCLR2 (10,3)	BCLR2 (7,2)	BCS (4,2)								BIT (2,2)	BIT (4,2)	BIT (5,3)	BIT (6,3)	BIT (5,2)	BIT (4,1)
6	BRSET3 (10,3)	BSET3 (7,2)	BNE (4,2)	ROR (6,2)	RORA (4,1)	RORX (4,1)	ROR (7,2)	ROR (6,1)			LDA (2,2)	LDA (4,2)	LDA (5,3)	LDA (6,3)	LDA (5,2)	LDA (4,1)
7	BRCLR3 (10,3)	BCLR3 (7,2)	BEQ (4,2)	ASR (6,2)	ASRA (4,1)	ASRX (4,1)	ASR (7,2)	ASR (6,1)		TAX (2,1)		STA (5,2)	STA (6,3)	STA (7,3)	STA (6,2)	STA (5,1)
8	BRSET4 (10,3)	BSET4 (7,2)	BHCC (4,2)	LSL (6,2)	LSLA (4,1)	LSLX (4,1)	LSL (7,2)	LSL (6,1)		CLC (2,1)	EOR (2,2)	EOR (4,2)	EOR (5,3)	EOR (6,3)	EOR (5,2)	EOR (4,1)
9	BRCLR4 (10,3)	BCLR4 (7,2)	BHCS (4,2)	ROL (6,2)	ROLA (4,1)	ROLX (4,1)	ROL (7,2)	ROL (6,1)		SEC (2,1)	ADC (2,2)	ADC (4,2)	ADC (5,3)	ADC (6,3)	ADC (5,2)	ADC (4,1)
A	BRSET5 (10,3)	BSET5 (7,2)	BPL (4,2)	DEC (6,2)	DECA (4,1)	DECX (4,1)	DEC (7,2)	DEC (6,1)		CLI (2,1)	ORA (2,2)	ORA (4,2)	ORA (5,3)	ORA (6,3)	ORA (5,2)	ORA (4,1)
B	BRCLR5 (10,3)	BCLR5 (7,2)	BMI (4,2)							SEI (2,1)	ADD (2,2)	ADD (4,2)	ADD (5,3)	ADD (6,3)	ADD (5,2)	ADD (4,1)
C	BRSET6 (10,3)	BSET6 (7,2)	BMC (4,2)	INC (6,2)	INCA (4,1)	INCX (4,1)	INC (7,2)	INC (6,1)		RSP (2,1)		JMP (3,2)	JMP (4,3)	JMP (5,3)	JMP (4,2)	JMP (3,1)
D	BRCLR6 (10,3)	BCLR6 (7,2)	BMS (4,2)	TST (6,2)	TSTA (4,1)	TSTX (4,1)	TST (7,2)	TST (6,1)		NOP (2,1)	BSR (REL) (8,2)	JSR (7,2)	JSR (8,3)	JSR (9,3)	JSR (8,2)	JSR (7,1)
E	BRSET7 (10,3)	BSET7 (7,2)	BIL (4,2)								LDX (2,2)	LDX (4,2)	LDX (5,3)	LDX (6,3)	LDX (5,2)	LDX (4,1)
F	BRCLR7 (10,3)	BCLR7 (7,2)	BIH (4,2)	CLR (6,2)	CLRA (4,1)	CLRX (4,1)	CLR (7,2)	CLR (6,1)		TXA (2,1)		STX (5,2)	STX (6,3)	STX (7,3)	STX (6,2)	STX (5,1)

LEGEND

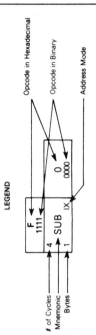

- **F** — Opcode in Hexadecimal
- **1111** — Opcode in Binary
- **SUB** — Mnemonic
- **IX** — Address Mode
- **0 / 0000** — (low nibble hex / binary)
- **4** — # of Cycles
- **1** — Bytes

Abbreviations for Address Modes

INH	Inherent
IMM	Immediate
DIR	Direct
EXT	Extended
REL	Relative
BSC	Bit Set/Clear
BTB	Bit Test and Branch
IX	Indexed (No Offset)
IX1	Indexed, 1 Byte (8-Bit) Offset
IX2	Indexed, 2 Byte (16-Bit) Offset

 MOTOROLA Semiconductor Products Inc.

MC68705R3

M6805 FAMILY

	MC6805P2	MC6805P4	MC6805R2	MC6805T2	MC6805U2
Technology	HMOS	HMOS	HMOS	HMOS	HMOS
Number of Pins	28	28	40	28	40
On-Chip RAM (Bytes)	64	112	64	64	64
On-Chip User ROM (Bytes)	1.1K	1.1K	2K	2.5K	2K
External Bus	None	None	None	None	None
Bidirectional I/O Lines	20	20	24	19	24
Unidirectional I/O Lines	None	None	6 Inputs	None	8 Inputs
Other I/O Features	Timer	Timer	Timer, A/D	Timer, PLL	Timer
External Interrupt Inputs	1	1	2	2	2
EPROM Version	MC68705P3	MC68705P3	MC68705R3	None	MC68705U3
STOP and WAIT	No	No	No	No	No

	MC68075P3	MC68705R3	MC68705U3	MC146805E2	MC146805F2	MC146805G2
Technology	HMOS	HMOS	HMOS	CMOS	CMOS	CMOS
Number of Pins	28	40	40	40	28	40
On-Chip RAM (Bytes)	112	112	112	112	64	112
On-Chip User ROM (Bytes)	1.8K EPROM	3.8K EPROM	3.8K EPROM	None	1K	2K
External Bus	None	None	None	Yes	None	None
Bidirectional I/O Lines	20	24	24	16	16	32
Unidirectional I/O Lines	None	6 Inputs	8 Inputs	None	4 Inputs	None
Other I/O Features	Timer	Timer, A/D	Timer	Timer	Timer	Timer
External Interrupt Inputs	1	2	2	1	1	1
EPROM Version	--	--	--	None	None	None
STOP and WAIT	No	No	No	Yes	Yes	Yes

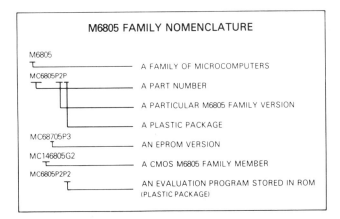

M6805 FAMILY NOMENCLATURE

M6805 — A FAMILY OF MICROCOMPUTERS

MC6805P2P
- A PART NUMBER
- A PARTICULAR M6805 FAMILY VERSION
- A PLASTIC PACKAGE

MC68705P3 — AN EPROM VERSION

MC146805G2 — A CMOS M6805 FAMILY MEMBER

MC6805P2P2 — AN EVALUATION PROGRAM STORED IN ROM (PLASTIC PACKAGE)

 MOTOROLA *Semiconductor Products Inc.*
Colvilles Road, Kelvin Estate-East Kilbridge/Glasgow-SCOTLAND   Printed in Switzerland 4. 82

Appendix 2

The 6805 Detail Instruction Set

Reproduced by courtesy of Motorola Limited

INSTRUCTION SET
DETAILED DEFINITION

0 EXECUTABLE INSTRUCTIONS

1 INTRODUCTION

In the pages that follow this section, the various Accumulator and Memory operations, together with the respective Mnemonic, provides a heading for each of the executable instructions. The STOP and WAIT instructions apply only to the CMOS M146805 Family. The pages are arranged in alphabetical order of the Mnemonic. A brief description of the operation is provided along with other applicable pertinent information, including: condition code status; Boolean Formula; Source Forms; usable Addressing Modes; number of execution cycles (both M6805 and M146805 Families); number of bytes required; and the opcode for each usable Addressing Mode. Paragraph D.2 contains a listing of the various nomeclature (abbreviations and signs) used in the operations.

2 NOMENCLATURE

The following nomenclature is used in the executable instructions which follow this paragraph.

(a) Operators:

( )	indirection. i.e., (SP) means the value pointed to by SP
←	is loaded with (read: 'gets')
•	boolean AND
v	boolean (inclusive) OR
⊕	boolean EXCLUSIVE OR
~	boolean NOT
−	negation (two's complement)

(b) Registers in the MPU:

ACCA	Accumulator
CC	Condition Code Register
X	Index Register
PC	Program Counter
PCH	Program Counter High Byte
PCL	Program Counter Low Byte
SP	Stack Pointer

(c) Memory and Addressing:

M Contents of any memory location (one byte)

Rel Relative address (i.e., the two's complement number stored in the second byte of machine code in a branch instruction.)

(d) Bits in the Condition Code Register:

C	Carry/Borrow, Bit 0
Z	Zero Indicator, Bit 1
N	Negative Indicator, Bit 2
I	Interrupt Mask, Bit 3
H	Half Carry Indicator, Bit 4

(e) Status of Individual Bits BEFORE Execution of an Instruction

An Bit n of ACCA (n = 7, 6, 5, 4, 3, 2, 1, 0)

Xn Bit n of X (n = 7, 6, 5, 4, 3, 2, 1, 0)

Mn Bit n of M (n = 7, 6, 5, 4, 3, 2, 1, 0). In read/modify/write instructions, Mn is used to represent bit n of M, A or X.

(f) Status of Individual Bits AFTER Execution of an Instruction:

Rn Bit n of the result (n = 7, 6, 5, 4, 3, 2, 1, 0)

(g) Source Forms:

P Operands with IMMediate, DIRect, EXTended and INDexed (0, 1, 2 byte offset) addressing modes

Q Operands with DIRect, INDexed (0 and 1 byte offset) addressing modes

dd Relative operands

DR Operands with DIRect addressing mode only.

(h) iff

abbreviation for if-and-only-if.

D-2

ADC

Add with Carry

ADC

Operation: ACCA ← ACCA + M + C

Description: Adds the contents of the C bit to the sum of the contents of ACCA and M, and places the result in ACCA.

**Condition
Codes:**

- H: Set if there was a carry from bit 3; cleared otherwise.
- I: Not affected.
- N: Set if the most significant bit of the result is set; cleared otherwise.
- Z: Set if all bits of the result are cleared; cleared otherwise.
- C: Set if there was a carry from the most significant bit of the result; cleared otherwise.

Boolean Formulae for Condition Codes:

$H = A3 \cdot M3vM3 \cdot R3vR3 \cdot A3$

$N = R7$

$Z = \overline{R7} \cdot \overline{R6} \cdot \overline{R5} \cdot \overline{R4} \cdot \overline{R3} \cdot \overline{R2} \cdot \overline{R1} \cdot \overline{R0}$

$C = A7 \cdot M7vM7 \cdot R7vR7 \cdot A7$

Source Form(s):	Addressing Mode	Cycles HMOS	Cycles CMOS	Bytes	Opcode
ADC P	Inherent				
	Relative				
	Accumulator				
	Index Register				
	Immediate	2	2	2	A9
	Direct	4	3	2	B9
	Extended	5	4	3	C9
	Indexed 0 Offset	4	3	1	F9
	Indexed 1-Byte	5	4	2	E9
	Indexed 2-Byte	6	5	3	D9

ADD

Add

ADD

Operation: ACCA ← ACCA + M

Description: Adds the contents of ACCA and the contents of M and places the result in ACCA.

**Condition
Codes:**

- H: Set if there was a carry from bit 3; cleared otherwise.
- I: Not affected.
- N: Set if the most significant bit of the result is set; cleared otherwise.
- Z: Set if all bits of the result are cleared; cleared otherwise.
- C: Set if there was a carry from the most significant bit of the result; cleared otherwise.

Boolean Formulae for Condition Codes:

$H = A3 \cdot M3vM3 \cdot R3vR3 \cdot A3$

$N = R7$

$Z = \overline{R7} \cdot \overline{R6} \cdot \overline{R5} \cdot \overline{R4} \cdot \overline{R3} \cdot \overline{R2} \cdot \overline{R1} \cdot \overline{R0}$

$C = A7 \cdot M7vM7 \cdot \overline{R7}v\overline{R7} \cdot A7$

**Source
Form(s):** ADD P

Addressing Mode	Cycles		Bytes	Opcode
	HMOS	CMOS		
Inherent				
Relative				
Accumulator				
Index Register				
Immediate	2	2	2	AB
Direct	4	3	2	BB
Extended	5	4	3	CB
Indexed 0 Offset	4	3	1	FB
Indexed 1-Byte	5	4	2	EB
Indexed 2-Byte	6	5	3	DB

AND   Logical AND   AND

Operation: ACCA — ACCA . M

Description: Performs logical AND between the contents of ACCA and the contents of M and places the result in ACCA. Each bit of ACCA after the operation will be the logical AND result of the corresponding bits of M and of ACCA before the operation.

Condition Codes:
- H: Not affected.
- I: Not affected.
- N: Set if the most significant bit of the result is set; cleared otherwise.
- Z: Set if all bits of the result are cleared; cleared otherwise.
- C: Not affected.

Boolean Formulae for Condition Codes:

$N = R7$

$Z = \overline{R7} \cdot \overline{R6} \cdot \overline{R5} \cdot \overline{R4} \cdot \overline{R3} \cdot \overline{R2} \cdot \overline{R1} \cdot \overline{R0}$

Source Form(s):   AND P

Addressing Mode	Cycles		Bytes	Opcode
	HMOS	CMOS		
Inherent				
Relative				
Accumulator				
Index Register				
Immediate	2	2	2	A4
Direct	4	3	2	B4
Extended	5	4	3	C4
Indexed 0 Offset	4	3	1	F4
Indexed 1-Byte	5	4	2	E4
Indexed 2-Byte	6	5	3	D4

ASL   Arithmetic Shift Left   ASL

Operation: $C \leftarrow b7 \;[\;\;\;\;\;\;]\; b0 \leftarrow 0$

Description: Shifts all bits of ACCA, X or M one place to the left. Bit 0 is loaded with a zero. The C bit is loaded from the most significant bit of ACCA, X or M.

Condition
Codes: H: Not affected.

I: Not affected.

N: Set if the most significant bit of the result is set; cleared otherwise.

Z: Set if all bits of the result are cleared; cleared otherwise.

C: Set if, before the operation, the most significant bit of ACCA, X or M was set; cleared otherwise.

Boolean Formulae for Condition Codes:

$N = R7$

$Z = \overline{R7} \cdot \overline{R6} \cdot \overline{R5} \cdot \overline{R4} \cdot \overline{R3} \cdot \overline{R2} \cdot \overline{R1} \cdot \overline{R0}$

$C = M7$

Comments: Same opcode as LSL

Source Form(s):	Addressing Mode	Cycles HMOS	Cycles CMOS	Bytes	Opcode
ASL Q, ASLA, ASLX	Inherent				
	Relative				
	Accumulator	4	3	1	48
	Index Register	4	3	1	58
	Immediate				
	Direct	6	5	2	38
	Extended				
	Indexed 0 Offset	6	5	1	78
	Indexed 1-Byte	7	6	2	68
	Indexed 2-Byte				

ASR   Arithmetic Shift Right   ASR

Operation:

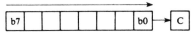

Description: Shifts all bits of ACCA, X or M one place to the right. Bit 7 is held constant. Bit 0 is loaded into the C bit.

Condition
Codes: H: Not affected.

I: Not affected.

N: Set if the most significant bit of the result is set; cleared otherwise.

Z: Set if all bits of the result are cleared; cleared otherwise.

C: Set if, before the operation, the least significant bit of ACCA, X or M was set; cleared otherwise.

Boolean Formulae for Condition Codes:

$N = R7$

$Z = \overline{R7} \cdot \overline{R6} \cdot \overline{R5} \cdot \overline{R4} \cdot \overline{R3} \cdot \overline{R2} \cdot \overline{R1} \cdot \overline{R0}$

$C = M0$

Source Form(s):	Addressing Mode	Cycles HMOS	Cycles CMOS	Bytes	Opcode
ASR Q, ASRA, ASRX	Inherent				
	Relative				
	Accumulator	4	3	1	47
	Index Register	4	3	1	57
	Immediate				
	Direct	6	5	2	37
	Extended				
	Indexed 0 Offset	6	5	1	77
	Indexed 1-Byte	7	6	2	67
	Indexed 2-Byte				

BCC

Branch if Carry Clear

BCC

Operation: PC ← PC + 0002 + Rel iff C = 0

Description: Tests the state of the C bit and causes a branch iff C is clear. See BRA instruction for further details of the execution of the branch.

**Condition
Codes:** Not affected.

Comments: Same opcode as BHS

**Source
Form(s):** BCC dd

Addressing Mode	Cycles		Bytes	Opcode
	HMOS	CMOS		
Inherent				
Relative	4	3	2	24
Accumulator				
Index Register				
Immediate				
Direct				
Extended				
Indexed 0 Offset				
Indexed 1-Byte				
Indexed 2-Byte				

BCLR n

Bit Clear Bit n

BCLR n

Operation: Mn ← 0

Description: Clear bit n (n = 0, 7) in location M. All other bits in M are unaffected.

**Condition
Codes:** Not affected.

**Source
Form(s):** BCLR n, DR

Addressing Mode	Cycles		Bytes	Opcode
	HMOS	CMOS		
Inherent				
Relative				
Accumulator				
Index Register				
Immediate				
Direct	7	5	2	11 + 2•n
Extended				
Indexed 0 Offset				
Indexed 1-Byte				
Indexed 2-Byte				

BCS

Branch if Carry Set

BCS

Operation: PC ← PC + 0002 + Rel iff C = 1

Description: Tests the state of the C bit and causes a branch iff C is set. See BRA instruction for further details of the execution of the branch.

**Condition
Codes:**   Not affected.

Comments: Same opcode as BLO

**Source
Form(s):**   BCS dd

Addressing Mode	Cycles HMOS	Cycles CMOS	Bytes	Opcode
Inherent				
Relative	4	3	2	25
Accumulator				
Index Register				
Immediate				
Direct				
Extended				
Indexed 0 Offset				
Indexed 1-Byte				
Indexed 2-Byte				

BEQ

Branch if Equal

BEQ

Operation: PC ← PC + 0002 + Rel iff Z = 1

Description: Tests the state of the Z bit and causes a branch iff Z is set. Following a compare or subtract instruction BEQ will cause a branch if the arguments were equal. See BRA instruction for further details of the execution of the branch.

**Condition
Codes:**   Not affected.

**Source
Form(s):**   BEQ dd

Addressing Mode	Cycles HMOS	Cycles CMOS	Bytes	Opcode
Inherent				
Relative	4	3	2	27
Accumulator				
Index Register				
Immediate				
Direct				
Extended				
Indexed 0 Offset				
Indexed 1-Byte				
Indexed 2-Byte				

BHCC

Branch if Half Carry Clear

BHCC

Operation: PC ← PC + 0002 + Rel iff H = 0

Description: Tests the state of the H bit and causes a branch iff H is clear. See BRA instruction for further details of the execution of the branch.

**Condition
Codes:**   Not affected.

**Source
Form(s):**   BHCC dd

Addressing Mode	Cycles HMOS	CMOS	Bytes	Opcode
Inherent				
Relative	4	3	2	28
Accumulator				
Index Register				
Immediate				
Direct				
Extended				
Indexed 0 Offset				
Indexed 1-Byte				
Indexed 2-Byte				

BHCS

Branch if Half Carry Set

BHCS

Operation: PC ← PC + 0002 + Rel iff H = 1

Description: Tests the state of the H bit and causes a branch iff H is set. See BRA instruction for further details of the execution of the branch.

**Condition
Codes:**   Not affected.

**Source
Form(s):**   BHCS dd

Addressing Mode	Cycles HMOS	CMOS	Bytes	Opcode
Inherent				
Relative	4	3	2	29
Accumulator				
Index Register				
Immediate				
Direct				
Extended				
Indexed 0 Offset				
Indexed 1-Byte				
Indexed 2-Byte				

BHI   Branch if Higher   # BHI

Operation: PC ← PC + 0002 + Rel iff (C v Z) = 0
                                          i.e., if ACCA > M (unsigned binary numbers)

Description: Causes a branch iff both C and Z are zero. If the BHI instruction is executed im-
                                mediately after execution of either of the CMP or SUB instructions, the branch will
                                occur if and only if the unsigned binary number represented by the minuend (i.e.,
                                ACCA) was greater than the unsigned binary number represented by the subtrahend
                                (i.e., M). See BRA instruction for further details of the execution of the branch.

**Condition
Codes:**   Not affected.

**Source
Form(s):**   BHI dd

Addressing Mode	Cycles		Bytes	Opcode
	HMOS	CMOS		
Inherent				
Relative	4	3	2	22
Accumulator				
Index Register				
Immediate				
Direct				
Extended				
Indexed 0 Offset				
Indexed 1-Byte				
Indexed 2-Byte				

BHS   Branch iff Higher or Same   # BHS

Operation: PC ← PC + 0002 + Rel iff C = 0

Description: Following an unsigned compare or subtract, BHS will cause a branch iff the register
                                was higher than or the same as the location in memory. See BRA instruction for fur-
                                ther details of the execution of the branch.

**Condition
Codes:**   Not affected.

Comments: Same opcode as BCC

**Source
Form(s):**   BHS dd

Addressing Mode	Cycles		Bytes	Opcode
	HMOS	CMOS		
Inherent				
Relative	4	3	2	24
Accumulator				
Index Register				
Immediate				
Direct				
Extended				
Indexed 0 Offset				
Indexed 1-Byte				
Indexed 2-Byte				

BIH   Branch iff Interrupt Line is High   BIH

Operation: PC ← PC + 0002 + Rel iff INT = 1

Description: Tests the state of the external interrupt pin and branches iff it is high. See BRA instruction for further details of the execution of the branch.

**Condition
Codes:**   Not affected.

Comments: In systems not using interrupts, this instruction and BIL can be used to create an extra I/O input bit. This instruction does NOT test the state of the interrupt mask bit nor does it indicate whether an interrupt is pending. All it does is indicate whether the INT line is high.

**Source
Form(s):**   BIH dd

Addressing Mode	Cycles		Bytes	Opcode
	HMOS	CMOS		
Inherent				
Relative	4	3	2	2F
Accumulator				
Index Register				
Immediate				
Direct				
Extended				
Indexed 0 Offset				
Indexed 1-Byte				
Indexed 2-Byte				

BIL   Branch if Interrupt Line is Low   BIL

Operation: PC ← PC + 0002 + Rel iff INT = 0

Description: Tests the state of the external interrupt pin and branches iff it is low. See BRA instruction for further details of the execution of the branch.

**Condition
Codes:**   Not affected.

Comments: In systems not using interrupts, this instruction and BIH can be used to create an extra I/O input bit. This instruction does NOT test the state of the interrupt mask bit nor does it indicate whether an interrupt is pending. All it does is indicate whether the INT line is Low.

**Source
Form(s):**   BIL dd

Addressing Mode	Cycles		Bytes	Opcode
	HMOS	CMOS		
Inherent				
Relative	4	3	2	2E
Accumulator				
Index Register				
Immediate				
Direct				
Extended				
Indexed 0 Offset				
Indexed 1-Byte				
Indexed 2-Byte				

BIT

Bit Test Memory with Accumulator

BIT

Operation: ACCA • M

Description: Performs the logical AND comparison of the contents of ACCA and the contents of M and modifies the condition codes accordingly. The contents of ACCA and M are unchanged.

Condition Codes:

H: Not affected.
I: Not affected.
N: Set if the most significant bit of the result of the AND is set; cleared otherwise.
Z: Set if all bits of the result of the AND are cleared; cleared otherwise.
C: Not affected.

Boolean Formulae for Condition Codes:

$N = R7$
$Z = \overline{R7} \cdot \overline{R6} \cdot \overline{R5} \cdot \overline{R4} \cdot \overline{R3} \cdot \overline{R2} \cdot \overline{R1} \cdot \overline{R0}$

Source Form(s): BIT P

Addressing Mode	Cycles HMOS	CMOS	Bytes	Opcode
Inherent				
Relative				
Accumulator				
Index Register				
Immediate	2	2	2	A5
Direct	4	3	2	B5
Extended	5	4	3	C5
Indexed 0 Offset	4	3	1	F5
Indexed 1-Byte	5	4	2	E5
Indexed 2-Byte	6	5	3	D5

BLO

Branch if Lower

BLO

Operation: PC ← PC + 0002 + Rel iff C = 1

Description: Following a compare, BLO will branch iff the register was lower than the memory location. See BRA instruction for further details of the execution of the branch.

Condition Codes: Not affected.

Comments: Same opcode as BCS

Source Form(s): BLO dd

Addressing Mode	Cycles HMOS	CMOS	Bytes	Opcode
Inherent				
Relative	4	3	2	25
Accumulator				
Index Register				
Immediate				
Direct				
Extended				
Indexed 0 Offset				
Indexed 1-Byte				
Indexed 2-Byte				

BLS
Branch iff Lower or Same
BLS

Operation: PC ← PC + 0002 + Rel iff (C v Z) = 1
i.e., if ACCA ← M (unsigned binary numbers)

Description: Causes a branch if (C is set) OR (Z is set). If the BLS instruction is executed immediately after execution of either of the instructions CMP or SUB, the branch will occur if and only if the unsigned binary number represented by the minuend (i.e., ACCA) was less than or equal to the unsigned binary number represented by the subtrahend (i.e., M). See BRA instruction for further details of the execution of the branch.

**Condition
Codes:**   Not affected.

**Source
Form(s):**   BLS dd

Addressing Mode	Cycles HMOS	Cycles CMOS	Bytes	Opcode
Inherent				
Relative	4	3	2	23
Accumulator				
Index Register				
Immediate				
Direct				
Extended				
Indexed 0 Offset				
Indexed 1-Byte				
Indexed 2-Byte				

BMC
Branch if Interrupt Mask is Clear
BMC

Operation: PC ← PC + 0002 + Rel iff I = 0

Description: Tests the state of the I bit and causes a branch iff I is clear. See BRA instruction for further details of the execution of the branch.

**Condition
Codes:**   Not affected.

Comments: This instruction does NOT branch on the condition of the external interrupt line. The test is performed only on the interrupt mask bit.

**Source
Form(s):**   BMC dd

Addressing Mode	Cycles HMOS	Cycles CMOS	Bytes	Opcode
Inherent				
Relative	4	3	2	2C
Accumulator				
Index Register				
Immediate				
Direct				
Extended				
Indexed 0 Offset				
Indexed 1-Byte				
Indexed 2-Byte				

BMI
Branch if Minus
BMI

Operation: PC ← PC + 0002 + Rel iff N = 1

Description: Tests the state of the N bit and causes a branch iff N is set. See BRA instruction for further details of the execution of the branch.

**Condition
Codes:** Not affected.

**Source
Form(s)** BMI dd

Addressing Mode	Cycles		Bytes	Opcode
	HMOS	CMOS		
Inherent				
Relative	4	3	2	2B
Accumulator				
Index Register				
Immediate				
Direct				
Extended				
Indexed 0 Offset				
Indexed 1-Byte				
Indexed 2-Byte				

BMS
Branch if Interrupt Mask Bit is Set
BMS

Operation: PC ← PC + 0002 + Rel iff I = 1

Description: Tests the state of the I bit and causes a branch iff I is set. See BRA instruction for further details of the execution of the branch.

**Condition
Codes:** Not affected.

Comments: This instruction does NOT branch on the condition of the external interrupt line. The test is performed only on the interrupt mask bit.

**Source
Form(s):** BMS dd

Addressing Mode	Cycles		Bytes	Opcode
	HMOS	CMOS		
Inherent				
Relative	4	3	2	2D
Accumulator				
Index Register				
Immediate				
Direct				
Extended				
Indexed 0 Offset				
Indexed 1-Byte				
Indexed 2-Byte				

BNE
Branch if Not Equal
BNE

Operation: PC ← PC + 0002 + Rel iff Z = 0

Description: Tests the state of the Z bit and causes a branch iff Z is clear. Following a compare or subtract instruction BNE will cause a branch if the arguments were different. See BRA instruction for further details of the execution of the branch.

Condition Codes: Not affected.

Source Form(s): BNE dd

Addressing Mode	Cycles HMOS	CMOS	Bytes	Opcode
Inherent				
Relative	4	3	2	26
Accumulator				
Index Register				
Immediate				
Direct				
Extended				
Indexed 0 Offset				
Indexed 1-Byte				
Indexed 2-Byte				

BPL
Branch if Plus
BPL

Operation: PC ← PC + 0002 + Rel iff N = 0

Description: Tests the state of the N bit and causes a branch iff N is clear. See BRA instruction for further details of the execution of the branch.

Condition Codes: Not affected.

Source Form(s): BPL dd

Addressing Mode	Cycles HMOS	CMOS	Bytes	Opcode
Inherent				
Relative	4	3	2	2A
Accumulator				
Index Register				
Immediate				
Direct				
Extended				
Indexed 0 Offset				
Indexed 1-Byte				
Indexed 2-Byte				

BRA   Branch Always   **BRA**

Operation: PC ← PC + 0002 + Rel

Description: Unconditional branch to the address given by the foregoing formula, in which Rel is
the relative address stored as a two's complement number in the second byte of
machine code corresponding to the branch instruction.

NOTE: The source program specifies the destination of any branch instruction by its
absolute address, either as a numerical value or as a symbol or expression which can
be evaluated by the assembler. The assembler obtains the relative address Rel from
the absolute address and the current value of the program counter.

**Condition
Codes:**   Not affected.

Addressing Mode	Cycles HMOS	Cycles CMOS	Bytes	Opcode
Inherent				
Relative	4	3	2	20
Accumulator				
Index Register				
Immediate				
Direct				
Extended				
Indexed 0 Offset				
Indexed 1-Byte				
Indexed 2-Byte				

**Source
Form(s):**   BRA dd

BRCLR n   Branch if Bit n is Clear   **BRCLR n**

Operation: PC ← PC + 0003 + Rel iff bit n of M is zero

Description: Tests bit n (n = 0, 7) of location M and branches iff the bit is clear.

**Condition
Codes:**
H: Not affected.
I: Not affected.
N: Not affected.
Z: Not affected.
C: Set if Mn = 1; cleared otherwise.

Boolean Formulae for Condition Codes:
C = Mn

Comments: The C bit is set to the state of the bit tested. Used with an appropriate rotate instruction, this instruction is an easy way to do serial to parallel conversions.

**Source
Form(s):**   BRCLR n, DR, dd

Addressing Mode	Cycles HMOS	Cycles CMOS	Bytes	Opcode
Inherent				
Relative	10	5	3	01 + 2•n
Accumulator				
Index Register				
Immediate				
Direct				
Extended				
Indexed 0 Offset				
Indexed 1-Byte				
Indexed 2-Byte				

BRN

Branch Never

BRN

Description: Never branches. Branch never is a 2 byte 4 cycle NOP.

**Condition
Codes:** Not affected.

Comments: BRN is included here to demonstrate the nature of branches on the M6805 Family. Each branch is matched with an inverse that varies only in the least significant bit of the opcode. BRN is the inverse of BRA. This instruction may have some use during program debugging.

**Source
Form(s):** BRN dd

Addressing Mode	Cycles HMOS	CMOS	Bytes	Opcode
Inherent				
Relative	4	3	2	21
Accumulator				
Index Register				
Immediate				
Direct				
Extended				
Indexed 0 Offset				
Indexed 1-Byte				
Indexed 2-Byte				

BRSET

Branch if Bit n is Set

BRSET

Operation: $PC \leftarrow PC + 0003 + Rel$ iff Bit n of M is not zero

Description: Tests bit n (n = 0, 7) of location M and branches iff the bit is set.

**Condition
Codes:**
H: Not affected.
I: Not affected.
N: Not affected.
Z: Not affected.
C: Set if Mn = 1; cleared otherwise.

Boolean Formulae for Condition Codes:
$C = Mn$

Comments: The C bit is set to the state of the bit tested. Used with an appropriate rotate instruction, this instruction is an easy way to provide serial to parallel conversions.

**Source
Form(s):** BRSET n, DR, dd

Addressing Mode	Cycles HMOS	CMOS	Bytes	Opcode
Inherent				
Relative	10	5	3	2•n
Accumulator				
Index Register				
Immediate				
Direct				
Extended				
Indexed 0 Offset				
Indexed 1-Byte				
Indexed 2-Byte				

BSET n

Set Bit in Memory

BSET n

Operation: Mn ← 1

Description: Set bit n (n = 0, 7) in location M. All other bits in M are unaffected.

**Condition
Codes:**   Not affected.

**Source
Form(s):**   BSET n, DR

Addressing Modes	Cycles HMOS	CMOS	Bytes	Opcode
Inherent				
Relative				
Accumulator				
Index Register				
Immediate				
Direct	7	5	2	10 + 2•n
Extended				
Indexed 0 Offset				
Indexed 1-Byte				
Indexed 2-Byte				

BSR

Branch to Subroutine

BSR

Operation: PC ← PC + 0002
(SP) ← PCL; SP ← SP − 0001
(SP) ← PCH; SP ← SP − 0001
PC ← PC + Rel

Description: The program counter is incremented by 2. The least (low) significant byte of the program counter contents is pushed onto the stack. The stack pointer is then decremented (by one). The most (high) signficant byte of the program counter contents is then pushed onto the stack. Unused bits in the Program Counter high byte are stored as 1's on the stack. The stack pointer is again decremented (by one). A branch then occurs to the location specified by the relative offset. See the BRA instruction for details of the branch execution.

**Condition
Codes:**   Not affected.

**Source
Form(s):**   BSR dd

Addressing Mode	Cycles HMOS	CMOS	Bytes	Opcode
Inherent				
Relative	8	6	2	AD
Accumulator				
Index Register				
Immediate				
Direct				
Extended				
Indexed 0 Offset				
Indexed 1-Byte				
Indexed 2-Byte				

CLC

Clear Carry Bit

CLC

Operation: C bit ← 0

Description: Clears the carry bit in the processor condition code register.

**Condition
Codes:**
    H: Not affected.
    I: Not affected.
    N: Not affected.
    Z: Not affected.
    C: Cleared.

Boolean Formulae for Condition Codes:
    C = 0

Source Form(s):		Addressing Mode	Cycles HMOS	Cycles CMOS	Bytes	Opcode
CLC		Inherent	2	2	1	98
		Relative				
		Accumulator				
		Index Register				
		Immediate				
		Direct				
		Extended				
		Indexed 0 Offset				
		Indexed 1-Byte				
		Indexed 2-Byte				

CLI

Clear Interrupt Mask Bit

CLI

Operation: I bit ← 0

Description: Clears the interrupt mask bit in the processor condition code register. This enables the microprocessor to service interrupts. Interrupts that were pending while the I bit was set will now begin to have effect.

**Condition
Codes:**
    H: Not affected.
    I: Cleared·
    N: Not affected.
    Z: Not affected.
    C: Not affected.

Boolean Formulae for Condition Codes:
    I = 0

Source Form(s):		Addressing Mode	Cycles HMOS	Cycles CMOS	Bytes	Opcode
CLI		Inherent	2	2	1	9A
		Relative				
		Accumulator				
		Index Registers				
		Immediate				
		Direct				
		Extended				
		Indexed 0 Offset				
		Indexed 1-Byte				
		Indexed 2-Byte				

CLR
Clear
CLR

Operation: X ← 00 or,
               ACCA ← 00 or,
               M ← 00

Description: The contents of ACCA, X or M are replaced with zeroes.

**Condition
Codes:**   H: Not affected.
             I: Not affected.
             N: Cleared.
             Z: Set.
             C: Not affected.

Boolean Formulae for Condition Codes:
               N = 0
               Z = 1

**Source
Form(s):**   CLR Q, CLRA, CLRX

Addressing Mode	Cycles HMOS	CMOS	Bytes	Opcode
Inherent				
Relative				
Accumulator	4	3	1	4F
Index Register	4	3	1	5F
Immediate				
Direct	6	5	2	3F
Extended				
Indexed 0 Offset	6	5	1	7F
Indexed 1-Byte	7	6	2	6F
Indexed 2-Byte				

CMP
Compare Accumulator with Memory
CMP

Operation: ACCA − M

Description: Compares the contents of ACCA and the contents of M and sets the condition codes, which may then be used for controlling the conditional branches. Both operands are unaffected.

**Condition
Codes:**   H: Not affected.
             I: Not affected.
             N: Set if the most significant bit of the result of the subtraction is set; cleared otherwise.
             Z: Set if all bits of the result of the subtraction are cleared; cleared otherwise.
             C: Set if the absolute value of the contents of memory is larger than the absolute value of the accumulator; cleared otherwise.

Boolean Formulae for Condition Codes:

$$N = R7$$
$$Z = \overline{R7} \cdot \overline{R6} \cdot \overline{R5} \cdot \overline{R4} \cdot \overline{R3} \cdot \overline{R2} \cdot \overline{R1} \cdot \overline{R0}$$
$$C = A7 \cdot M7 v M7 \cdot \overline{R7} v \overline{R7} \cdot A7$$

Source Form(s): CMP P

Addressing Mode	Cycles HMOS	Cycles CMOS	Bytes	Opcode
Inherent				
Relative				
Accumulator				
Index Register				
Immediate	2	2	2	A1
Direct	4	3	2	B1
Extended	5	4	3	C1
Indexed 0 Offset	4	3	1	F1
Indexed 1-Byte	5	4	2	E1
Indexed 2-Byte	6	5	3	D1

COM   Complement   COM

Operation:
$$X \leftarrow \sim X = \$FF - X \text{ or,}$$
$$ACCA \leftarrow \sim ACCA = \$FF - ACCA \text{ or,}$$
$$M \leftarrow \sim M = \$FF - M$$

Description: Replaces the contents of ACCA, X or M with the one's complement. Each bit of the operand is replaced with the complement of that bit.

Condition Codes:

H:	Not affected.
I:	Not affected.
N:	Set if the most significant bit of the result is set; cleared otherwise.
Z:	Set if all bits of the result are cleared; cleared otherwise.
C:	Set.

Boolean Formulae for Condition Codes:

$$N = R7$$
$$Z = \overline{R7} \cdot \overline{R6} \cdot \overline{R5} \cdot \overline{R4} \cdot \overline{R3} \cdot \overline{R2} \cdot \overline{R1} \cdot \overline{R0}$$
$$C = 1$$

Source Form(s): COM Q, COMA, COMX

Addressing Mode	Cycles HMOS	Cycles CMOS	Bytes	Opcode
Inherent				
Relative				
Accumulator	4	3	1	43
Index Register	4	3	1	53
Immediate				
Direct	6	5	2	33
Extended				
Indexed 0 Offset	6	5	1	73
Indexed 1-Byte	7	6	2	63
Indexed 2-Byte				

CPX   **Compare Index Register with Memory**   # CPX

Operation: X – M

Description: Compares the contents of X to the contents of M and sets the condition codes, which may then be used for controlling the conditional branches. Both operands are unaffected.

Condition
Codes: H: Not affected.

I: Not affected.

N: Set if the most significant bit of the result of the subtraction is set; cleared otherwise.

Z: Set if all bits of the result of the subtraction are cleared; cleared otherwise.

C: Set if the absolute value of the contents of memory is larger than the absolute value of the index register; cleared otherwise.

Boolean Formulae for Condition Codes:

$N = R7$

$Z = \overline{R7} \cdot \overline{R6} \cdot \overline{R5} \cdot \overline{R4} \cdot \overline{R3} \cdot \overline{R2} \cdot \overline{R1} \cdot \overline{R0}$

$C = X7 \cdot M7 \vee M7 \cdot \overline{R7} \vee \overline{R7} \cdot X7$

Source
Form(s):   CPX P

Addressing Mode	Cycles HMOS	Cycles CMOS	Bytes	Opcode
Inherent				
Relative				
Accumulator				
Index Register				
Immediate	2	2	2	A3
Direct	4	3	2	B3
Extended	5	4	3	C3
Indexed 0 Offset	4	3	1	F3
Indexed 1-Byte	5	4	2	E3
Indexed 2-Byte	6	5	3	D3

DEC   **Decrement**   # DEC

Operation: X ← X-01 or,

ACCA ← ACCA-01 or,

M ← M-01

Description: Subtract one from the contents of ACCA, X or M. The N and Z bits are set or reset according to the result of this operation. The C bit is not affected by this operation.

Condition
Codes: H: Not affected.

I: Not affected.

N: Set if the most significant bit of the result is set; cleared otherwise.

Z: Set if all bits of the result are cleared; cleared otherwise.

C: Not affected.

Boolean Formulae for Condition Codes:

$N = R7$

$Z = \overline{R7} \cdot \overline{R6} \cdot \overline{R5} \cdot \overline{R4} \cdot \overline{R3} \cdot \overline{R2} \cdot \overline{R1} \cdot \overline{R0}$

Source Form(s):   DEC Q, DECA, DECX, DEX

Addressing Mode	Cycles		Bytes	Opcode
	HMOS	CMOS		
Inherent				
Relative				
Accumulator	4	3	1	4A
Index Register	4	3	1	5A
Immediate				
Direct	6	5	2	3A
Extended				
Indexed 0 Offset	6	5	1	7A
Indexed 1-Byte	7	6	2	6A
Indexed 2-Byte				

EOR   Exclusive Or Memory with Accumulator   EOR

Operation: ACCA ← ACCA ⊕ M

Description: Performs the logical EXCLUSIVE OR between the contents of ACCA and the contents of M, and places the result in ACCA. Each bit of ACCA after the operation will be the logical EXCUSIVE OR of the corresponding bit of M and ACCA before the operation.

Condition Codes:

H: Not affected.

I: Not affected.

N: Set if the most significant bit of the result is set; cleared otherwise.

Z: Set if all bits of the result are cleared; cleared otherwise.

C: Not affected.

Boolean Formulae for Condition Codes:

$N = R7$

$Z = \overline{R7} \cdot \overline{R6} \cdot \overline{R5} \cdot \overline{R4} \cdot \overline{R3} \cdot \overline{R2} \cdot \overline{R1} \cdot \overline{R0}$

Source Form(s):   EOR P

Addressing Mode	Cycles		Bytes	Opcode
	HMOS	CMOS		
Inherent				
Relative				
Accumulator				
Index Register				
Immediate	2	2	2	A8
Direct	4	3	2	B8
Extended	5	4	3	C8
Indexed 0 Offset	4	3	1	F8
Indexed 1-Byte	5	4	2	E8
Indexed 2-Byte	6	5	3	D8

INC
Increment
INC

Operation: X ← X + 01 or,
ACCA ← ACCA + 01 or,
M ← M + 01

Description: Add one to the contents of ACCA, X or M. The N and Z bits are set or reset according to the result of this operation. The C bit is not affected by this operation.

**Condition
Codes:**

H: Not affected.
I: Not affected.
N: Set if the most significant bit of the result is set; cleared otherwise.
Z: Set if all bits of the result are cleared; cleared otherwise.
C: Not affected.

Boolean Formulae for Condition Codes:
$$N = R7$$
$$Z = \overline{R7} \cdot \overline{R6} \cdot \overline{R5} \cdot \overline{R4} \cdot \overline{R3} \cdot \overline{R2} \cdot \overline{R1} \cdot \overline{R0}$$

**Source
Form(s):** INC Q, INCA, INCX, INX

Addressing Mode	Cycles HMOS	Cycles CMOS	Bytes	Opcode
Inherent				
Relative				
Accumulator	4	3	1	4C
Index Register	4	3	1	5C
Immediate				
Direct	6	5	2	3C
Extended				
Indexed 0 Offset	6	5	1	7C
Indexed 1-Byte	7	6	2	6C
Indexed 2-Byte				

JMP
Jump
JMP

Operation: PC ← effective address

Description: A jump occurs to the instruction stored at the effective address. The effective address is obtained according to the rules for EXTended, DIRect or INDexed addressing.

**Condition
Codes:** Not affected.

**Source
Form(s):** JMP P

Addressing Mode	Cycles HMOS	Cycles CMOS	Bytes	Opcode
Inherent				
Relative				
Accumulator				
Index Register				
Immediate				
Direct	3	2	2	BC
Extended	4	3	3	CC
Indexed 0 Offset	3	2	1	FC
Indexed 1-Byte	4	3	2	EC
Indexed 2-Byte	5	4	3	DC

JSR   Jump to Subroutine   JSR

Operation: PC ← PC + N
(SP) ← PCL; SP ← SP − 0001
(SP) ← PCH ; SP ← SP − 0001
PC ← effective address

Description: The program counter is incremented by N (N = 1, 2 or 3 depending on the address-ing mode), and is then pushed onto the stack (least significant byte first). Unused bits in the Program Counter high byte are stored as 1's on the stack. The stack pointer points to the next empty location on the stack. A jump occurs to the instruc-tion stored at the effective address. The effective address is obtained according to the rules for EXTended, DIRect, or INDexed addressing.

Condition
Codes: Not affected.

Source
Form(s):   JSR P

Addressing Mode	Cycles HMOS	Cycles CMOS	Bytes	Opcode
Inherent				
Relative				
Accumulator				
Index Register				
Immediate				
Direct	7	5	2	BD
Extended	8	6	3	CD
Indexed 0 Offset	7	5	1	FD
Indexed 1-Byte	8	6	2	ED
Indexed 2-Byte	9	7	3	DD

LDA   Load Accumulator from Memory   LDA

Operation: ACCA ← M

Description: Loads the contents of memory into the accumulator. The condition codes are set according to the data.

Condition
Codes:
H: Not affected.
I: Not affected.
N: Set if the most significant bit of the accumulator is set; cleared otherwise.
Z: Set if all bits of the accumulator are cleared; cleared otherwise.
C: Not affected.

Boolean Formulae for Condition Codes:

$$N = R7$$
$$Z = \overline{R7} \cdot \overline{R5} \cdot \overline{R4} \cdot \overline{R3} \cdot \overline{R2} \cdot \overline{R1} \cdot \overline{R0}$$

Source
Form(s):   LDA P

Addressing Mode	Cycles HMOS	Cycles CMOS	Bytes	Opcode
Inherent				
Relative				
Accumulator				
Index Register				
Immediate	2	2	2	A6
Direct	4	3	2	B6
Extended	5	4	3	C6
Indexed 0 Offset	4	3	1	F6
Indexed 1-Byte	5	4	2	E6
Indexed 2-Byte	6	5	3	D6

LDX   Load Index Register from Memory   # LDX

Operation: X ← M

Description: Loads the contents of memory into the index register. The condition codes are set according to the data.

**Condition
Codes:**   H: Not affected.
             I: Not affected.
             N: Set if the most significant bit of the index register is set; cleared otherwise.
             Z: Set if all bits of the index register are cleared; cleared otherwise.
             C: Not affected.

Boolean Formulae for Condition Codes:

$$N = R7$$
$$Z = \overline{R7} \cdot \overline{R6} \cdot \overline{R5} \cdot \overline{R4} \cdot \overline{R3} \cdot \overline{R2} \cdot \overline{R1} \cdot \overline{R0}$$

**Source
Form(s):**   LDX P

Addressing Mode	Cycles HMOS	Cycles CMOS	Bytes	Opcode
Inherent				
Relative				
Accumulator				
Index Register				
Immediate	2	2	2	AE
Direct	4	3	2	BE
Extended	5	4	3	CE
Indexed 0 Offset	4	3	1	FE
Indexed 1-Byte	5	4	2	EE
Indexed 2-Byte	6	5	3	DE

LSL   Logical Shift Left   # LSL

Operation:

C ← b7 [ ] [ ] [ ] [ ] b0 ← 0

Description: Shifts all bits of the ACCA, X or M one place to the left. Bit 0 is loaded with a zero. The C bit is loaded from the most signficant bit of ACCA, X or M.

**Condition
Codes:**   H: Not affected.
             I: Not affected.
             N: Set if the most significant bit of the result is set; cleared otherwise.
             Z: Set if all bits of the result are cleared; cleared otherwise.
             C: Set if, before the operation, the most significant bit of ACCA, X or M was set; cleared otherwise.

Boolean Formulae for Condition Codes:

$$N = R7$$
$$Z = \overline{R7} \cdot \overline{R6} \cdot \overline{R5} \cdot \overline{R4} \cdot \overline{R3} \cdot \overline{R2} \cdot \overline{R1} \cdot \overline{R0}$$
$$C = M7$$

Comments: Same as ASL

**Source
Form(s):**   LSL Q, LSLA, LSLX

Addressing Mode	Cycles		Bytes	Opcode
	HMOS	CMOS		
Inherent				
Relative				
Accumulator	4	3	1	48
Index Register	4	3	1	58
Immediate				
Direct	6	5	2	38
Extended				
Indexed 0 Offset	6	5	1	78
Indexed 1-Byte	7	6	2	68
Indexed 2-Byte				

LSR   Logical Shift Right   LSR

Operation: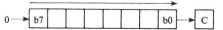

Description: Shifts all bits of ACCA, X or M one place to the right. Bit 7 is loaded with a zero. Bit 0 is loaded into the C bit.

**Condition
Codes:**

H: Not affected.
I: Not affected.
N: Cleared.
Z: Set if all bits of the result are cleared; cleared otherwise.
C: Set if, before the operation, the least significant bit of ACCA, X or M was set; cleared otherwise.

Boolean Formulae for Condition Codes:

$N = 0$
$Z = \overline{R7} \cdot \overline{R6} \cdot \overline{R5} \cdot \overline{R4} \cdot \overline{R3} \cdot \overline{R2} \cdot \overline{R1} \cdot \overline{R0}$
$C = M0$

**Source
Form(s):**   LSR Q, LSRA, LSRX

Addressing Mode	Cycles		Bytes	Opcode
	HMOS	CMOS		
Inherent				
Relative				
Accumulator	4	3	1	44
Index Register	4	3	1	54
Immediate				
Direct	6	5	2	34
Extended				
Indexed 0 Offset	6	5	1	74
Indexed 1-Byte	7	6	2	64
Indexed 2-Byte				

NEG   Negate   NEG

Operation: $-X \rightarrow X = 00 - X$ or,
$- ACCA \rightarrow ACCA = 00 - ACCA$ or,
$-M \rightarrow M = 00 - M$

Description: Replaces the contents of ACCA, X or M with its two's complement. Note that $80 is
left unchanged.

**Condition
Codes:**   H: Not affected.
I: Not affected.
N: Set if the most significant bit of the result is set; cleared otherwise.
Z: Set if all bits of the result are cleared; cleared otherwise.
C: Set if there would be a borrow in the implied subtraction from zero; the C
bit will be set in all cases except when the contents of ACCA, X or M be-
fore the NEG is 00.

Boolean Formulae for Condition Codes:
$N = R7$
$Z = \overline{R7} \cdot \overline{R6} \cdot \overline{R5} \cdot \overline{R4} \cdot \overline{R3} \cdot \overline{R2} \cdot \overline{R1} \cdot \overline{R0}$
$C = R7vR6vR5vR4vR3vR2vR1vR0$

Source Form(s): NEG Q, NEGA, NEGX	Addressing Mode	Cycles HMOS	CMOS	Bytes	Opcode
	Inherent				
	Relative				
	Accumulator	4	3	1	40
	Index Register	4	3	1	50
	Immediate				
	Direct	6	5	2	30
	Extended				
	Indexed 0 Offset	6	5	1	70
	Indexed 1-Byte	7	6	2	60
	Indexed 2-Byte				

NOP   No Operation   NOP

Description: This is a single-byte instruction which causes only the program counter to be incremented. No other registers are changed.

**Condition
Codes:**   Not affected.

Source Form(s): NOP	Addressing Mode	Cycles HMOS	CMOS	Bytes	Opcode
	Inherent	2	2	1	9D
	Relative				
	Accumulator				
	Index Register				
	Immediate				
	Direct				
	Extended				
	Indexed 0 Offset				
	Indexed 1-Byte				
	Indexed 2-Byte				

ORA   Inclusive OR   ORA

Operation: ACCA ← ACCA V M

Description: Performs logical OR between the contents of ACCA and the contents of M and place the result in ACCA. Each bit of ACCA after the operation will be the logical (inclusive) OR result of the corresponding bits of M and ACCA before the operation.

Condition Codes:

H: Not affected.
I: Not affected.
N: Set if the most significant bit of the result is set; cleared otherwise.
Z: Set if all bits of the result are cleared; cleared otherwise.
C: Not affected.

Boolean Formulae for Condition Codes:

$$N = R7$$
$$Z = \overline{R7} \cdot \overline{R6} \cdot \overline{R5} \cdot \overline{R4} \cdot \overline{R3} \cdot \overline{R2} \cdot \overline{R1} \cdot \overline{R0}$$

Source Form(s):   ORA P

Addressing Mode	Cycles HMOS	Cycles CMOS	Bytes	Opcode
Inherent				
Relative				
Accumulator				
Index Register				
Immediate	2	2	2	AA
Direct	4	3	2	BA
Extended	5	4	3	CA
Indexed 0 Offset	4	3	1	FA
Indexed 1-Byte	5	4	2	EA
Indexed 2-Byte	6	5	3	DA

ROL   Rotate Left thru Carry   ROL

Operation:

| C | ← | b7 | | | | | | | b0 | ← | C |

Description: Shifts all bits of the ACCA, X or M one place to the left. Bit 0 is loaded from the C bit. The C bit is loaded from the most significant bit of ACCA, X or M.

Condition Codes:

H: Not affected.
I: Not affected.
N: Set if the most significant bit of the result is set; cleared otherwise.
Z: Set if all bits of the result are cleared; cleared otherwise.
C: Set if, before the operation, the most significant bit of ACCA, X or M was set; cleared otherwise.

Boolean Formulae for Condition Codes:

$$N = R7$$
$$Z = \overline{R7} \cdot \overline{R6} \cdot \overline{R5} \cdot \overline{R4} \cdot \overline{R3} \cdot \overline{R2} \cdot \overline{R1} \cdot \overline{R0}$$
$$C = M7$$

Source Form(s):   ROL Q, ROLA, ROLX

Addressing Mode	Cycles HMOS	CMOS	Bytes	Opcode
Inherent				
Relative				
Accumulator	4	3	1	49
Index Register	4	3	1	59
Immediate				
Direct	6	5	2	39
Extended				
Indexed 0 Offset	6	5	1	79
Indexed 1-Byte	7	6	2	69
Indexed 2-Byte				

ROR   Rotate Right Thru Carry   ROR

Operation: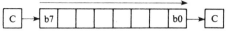

Description: Shifts all bits of ACCA, X or M one place to the right. Bit 7 is loaded from the C bit. Bit 0 is loaded into the C bit.

Condition Codes:

H: Not affected.
I: Not affected.
N: Set if the most significant bit of the result is set; cleared otherwise.
Z: Set if all bits of the result are cleared; cleared otherwise.
C: Set if, before the operation, the least significant bit of ACCA, X or M was set; cleared otherwise.

Boolean Formulae for Condition Codes:

$N = R7$
$Z = \overline{R7} \cdot \overline{R6} \cdot \overline{R5} \cdot \overline{R4} \cdot \overline{R3} \cdot \overline{R2} \cdot \overline{R1} \cdot \overline{R0}$
$C = M0$

Source Form(s): ROR Q, RORA, RORX

Addressing Mode	Cycles HMOS	CMOS	Bytes	Opcode
Inherent				
Relative				
Accumulator	4	3	1	46
Index Register	4	3	1	56
Immediate				
Direct	6	5	2	36
Extended				
Indexed 0 Offset	6	5	1	76
Indexed 1-Byte	7	6	2	66
Indexed 2-Byte				

RSP   Reset Stack Pointer   RSP

Operation: SP ← $7F

Description: Resets the stack pointer to the top of the stack.

Condition Codes: Not affected.

Source
Form(s):   RSP

Addressing Mode	Cycles HMOS	CMOS	Bytes	Opcode
Inherent	2	2	1	9C
Relative				
Accumulator				
Index Register				
Immediate				
Direct				
Extended				
Indexed 0 Offset				
Indexed 1-Byte				
Indexed 2-Byte				

RTI   Return from Interrupt   RTI

Operation: SP ← SP + 0001 ; CC ← (SP)
SP ← SP + 0001 ; ACCA ← (SP)
SP ← SP + 0001 ; X ← (SP)
SP ← SP + 0001 ; PCH ← (SP)
SP ← SP + 0001 ; PCL ← (SP)

Description: The Condition Codes, Accumulator, Index Register and the Program Counter are restored according to the state previously saved on the stack. Note that the interrupt mask bit (I bit) will be reset if and only if the corresponding bit stored on the stack is zero.

Condition
Codes: Set or cleared according to the first byte pulled from the stack.

Source
Form(s):   RTI

Addressing Mode	Cycles HMOS	CMOS	Bytes	Opcode
Inherent	9	9	1	80
Relative				
Accumulator				
Index Register				
Immediate				
Direct				
Extended				
Indexed 0 Offset				
Indexed 1-Byte				
Indexed 2-Byte				

RTS   Return from Subroutine   RTS

Operation: SP ← SP + 0001 ; PCH ← (SP)
SP ← SP + 0001 ; PCL ← (SP)

Description: The stack pointer is incremented (by one). The contents of the byte of memory, pointed to by the stack pointer, are loaded into the high byte of the program counter. The stack pointer is again incremented (by one). The byte pointed to by the stack pointer is loaded into the low byte of the program counter.

Condition
Codes: Not affected.

Source		Addressing Mode	Cycles HMOS	Cycles CMOS	Bytes	Opcode
Form(s):	RTS	Inherent	6	6	1	81
		Relative				
		Accumulator				
		Index Register				
		Immediate				
		Direct				
		Extended				
		Indexed 0 Offset				
		Indexed 1-Byte				
		Indexed 2-Byte				

SBC   Subtract with Carry   SBC

Operation: $ACCA \leftarrow ACCA - M - C$

Description: Subtracts the contents of M and C from the contents of ACCA, and places the result in ACCA.

Condition
Codes:
- H: Not affected.
- I: Not affected.
- N: Set if the most significant bit of the result is set; cleared otherwise.
- Z: Set if all bits of the result are cleared; cleared otherwise.
- C: Set if the absolute value of the contents of memory plus the previous carry is larger than the absolute value of the accumulator; cleared otherwise.

Boolean Formulae for Condition Codes:

$N = R7$

$Z = \overline{R7} \cdot \overline{R6} \cdot \overline{R5} \cdot \overline{R4} \cdot \overline{R3} \cdot \overline{R2} \cdot \overline{R1} \cdot \overline{R0}$

$C = A7 \cdot M7 v M7 \cdot \overline{R7} v \overline{R7} \cdot A7$

Source		Addressing Mode	Cycles HMOS	Cycles CMOS	Bytes	Opcode
Form(s):	SBC P	Inherent				
		Relative				
		Accumulator				
		Index Register				
		Immediate	2	2	2	A2
		Direct	4	3	2	B2
		Extended	5	4	3	C2
		Indexed 0 Offset	4	3	1	F2
		Indexed 1-Byte	5	4	2	E2
		Indexed 2-Byte	6	5	3	D2

SEC   Set Carry Bit   SEC

Operation: C bit $\leftarrow 1$

Description: Sets the carry bit in the processor condition code register.

Condition
Codes: H: Not affected.
             I: Not affected.
             N: Not affected.
             Z: Not affected.
             C: Set.

Boolean Formulae for Condition Codes:
             C = 1

Source
Form(s):   SEC

Addressing Mode	Cycles HMOS	Cycles CMOS	Bytes	Opcode
Inherent	2	2	1	99
Relative				
Accumulator				
Index Register				
Immediate				
Direct				
Extended				
Indexed 0 Offset				
Indexed 1-Byte				
Indexed 2-Byte				

SEI   Set Interrupt Mask Bit   SEI

Operation: I bit ← 1

Description: Sets the interrupt mask bit in the processor condition code register. The microprocessor is inhibited from servicing interrupts, and will continue with execution of the instructions of the program until the interrupt mask bit is cleared.

Condition
Codes: H: Not affected.
             I: Set
             N: Not Affected.
             Z: Not affected.
             C: Not affected.

Boolean Formulae for Condition Codes:
             I = 1

Source
Form(s):   SEI

Addressing Mode	Cycles HMOS	Cycles CMOS	Bytes	Opcode
Inherent	2	2	1	9B
Relative				
Accumulator				
Index Register				
Immediate				
Direct				
Extended				
Indexed 0 Offset				
Indexed 1-Byte				
Indexed 2-Byte				

STA

Store Accumulator in Memory

STA

Operation: M ← ACCA

Description: Stores the contents of ACCA in memory. The contents of ACCA remain the same.

**Condition
Codes:**

H: Not affected.
I: Not affected.
N: Set if the most significant bit of the accumulator is set; cleared otherwise.
Z: Set if all bits of the accumulator are clear; cleared otherwise.
C: Not Affected.

Boolean Formulae for Condition Codes:

$$N = A7$$
$$Z = \overline{A7} \cdot \overline{A6} \cdot \overline{A5} \cdot \overline{A4} \cdot \overline{A3} \cdot \overline{A2} \cdot \overline{A1} \cdot \overline{A0}$$

**Source
Form(s):**   STA P

Addressing Mode	Cycles HMOS	Cycles CMOS	Bytes	Opcode
Inherent				
Relative				
Accumulator				
Index Register				
Immediate				
Direct	5	4	2	B7
Extended	6	5	3	C7
Indexed 0 Offset	5	4	1	F7
Indexed 1-Byte	6	5	2	E7
Indexed 2-Byte	7	6	3	D7

STOP

Enable IRQ, Stop Oscillator

STOP

Description: Reduces power consumption by eliminating all dynamic power dissipation. Results in: (1) timer prescaler to clear; (2) disabling of timer interrupts (3) timer interrupt flag bit to clear; (4) external interrupt request enabling; and (5) inhibiting of oscillator.

When $\overline{RESET}$ or $\overline{IRQ}$ input goes low: (1) oscillator is enabled, (2) a delay of 1920 instruction cycles allows oscillator to stabilize, (3) the interrupt request vector is fetched, and (4) service routine is executed.

External interrupts are enabled following the RTI command.

**Condition
Codes:**

H: Not Affected.
I: Cleared.
N: Not Affected.
Z: Not Affected.
C: Not Affected.

**Source
Form(s):**   STOP

Addressing Mode	Cycles HMOS	Cycles CMOS	Bytes	Opcode
Inherent	—	2	1	8E
Relative				
Accumulator				
Index Register				
Immediate				
Direct				
Extended				
Indexed 0 Offset				
Indexed 1-Byte				
Indexed 2-Byte				

STX

Store Index Register in Memory

STX

Operation: M ← X

Description: Stores the contents of X in memory. The contents of X remain the same.

Condition Codes:

H: Not Affected.
I: Not affected.
N: Set if the most significant bit of the index register is set; cleared otherwise.
Z: Set if all bits of the index register are clear; cleared otherwise.
C: Not affected.

Boolean Formulae for Condition Codes:

$$N = X7$$
$$Z = \overline{X7} \cdot \overline{X6} \cdot \overline{X5} \cdot \overline{X4} \cdot \overline{X3} \cdot \overline{X2} \cdot \overline{X1} \cdot \overline{X0}$$

Source Form(s):   STX P

Addressing Mode	Cycles HMOS	Cycles CMOS	Bytes	Opcode
Inherent				
Relative				
Accumulator				
Index Register				
Immediate				
Direct	5	4	2	BF
Extended	6	5	3	CF
Indexed 0 Offset	5	4	1	FF
Indexed 1-Byte	6	5	2	EF
Indexed 2-Byte	7	6	3	DF

SUB

Subtract

SUB

Operation: ACCA ← ACCA − M

Description: Subtracts the contents of M from the contents of ACCA and places the result in ACCA.

Condition Codes:

H: Not affected.
I: Not affected.
N: Set if the most significant bit of the result is set; cleared otherwise.
Z: Set if all bits of the results are cleared; cleared otherwise.
C: Set if the absolute value of the contents of memory are larger than the absolute value of the accumulator; cleared otherwise.

Boolean Formulae for Condition Codes:

$$N = R7$$
$$Z = \overline{R7} \cdot \overline{R6} \cdot \overline{R5} \cdot \overline{R4} \cdot \overline{R3} \cdot \overline{R2} \cdot \overline{R1} \cdot \overline{R0}$$
$$C = A7 \bullet M7 v M7 \bullet \overline{R7} v \overline{R7} \bullet A7$$

Source Form(s):   SUB P

Addressing Mode	Cycles HMOS	Cycles CMOS	Bytes	Opcode
Inherent				
Relative				
Accumulator				
Index Register				
Immediate	2	2	2	A0
Direct	4	3	2	B0
Extended	5	4	3	C0
Indexed 0 Offset	4	3	1	F0
Indexed 1-Byte	5	4	2	E0
Indexed 2-Byte	6	5	3	D0

SWI   Software Interrupt   SWI

Operation: PC ← PC + 0001
                     (SP) ← PCL ; SP ← SP − 0001
                     (SP) ← PCH ; SP ← SP − 0001
                     (SP) ← X ; SP ← SP − 0001
                     (SP) ← ACCA ; SP ← SP − 0001
                     (SP) ← CC ; SP ← SP − 0001
                     I bit ← 1
                     PCH ← n − 0003
                     PCL ← n − 0002

Description: The program counter is incremented (by one). The Program Counter, Index Register
                     and Accumulator are pushed onto the stack. The Condition Code register bits are
                     then pushed onto the stack with bits H, I, N, Z and C going into bit positions 4
                     through 0 with the top three bits (7, 6 and 5) containing ones. The stack pointer is
                     decremented by one after each byte is stored on the stack.

                     The interrupt mask bit is then set. The program counter is then loaded with the ad-
                     dress stored in the software interrupt vector located at memory locations n − 0002
                     and n − 0003, where n is the address corresponding to a high state on all lines of the
                     address bus.

Condition
Codes: H: Not affected.
                     I: Set.
                     N: Not affected.
                     Z: Not affected.
                     C: Not affected.

Boolean Formulae for Condition Codes:
                     I = 1

Caution: This instruction is used by Motorola in some of its software products and may be
                     unavailable for general use.

Source
Form(s):   SWI

Addressing Mode	Cycles		Bytes	Opcode
	HMOS	CMOS		
Inherent	11	10	1	83
Relative				
Accumulator				
Index Register				
Immediate				
Direct				
Extended				
Indexed 0 Offset				
Indexed 1-Byte				
Indexed 2-Byte				

TAX   Transfer Accumulator to Index Register   TAX

Operation: X ← ACCA

Description: Loads the index register with the contents of the accumulator. The contents of the
                     accumulator are unchanged.

**Condition
Codes:**   Not affected.

**Source
Form(s):**   TAX

Addressing Mode	Cycles		Bytes	Opcode
	HMOS	CMOS		
Inherent	2	2	1	97
Relative				
Accumulator				
Index Register				
Immediate				
Direct				
Extended				
Indexed 0 Offset				
Indexed 1-Byte				
Indexed 2-Byte				

TST   Test for Negative or Zero   TST

Operation: X − 00 or,
ACCA − 00 or,
M − 0

Description: Sets the condition codes N and Z according to the contents of ACCA, X or M.

**Condition
Codes:**

H: Not affected.

I: Not affected.

N: Set if the most significant bit of the contents of ACCA, X or M is set; cleared otherwise.

Z: Set if all bits of ACCA, X or M are clear; cleared otherwise.

C: Not affected.

Boolean Formulae for Condition Codes:

$N = M7$

$Z = \overline{M7} \cdot \overline{M6} \cdot \overline{M5} \cdot \overline{M4} \cdot \overline{M3} \cdot \overline{M2} \cdot \overline{M1} \cdot \overline{M0}$

**Source
Form(s):**   TST Q, TSTA, TSTX

Addressing Mode	Cycles		Bytes	Opcode
	HMOS	CMOS		
Inherent				
Relative				
Accumulator	4	3	1	4D
Index Register	4	3	1	5D
Immediate				
Direct	6	4	2	3D
Extended				
Indexed 0 Offset	6	4	1	7D
Indexed 1-Byte	7	5	2	6D
Indexed 2-Byte				

TXA   Transfer Index Register to Accumulator   TXA

Operation: ACCA ← X

Description: Loads the accumulator with the contents of the index register. The contents of the index register are unchanged.

Condition Codes: Not affected.

Source Form(s):   TXA

Addressing Mode	Cycles		Bytes	Opcode
	HMOS	CMOS		
Inherent	2	2	1	9F
Relative				
Accumulator				
Index Register				
Immediate				
Direct				
Extended				
Indexed 0 Offset				
Indexed 1-Byte				
Indexed 2-Byte				

WAIT   Enable Interrupt, Stop Processor   WAIT

Description: Reduces power consumption by eliminating dynamic power dissipation in all circuits except the timer and timer prescaler. Causes enabling of external interrupts and stops clocking or processor circuits.

Timer interrupts may be enabled or disabled by programmer prior to execution of WAIT.

When RESET or IRQ input goes low, or timer counter reaches zero with counter interrupt enabled: (1) processor clocks are enabled, and (2) interrupt request, reset, and timer interrupt vectors are fetched.

Interrupts are enabled following the RTI command.

Condition Codes:
H: Not affected.
I: Cleared.
N: Not affected.
Z: Not affected.
C: Not affected.

Source Form(s):   WAIT

Addressing Mode	Cycles		Bytes	Opcode
	HMOS	CMOS		
Inherent	—	2	1	8F
Relative				
Accumulator				
Index Register				
Immediate				
Direct				
Extended				
Indexed 0 Offset				
Indexed 1-Byte				
Indexed 2-Byte				

Appendix 3

The 1414 Alphanumeric Display Data Sheet

Reproduced by courtesy of Hewlett Packard Limited, Miller House, The Ring, Bracknell, Berkshire RG12 1XN, UK and PO Box 10310, Palo Alto. CA 94303-0890, USA. Also manufactured by Siemens-Litronix, 19000 Homestead Road, Cupertino, CA 95014, USA and supplied by RS Components Limited, PO Box 99, Corby, Northants, NN17 9RS, UK.

FOUR CHARACTER
2.85mm (0.112 in.)
SMART
ALPHANUMERIC DISPLAY

HPDL-1414

TECHNICAL DATA   SEPTEMBER 1985

Features

- **SMART ALPHANUMERIC DISPLAY**
  Built-in RAM, ASCII Decoder and
  LED Drive Circuitry

- **WIDE OPERATING TEMPERATURE RANGE**
  −40° C to +85° C

- **FAST ACCESS TIME**
  160 ns

- **EXCELLENT ESD PROTECTION**
  Built-in Input Protection Diodes

- **CMOS IC FOR LOW POWER CONSUMPTION**

- **FULL TTL COMPATIBILITY OVER OPERATING**
  TEMPERATURE RANGE
  $V_{IL} = 0.8$ V
  $V_{IH} = 2.0$ V

- **WAVE SOLDERABLE**

- **RUGGED PACKAGE CONSTRUCTION**

- **END-STACKABLE**

- **WIDE VIEWING ANGLE**

Typical Applications

- **PORTABLE DATA ENTRY DEVICES**
- **MEDICAL EQUIPMENT**
- **PROCESS CONTROL EQUIPMENT**
- **TEST EQUIPMENT**
- **INDUSTRIAL INSTRUMENTATION**
- **COMPUTER PERIPHERALS**
- **TELECOMMUNICATION INSTRUMENTATION**

Description

The HPDL-1414 is a smart 2.85 mm (0.112") four character, sixteen-segment, red GaAsP display. The on-board CMOS IC contains memory, ASCII decoder, multiplexing circuitry and drivers. The monolithic LED characters are magnified by an immersion lens which increases both character size and luminous intensity. The encapsulated dual-in-line package provides a rugged, environmentally sealed unit.

The HPDL-1414 incorporates many improvements over competitive products. It has a wide operating temperature range, very fast IC access time and improved ESD protection. The display is also fully TTL compatible, wave solderable and highly reliable. This display is ideally suited for industrial and commercial applications where a good-looking, easy-to-use alphanumeric display is required.

Absolute Maximum Ratings

Supply Voltage, V_{CC} to Ground . . . . −0.5 V to 7.0V
Input Voltage, Any Pin to Ground . . . . −0.5 V to 7.0V
Free Air Operating
   Temperature Range, T_A . . . . −40°C to +85°C
Relative Humidity (non-condensing) at 65°C 90%
Storage Temperature, T_S . . . . −40°C to +85°C
Maximum Solder Temperature, 1.59 mm (0.063 in.)
   below Seating Plane, t< 5 sec. . . . . 260°C

Package Dimensions

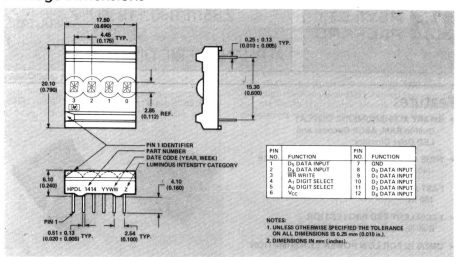

NOTES:
1. UNLESS OTHERWISE SPECIFIED THE TOLERANCE ON ALL DIMENSIONS IS 0.25 mm (0.010 in.).
2. DIMENSIONS IN mm (inches).

PIN NO.	FUNCTION	PIN NO.	FUNCTION
1	D_5 DATA INPUT	7	GND
2	D_4 DATA INPUT	8	D_0 DATA INPUT
3	WR WRITE	9	D_1 DATA INPUT
4	A_1 DIGIT SELECT	10	D_2 DATA INPUT
5	A_0 DIGIT SELECT	11	D_3 DATA INPUT
6	V_{CC}	12	D_6 DATA INPUT

Recommended Operating Conditions

Parameter	Symbol	Min.	Nom.	Max.	Units
Supply Voltage	V_{CC}	4.5	5.0	5.5	V
Input Voltage High	V_{IH}	2.0			V
Input Voltage Low	V_{IL}			0.8	V

DC Electrical Characteristics Over Operating Temperature Range

TYPICAL VALUES

Parameter	Symbol	Units	−40°C	−20°C	25°C	85°C	Test Condition
I_{CC} 4 digits on (10 seg/digit)[1,2]	I_{CC}	mA	90	85	70	60	V_{CC} = 5.0 V
I_{CC} Blank	I_{CC} ($\overline{BL}$)	mA	1.8	1.5	1.2	1.1	V_{CC} = 5.0 V, $\overline{BL}$ = 0.8 V
Input Current, Max.	I_{IL}	µA	23	20	17	12	V_{CC} = 5.0 V, V_{IN} = 0.8 V

GUARANTEED MAXIMUM VALUES

Parameter	Symbol	Units	25°C V_{CC} = 5.0 V	Maximum Over Operating Temperature Range V_{CC} = 5.5 V
I_{CC} 4 digits on (10 seg/digit)[1,2]	I_{CC}	mA	90	130
I_{CC} Blank	I_{CC} ($\overline{BL}$)	mA	2.3	4.0
Input Current, Max.	I_{IL}	µA	30	50
Power Dissipation[3]	P_D	mW	450	715

Notes:
1. "%" illuminated in all four characters.
2. Measured at five seconds.
3. Power dissipation = $V_{CC} \cdot I_{CC}$ (10 seg.).

AC Timing Characteristics Over Operating Temperature Range at $V_{CC} = 4.5$ V

Parameter	Symbol	-20°C t_{MIN}	25°C t_{MIN}	70°C t_{MIN}	Units
Address Setup Time	t_{AS}	90	115	150	ns
Write Delay Time	t_{WD}	10	15	20	ns
Write Time	t_W	80	100	130	ns
Data Setup Time	t_{DS}	40	60	80	ns
Data Hold Time	t_{DH}	40	45	50	ns
Address Hold Time	t_{AH}	40	45	50	ns
Access Time		130	160	200	ns
Refresh Rate		420-790	310-630	270-550	Hz

Optical Characteristics

Parameter	Symbol	Test Condition	Min.	Typ.	Units
Peak Luminous Intensity per digit, 8 segments on (character average)	Iv Peak	$V_{CC} = 5.0$ V "✳" illuminated in all 4 digits.	0.4	1.0	mcd
Peak Wavelength	λpeak			655	nm
Dominant Wavelength	λd			640	nm
Off Axis Viewing Angle				±40	degrees
Digit Size				2.85	mm

Timing Diagram

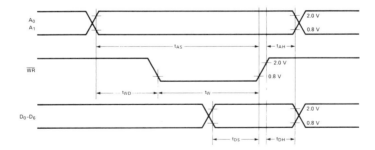

Magnified Character Font Description

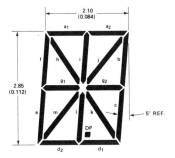

Relative Luminous Intensity vs. Temperature

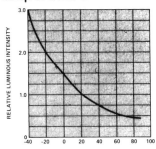

Electrical Description

Figure 1 shows the internal block diagram of the HPDL-1414. It consists of two parts: the display LEDs and the CMOS IC. The CMOS IC consists of a four-word ASCII memory, a 64-word character generator, 17 segment drivers, four digit drivers, and the scanning circuitry necessary to multiplex the four monolithic LED characters. In normal operation, the divide-by-four counter sequentially accesses each of the four RAM locations and simultaneously enables the appropriate display digit driver. The output of the RAM is decoded by the character generator which, in turn, enables the appropriate display segment drivers. Seven-bit ASCII data is stored in RAM. Since the display uses a 64-character decoder, half of the possible 128 input combinations are invalid. For each display location where D5=D6 in the ASCII RAM, the display character is blanked.

Data is loaded into the display through the DATA inputs (D6-D0), ADDRESS inputs (A1-A0), and WRITE ($\overline{WR}$). After a character has been written to memory, the IC decodes the ASCII data, drives the display and refreshes it without any external hardware or software.

The HPDL-1414 uses 12 pins to control the CMOS IC. Figure 1 shows the effect these inputs have on the display.

DATA INPUTS (D_0-D_6, pins 1, 2, 8-12)	Seven bit ASCII data is entered into memory via the DATA inputs.
ADDRESS INPUTS (A_1-A_0, pins 4 and 5)	Each location in memory has a distinct address. ADDRESS inputs enable the designer to select a specific location in memory to store data. Address 00 accesses the far right display location. Address 11 accesses the far left location.
WRITE ($\overline{WR}$, pin 3)	Data is written into the display when the $\overline{WR}$ input is low.
V_{CC} and GND (pins 6 and 7)	These pins supply power to the display.

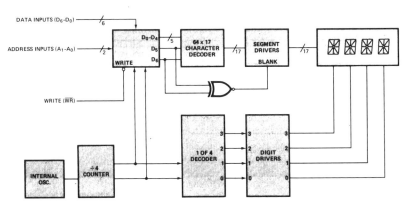

Figure 1. HPDL-1414 Internal Block Diagram

$\overline{WR}$	A_1	A_0	D_6	D_5	D_4	D_3	D_2	D_1	D_0	DIG_3	DIG_2	DIG_1	DIG_0
L	L	L	a	a	a	a	a	a	a	NC	NC	NC	A
L	L	H	b	b	b	b	b	b	b	NC	NC	B	NC
L	H	L	c	c	c	c	c	c	c	NC	C	NC	NC
L	H	H	d	d	d	d	d	d	d	D	NC	NC	NC
H	X	X	X	X	X	X	X	X	X	Previously Written Data			

L = LOGIC LOW INPUT   "a" = ASCII CODE CORRESPONDING TO SYMBOL "A"
H = LOGIC HIGH INPUT   NC = NO CHANGE
X = DON'T CARE

Figure 2. Write Truth Table

Using the HPDL-1414 with Microprocessors

Figures 3 and 4 show how to connect the HPDL-1414 to a Motorola 6800 or an Intel 8085. The major differences between the two circuits are:

1. The 6800 requires two latches to store the ADDRESS and ASCII DATA information to increase the address and data input hold times.
2. The 6800 requires a flip-flop to delay the display WRITE signal to increase the address input setup time.

ADDRESS inputs (A_1 and A_0) are connected to microprocessor addresses A_1 and A_0. A 74LS138 may be used to generate individual display WRITE signals. Higher order microprocessor address lines are connected to the 74LS138. The microprocessor write line must be wired to one of the active low enable inputs of the 74LS138. Both figures are formatted with address 0 being the far right display character.

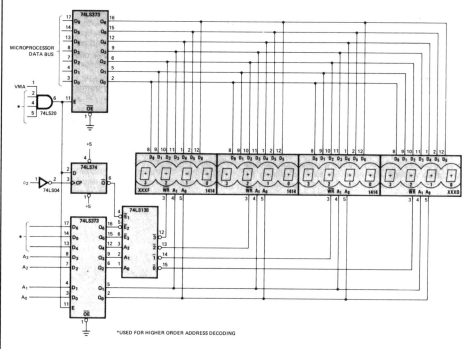

Figure 3: Memory Mapped Interface for the 6800

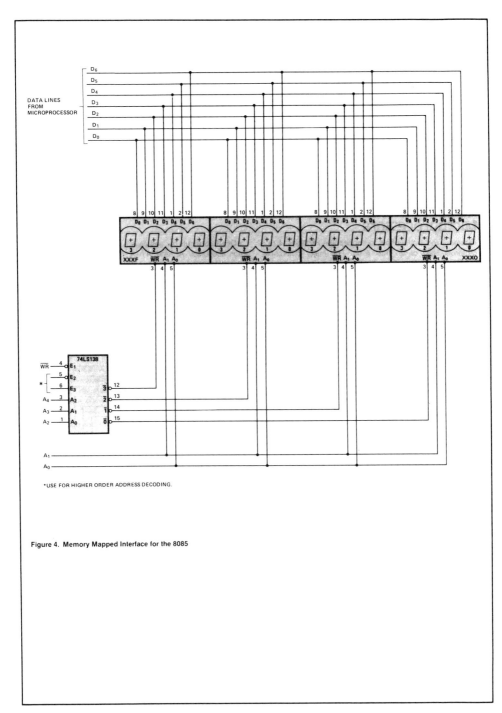

DATA LINES FROM MICROPROCESSOR

*USE FOR HIGHER ORDER ADDRESS DECODING.

Figure 4. Memory Mapped Interface for the 8085

BITS		D_3	0	0	0	0	0	0	0	0	1	1	1	1	1	1	1	1
		D_2	0	0	0	0	1	1	1	1	0	0	0	0	1	1	1	1
		D_1	0	0	1	1	0	0	1	1	0	0	1	1	0	0	1	1
		D_0	0	1	0	1	0	1	0	1	0	1	0	1	0	1	0	1
D_6 D_5 D_4	HEX	0	1	2	3	4	5	6	7	8	9	A	B	C	D	E	F
0 1 0	2	(space)	!	"	#	$	%	&	'	(	)	*	+	,	−	.	/
0 1 1	3	0	1	2	3	4	5	6	7	8	9	:	;	<	=	>	?
1 0 0	4	@	A	B	C	D	E	F	G	H	I	J	K	L	M	N	O
1 0 1	5	P	Q	R	S	T	U	V	W	X	Y	Z	[	\	]	^	_

Figure 5. HPDL-1414 ASCII Character Set

Mechanical and Electrical Considerations

The HPDL-1414 is a 12 pin dual-in-line package which can be stacked horizontally and vertically to create arrays of any size. The HPDL-1414 is designed to operate continuously from −40°C to +85°C for all possible input conditions.

The HPDL-1414 is assembled by die attaching and wire bonding the four GaAsP/GaAs monolithic LED chips and the CMOS IC to a high temperature printed circuit board. An immersion lens is formed by placing the PC board assembly into a nylon lens filled with epoxy. A plastic cap creates an air gap to protect the CMOS IC. Backfill epoxy environmentally seals the display package. This package construction gives the display a high tolerance to temperature cycling.

The inputs to the CMOS IC are protected against static discharge and input current latchup. However, for best results, standard CMOS handling precautions should be used. Prior to use, the HPDL-1414 should be stored in anti-static tubes or conductive material. A grounded conductive assembly area should be used, and assembly personnel should wear conductive wrist straps. Lab coats made of synthetic materials should be avoided since they may collect a static charge. Input current latchup is caused when the CMOS inputs are subjected either to a voltage below ground (V_{IN} < ground) or to a voltage higher than V_{CC} (V_{IN} > V_{CC}), and when a high current is forced into the input.

Soldering and Post Solder Cleaning Instructions for the HPDL-1414

The HPDL-1414 may be hand soldered or wave soldered with SN63 solder. Hand soldering may be safely performed only with an electronically temperature-controlled and securely grounded soldering iron. For best results, the iron tip temperature should be set at 315°C (600°F). For wave soldering, a rosin-based RMA flux or a water soluble organic acid (OA) flux can be used. The solder wave temperature should be 245°C ±5°C (473°F ±9°F), and the dwell in the wave should be set at 1 1/2 to 3 seconds for optimum soldering. Preheat temperature should not exceed 93°C (200°F) as measured on the solder side of the PC board.

Post solder cleaning may be performed with a solvent or aqueous process. For solvent cleaning, Allied Chemical Genesolv DES, Baron Blakeslee Blaco-Tron TES or DuPont Freon TE can only be used. These solvents are azeotropes of trichlorotrifluoroethane FC-113 with low concentrations of ethanol (5%). The maximum exposure time in the solvent vapors at boiling temperature should not exceed 2 minutes. Solvents containing high concentrations of alcohols, pure alcohols, isopropanol or acetone should not be used as they will chemically attack the nylon lens. Solvents containing trichloroethane FC-111 or FC-112 and trichloroethylene (TCE) are not recommended.

An aqueous cleaning process is highly recommended. A saponifier, such as Kester Bio-kleen Formula 5799 or equivalent, may be added to the wash cycle of an aqueous process to remove rosin flux residues. Organic acid flux residues must be thoroughly removed by an aqueous cleaning process to prevent corrosion of the leads and solder connections. The optimum water temperature is 60°C (140°F). The maximum cumulative exposure of the HPDL-1414 to wash and rinse cycles should not exceed 15 minutes.

Optical Considerations/
Contrast Enhancement

The HPDL-1414 display uses a precision aspheric immersion lens to provide excellent readability and low off-axis distortion. The aspheric lens produces a magnified character height of 2.85 mm (0.112 in.) and a viewing angle of ±40 degrees. These features provide excellent readability at distances of up to 1.5 meters (4 feet).

Each HPDL-1414 display is tested for luminous intensity and marked with an intensity category on the side of the display package. To ensure intensity matching for multiple package applications, mixing intensity categories for a given panel is not recommended.

The HPDL-1414 display is designed to provide maximum contrast when placed behind an appropriate contrast enhancement filter. Some suggested filters are Panelgraphic Ruby Red 60, Panelgraphic Dark Red 63, SGL Homalite H100-1650, Rohm and Haas 2423, Chequers Engraving 118, and 3M R6510. For further information on contrast enhancement, see Hewlett-Packard Application Note 1015.

For more information call your local HP sales office listed in the telephone directory white pages. Ask for the Components Department. Or write to Hewlett-Packard: **U.S.A.** — P.O. Box 10301, Palo Alto, CA 94303-0890. **Europe** — P.O. Box 999 1180 AZ Amstelveen. The Netherlands. **Canada** — 6877 Goreway Drive. Mississauga. L4V 1M8. Ontario. **Japan** — Yokogawa-Hewlett-Packard Ltd.. 3-29-21. Takaido-Higashi. Suginami-ku. Tokyo 168. **Elsewhere** in the world. write to Hewlett-Packard Intercontinental. 3495 Deer Creek Road, Palo Alto. CA 94304.

Appendix 4

The 590 Semiconductor Temperature Sensor

Reproduced by courtesy of RS Components Limited, PO Box 99, Corby, Northants, NN17 9RS, UK and Analog Devices Ltd, Central Avenue, East Molesey, Surrey, KT8 OSN, UK, also manufactured by Intersil, Inc, 10710 N. Tantau Avenue, Cupertino, CA 95014, USA.

Issued July 1983 **3992**

Semiconductor temperature sensor

Stock number 308-809

The RS590 semiconductor temperature sensor is functionally a two terminal I.C. which produces an output current proportional to absolute temperature. For supply voltages between +4V and +30V d.c. the device acts as a high impedance constant current regulator passing μA per degree Kelvin. Linearisation circuitry, precision voltage amplifiers, resistance measuring circuitry or cold junction compensation are not required for basic temperature measurement.

The RS590 is ideal in remote sensing applications. The device is virtually insensitive to voltage drops over long lines due to its high impedance current output provided the connection cable used is a twisted pair and well insulated.

Specification

Typical at +25°C (298.2°K) and V_S = 5V unless otherwise stated.

Absolute maximum ratings

Forward voltage (+ to —) _____ +44V
Reverse voltage (+ to —) _____ —20V
Breakdown voltage (Case to + or —) _____ ±200V
Rated performance temperature range
_____ —55°C to + 150°C
Storage temperature range _____ —65°C to + 175°C
Lead temperature (soldering, 10 sec) _____ +300°C

Power supply

Operating voltage range _____ + 4V to + 30V

PIN CONNECTIONS

TO 52 Package

PIN VIEW

Output

Nominal current output _____ 298.2μA
Nominal temperature coefficient _____ 1μA/°C
Calibration error _____ ±2.5°C max
Absolute error[2] (over rated performance temperature range)
    Without external calibration adjustment
        ±5.5°C max
  With + 25°C calibration error set to zero
      ±2.0°C max
  Nonlinearity _____ ±0.8°C max
  Repeatability _____ ±0.1°C max
  Long term drift[1] _____ ±0.1°C max
Current noise _____ 40pA/$\sqrt{Hz}$
Power supply rejection
  +4V ≤ V_S ≤ +5V _____ 0.5μA/V
  +5V ≤ V_S ≤ +15V _____ 0.2μA/V
  + 15V ≤ V_S ≤ + 30V _____ 0.1μA/V
Case isolation to either lead _____ $10^{10}\Omega$
Effective shunt capacitance _____ 100pF
Electrical Turn-on time[2] _____ 20μs
Reverse bias leakage current[3]
  (Reverse voltage = 10V) _____ 10pA

1 Conditions: constant + 5V, constant + 125°C
2 Does not include self heating effects
3 Leakage current doubles every 10°C

Operation

As previously stated the output of the RS590 is basically a proportional to absolute temperature (PTAT) current regulator i.e. the output is equal to a scale factor multiplied by the temperature of the sensor in degrees Kelvin.

Calibration error

The difference between the indicated temperature and actual temperature is called the calibration error. Since this is a scale factor error, it is relatively simple to trim out. Fig. 1 shows the most elementary way of accomplishing this.

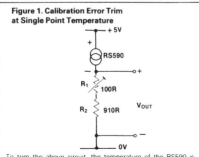

Figure 1. Calibration Error Trim at Single Point Temperature

To trim the above circuit, the temperature of the RS590 is measured by a reference temperature sensor and R₁ is trimmed so that V_{OUT}=1mV/ °K at that temperature.

Each RS590 is tested for error over the temperature range with callibration error trimmed out.
This error consists of a slope error and some curvature, mostly at the temperature extremes. Fig. 2 shows a typical temperature curve before and after calibration error trimming.

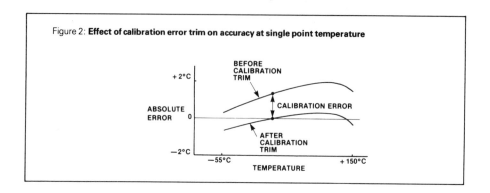

Figure 2: **Effect of calibration error trim on accuracy at single point temperature**

Nonlinearity

Nonlinearity as it applies to the RS590 is the maximum deviation of current over the entire temperature range from a best fit straight line. Fig. 3 shows the nonlinearity of the typical RS590 from Fig. 2.

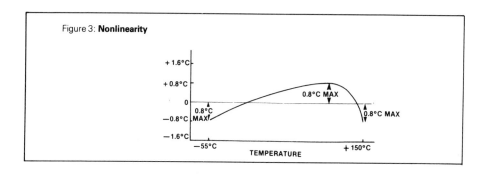

Figure 3: **Nonlinearity**

Fig 4A. shows a circuit in which nonlinearity is the major contribution to error over temperature. The circuit is trimmed by adjusting R_1 for a 0V output with RS590 at 0°C. R_2 is then adjusted for 10V out with the sensor at 100°C. Other pairs of temperatures may be used with this procedure as long as they are measured accurately by a reference sensor. Note that for +15V output (150°C) the V+ supply to the op-amp must be greater than 17V. Also note that V− should be at least −4V: if V− is ground there is no voltage applied across the device.
Note: Resistor values are typical and may need alteration depending upon magnitude of V−.

3992

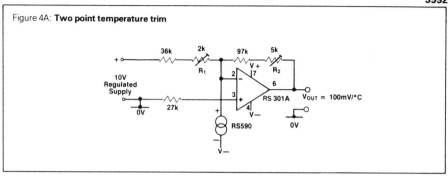

Figure 4A: **Two point temperature trim**

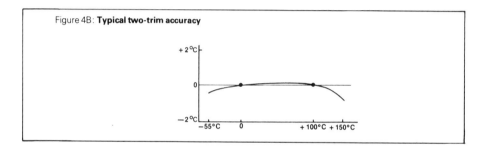

Figure 4B: **Typical two-trim accuracy**

Series/Parallel connection

Several RS590 devices may be connected in series as shown in Fig. 5. This configuration allows the minimum of all the sensed temperatures to be indicated. Connecting the sensors in parallel (Fig. 6) indicates the average of the sensed temperatures.

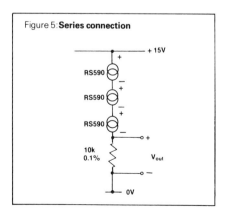

Figure 5: **Series connection**

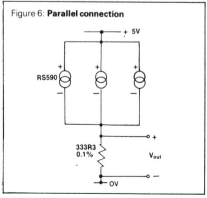

Figure 6: **Parallel connection**

3992

Differential temperature measurement

Fig. 7 illustrates one method by which differential temperature measurements can be made.

R_1 and R_2 may be used to trim the output of the op-amp to indicate a desired temperature difference.

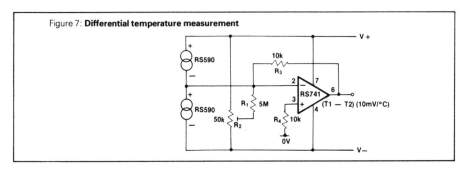

Figure 7: **Differential temperature measurement**

Temperature control

The RS590 may also be used in temperature control circuits (see Fig. 8). R_H and R_L are selected to set the high and low limits for R_{SET}. The RS590 is powered from a 12V stabilised source which isolates it from supply variations while maintaining a reasonable voltage across it. C_1 may be needed to filter extraneous noise. The value of R_B is determined by the ß of the transistor and the current requirements of the load.

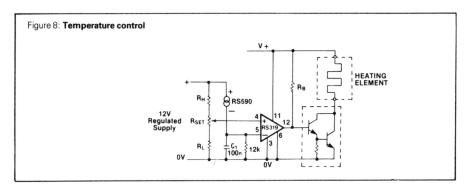

Figure 8: **Temperature control**

R.S. Components Ltd. PO Box 99, Corby, Northants, NN17 9RS   Telephone: 0536 201234
◑ An Electrocomponents Group Company   ©RS Components Ltd. 1984

Appendix 5

The Cross-editor/Assembler 6805 Source Listing

The source and object listings presented in this book were generated using the software presented here, compiled and run on the following hardware environment.

Apple //e processor with Apple 80-column card
Single disc drive under DOS 3.3
Grappler printer interface card to Epson FX-105 printer

The listings are given in their BASIC interpreted form. It is recommended that these be compiled and that the assembler be split into separate Pass 1 and Pass 2 files. In this case Pass 1 variables T, PR, LI, SA, LK, ER, L3, KK, TA%(256), OC%(85), D$, OB$, HF$, MF$, TA$(256), E$(2), N$(85), PS$(8), SF$(10), PC, MPC, NB, and CS should be defined as common for sending to Pass 2.

A copy of the compiled Editor, Assembler, 6805-EPROM Programmer (see Chapter 10) and Simulator is available directly from the author on receipt of a SSDD soft-sectored disk and return postage.

Commercial assemblers are available for other operating systems, some sources of which are:

Avocet Systems Inc, 10 Summer Street, PO Box 490, Rockport, ME, 04856, USA (CP/M and PCDOS/MDOS). Also supply programmers.

Crossware Productions, Melbourn, Royston, Herts, SG8 6BA, UK
(BBC DFS)

TEC, PO Box 53, West Gloverny, VT, 05875, USA (PCDOS/MDOS). Also supply IBM PC compatible programmer and simulator.

Thorson Engineering Co, 6225-76th St. S. E. Snohomish, WA, 98290, USA. (PCDOS/MDOS). Also supply IBM PC compatible in-circuit emulator and programmer.

```
0    REM ********************************************************************
1    REM *S.J.Cahill                                                       *
2    REM *University of Ulster                                             *
3    REM *Intelligent Text Editor, preceeding Pass1 Assembler              *
4    REM *27th September, 1984 version                                     *
5    REM ********************************************************************
50   L = 0
60   D$ = CHR$ (13) + CHR$ (4)
100  DIM LI(256): DIM LA$(256): DIM NM$(256): DIM OP$(256): DIM CM$(256)
150  PRINT D$ PR#3: REM *Turn on 80-column card
200  HOME
210  PRINT "Text editor": PRINT "Copywrite S.J.Cahill; 1983"
215  PRINT
220  INVERSE : PRINT "LOAD": NORMAL
230  PRINT "Loads in named file to buffer from disc"
235  PRINT
240  INVERSE : PRINT "APPEND": NORMAL
250  PRINT "Appends text to file in buffer"
255  PRINT
260  INVERSE : PRINT "LIST": NORMAL
270  PRINT "Lists file in buffer"
275  PRINT
280  INVERSE : PRINT "MERGE": NORMAL
290  PRINT "Merges file from disc onto end of text"
295  PRINT
300  INVERSE : PRINT "SAVE": NORMAL
310  PRINT "Saves buffer text onto disc"
315  PRINT
320  INVERSE : PRINT "EXIT": NORMAL
330  PRINT "Exits from current mode"
331  PRINT
332  INVERSE : PRINT "DELETE": NORMAL
334  PRINT "Deletes specified lines from file"
335  PRINT
336  INVERSE : PRINT "ASSEMBLE";: NORMAL : PRINT
338  PRINT "Go to the Assembler"
340  INPUT Z$
345  Z$ = LEFT$ (Z$,2)
350  IF Z$ = "AP" THEN  GOSUB 5000
360  IF Z$ = "LI" THEN  GOSUB 9000
380  IF Z$ = "SA" THEN  GOSUB 6000
390  IF Z$ = "LO" THEN  GOSUB 6200
400  IF Z$ = "ME" THEN  GOSUB 6220
410  IF Z$ = "DE" THEN  GOSUB 6400
425  IF Z$ = "AS" THEN  7000
430  IF Z$ = "EX" AND  RIGHT$ (FI$,1) > < "E" THEN  STOP
440  IF Z$ = "EX" THEN  PRINT : INPUT "Have you saved this file? ";S$
450  IF LEFT$ (S$,1) = "Y" THEN  STOP
480  GOTO 200
5000  REM *Append lines
5001  HOME : INVERSE : PRINT "MAXIMUM FILE LENGTH 255 LINES": NORMAL : PRINT
5002  L$ = "":S$ = ""
5003  POKE 51,63
5004  CALL 64874
5006  FOR I = 512 TO 766
5008  Z$ = CHR$ (( PEEK (I) - 128))
5010  IF Z$ = CHR$ (13) THEN I = 766: GOTO 5014
5012  L$ = L$ + Z$
```

```
5014 NEXT
5015 IF L$ = "" THEN 5004
5019 REM Now look for line number
5020 FOR I1 = 1 TO LEN (L$)
5030 Z$ = MID$ (L$,I1,1)
5040 IF Z$ = CHR$ (32) AND S$ = "" THEN 5080
5050 IF Z$ = CHR$ (32) THEN I2 = I1 + 1:I1 = LEN (L$): GOTO 5080
5060 IF ( ASC (Z$) < 48) OR ( ASC (Z$) > 57) THEN 5490
5075 S$ = S$ + Z$
5080 IF S$ = L$ THEN I2 = LEN (L$)
5080 NEXT I1
5090 LI(L) = VAL (S$)
5095 IF I2 > LEN (L$) THEN LA$(L) = "":NM$(L) = "":OP$(L) = "":CM$(L) = "": GOTO 5419
5099 REM Now look for a label
5100 IF MID$ (L$,I2,1) = CHR$ (32) THEN LA$(L) = "": GOTO 5165
5105 IF MID$ (L$,I2,1) = "*" THEN LA$(L) = "*":NM$(L) = "":OP$(L) = "":I2 = I2 + 1: GOTO 5310
5110 S$ = ""
5120 FOR I1 = I2 TO LEN (L$)
5130 Z$ = MID$ (L$,I1,1)
5140 IF Z$ = CHR$ (32) THEN LA$(L) = S$:I2 = I1 + 1:I1 = LEN (L$): GOTO 5160
5150 S$ = S$ + Z$
5160 NEXT I1
5164 REM Now look for the mnemonic
5165 S$ = ""
5170 FOR I1 = I2 TO LEN (L$)
5180 Z$ = MID$ (L$,I1,1)
5190 IF Z$ = CHR$ (32) AND S$ = "" THEN 5220
5200 IF Z$ = CHR$ (32) THEN NM$(L) = S$:I2 = I1 + 1:I1 = LEN (L$): GOTO 5220
5210 S$ = S$ + Z$
5215 IF I1 = LEN (L$) THEN NM$(L) = S$:OP$(L) = "":CM$(L) = "": GOTO 5350
5220 NEXT
5229 REM Now look for the operand, if any!
5230 S$ = ""
5240 FOR I1 = I2 TO LEN (L$)
5250 Z$ = MID$ (L$,I1,1)
5260 IF S$ = "" AND Z$ = CHR$ (32) THEN 5300
5265 IF NM$(L) = "FCC" AND S$ > < "" AND Z$ = LEFT$ (S$,1) THEN OP$(L) = S$ + Z$:I2 = I1 + 1:I1 = LEN (L$): GOTO 5300
5270 IF NM$(L) > < "FCC" AND CHR$ (32) THEN OP$(L) = S$:I2 = I1 + 1:I1 = LEN (L$): GOTO 5300
5280 IF Z$ = "*" THEN OP$(L) = "":I2 = I1:I1 = LEN (L$): GOTO 5300
5290 S$ = S$ + Z$
5295 IF I1 = LEN (L$) THEN OP$(L) = S$:CM$(L) = "": GOTO 5350
5300 NEXT
5309 REM Now look for the comment
5310 S$ = ""
5315 IF I2 > LEN (L$) THEN 5419
5320 FOR I1 = I2 TO LEN (L$)
5330 IF S$ = "" AND MID$ (L$,I1,1) = CHR$ (32) THEN 5350
5340 CM$(L) = RIGHT$ (L$, LEN (L$) + 1 - I1):I1 = LEN (L$)
5350 NEXT
5415 REM Check, is this a new line?
5419 IF L = 0 THEN 5470
5420 FOR I1 = 0 TO L - 1
5421 IF LI(I1) < = LI(L) THEN 5430
5422 V = LI(L):W$ = LA$(L):X$ = NM$(L):Y$ = OP$(L):Z$ = CM$(L)
5423 FOR I2 = L TO I1 STEP -1
5424 LI(I2) = LI(I2 - 1):LA$(I2) = LA$(I2 - 1):NM$(I2) = NM$(I2 - 1):OP$(I2) = OP$(I2 - 1):CM$(I2) = CM$(I2 - 1)
5425 NEXT I2
```

Listing A5.1

```
5426 LI(I1) = V:LA$(I1) = W$:NM$(I1) = X$:OP$(I1) = Y$:CM$(I1) = Z$
5427 I1 = L - 1: GOTO 5460
5430 IF LI(I1) > < LI(L) THEN 5460
5440 LA$(I1) = LA$(L):NM$(I1) = NM$(L):OP$(I1) = OP$(L):CM$(I1) = CM$(L)
5445 LI(L) = Ø:LA$(L) = "":NM$(L) = "":OP$(L) = "":CM$(L) = ""
5450 L = L - 1:I1 = L
5460 NEXT
5470 L = L + 1
5480 GOTO 5002
5490 L$ = LEFT$ (L$,2)
5495 IF L = 256 THEN INVERSE : PRINT "MAXIMUM FILE LENGTH = 255 LINES": NORMAL : GOTO 5002
5500 IF L$ = "EX" THEN RETURN
5501 IF L$ = "LI" THEN GOSUB 5510
5502 GOTO 5002
5510 INPUT "Starting line number?";I1
5520 INPUT "End line number?";I2
5525 PRINT : INPUT "Hard copy? ";S$
5527 PRINT : IF LEFT$ (S$,1) = "Y" THEN 5600
5530 PRINT "Press Space to advance; P to Pause"
5531 REM PRINT CHR$ (12) CHR$ (21)
5532 REM PRINT CHR$ (4);"PR#1"
5533 REM PRINT CHR$ (15)
5534 REM PRINT CHR$ (27)"Q" CHR$ (100)
5535 FOR I = Ø TO L
5540 X = PEEK (49168): IF PEEK (49152) > < 32 THEN 5540
5550 IF LI(I) < I1 THEN 5580
5560 IF LI(I) > I2 OR LI(I) = Ø THEN I = L: GOTO 5580
5565 IF LA$(I) = "*" THEN PRINT LI(I);;: *";CM$(I): GOTO 5579
5570 PRINT LI(I);;: ";NM$(I);;: ";OP$(I);;: ";CM$(I)
5579 FOR X = Ø TO 100: NEXT
5580 NEXT
5585 GET X$
5590 RETURN
5600 REM Printer list routine
5610 PRINT CHR$ (21) CHR$ (12): REM *Turn off 80-column card
5620 PRINT D$;"PR#1": REM Turn on Grappler
5625 PRINT CHR$ (9); CHR$ (25): REM *Avoids interference between grappler control & printer control
5630 PRINT CHR$ (27);"Q"; CHR$ (80)
5640 PRINT CHR$ (27);"N"; CHR$ (3): REM Skip 3 lines at perforation
5650 S$ = "List " + FL$
5660 PRINT CHR$ (14) TAB( (40 - LEN (S$)) / 2);S$
5670 PRINT
5675 FOR I = Ø TO L
5680 IF LI(I) < I1 THEN 5710
5690 IF LI(I) > I2 OR LI(I) = Ø THEN I = L: GOTO 5710
5695 IF LA$(I) = "*" THEN PRINT LI(I) TAB( 4);"*";CM$(I): GOTO 5710
5700 PRINT CHR$ (27);"D"; CHR$ (6); CHR$ (16); CHR$ (22); CHR$ (34); CHR$ (Ø);LI(I); CHR$ (9);LA$(I); CHR$ (9);NM$(I); CHR$ (9);OP$(I); CHR$ (9);CM$(I)
5710 NEXT
5720 PRINT CHR$ (12): REM Form Feed
5730 PRINT D$; "PR#3"
5740 RETURN
6000 REM Save subroutine
6020 PRINT : INPUT "Is this a new file for this run? ";Z$
6030 IF RIGHT$ (Z$,1) = "N" THEN 6055
6040 PRINT : INPUT "File name please ",FI$
6050 FI$ = FI$ + "-SOURCE"
6055 PRINT D$"OPEN";FI$
```

```
6060    PRINT D$"DELETE";FI$
6070    PRINT D$"OPEN";FI$
6080    PRINT D$"WRITE";FI$
6085    PRINT L
6090    FOR I = Ø TO L - 1
6100    PRINT CHR$ (34) + LA$(I) + CHR$ (34) + NM$(I) + CHR$ (34): PRINT CHR$ (34) + OP$(I) + CHR$ (3
        4): PRINT CHR$ (34) + CM$(I) + CHR$ (34)
6110    NEXT
6120    PRINT D$"CLOSE";FI$
6130    RETURN
6200    REM Load/Merge subroutine
6210    L = Ø
6220    HOME : REM Merge entry point
6225    PRINT CHR$ (21) CHR$ (12)
6230    PRINT D$"CATALOG"
6240    PRINT : INPUT "Name of file please ";FI$
6250    PRINT D$"OPEN";FI$
6260    PRINT D$"READ";FI$
6270    INPUT L1
6275    I1 = L
6280    FOR I = L TO L + L1 - 1
6290    LA$(I1) = "":NM$(I1) = "":OP$(I1) = "":CM$(I1) = ""
6292    INPUT LA$(I1): INPUT NM$(I1): INPUT OP$(I1): INPUT CM$(I1)
6294    IF LA$(I1) = "" AND NM$(I1) = "" AND OP$(I1) = "" AND CM$(I1) = "" THEN 63ØØ
6296    I1 = I1 + 1
6300    NEXT
6310    PRINT D$"CLOSE";FI$
6320    L = I1
6325    RETURN
6330    PRINT D$"PR#3"
6400    PRINT : INPUT "Delete from? ";I1
6410    PRINT : INPUT "to? ";I2
6420    J = Ø
6430    FOR I = Ø TO L - 1
6440    IF LI(I) < I1 THEN J = J + 1: GOTO 6470
6450    IF LI(I) = < I2 THEN 6465
6460    LI(J) = LI(I):LA$(J) = LA$(I):NM$(J) = NM$(I):OP$(J) = OP$(I):CM$(J) = CM$(I):J = J + 1
6465    LI(I) = Ø
6470    NEXT
6475    L = L - (I - J)
6480    PRINT : PRINT "Lines ";I1;" to ";I2;" deleted": PRINT
6490    RETURN
7000    REM *Goes to the Assembler
7010    HOME
7020    INPUT "Enter 6800 or 6805 for 6800/1/2 and 6804/5 types respectively ";A$
7030    FI$ = "ASSEMBLE" + A$
7050    PRINT CHR$ (4)"RUN";FI$
9000    HOME
9010    PRINT D$"CATALOG"
9020    PRINT : INPUT "Name of file please ";FI$
9022    IF RIGHT$ (FI$,1) = CHR$ (32) THEN FI$ = LEFT$ (FI$, LEN (FI$) - 1): GOTO 9022
9025    HOME
9030    PRINT : INPUT "Hard copy? ";PR$
9040    PR$ = RIGHT$ (PR$,1)
9050    IF PR$ > < "Y" THEN HOME : GOTO 9210
```

Listing A5.1 *(continued)*

```
9055  PRINT CHR$ (12) CHR$ (21)
9057  HOME
9060  PRINT "Move paper to top of form, & hit key"
9065  GET X$
9067  PRINT
9070  PRINT CHR$ (4);"PR#1"
9080  PRINT CHR$ (27)"Q" CHR$ (120)
9090  PRINT CHR$ (27)"C" CHR$ (66)
9100  PRINT CHR$ (27)"N" CHR$ (3)
9110  PRINT CHR$ (15)
9210  PRINT CHR$ (14) TAB( 20 - LEN (FI$) / 2);FI$
9220  IF RIGHT$ (FI$,1) = "E" THEN GOTO 10000
9230  IF RIGHT$ (FI$,1) = "T" THEN 11000
9235  IF RIGHT$ (FI$,1) = "X" THEN 12000
9240  PRINT "Illegal file type": GOTO 9010
9999  REM *Source-file list routine
10000 HOME
10010 IF PR$ > < "Y" THEN  PRINT "Key P to Pause, X to eXit"
10020 POKE 34,1
10030 PRINT D$"OPEN";FI$
10040 PRINT D$"READ";FI$
10050 INPUT L
10060 FOR I9 = 10 TO 10 * L STEP 10
10065 X = PEEK (49385)
10070 INPUT LA$,NM$,OP$,CM$
10080 PRINT LEFT$ ( STR$ (I9) + "    ",5); GOTO 10130
10090 IF NM$ = "" THEN  PRINT "*";: GOTO 10130
10100 PRINT LEFT$ (LA$ + "    ",9); LEFT$ (NM$ + "    ",6);
10110 IF LEN (OP$) > 16 THEN  PRINT OP$;"  ";: GOTO 10130
10120 PRINT LEFT$ (OP$ + "    ",18);
10130 PRINT CM$
10140 IF PEEK (49152) = 216 THEN I9 = L * 10: GOTO 10160
10150 IF PEEK (49152) = 208 THEN 10150
10160 NEXT I9
10170 PRINT D$"CLOSE";FI$
10180 X = PEEK (49384):X = PEEK (49168)
10190 PRINT D$"PR#0": PRINT : PRINT "Any key to continue"
10200 GET X$
10210 X = PEEK (49168)
10220 PRINT D$"PR#3"
10230 POKE 34,0
10240 IF PR$ = "Y" THEN  PRINT CHR$ (18)
10250 RETURN
11000 HOME
11005 IF PR$ > < "Y" THEN  PRINT "Key P to Pause, X to eXit"
11010 PRINT "Line Machine code"; SPC( 9);"Source code"; SPC( 16);"Comment"
11020 POKE 34,3
11040 PRINT D$"OPEN";FI$
11050 PRINT D$"READ";FI$
11060 FOR I9 = 10 TO 65530 STEP 10
11065 X = PEEK (49385)
11070 INPUT MC$,LA$,NM$,OP$,CM$
11075 IF OP$ = "*" THEN I9 = 65530: GOTO 11250
11080 PRINT LEFT$ ( STR$ (I9) + "    ",5);
11085 IF NM$ = "FCB") THEN  PRINT "*";: GOTO 11210
11090 IF (NM$ = "FCB") + (NM$ = "FDB") + (NM$ = "FCC") > 0 THEN  INVERSE : PRINT MC$;: NORMAL : PRINT : PRINT CHR$ (13) SPC( 17)
      ;: GOTO 11180
```

```
11100  IF NM$ > < "SPC" THEN 11130
11110  FOR II = 1 TO  VAL (OP$): PRINT : NEXT
11120  GOTO 11230
11130  IF NM$ > < "PAGE" THEN 11150
11140  IF PR$ = "Y" THEN  PRINT  CHR$ (12): GOTO 11230
11150  IF (NM$ = "ORG") + (NM$ = "EQU") + (NM$ = "RMB") = Ø THEN  INVERSE
11160  PRINT MC$;
11170  NORMAL
11180  PRINT  SPC( 1); LEFT$ (LA$ + "         ",8); LEFT$ (NM$ + "    ",6);
11190  IF  LEN (OP$) > 12 THEN  PRINT OP$; "  ";: GOTO 11210
11200  PRINT  LEFT$ (OP$ + "              ",14);
11210  PRINT CM$
11230  IF  PEEK (49152) = 216  THEN I9 = 65530: GOTO 11250
11240  IF  PEEK (49152) = 208  THEN 11240
11250  NEXT I9
11260  PRINT D$"CLOSE";FI$
11265  X =  PEEK (49384):X =  PEEK (49168)
11270  PRINT D$"PR#Ø": PRINT : PRINT "Any key to continue"
11280  GET X$
11285  X =  PEEK (49168)
11290  PRINT D$"PR#3"
11300  IF PR$ = "Y" THEN  PRINT  CHR$ (18)
11350  POKE 34,Ø
11999  RETURN
12000  HOME
12010  IF PR$ > < "Y" THEN  PRINT "Key P to Pause, X to eXit"
12020  POKE 34,1
12030  PRINT D$"OPEN";FI$
12040  PRINT D$"READ";FI$
12050  FOR I9 = 1 TO 65530
12060  X =  PEEK (49385)
12070  INPUT L$
12080  IF L$ = "59" THEN I9 = 65530: GOTO 12130
12090  PRINT "<"; MID$ (L$,5,4);">"; + MID$ (L$,9,( LEN (L$) - 1Ø))
12100  REM *     LEFT$ (L$,4) + "<"; + MID$ (L$,5,4) + ">"; + MID$ (L$,9,( LEN(L$) - 1Ø)) + " " + RIGHT$ (L$,2)
12110  IF  PEEK (49152) = 216  THEN I9 = 65530: GOTO 12130
12120  IF  PEEK (49152) = 208  THEN 12120
12130  NEXT
12140  PRINT D$"CLOSE";FI$
12150  X =  PEEK (49384):X =  PEEK (49166)
12160  PRINT D$"PR#Ø": PRINT : PRINT "Any key to continue"
12170  GET X$
12180  X =  PEEK (49166)
12190  PRINT D$"PR#3"
12200  POKE 34,Ø
12210  IF PR$ = "Y" THEN  PRINT  CHR$ (18)
12220  RETURN
```

Listing A5.1 *(continued)*

```
0    REM ***************************************************************
1    REM *S.J.Cahill                                                  *
2    REM *University of Ulster                                        *
3    REM *Pass1 & Pass2 6805 assembler                                *
4    REM *22nd January, 1985 version                                  *
5    REM ***************************************************************
10   PRINT CHR$ (4)"MAXFILES1"
15   HIMEM: PEEK (115) + 256 *   PEEK (116)
100  D$ =   CHR$ (4)
120  DIM LA$(256),NM$(256),OP$(256),CM$(256),TA$(256),TA%(256),AM%(256),MC%(256),ER$(2),H(3)
125  DIM N$(85),OC%(85)
130  DATA "EQU","ORG","SPC","PAGE","RMB","FCB","FCC","FDB"
140  FOR I = 1 TO 8: READ PS$(I):   NEXT
180  PRINT  CHR$ (12) CHR$ (21)
190  POKE 34,0
200  E$(0) = "Illegal address mode in line "
210  E$(1) = "Incorrect operand in line "
220  E$(2) = "Illegal instruction in line "
300  DATA "BRA","BRN","BHI","BLS","BCC","BCS","BLO","BHS","BNE","BEQ","BHCC","BHCS","BPL","BMI","BMC","BMS","BIL","BIH"
310  DATA "NEG","COM","LSR","ROR","ASR","LSL","ROL","DEC","INC","TST","CLR"
320  DATA "NEGA","COMA","LSRA","RORA","ASRA","LSLA","ROLA","DECA","INCA","TSTA","CLRA"
330  DATA "NEGX","COMX","LSRX","RORX","ASRX","LSLX","ROLX","DECX","INCX","TSTX","CLRX"
340  DATA "RTI","RTS","SWI","STOP","WAIT"
350  DATA "TAX","CLC","SEC","CLI","SEI","RSP","NOP","TXA"
360  DATA "SUB","CMP","SBC","CPX","AND","BIT","LDA","STA","EOR","ADC","ORA","ADD","JMP","BSR","JSR","LDX","STX"
400  DATA 32,3,34,35,36,37,38,39,40,41,42,43,44,45,46,47
410  DATA 32,35,36,38,39,40,41,42,44,45,47
420  DATA 64,67,68,70,71,72,73,74,76,77,79
430  DATA 80,83,84,86,87,88,89,90,92,93,95
450  DATA 128,129,131,142,143
460  DATA 151,152,153,154,155,156,157,159
470  DATA 160,161,162,163,164,165,166,167,168,169,170,171,172,173,173,174,175
480  FOR I1 = 0 TO 85: READ N$(11):   NEXT
490  FOR I9 = 0 TO 85: READ OC%(19):   NEXT
500  REM Menue
505  HOME
510  INVERSE :  PRINT "ASSEMBLE":  NORMAL
520  PRINT "Loads named source-file, assembles":  PRINT "and saves hex file (on no error)"
530  PRINT
570  INVERSE :  PRINT "6805 PROGRAM":  NORMAL
580  PRINT "Programs 6805 in slot 5"
590  PRINT
600  INVERSE :  PRINT "PROGRAM EPROM":  NORMAL
610  PRINT "Programs EPROM in slot 4"
620  PRINT
630  INVERSE :  PRINT "EDIT":  NORMAL
640  PRINT "Return to Editor, to change Source code"
650  INVERSE :  PRINT "EXIT":  NORMAL
660  PRINT "Terminate"
670  PRINT
680  PRINT
690  INPUT Z$
700  Z$ =  LEFT$ (Z$,1)
710  IF Z$ = "A" THEN 900
720  IF Z$ = "T" THEN  PRINT D$"RUNTEXT EDITOR"
730  IF Z$ = "E" THEN STOP
740  IF Z$ = "E" THEN  PRINT D$"RUNEPROM PROG"
800  GOTO 505: REM *Illegal command
```

```
900  HOME
901  PR = 0:LI = 0:SA = 1
905  INVERSE : PRINT "PRINT": NORMAL
910  PRINT "Hard copy (list to VDU on default)"
915  PRINT
920  INVERSE : PRINT "LISTNO": NORMAL
925  PRINT "Only error messages to VDU"
930  PRINT
935  INVERSE : PRINT "MACHINE FILE": NORMAL
940  PRINT "Default Machine file not generated"
945  PRINT
950  INVERSE : PRINT "GO": NORMAL
955  PRINT "Go and assemble"
960  PRINT : INPUT Z$
962  Z$ = LEFT$ (Z$,1)
965  IF Z$ = "P" THEN PR = 1: GOTO 960
970  IF Z$ = "L" THEN LI = 1: GOTO 960
975  IF Z$ = "M" THEN SA = 0: GOTO 960
980  IF Z$ = "G" THEN 1000: GOTO 960
985  PRINT "Illegal option": GOTO 960
1000 POKE 34,0: HOME
1010 PRINT "6805 Assembler": PRINT "Copywrite S.J.Cahill; 1984"
1020 PRINT
1030 INVERSE : PRINT "ASSEMBLE SOURCE FILE TO OBJECT CODE": NORMAL
1040 PRINT
1060 GOSUB 20000
1070 L3 = 0
1074 IF PR = 1 THEN PRINT CHR$ (27)"Q" CHR$ (80): PRINT CHR$ (27)"C" CHR$ (27) CHR$ (66): PRINT CHR$ (80): PRINT CHR$ (27)"N" CHR$
     (3)
1076 IF PR = 0 THEN PRINT D$"PR#3"
1080 FOR KK = 0 TO LK - 1
1110 PRINT D$"OPEN";SF$(KK)
1120 PRINT D$" READ ";SF$(KK)
1130 INPUT L
1140 I1 = 1
1150 FOR I = 1 TO L
1160 LA$(I1) = "":NM$(I1) = "":OP$(I1) = "":CM$(I1) = ""
1165 INPUT LA$(I1),NM$(I1),OP$(I1),CM$(I1)
1170 IF LA$(I1) + NM$(I1) + OP$(I1) + CM$(I1) = "" THEN 1200
1190 I1 = I1 + 1
1200 NEXT
1210 PRINT D$"CLOSE";SF$(KK)
1220 L = I1 - 1
1235 IF KK = 0 THEN PRINT CHR$ (14) TAB( (40 - LEN (OB$)) / 2);OB$
1240 POKE 34,0: HOME : PRINT "1st Pass ";SF$(KK): POKE 34,3
1250 REM Build up label table from EQU's
1257 PA = 1
1260 FOR L1 = 1 TO L:L2 = L1 + L3
1275 IF NM$(L1) > < "EQU" THEN 1330
1280 IF PR = 0 THEN X = PEEK (37): PRINT : PRINT L2 * 10;"  ": POKE 37,X
1290 IF LA$(L1) = "" THEN PRINT "EQU with no label in line ";L2 * 10: GOTO 1330
1300 IF OP$(L1) = "" THEN OD$ = "0"
1310 OD$ = OP$(L1): GOSUB 11020
1320 TA$(T) = LA$(L1):TA%(T) = DE - 32767
1330 T = T + 1
1340 REM Build up all non-EQU labels
```

Listing A5.2

```
1345 FOR L1 = 1 TO L:L2 = L1 + L3
1347 IF PR = 0 THEN X = PEEK (37): POKE 37,1: PRINT : PRINT L2 * 10;"          ": POKE 37,X: PRINT
1350 IF NM$(L1) = "": THEN AM%(L1) = 900: GOTO 1520: REM A comment line
1360 IF LA$(L1) > < "" AND NM$(L1) > < "EQU" THEN TA$(T) = LA$(L1):TA%(T) = PC - 32767:T = T + 1
1370 REM Now distinguish between pseudo and true operators
1380 X = 0
1390 FOR J = 1 TO 8
1400 IF NM$(L1) = PS$(J) THEN X = J:AM%(L1) = X * 100:J = 8
1410 NEXT
1420 ON X GOTO 1520,1450,1520,1470,1490,1490,1512,1490
1430 GOTO 1540: REM Go to real operator
1440 REM Pseudo operations
1450 OD$ = OF$(L1): GOSUB 11020: REM ORG
1460 PC = DE: GOTO 1520
1470 OD$ = OF$(L1): GOSUB 11020: REM RMB
1480 PC = PC + DE: GOTO 1520
1490 OD$ = OF$(L1): GOSUB 11400: REM FCB, FDB
1500 PC = PC + COMMA + 1
1510 IF NM$(L1) = "FDB" THEN PC = PC + COMMA + 1
1511 GOTO 1520
1512 X = LEN (OF$(L1)) - 2:PC = PC + X: REM FCC
1520 NEXT
1530 GOTO 1735
1540 REM Machine codeable operations
1545 IF LEFT$ (OF$(L1),1) = "", THEN OP$(L1) = "0" + OF$(L1)
1550 IF OP$(L1) = "" THEN PC = PC + 1:AM%(L1) = 15: GOTO 1730: REM Inherent
1560 IF LEFT$ (NM$(L1),1) > < "B" OR NM$(L1) = "BIT" THEN 1620
1570 REM Branch; Bit modify; or Branch on bit
1575 OD$ = OF$(L1): GOSUB 11400: REM How many zones?
1580 AM%(L1) = 20 + COMMA
1590 PC = PC + 2
1600 IF COMMA = 2 THEN PC = PC + 1
1610 GOTO 1730
1620 IF LEFT$ (OF$(L1),1) = "#" THEN PC = PC + 2:AM%(L1) = 0: GOTO 1730: REM Immediate
1630 REM Three indexed modes
1640 IF RIGHT$ (OF$(L1),2) > < ",X" THEN 1700
1650 OD$ = LEFT$ (OF$(L1), LEN (OF$(L1)) - 2): GOSUB 11020
1660 IF DE = 0 THEN PC = PC + 1:AM%(L1) = 5: GOTO 1730
1670 IF DE < 256 THEN PC = PC + 2:AM%(L1) = 4: GOTO 1730
1680 PC = PC + 3:AM%(L1) = 3: GOTO 1730
1690 REM Direct or extended
1700 OD$ = OF$(L1): GOSUB 11020
1710 IF DE < 256 THEN PC = PC + 2:AM%(L1) = 1: GOTO 1730
1720 PC = PC + 3:AM%(L1) = 2
1730 NEXT L1
1735 L3 = L3 + L
1738 A$ = "AM" + STR$ (KK)
1740 PRINT D$"OPEN";A$
1750 PRINT D$"WRITE";A$
1760 FOR I = 1 TO L
1770 PRINT AM%(I)
1780 NEXT
1790 PRINT D$"CLOSE";A$
1800 NEXT KK: REM *Next file
2000 CS = 0:MF$ = "":PC = 0:NB = 0:MPC = 0:PA = 2:L3 = 0
2005 POKE 34,0: HOME : IF PR = 0 THEN PRINT "2nd Pass"
2010 IF SA + ER > 0 THEN 2150
2020 HF$ = LEFT$ (OB$, LEN (OB$) - 6) + "HEX"
```

```
2040 PRINT D$"OPEN";HF$
2050 PRINT D$"WRITE";HF$
2060 DE = LEN (HF$) + 3:CS = DE: GOSUB 50200
2065 MF$ = "SO" + HEX$
2070 FOR I = 1 TO LEN (HF$)
2080 X$ = MID$ (HF$,I,1)
2090 MF$ = MF$ + X$:CS = CS + ASC (X$)
2100 NEXT
2110 DE = 255 - (CS - INT (CS / 256) * 256): GOSUB 50200
2120 PRINT MF$ + HEX$
2130 PRINT D$"CLOSE";HF$
2140 CS = 0:MF$ = ""
2150 FOR KK = 0 TO LK - 1
2160 IF LK = 1 THEN 2300
2170 PRINT D$"OPEN";SF$(KK)
2180 PRINT D$"READ";SF$(KK)
2190 INPUT L
2200 I1 = 1
2210 FOR I = 1 TO L
2220 LA$(I1) = "":NM$(I1) = "":OP$(I1) = "":CM$(I1) = ""
2230 INPUT LA$(I1),NM$(I1),OP$(I1),CM$(I1)
2240 IF LA$(I1) + NM$(I1) + OP$(I1) + CM$(I1) = "" THEN 2260
2250 I1 = I1 + 1
2260 NEXT
2270 PRINT D$"CLOSE";SF$(KK)
2280 L = I1 - 1
2282 A$ = "AM" + STR$ (KK)
2285 PRINT D$"OPEN";A$
2290 PRINT D$"READ";A$
2294 FOR I = 1 TO L: INPUT AM%(I): NEXT
2296 PRINT D$"CLOSE";A$
2305 IF PR = 1 THEN PRINT : PRINT "2nd Pass ";SF$(KK): GOTO 2330
2310 IF KK > < 0 THEN 3010
2310 POKE 34,0: HOME
2320 PRINT "2nd Pass " SPC( 5);"Key P to Pause, any key to continue"
2330 PRINT "Line Machine code"; SPC( 8);"Source code"; SPC( 18);"Comment"
2340 IF PR = 0 THEN POKE 34,2
3010 FOR L1 = 1 TO L:L2 = L1 + L3
3020 IF AM%(L1) > 99 THEN 7000: REM Pseudo operation
3040 DE = PC: GOSUB 50300
3050 MC$(L1) = HEX$ + " ": REM Hex value of Program counter
3060 IF AM%(L1) < 20 THEN GOSUB 6010: REM Not Branch or Bit mod
3070 IF AM%(L1) > 19 THEN GOSUB 5500: REM Sub to evaluate Branch & Bit mod
3500 GOSUB 8000
3510 GOSUB 9000
4000 NEXT
4001 L3 = L3 + L
4020 IF KK = 1 THEN PRINT D$"OPEN";OB$
4030 IF KK > 1 THEN PRINT D$"APPEND";OB$
4035 PRINT D$"WRITE";OB$
4040 FOR I = 1 TO L
4050 PRINT MC$(I);LA$(I);NM$(I);OP$(I);CM$(I)
4060 NEXT
4070 IF KK = LK - 1 THEN PRINT "*";"";"";"";""
4080 PRINT D$"CLOSE";OB$
4090 NEXT KK: REM *Next file
4092 FOR I = 0 TO LK - 1
```

Listing A5.2 (*continued*)

```
4094 A$ = "AM" + STR$ (I)
4096 PRINT D$"DELETE",A$
4098 NEXT
4099 IF SA  >  < Ø THEN  PRINT  PRINT D$"DELETE";HF$: GOTO 4105: REM  *Delete Hex file if not wanted
4100 IF (ER + SA = Ø) AND NB >  < Ø THEN  GOSUB 9030: REM *Finish off the HEX file
4101 PRINT D$"APPEND";HF$
4102 PRINT D$"WRITE";HF$
4103 PRINT "S9"
4104 PRINT D$"CLOSE";HF$
4105 PRINT : PRINT "Assembly complete with ";ER;" errors"
4110 IF PR = 1 THEN  PRINT  CHR$ (12): PRINT  CHR$ (27)"J" CHR$ (255):  PRINT D$"PR#Ø"
4130 PRINT "Key to continue ": GET X
4140 POKE 34,Ø
4140 PRINT  CHR$ (13)  CHR$ (4)"RUN TEXT EDITOR"
5494 REM *Subroutine to evaluate Branch & Bit mod
5495 REM  *Entry:AM%(L1);NM(L1);OP$(L1);MC$(L1);MF$;PC;NB;ER
5496 REM  *Exit :MC$;MF$;PC;NB;CS;ER: All other entry variables unchanged
5497 REM  *Global variables, N$(I);OC(I):OD$;L1;DE;HEX$;OFFSET$;OFFSET
5498 REM  *Local variables, S$;S1$;S2$;S3$;I1;X1
5499 REM  *Subroutines 11020;50200;50400
5500 ON AM%(L1) - 20 GOTO 5700,5850
5510     X1 = - 1: REM *Simple Branch
5515     PC = PC + 2
5520     FOR I1 = Ø TO 85
5530     : IF NM$(L1) = N$(I1) THEN DE = OC%(I1):X1 = I1:I1 = 85
5540     NEXT
5550     IF X1 = - 1 THEN E$ = E$(2): GOTO 51000
5560     GOSUB 51100
5580     OD$= OP$(L1)
5590     GOSUB 11020
5605     GOSUB 50400
5610     MC$(L1) = MC$(L1) + "-" + OFFSET$ + "- "
5612     IF (SA + ER) >  < Ø THEN  RETURN
5615     CS = CS + OFFSET
5620     MF$ = MF$ + OFFSET$
5630     NB = NB + 2
5640     RETURN
5700     S$ = ""
5702     FOR I1 = 1 TO LEN (OP$(L1))
5703     Z$ = MID$ (OP$(L1),I1,1)
5704     IF Z$ = "," THEN X1 = I1:I1 =  LEN (OP$(L1)): GOTO 5708
5706     S$ = S$ + Z$
5708     NEXT
5710     OD$ = S$: GOSUB 11020
5720     IF DE <  8 AND DE >  = Ø THEN 5740
5730     E$ = E$(1): GOTO 51020
5740     IF NM$(L1) = "BCLR" THEN DE = 17 + 2 * DE: GOTO 5770
5750     IF NM$(L1) = "BSET" THEN DE = 16 + 2 * DE: GOTO 5770
5760     E$ = E$(2): GOSUB 51010
5765     GOTO 5790
5770     GOSUB 51100
5790     OD$ = RIGHT$ (OP$(L1), LEN (OP$(L1)) - X1): GOSUB 11020
5800     GOSUB 5115Ø
5820     PC = PC + 2:NB = NB + 2
5830     RETURN
5850     PC = PC + 3:S$ = "": REM *Branch on bit
5852     FOR I1 = 1 TO  LEN (OP$(L1))
5853     Z$ =  MID$ (OP$(L1),I1,1)
```

```
5854    IF Z$ = ",", THEN X1 = II:II = LEN (OP$(L1)): GOTO 5858
5856    S$ = S$ + Z$
5858    NEXT
5859    OD$ = S$: GOSUB 11020
5860    IF DE < 8 AND DE > = 0 THEN 5880
5870    E$ = E$(1): GOTO 51020
5880    IF NM$(L1) = "BRCLR" THEN DE = 1 + 2 * DE: GOTO 5910
5890    IF NM$(L1) = "BRSET" THEN DE = 2 * DE: GOTO 5910
5900    E$ = E$(2): GOSUB 51010
5905    GOTO 5940
5910    GOSUB 51100
5940    S1$ = RIGHT$ (OP$(L1), LEN (OP$(L1)) - X1):S2$ = ""
5945    FOR II = 1 TO LEN (S1$)
5950    :Z$ = MID$ (S1$,II,1)
5960    : IF Z$ = ",", THEN X1 = II:II = LEN (S1$): GOTO 5970
5965    :S2$ = S2$ + Z$
5970    NEXT
5972    IF S2$ = "" THEN S2$ = "0": REM *S2$=Address
5975    IF RIGHT$(S1$,1) = "," THEN S3$ = "0": GOTO 5980: REM *If a null target field then assume lies at zero
5977    S3$ = RIGHT$(S1$, LEN (S1$) - X1)
5980    OD$ = S2$: GOSUB 11020
5981    CS = CS + DE
5984    GOSUB 50200
5985    MC$(L1) = MC$(L1) + "-" + HEX$: IF (SA + ER) = 0 THEN MF$ = MF$ + HEX$: REM *Add to machine & hex files
5987    OD$ = S3$: GOSUB 11020
5989    GOSUB 50400
5990    CS = CS + DE
5994    MC$(L1) = MC$(L1) + OFF$:MF$ = MF$ + OFFSET$
5998    NB = NB + 3: RETURN
6000    REM *Subroutine to evaluate all non-Branch & Bit mod instructions
6001    REM *Entry:AM%(L1):NM(L1);OP$(L1):MF$:PC;NB;ER
6002    REM *Exit:MC$;MF$;PC;NB;CS;ER: All other entry variables unchanged
6003    REM *Global variables, N$(I);OC(I);OD$;L1;L2;DE;HEX$
6005    REM *Local variables, I1;X1
6006    REM *Subroutines 11020;50200;50300
6010    X1 = 0
6020    FOR I1 = 18 TO 85: REM *Find instruction
6030    :IF NM$(L1) = N$(I1) THEN DE = OC%(I1):X1 = I1:J1 = 85
6040    NEXT
6042    REM *Error handling
6045    IF X1 > = 0 THEN 6090
6050    E$ = E$(2): GOSUB 51010
6060    IF AM%(L1) = 5 OR AM%(L1) = 15 THEN MC$(L1) = MC$(L1) + "     ":PC = PC + 1: RETURN : REM  Assume Inherent or IX0
6070    IF AM%(L1) = 2 OR AM%(L1) = 3 THEN MC$(L1) = MC$(L1) + "-****":PC = PC + 3: RETURN : REM  *Assume Extended or IX2
6080    MC$(L1) = MC$(L1) + "-*":PC = PC + 2: RETURN
6085    REM *
6090    ON AM%(L1) GOTO 6200, 6300, 6400, 6500, 6600
6092    IF AM%(L1) = 15 GOTO 6700
6095    PC = PC + 2: REM *Immediate
6100    IF DE < 160 OR DE = 167 OR DE = 172 OR DE = 173 OR DE = 175 THEN E$ = E$(0): GOTO 51000
6110    GOSUB 51100
6140    OD$ = RIGHT$ (OP$(L1), LEN (OP$(L1)) - 1): GOSUB 11020
6145    IF DE > 255 THEN PRINT "Immediate operand overload in line ";L2 * 10:ER = ER + 1:MC$(L1) = MC$(L1) + "-**  ": RETURN

6150    GOSUB 51150
6180    NB = NB + 2
6190    RETURN
```

Listing A5.2 (continued)

```
6199    REM *Direct
6200    DE = DE + 16:PC = PC + 2
6210    IF (DE > 63 AND DE < 176) OR DE > 197 THEN E$ = E$(0): GOTO 51000
6220    GOSUB 51100
6240    OD$ = OP$(L1): GOSUB 11020
6250    IF DE > 255 THEN  PRINT "Non-direct address in line ";L2 * 10:ER = ER + 1:MC$(L1) = MC$(L1) + '-**  ": RETURN
6260    GOSUB 51150
6280    NB = NB + 2
6290    RETURN
6299    REM *Extended
6300    PC = PC + 3:DE = DE + 32
6310    IF DE < 192 OR DE > 207 THEN E$ = E$(0): GOTO 51020
6320    GOSUB 51100
6340    OD$ = OP$(L1): GOSUB 51170
6370    NB = NB + 3
6380    RETURN
6399    REM *Index mode2
6400    PC = PC + 3:DE = DE + 48
6410    IF DE < 208 OR DE > 223 THEN E$ = E$(0): GOTO 51020
6420    GOSUB 51100
6440    OD$ = LEFT$ (OP$(L1), LEN (OP$(L1)) - 2): GOSUB 11020
6450    GOSUB 51170
6470    NB = NB + 3
6480    RETURN
6499    REM *Index mode 1
6500    PC = PC + 2:DE = DE + 64
6510    IF DE < 96 OR (DE > 111 AND DE < 224) OR DE > 239 THEN E$ = E$(0): GOTO 51000
6520    GOSUB 51100
6540    OD$ = LEFT$ (OP$(L1), LEN (OP$(L1)) - 2): GOSUB 11020
6550    GOSUB 51150
6570    NB = NB + 2
6580    RETURN
6599    REM *Index mode 0
6600    PC = PC + 1:DE = DE + 80
6610    IF (DE > 127 AND DE < 240) OR DE < 112 THEN E$ = E$(0): GOTO 51030
6620    GOSUB 51200
6640    NB = NB + 1
6650    RETURN
6699    REM *Inherent
6700    PC = PC + 1
6710    IF DE < 64 OR (DE > 95 AND DE < 128) OR DE > 159 THEN E$ = E$(0): GOTO 51030
6720    GOSUB 51200
6750    NB = NB + 1
6760    RETURN
7000    ON AM%(L1) / 100 GOTO 7150,7100,7300,7400,7500,7600,7800,7600,7050
7049    REM *Comment
7050    IF LI = 0 THEN  PRINT  LEFT$ ( STR$ (L2 * 10) + "          ", 5);"*";CM$(L1)
7060    GOTO 4000
7099    REM *ORG
7100    OD$ = OP$(L1): GOSUB 11020
7110    PC = DE
7115    GOSUB 50300
7117    MC$(L1) = "          <" + HEX$ + "> "
7120    GOSUB 8000
7130    GOSUB 9000
7140    GOTO 4000
7149    REM *EQU
```

```
7150 OD$ = OP$(L1): GOSUB 11020
7160 GOSUB 50300
7170 MC$(L1) = "     <" + HEX$ + "> "
7180 GOSUB 8000
7190 GOTO 4000
7300 IF OP$(L1) = "" THEN OP$(L1) = "1": REM *SPC
7310 OD$ = OP$(L1):: GOSUB 11020
7320 FOR I2 = 1 TO DE
7330 PRINT
7340 NEXT
7360 GOTO 4000
7400 IF PR = 1 THEN PRINT CHR$ (12): REM *PAGE
7420 GOTO 4000
7500 DE = PC: GOSUB 50300: REM *RMB
7505 MC$(L1) = "     <" + HEX$ + "> "
7510 OD$ = OP$(L1): GOSUB 11020
7515 PC = PC + DE
7520 DE = PC - 1: GOSUB 50300
7530 MC$(L1) = MC$(L1) + "<" + HEX$ + ">"
7540 GOSUB 8000
7550 GOTO 4000
7600 OD$ = "":Z$ = "": REM *FCB;FDB
7605 DE = PC: GOSUB 50300
7607 MC$(L1) = HEX$ + "  ": REM *HEX value of Program counter
7610 FOR I = 1 TO LEN (OP$(L1))
7630 IF MID$ (OP$(L1),I,1) > < "," AND I > < LEN (OP$(L1)) THEN OD$ = OD$ + MID$ (OP$(L1),I,1): GOTO 7740
7635 IF MID$ (OP$(L1),I,1) > < "," THEN OD$ = OD$ + MID$ (OP$(L1),I,1)
7640 GOSUB 11020
7660 X = (NM$(L1) = "FDB"):PC = PC + 1 + X:NB = NB + 1 + X
7670 IF X = 1 THEN 7700
7680 CS = CS + DE: GOSUB 50200
7690 GOTO 7710
7700 CS = CS + INT (DE / 256) + (DE - INT (DE / 256) * 256): GOSUB 50300
7710 MC$(L1) = MC$(L1) + HEX$: IF SA + ER = 0 THEN MF$ = MF$ + HEX$
7730 OD$ = ""
7740 NEXT
7750 GOSUB 8000
7755 GOSUB 9000
7760 GOTO 4000
7800 DE = PC: GOSUB 50300
7805 MC$(L1) = HEX$ + "  ": REM *HEX value of Program counter
7807 FOR I = 2 TO LEN (OP$(L1)) - 1
7810 DE = ASC ( MID$ (OP$(L1),I,1))
7820 PC = PC + 1:NB = NB + 1
7840 NEXT
7850 GOSUB 8000
7855 GOSUB 9000
7860 GOTO 4000
7999 REM *Prints source code for EQU & ORG operations
8000 IF LI = 1 THEN RETURN
8005 X = PEEK (49168): IF PEEK (49152) = 80 THEN 8005
8010 PRINT LEFT$ ( STR$ (L2 * 10) + ": ",5);
8022 IF (AM%(L1) = 600) + (AM%(L1) = 700) + (AM%(L1) = 800) = 1 THEN INVERSE : PRINT MC$(L1);: NORMAL : PRINT CHR$ (13)
     SPC( 17);: GOTO 8040
8025 IF AM%(L1) < 100 THEN INVERSE
8030 PRINT MC$(L1);
```

Listing A5.2 (continued)

```
8035    NORMAL
8040    PRINT SPC( 1); LEFT$ (LA$(L1) + "              ",8); LEFT$ (NM$(L1) + "          ",6);
8050    IF LEN (OP$(L1)) > 12 THEN  PRINT OP$(L1);",";: GOTO 8070
8060    PRINT LEFT$ (OP$(L1) + "              ",14);
8070    PRINT CM$(L1)
8080    RETURN
8999    REM *Machine file subroutine
9000    IF ER + SA > 0 THEN  RETURN
9010    IF NB < 32 AND NM$(L1) > < "ORG" THEN  RETURN
9020    IF NM$(L1) = "ORG" AND MF$ = "" THEN MPC = PC: RETURN
9030    DE = NB + 3:CS = CS + DE: GOSUB 50200
9040    Z$ = "S1" + HEX$
9050    DE = MPC:CS = CS + INT (DE / 256) + (DE - INT (DE / 256) * 256): GOSUB 50300
9060    Z$ = Z$ + HEX$: DE = MF$
9070    DE = 255 - (CS - INT (CS / 256) * 256): GOSUB 50200
9080    MF$ = Z$ + HEX$
9090    PRINT D$"APPEND";HF$
9100    PRINT D$"WRITE";HF$
9110    PRINT MF$
9120    PRINT D$"CLOSE";HF$
9130    MF$ = "":MPC = PC:NB = 0
9135    CS = 0
9140    RETURN
11000   REM Operand evaluation subroutine
11010   REM First examine for arithmetic expression
11020   ZZ = -1
11025   FOR J1 = 1 TO LEN (OD$) -1
11030   H1 = ASC ( MID$ (OD$,J1,1))
11050   IF H1 = 43 OR H1 = 45 OR H1 = 42 OR H1 = 47 THEN ZZ = J1:J1 = LEN (OD$)
11060   NEXT
11070   IF ZZ = -1 THEN 11200
11080   S1$ = OD$
11090   OD$ = LEFT$ (S1$,ZZ - 1): GOSUB 11200
11110   OD$ = RIGHT$ (S1$, LEN (S1$) - ZZ): GOSUB 11200
11100   N1 = DE
11120   IF H1 = 43 THEN DE = N1 + DE: GOTO 11160
11130   IF H1 = 45 THEN DE = N1 - DE: GOTO 11160
11140   IF H1 = 42 THEN DE = N1 * DE: GOTO 11160
11150   DE = INT (N1 / DE)
11160   IF DE > 65535 OR DE < 0 THEN  PRINT "Over/under range error in line ";L2 * 10;": GOTO 11310
11170   RETURN
11200   S$ = LEFT$ (OD$,1)
11210   IF ASC (S$) > 47 AND ASC (S$) < 58 THEN DE = VAL (OD$): RETURN
11220   IF S$ > < "$" THEN 11230
11222   HEX$ = OD$: GOSUB 50200
11225   GOTO 11310
11230   IF S$ = "" THEN DE = ASC ( RIGHT$ (OD$,1)): RETURN
11240   IF S$ > < "%" THEN 11260
11250   BIN$ = OD$: GOSUB 50100
11255   GOTO 11310
11260   DE = -1
11270   FOR I9 = 0 TO T -1
11280   IF TA$(I9) = OD$ THEN DE = TA%(I9) + 32767:I9 = T
11290   NEXT
11300   IF DE = -1 AND PA = 2 THEN  PRINT "Undefined label in line ";L2 * 10;"; 0 default":DE = 0:ER = ER + 1: RETURN
11305   IF DE = -1 THEN DE = 512: RETURN
11310   IF DE > 65535 OR DE < 0 THEN  PRINT "Out of range in ";L2 * 10;"; 0 default":DE = 0:ER = ER + 1
11320   RETURN
```

```
11400   REM Evaluates number of commas in operand field
11410   REM Entry:OD$=operand
11420   REM Exit :COMMA=number of commas
11430   COMMA = 0
11440   FOR II = 1 TO LEN (OD$)
11450   IF MID$ (OD$,II,1) = ",", THEN COMMA = COMMA + 1
11460   NEXT
11470   RETURN
20000   INPUT "Number of Source files to be linked? ";LK
20010   FOR I = 0 TO LK - 1
20020   HOME
20025   PRINT D$"CATALOG"
20030   PRINT : INPUT "Name of Source file please   ";SF$(I)
20040   IF RIGHT$ (SF$(I),1) = "." THEN SF$(I) = LEFT$ (SF$(I), LEN (SF$(I)) - 1): GOTO 20040
20050   IF RIGHT$ (SF$(I),6) > < "SOURCE" THEN VTAB 24: PRINT "Must be ";: FLASH : PRINT "SOURCE FILE": NORMAL : GOTO 20
025
20060   NEXT
20065   HOME
20070   INPUT "Please name resultant Object file ";OB$
20085   OB$ = OB$ + "-OBJECT"
20090   RETURN
49999   REM Hex to decimal conversion; Entry-HEX$ = $nnnn of any length; Exit-DE = decimal
50000   DE = 0
50010   FOR I9 = 2 TO LEN (HEX$)
50020   AS = ASC ( MID$ (HEX$,I9,1))
50030   IF AS < 48 OR (AS > 57 AND AS < 65) OR AS > 70 THEN  PRINT "Illegal hex digit in line ";L2 * 10;": "; 0 default":DE =
0:ER = ER + 1: RETURN
50040   DE = DE * 16 + (AS > 64) * (AS - 55) + (AS < 58) * (AS - 48)
50050   NEXT
50060   RETURN
50099   REM Binary to decimal subroutine; Entry-BIN$, %nnnn any length; Exit-DE
50100   DE = 0
50110   FOR I9 = 2 TO LEN (BIN$)
50120   AS = ASC ( MID$ (BIN$,I9,1))
50130   IF AS > 49 OR AS < 48 THEN  PRINT "Illegal binary digit in line ";L2 * 10;"; 0 default":DE = 0:ER = ER + 1: RETURN
50140   DE = DE * 2 + (AS - 48)
50150   NEXT
50160   RETURN
50196   REM Decimal to 2-digit hex conversion
50197   REM Entry: DE<256
50198   REM Exit : HEX$; DE unchanged
50199   REM Local variables used: H1,H2
50200   IF DE > 256 THEN  PRINT "HEX >$FF in line ";L2 * 10:HEX$ = "**":ER = ER + 1: RETURN
50210   H2 = INT (DE / 16):H1 = DE - H2 * 16
50220   H1 = (H1 + (H1 > 9) * 7) + 48
50230   H2 = (H2 + (H2 > 9) * 7) + 48
50240   HEX$ = CHR$ (H2) + CHR$ (H1)
50250   RETURN
50296   REM Decimal to 4-digit hex conversion
50297   REM Entry: DE<65536
50298   REM Exit : HEX$; DE destroyed
50299   REM Local variables used: I9,H(0-3)
50300   HEX$ = ""
50310   FOR I9 = 3 TO 0 STEP - 1
50320   H(I9) = INT (DE / 16 ^ I9):DE = DE - H(I9) * 16 ^ I9
50330   HEX$ = HEX$ + CHR$ ((H(I9) + (H(I9) > 9) * 7) + 48)
```

Listing A5.2 (continued)

```
50340    NEXT
50350    RETURN
50396 REM * Subroutine calculates Branch offset
50397 REM * Entry:DE=operand: PC=current position
50398 REM * Exit :OFFSET$ in hex: DE;PC no change
50399 REM * Local variables used, none:Subroutines used, 50200
50400    OFFSET = DE - PC
50410    IF OFFSET > 127 OR OFFSET < - 128 THEN  PRINT "Out-of-range Branch in line ";L2 * 10:OFFSET$ = "**":ER = ER + 1:  RETURN
50420    IF OFFSET < 0 THEN OFFSET = 256 + OFFSET
50430    DE = OFFSET: GOSUB 50200
50440    OFFSET$ = HEX$
50450    RETURN
51000    MC$(L1) = MC$(L1) + "??-**  ":  GOTO 51070
51010    MC$(L1) = MC$(L1) + "??:":  GOTO 51070
51020    MC$(L1) = MC$(L1) + "??-***":  GOTO 51070
51030    MC$(L1) = MC$(L1) + "??  ":  GOTO 51070
51040    MC$(L1) = MC$(L1) + "??-":  GOTO 51070
51070    PRINT E$;L2 * 10:ER = ER + 1:  RETURN
51100    CS = CS + DE:  GOSUB 50200
51110    MC$(L1) = MC$(L1) + HEX$:  GOTO 51300
51150    CS = CS + DE:  GOSUB 50200
51160    MC$(L1) = MC$(L1) + "-" + HEX$ + "  ":  GOTO 51300
51170    CS = CS + INT (DE / 256) + (DE - INT (DE / 256) * 256):  GOSUB 50300
51180    MC$(L1) = MC$(L1) + "-" + HEX$:  GOTO 51300
51200    CS = CS + DE:  GOSUB 50200
51210    MC$(L1) = MC$(L1) + HEX$ + "  ":  GOTO 51300
51300    IF (SA + ER) = 0 THEN MF$ = MF$ + HEX$:  RETURN
51310    RETURN
```

Listing A5.2 *(continued)*

Index